WOMEN
AND
VIOLENCE

WOMEN
AND
VIOLENCE

Miriam F. Hirsch, Ed.D., ACSW

Miriam F.

Professor of Sociology
Springfield College
Springfield, Massachusetts

 VAN NOSTRAND REINHOLD COMPANY
 NEW YORK   CINCINNATI   ATLANTA   DALLAS   SAN FRANCISCO
①   LONDON   TORONTO   MELBOURNE

Van Nostrand Reinhold Company Regional Offices:
New York   Cincinnati   Atlanta   Dallas   San Francisco

Van Nostrand Reinhold Company International Offices:
London   Toronto   Melbourne

Library of Congress Catalog Card Number: 80-17964
ISBN: 0-442-26148-9

Manufactured in the United States of America

Published by Van Nostrand Reinhold Company
135 West 50th Street, New York, N.Y. 10020

Published simultaneously in Canada by Van Nostrand Reinhold Ltd.

15 14 13 12 11 10 9 8 7 6 5 4 3 2 1

Library of Congress Cataloging in Publication Data

Hirsch, Miriam F.
  Women and violence.

  Includes bibliographical references and index.
  1. Women—Psychology. 2. Aggressiveness
(Psychology) 3. Women—Crimes against. 4. Sex
discrimination against women. I. Title.
HQ1206.H53   305.4′2   80-17964
ISBN 0-442-26148-9

Preface

This book had its beginning with my birth. I was born female, felt like a second-class citizen and always wondered why I wanted to be a boy. I saw my uncle beat his wife and his children in sudden, unexplained, uncontrolled rage, and wondered why he did so. I was insulted and uncomfortable with the jokes about women depicting them in stereotypical ways, and wondered why I felt angry, hurt, and overwhelmed. I wondered why I felt I had to work harder to prove that I could succeed and why I was paid less than some of the men with less ability and fewer credentials. I wondered why, in order to be heard, I had to have a man speak for me, and why women were being raped and beaten but no one cried out. I know why now, and my understanding of all this is the thread that runs through the book.

I dedicate this book to the man in my life, my husband, Lester Hirsch, a gentle, supportive man. If all men were like him, there would be no violence against women.

My thanks to the librarians at Springfield College, who never tired of my constant presence and questions. A special thanks to Laurina Cashin and Ron Catabia for their unwavering help and untiring work. I am also grateful to the librarians at Baystate Medical Center in Springfield, Massachusetts.

I would also like to thank Harriet Chaiken, who typed the manuscript, Judy Jackson for helping me to find some of the pertinent information on women and crime, and last but not least, my husband, who painstakingly helped to edit the manuscript, as well as giving me his unconditional support.

MIRIAM F. HIRSCH

Introduction

Violence is embedded in the fabric of the American society. The United States was spawned in violence and continues to be a basically violent society. According to a study by the National Commission on the Causes and Prevention of Violence in 1968, America has made heroes of people such as Jesse James, John Dillinger, and others who thwarted the law. Although there was a decrease in the rate of crime and that of violent behavior in the 1930s, and a lessening of crime during World War II when people shared common goals, violence began to increase in the 1960s and has been ascending ever since (Silberman, 1978).

A president, John F. Kennedy, his brother, Robert, and the civil rights leader, Martin Luther King, were all assassinated within a five-year period. If someone really rocks the boat, so to speak, annihilation is not uncommon. Labor leader, Jimmy Hoffa, disappeared and is presumed dead, and Karen Silkwood, a young woman killed in an automobile accident of suspicious origin, is thought to have been "fingered" because she sought to call national attention to the dangers inherent in a facility processing nuclear materials.

The rate of murder per 100,000 people in 1978 was triple that of 1938 (Herbers, 1979). It was originally thought that crime and violence would decrease because of a decrease in the numbers of young people; however, this did not happen. The FBI reports that there was a 1.3 percent increase in crime in 1978 over 1977, and that revolvers were the weapons used in 49 percent of the murders, while 14 percent of the victims died as a result of the use of shot-guns and rifles (*Uniform Crime Reports for the United States,* 1979). Rape increased by 11 percent early in 1979 (*Uniform Crime Reports for the United States,* 1979). Crime, particularly serious crime, continues to rise steadily, not only in cities, but also in rural areas and in what was once considered a peaceful haven, the small town.

Fraternities continue their destructive initiation rites, and there continue to be accusations of violence in Marine boot camp, sometimes to the point of murder. Paddling is still permissible by law in school systems throughout the country. Giving a teacher or principal the right to paddle, legitimizes violence as a method of relating to individuals, particularly those whose power is minimal or at worst, completely lacking.

Child abuse abounds, and its increase has prompted concerned citizens to strive for its reduction by publicizing the epidemic, as well as by establishing services both for abused children and for their abusers. It is estimated that 6.5 million children are the objects of abuse by members of their family every year (*U.S. News & World Report,* January 15, 1979, p. 60). One young girl ran away from home because her mother, who was beaten by her son, then proceeded to beat on the daughter. This is a classic example of displacement, whereby a person takes out frustration on another less powerful.

Family violence also includes husbands beating their wives, and in a smaller number of instances, wives battering their husbands. It is estimated that, although rapes are reported to occur once every eight minutes (*Uniform Crime Reports for the United States,* 1978), wife battering is three times as frequent, although most often not reported.

Violence in the school has reached epidemic proportions. In Dade County, Florida, 1153 attacks were reported, while in New York City high schools there were 2420 assaults, mostly against teachers and the administrative staff (*Time,* January 23, 1978, p. 73).

Even psychiatrists are battered. Between 1973 and 1975, there was a 20 to 30 percent increase in assaults on doctors at one institution alone, the Massachusetts Mental Health Center in Boston (*Time,* June 9, 1975, p. 41).

Although violence is generally on the increase in the United States, crimes against women, rape, wife battering, and attacks on older women, are also on the increase. Emotional violence, which is a function of discriminatory practices against females in work, in medical and psychiatric treatment, as well as in the manner in which access to open participation in the society is blocked, continues to exist. Women by definition are a minority, and as minorities they have become and always were legitimate objects of hostility.

A minority group has been defined by Louis Wirth as,

> . . . a group of people who, because of their physical or cultural characteristics, are singled out from others in the society in which they live for dif-

ferential and unequal treatment and who therefore regard themselves as objects of collective discrimination (Wirth, 1945, p. 347).

The basic, and I believe, most important characteristic of a minority which differentiates it from the dominant group is that of power. Power, by definition, is the ability to have control over one's destiny, and also to an extent to be able to control the future of other people. This women did not have, and to a great degree still do not have. Few women were admitted into law schools as well as medical schools; few were encouraged to become professionals or had access to educational institutions which would prepare them for a career in such male-dominated fields as engineering and science. Stromberg and Harkess (1978) point out that the first medical school established in the United States in 1767 did not accept women. The year 1847 marked the entrance of women into a school of medicine but women were excluded from the American Medical Association until 1915. Apparently as late as 1973 half of the physicians interviewed felt that women were discriminated against.

Whereas women make up about 7 percent of the physicians in the United States, only about 3 percent of the lawyers are female. Harvard University did not admit women into its law school until 1950 and not until 1969 did Notre Dame University open its doors to women interested in law. Law has always been considered a masculine field. Only about ten percent of the engineers and scientists were women in 1973 (Stromberg and Harkess, 1978). Marriage was stressed as the ultimate goal for women, and marriage was supposed to be the one and only "career" for females. Even those who succeeded in entering a profession were treated differentially, and differential treatment by definition means discrimination.

The declaration of International Women's Year for 1975 and the International Women's Year Conference held in Mexico City on June 19 through July 2 of that year were indications of a growing awareness of the plight of women not only in the United States but world wide. The conference was initiated by the United States in the U.N. Commission on the Status of Women and cosponsored by eleven developing countries of Asia, Africa, and Latin America. In some countries women comprise 80 to 90 percent of the 700 million illiterates of the world. Deprivation of education locks women into low status although they represent 34 percent of the gainfully employed workers throughout the world. The Commission recognized that all people must be used productively so that development can take place within nations.

Where are women today in the United States? Someone once said that it is simple to define a job that is particularly designed for women. It is any work which pays less than a man is willing to accept for doing a comparable job—and so it is. In spite of the passage of the Equal Pay Act of 1963 and its subsequent amendment in 1974 to extend coverage to about 7 million additional employees, and in spite of the affirmative action program, women are still getting second best, even though they are trying harder. Although there are now women capably trained to fly commercial aircraft, they are still being discouraged by the major airlines from doing so.

Women are consistently paid less for their work. They are often employed in low-paying positions, but even when they are doing the same type of job, their reimbursement for their labors is less than that of men. In 1977 the median earnings for women who worked full time was $8618 compared to $14,626 earned by men (U.S. Bureau of the Census, *Current Reports,* Series P-60, No. 116). Women are earning about 61 percent of what men earn. It is interesting to note that in 1955 the percentage of earnings for women was 64 percent that of males, but this differential has increased over the years, and even when one controls for the number of hours employed as well as educational level, we find that the differential continues to exist (*Manpower Report of the President,* April, 1975). The average salary of women in teaching is 85 percent of what men earn (Fogg, October 11, 1979), and teaching has been considered a female profession.

Sex discrimination suits against colleges and universities are rapidly increasing in reference to hiring policies, salaries, promotion, and the granting of tenure. Examples are Tufts University and Boston University, both in the state which is considered to be the cradle of democracy. Middle Tennessee State University, Rutgers University and Duke University are among many others throughout the country which have also faced similar charges.

Although our society is riddled with the cancer of discrimination against and rejection of the aged, negative attitudes toward older women in the work force tend to be more intense than toward men of comparable age. Mature stewardesses fought and won the battle to remain employed. Despite laws to the contrary, and despite the fact that mature women have been proven to be dependable, conscientious, and competent workers, distinct discrimination exists according to a study by the Labor Department's Manpower Administration. (Note it is still manpower, not personpower, although some women have decided that it is no longer a manhole but a personhole because you never know whom you may find down in the sewer.)

Although women finally got the right to vote in 1920, fifty-four years after black men, they are still attempting to pass an Equal Rights Amendment to the Constitution of the United States which would read that "Equality of rights under the law shall not be denied or abridged by the United States or by any State on account of sex." Apparently, giving women the same equality under the law that men have is so threatening that, although the ERA amendment was passed by Congress on March 22, 1972, it still has not been ratified by the three-fourths of the states needed for it to become effective. It is interesting to note that an equal rights amendment to the Constitution was first submitted to Congress in 1923 and each session subsequent to that year.

For too long women have been locked into traditional roles of wife and mother, with little or no identity of their own outside of these parameters. Even at death a woman's identity is derived from that of her husband, as seen in the obituary columns which are often headed, "Mrs. George Brown" unless she was a widow, at which time her death notice reads, "Mrs. Jane Brown, widow of Mr. George Brown."

Married women also were particularly discriminated against and were deprived of an identity of their own. Until recently credit cards were difficult to obtain for married women in their own names. I, myself, struggled with a large department store in Boston because they insisted on issuing a charge account to me in my husband's name, even though he has never shopped and will never shop there, and even though I was financially self-supporting. After claiming discrimination, and with a veiled threat of taking legal action, I won my battle, only to be told that I could use the credit card if it were issued in my husband's name, but that he was not able to use the card issued in my name. Sex discrimination in credit was outlawed by the United States Congress in October, 1975. It prohibits a retail store, bank, or credit union from refusing to grant credit to a woman on the basis of her sex or marital status, although it does not prohibit the questions regarding the former. The law also prohibits denial of separate billing and separate credit cards to married couples if they so desire.

In renewing my library card, which had been originally issued twenty years ago to me as Mrs. Lester Hirsch (a title I am very comfortable with), I was asked to have my husband sign his name to my renewal application because he was responsible for me and my debts. At this time I again cried discrimination, insisted on having a new card issued, and not only that but had it issued to Dr. Miriam F. Hirsch, to the utter dismay of the librarian, who was shocked to find that I had a doctorate, and who needed to check with the head librarian because to issue the card in my name was a violation of regulations.

Another experience of visiting a ladies' room in a bus station in one of the largest cities in New England, only to find that if I didn't have a dime I would not be able to perform a natural function—a bus depot which had many toilet facilities available to men without charge—gave me what is called colloquially "a gut reaction." I would venture to guess that most women in the United States have had all of these experiences and many more; but perhaps some women are not really aware of the subtle message which is being relayed—"you have come a long way, baby, but you still have a long way to go."

Women throughout history have never had the right to control their own bodies. This right was challenged by men who made the laws and who determined that women are basically creatures of reproduction, put on the earth so that males could make a statement about their masculinity. Not only were women to reproduce, but the product of the reproduction had to be male. Many a wife was harassed and chastised for giving birth to a female child. The Shah of Iran divorced his first wife because she bore him only female children. Although scientists have established the fact that sex is determined by the sperm cell, a woman is often still blamed if the sex of the child is not to its father's liking.

It was also considered the responsibility of the woman to prevent a pregnancy that was unwanted. This resulted in a "catch 22" situation, especially when, for example, the sale, and in a state such as Connecticut, the use of birth control devices, was still illegal until 1965. If you couldn't prevent pregnancy, you tried to relieve yourself of an unwanted one by jumping up and down, falling down stairs, or inserting pointed objects into the mouth of the uterus. All because abortion was also illegal. If you survived, you were lucky. As a result of the Hyde amendment, Medicaid payments did not cover abortions for a period, and poor women with unwanted pregnancies were powerless to get terminations under hygienic conditions. (The New York State Federal

District Court found the amendment unconstitutional in January 1980.)

When oral contraceptives were placed on the market, women readily accepted their use without questioning their safety. Diaphragms did prevent pregnancy, but only motivated women used them since their use required thinking ahead and protecting oneself before the sexual act occurred. Women's minority status influenced the wholesale dispensing of birth control pills, and of estrogen for menopausal women without, I feel, due concern for the consequences, and without sharing with the users the potentially destructive side effects that were possible. And so it wasn't until a number of deaths had resulted that a hue and cry began to be heard. If this had happened to men, would they have waited so long to react? I wonder.

As minority group people, there are many stereotypes associated with women. Stereotyping by definition means having ideas about people which are basically exaggerated, and which help a person to rationalize behavior towards a category of people; in the case which I am discussing, that category is women.

One stereotype which has been difficult for women to cope with is that which basically supports the concept that all women are born to be mothers and that is their destiny. However, due to the basic hostility that many men feel towards women, women were accused of being super mothers and thereby being responsible for the neurosis of their sons. In the 1940s Philip Wylie attacked American mothers for what he perceived as too much affection and smothering with the end result being the emasculation of their sons (Wylie, 1942). The Jewish mother was particularly attacked for too much mothering, while the black mother was attacked because she represented a matriarchal family system. Mothers-in-law are the butt of many jokes but do we ever hear a joke about fathers-in-law?

Freud stated that humor is meaningful and expresses an element of the true feeling of the joke teller. Obscene wit, particularly the "smutty joke was originally directed toward women and may be equated with attempts at seduction" (Freud, 1960, p. 97). This type of humor functions to attack the person of the opposite sex, usually women. Many of the jokes that we hear which have sexual connotations are directed against women. Jokes about rape and wife beating are certainly examples of attempts to legitimize hostile acts against females. Why would anyone think these jokes were funny if they did not basically believe in the message the humor was presenting or wishfully hope that it was true?

Women as sex objects is another stereotypical view of females. Because they are viewed as sex objects, women are perceived as basically sexual in nature, wanting to be overpowered by men and serving the purpose of satisfying the sexual needs of the male, be it stranger, lover, or husband. This resulted in the myth that women were really not interested in sex, and it was therefore unnecessary for them to be orgasmic. Women who presented themselves as sexually interested were regarded in a negative fashion. Women were sexual creatures, seductive in their behavior, wanting to ensnare men, but not interested in sexual gratification.

As sex objects, women are portrayed as submissive objects of abuse and violence in advertising, a situation which gained momentum in the 1960s, particularly in the record industry. One billboard in Los Angeles advertising a new Rolling Stones album called *Black and Blue* portrayed a woman in tattered clothes with chains around her wrists. Her expression was one of pure sexual excitement. The caption read, "She Loves It." This obviously hostile poster prompted the formation of an organization called Women Against Violence Against Women. Their thesis is that violence in the media is closely correlated with the violence that occurs in a society, and that depicting women in pornographic and abusive situations reinforces the basic assumption that they are legitimate objects of abusive behavior. Another record album pictured a woman sprawled in a seductive posture on the sidewalk. Her purse contents were strewn beside her and her clothes had been torn. Although there was no blood, no bruises, the message was obvious— that she is sexually seductive. Next to her body was a package of cigarettes called Lucky Strike.

Even fashions are sold with sex and violence. The May, 1975 issue of *Vogue Magazine* entitled, "The Story of OHHH," reported the following. Included in the spread were

> ... shots of a woman wincing in pain as a man bit her left ear, and another of a man ramming a hand into a woman's breast. (*Time,* February 7, 1977, p. 58).

Another picture printed in a magazine portrayed a woman's head being forced into a toilet bowl. Not only are women considered legitimate objects of abuse but in addition contempt for them is fairly obvious.

Hatred of women was identified as one of the motives for the Hillside strangler's brutal killing of at least ten women. Then there was the "classic rape" situation in the Fall of 1979, in which a University of Rhode Island woman student was allegedly hauled off to the men's dormitory screaming, and then was raped. Who was charged with the sexual assault? None other than members of the University's soccer team; upstanding, all-American "boys." One of the members of the team allegedly assaulted the same woman again nine days after the first attack.

One of the country's largest motorcycle gangs was recently accused of forcing girls into slavery by sexually abusing them, brutalizing them physically, and forcing them into prostitution and drug activities. Sometimes a young girl will be abused sexually by as many as 50 to 200 members of the gang in sequence, and if she is married, a young woman will be physically assaulted for refusing to participate in a wife-swapping deal.

Hatred of women also takes the form of expressing obscenities, exposing one's genitals for shock value, and at one fraternity party at Duke University, a group of women also accused the men of tearing at their clothes and dumping feces in one of the women's laps.

Then there is the cover of *Hustler Magazine,* showing a woman going through a meat grinder, and in another publication a woman's nipples being torn off by clippers. Motive—obviously to sexually excite men. Message—women are okay objects to brutalize.

The myth that women enjoy being "manhandled" goes along with the stereotype of women as sex objects. Finnair, the Finnish Airline, attempted to get Americans to use its services with an ad which was withdrawn after an outcry by the National Organization for Women. The ad read

> How Vilho Vatanen, the Finn, created the world's first sauna when he locked his wife in the smoke house, set it on fire, beat her soundly, with birch leaves, and discovered she loved it (*Time,* March 20, 1978, p. 63).

Meanwhile, wife beating has become such a serious problem in the United States that Sylvia Porter estimates it results in an economic loss of three to five billion dollars each year (Porter, November 1, 1979). Margaret Trudeau, the wife of the Prime Minister of Canada, Pierre

Trudeau, was beaten by her husband. He hit her, gave her a black eye, and according to the columnist writing the story, she loved it. Said Margaret, "Actually, I was quite pleased. It was the first time in a very long while that I'd been able to get a response from Pierre. He got all his hostility out and he hasn't shown me so much attention in years! It showed he really loved me . . ." (Markfield, March 27, 1979).

The thought that good sex is closely dependent on hostility is supported by C. A. Tripp, a psychologist, who has done research on sex. Masters and Johnson found an astonishing number of people whose fantasies had violent aspects to them. Robert J. Stoller, a psychoanalyst, is reported by *Time* (June 4, 1979, p. 64) to support the point of view that without hostility, sex for many people is ungratifying. Stoller is reported as presenting the view that people are basically sadomasochistic when it comes to sex. They bring to the sexual relationship a need to inflict pain on other people in order to compensate for past hurts inflicted on them. They are attempting to work through difficulties which occurred in childhood. Many people can compensate for this hostility by expressing affection. If Stoller is correct, we can expect women to continue to be the objects towards whom sexual hostility is expressed. Why? Because it is males who are encouraged to express their sexual feelings, because it is males who are imbued with compulsive masculinity, which basically is an attempt to overcome their feelings of being inadequate, and it is females who are socialized to be passive and receptive, nonassertive and nurturing. Females, therefore, would not tend to behaviorize their hostile feelings.

The hostility that men feel towards women is not only reflective of our own society. The mutilation of female children by circumcision is still being practiced throughout the world, and in particular, in thirty African countries. It is estimated that between 30 to 60 million females have been subjected to this procedure (*New Statesman,* August 24, 1979). Circumcision is supposed to desensitize the girl sexually so that she can be a better mother.

Circumcision for females consists of partial or full removal of the clitoris. The procedure is often done just before the girl arrives at puberty and is performed in a nonmedical setting by nonmedical personnel.

Clitoridectomy means removing the clitoris and is sometimes followed by infibulation, sewing the genitals so that only a tiny opening remains as access to the vagina. The International Tribunal on Crimes

Against Women held in 1976 documented cases of clitoridectomy, excision, and infibulation. Girls are subjected to these procedures just prior to beginning puberty. While some women hold the victim down, another woman, often a family member, cuts into the genital with the neck of a broken bottle or other crude device, making an unhygienic incision. When the clitoris is entirely removed, while the girl hemorrhages, cries of joy emanate from the participants, though not from the victim. The castrated female is then forced to walk through the town dressed in white but with breasts bared. Urinating becomes difficult and often complications occur (Russell and Van de Ven, 1976). The medical journal, *Obstetrics and Gynecology,* presented a case in 1974 (Onuigbo and Twomey) of an Ibo woman in Nigeria whose ritual circumcision resulted in the formation of a stone. Many women have had to have repairs made because after removal of the clitoris and the labia minora the remaining parts adhere. In some countries the woman is completely sewn up if her husband is gone for a length of time. This ensures him his wife's faithfulness.

This brings us to the belief that a woman who marries becomes the property of her husband, a belief which not only exists in other countries but is also found in our own democratic society. Rape becomes a violation of a man's property. The Code of Hammurabi (early 17th century B.C.) contains the earliest law which criminalizes rape. Death was the penalty meted out to a man who raped a virgin residing with her father. Early Hebrew laws also included penalties for rape. A man who raped an engaged woman in the field was condemned to death, while if the rape occurred within the city walls and the woman did not scream, both would be condemned to die. The rape of an unbetrothed woman was treated differently. In this case the offender would have to pay money to her father and marry her. The father was thereby compensated for the violation of his property.

Recently a member of the Saudi Arabian royal family was reported to have killed his daughter in a swimming pool because she had premarital sexual relations (*Time,* February 13, 1978, p. 46).

If women become the property of men at marriage, then their husbands have sexual access to them even if contrary to their own desires, and the law has supported this concept. If the couple are estranged or in the process of getting a divorce, rape charges can more easily find support in the legal system. Battering one's wife is just now becoming illegal.

I was recently given as a gift a set of pans for baking French bread. To my dismay, the directions for preparing the bread included a statement which said that women like to be beaten. "Don't be afraid ιo manhandle the dough—the rougher you are with it the more tender the bread—it's sort of like a woman in this respect." The myth of women as masochists continues to exist today.

Women are supposed to be dominated by men. Is that not the reason why men should be older than the women they marry, better educated, and make more money? John Knox (*The First Blast of the Trumpet Against the Monstruous Regiment of Women*) said in the 16th century:

> To promote a woman to bear rule, superiority, dominion, or empire above any realm, nation or city is repugnant to nature; contumely to God, a thing most contrarious to His revealed will and approved ordinances; and finally, it is the subversion of good order, of all equity and justice (p. B1).

The biblical story of Adam and Eve defines women as inherently evil and therefore legitimate objects of hostility and aggression. The danger of women was evident in their persecution as witches. Evil, because they caused terrible things to happen to other people, but also because they were said to copulate with the Devil. Women were not only seen as having strange evil powers but also as usual, to be sexual in their very nature.

We are aware today that many of those accused of witchcraft displayed symptoms which today we label hysteria. We are also aware of the fact that hysteria, when it was finally accepted as a disease entity, was seen as associated with the uterus and mainly found in women.

Another stereotype associated with women is that they are sneaky, can't be trusted and gossip a great deal.

> Nature doth paint them further to be weak, frail, impatient, feeble and foolish; and experience hath declared them to be unconstant, variable, cruel, and lacking the spirit of counsel (John Knox: *The First Blast of the Trumpet Against the Monstruous Regiment of Women*, p. B2).

> Thus through a woman was the secret known;
> Tell us, and in effect you tell the town. (John Dryden, *Wife of Bath's Tale*, p. 875).

Women are also thought to be illogical and to be concerned with trivia. George Bernard Shaw said, "You sometimes have to answer a woman according to her womanishness, just as you have to answer a fool according to his folly" (*An Unsocial Socialist* p. 253).

Stereotyping becomes a part of the child's repertoire by the time the age of four is reached. All new information is then interpreted through this framework (Frieze et al., 1978). It is no wonder that by the time we become an adult, we are behaving according to sexual scripts and viewing others stereotypically.

Women are also viewed as innately good and basically submissive. Although in a way this contradicts the stereotype of the woman as sexually seductive, the two stereotypes tend to exist side by side in spite of their disparity. The good girl is one who is not too sexually demanding (otherwise she would be too sexy), but has the right amount of behavioral as well as physical attributes to be attractive to men. Being good is rewarding; the basic reward being that of marriage and male protection (Fox, 1977). When she marries, a woman must become less sexually seductive and play the role of a good wife and mother, being submissive to her husband, who will protect her economically and in all other ways.

As minority group members, women are discriminated against, powerless, stereotyped and mistreated.

Why are women and children the victims of abuse? Every society culturally defines certain groups as acceptable objects of hostility (Simpson and Yinger, 1965). Such a group must be visibly different and distinct. Violence most often takes place between people whose status in society is different—one superior and the other subordinate (Grimshaw, 1970). The structure of the family gives the male the power over the female and therefore reinforces the subordinate position of the wife, which can then increase her chances of being the target of abuse.

Women, because of their differences and their historically subordinate position in our society, comprise a group which our society has defined as an acceptable object of hostility. Words in the English language which indicate femaleness are often used in a discrediting manner. Shrew is defined as "a woman of violent temper and speech" (Random House Dictionary, 1966, p. 1321). There is not a comparable word for man. Adams and Ware (1979) show that language is reflective of society and functions to socially mirror a culture. They cite the finding that there are 500 English words for prostitute. The comparable word for man has only 65 variations. Words for describing women in sexually derogatory ways are more extensive than those which describe men similarly. The fact that there is so much emphasis on women and sexuality linguistically indicates the degree of concern the society has about women and their sexuality (Schulz, 1975). Referring to adult women as "girls" is placing them in a position of powerlessness, since they are being referred to as nonadults. Adult men are generally not considered "boys." It is sad that like other minorities, women have been socialized to accept the stereotypes that the dominant group, men, are perpetuating. It is not uncommon to hear women refer to themselves as "girls" and to view the use of the word women as unflattering. Are we to assume that being an adult female is a negative status?

Adams and Ware (1979) also point out that the generic use of the word *men* and the use of the masculine pronouns to include females, places maleness as the point of reference, puts women in the position of "losing their linguistic identity," and helps to continue sexist attitudes and behavior. Sexual exploitation of females is also evident in the language usage among males (Kutner and Brogan, 1974). Men, more than women, expressed more words which referred to women as sex objects and male dominance in sexual intercourse. Is it not true that the way we speak is the way we think?

Sexual harassment of women at work is not a new phenomenon. Touching of women in a sexually seductive manner, as well as making promotion or even retention of the job contingent on the giving of sexual favors has finally been publicly noted by the federal government as discriminatory.

As stated earlier, women are legitimate objects of violence because of their minority group status. The roles that women are expected to play are influential in encouraging self-destruction as well as setting them up as victims.

What is meant by roles? A "role," by definition, is a set of behavior patterns expected of a person occupying a specific social position (status), such as wife, mother, student, etc. These roles are often accompanied by privileges and obligations which help the individual to know what she should do, what kinds of obligations she has, and to whom, as well as upon whom she has a right to make particular demands. To be a wife, for instance, is to possess a status role. The role of wife is changing rapidly in our society but still includes behaviors such as keeping house and having and caring for children, etc. A wife is obligated to her husband and children to perform certain duties, and rightfully expects from them love, devotion, etc. Since roles are complementary, social interaction does not become chaotic, because for every role associated with every status one occupies, there are also reciprocal behaviors associated with the complementary roles. Expectations of role behavior often come with conflicting pressures, particularly if inconsistent or contradictory behaviors are required. For example, in order to be feminine in our society a woman must be non-aggressive and noncompetitive, characteristics which are needed for success in the working world. What happens, therefore, to the woman who becomes a professional, and who "makes it" in our society?

Robert Ezra Park (1955), a noted sociologist of the Chicago school, stated that the concept of self was very directly linked to the roles one plays in the status one occupies. An individual, stated Park, becomes a person through being recognized by the community in which she lives. The value which society places on the role and status of an individual is instrumental in the kind of self-concept she will develop.

One's sex, male or female, is what sociologists consider an ascribed status, a status which is determined by birth rather than achievement. The status of female or male is associated with roles which are basically culturally determined. Slater (1970) states that there is no way of behaving, or quality of personality, that is considered masculine or feminine in every single society. There are cultures in which women carry heavy loads and are thought to be stronger than men. There are those cultures in which our stereotype of women as not being practical and as having intuition is associated with men. In the United States, states Slater, being passive is associated with femininity and being active with masculinity, but male speech and movement are expected to be slow, and those males who move and speak too fast are often labelled effeminate.

If, as is generally accepted, roles are learned, then the roles of femininity and masculinity are also learned.

A person learns to define herself by the way other people see her. While others are defining us they are also relaying a message which tells us what behaviors are deemed to be appropriate for us as particular types of people (Heiss, 1968). Role models are influential in teaching us how those who are like us should behave.

The roles that women are expected to play are subservient ones. They are roles which our society imbues with little status and often less value than masculine roles. Being "just a housewife" does not have the status that a work role has. Almost anyone can be a mother. A man is not just a husband and father, as Betty Friedan (1963) pointed out. He also has status in the work-related area. Unlike women, his identity, then, is not derived only in terms of someone else. Why do students often call their male professors "Doctor" regardless of whether or not the person has a doctorate, but automatically call a woman professor with a doctorate who happens to be married, Mrs.? It would appear that in our society a woman's marital status supercedes her earned degrees.

Feminine roles appear to cause depression in women. Women are more often depressed than men, and married women more often develop psychiatric problems than unmarried women. Discrimination both socially and economically has a negative effect on women as does discrimination against other minority groups.

Women as individuals have rebelled against the traditional roles assigned to them. A striking example of this is Deborah Sampson, who donned her brother's clothes and enlisted in the army in April, 1783, as her contribution to the Revolution, only to be honorably discharged six months later after being discovered a female while being treated for a bullet wound. Interestingly enough, in spite of her contribution to the service of her country, she and her family fought a long and arduous battle to receive veterans' benefits.

As women move out of their traditional roles, they become what is called "marginal women, neither fish nor fowl." They threaten the male world and its dominance and suffer as a result.

"Violence is developed in the family as it is in society by a superior status group (husbands) on an inferior status group (wives and children) when the legitimacy of the superior group's status is questioned" (Gelles, 1972, p. 137). Challenges to one's superior position which are symbolic also result in violent behavior. It is therefore legitimate to suggest that the growing increase in the status and independence of women, as a result of the pill and the passage of the Equal Rights Amendment by many states, may create anxiety in those men who are troubled by "compulsive masculinity" and who therefore perceive these changes as a threat to their position of superiority. Our society socially patterns antipathy between men and women.

It would seem as if there was a conflict of identity in the boy children, to unconscious fear of being feminine, which leads to protest masculinity, exaggeration of the differences between men and women, antagonism against and fear of women, male solidarity, and hence back to isolation of women (Whiting, 1965, p. 137).

The thesis that "compulsive masculinity" leads to violence implies that there is a tremendous need in our society for men to demonstrate their masculinity as a method of dealing with the anxiety around the natural identification with mother. In other words, the young male develops compulsive masculinity in reaction to his fear of being feminine. Note how pejorative it is to call a boy a "sissy." One finds, therefore, that in many cases the use of violence is felt by the offender as a requirement for the male role according to some researchers.

Violence or at least the fear of violence is a part of every woman's life. Each woman knows someone who has been the victim of a violent episode if she herself has not been involved at one time or another. If the abuse has not been physical, then it was psychological. Women are assaulted every day by their portrayal in the media and on the job by the attitudes that prevail and become actualized into messages which say, "You're not okay because you are female."

I have attempted to discuss in this book those areas of violence perpetrated by but mainly against women. Victims of violence we are; but perhaps continuing to publicly acclaim our indignation will help to ameliorate an injustice perpetrated against one-half of the human race.

References

Anon. Advertising for Trouble. *Time.* p. 63 (March 20, 1978).

———. Battered Families: A Growing Nightmare. *U.S. News and World Report.* p. 60 (January 15, 1979).

———. Battered Psychiatrists. *Time.* p. 41 (June 9, 1975).

———. Bedroom Battle. *Time.* p. 64 (June 4, 1979).

———. Crimes Against Thirty Million. *New Statesman.* pp. 266–268 (August 24, 1979).

———. *Manpower Report of the President.* U.S. Department of Labor, Manpower Administration. Washington, D.C.: U.S. Government Printing Office, April 1975.

———. Money Income and Poverty Status of Families and Persons in the United States: 1977 (Advanced Reports). U.S. Bureau of the Census. *Current Population Reports Series* P-60 no. 116.

———. Really Socking it to Women. *Time.* p. 58 (February 7, 1977).

————. The ABCs of School Violence. *Time*. p. 73 (January 23, 1978).

————. Tragic Princess. *Time*. p. 46 (February 13, 1978).

————. The Story of OHHH. *Vogue Magazine*. p. 102–115 (May 1975).

————. *Uniform Crime Reports for the United States*. Washington, D.C.: U.S. Government Printing Office, 1978.

————. *Uniform Crime Reports for the United States*. Washington, D.C.: U.S. Government Printing Office, 1979.

Adams, Karen L. and Ware, Norma C. Sexism and the English Language: the Linguistic Implications of Being a Woman, in Jo Freeman (ed.). *Women: A Feminist Perspective*. Palo Alto, Calif.: Mayfield, 1979.

Dryden, John. "Wife of Bath's Tale" in *Dryden's Poetical Works*. Boston: Houghton Mifflin, 1909.

Fogg, Susan. Statistics Show Women Make Up 41.2 Percent of U.S. Labor Force. Newhouse Wire Service (October 11, 1979).

Fox, Greer Litton. Nice girl: social control of women through a value construct. *Signs* 2:805–817 (Summer 1977).

Freud, Sigmund. The purposes of jokes, in *The Complete Psychological Works of Sigmund Freud,* James Strachey (ed.). London: The Hogarth Press and the Institute of Psycho-analysis, Vol VIII 1960, pp. 90–116.

Friedan, Betty. *The Feminine Mystique*. New York: Dell, 1963.

Frieze, Irene, Parsons, Jacquelynne E., Johnson, Paula B., Ruble, Diane N., Zellman, Gail L., in collaboration with Esther Sales. *Women and Sex Roles*. New York: W. W. Norton, 1978.

Gelles, Richard J. *The Violent Home: A Study of Physical Aggression Between Husbands and Wives*. Beverly Hills, California: Sage, 1972.

Grimshaw, Allen D. Interpreting collective violence: an argument for the importance of social structure. *Annals* 391:9–20 (September, 1970).

Heiss, Jerold (ed.). *Family Roles and Interaction: An Anthology*. Chicago: Rand McNally, 1968.

Herbers, John. Nation's crime rate rises again: growing social unrest is blamed. *New York Times* p. 1 (October 28, 1979).

Knox, John. *The First Blast of the Trumpet Against the Monstruous Regiment of Women* 1558. University Microfilm-English Books.

Kutner, Nancy G. and Brogan, Donna. An investigation of sex-related slang vocabulary and sex-role orientation among male and female university students. *Journal of Marriage and the Family* 36:474–484 (August 1974).

Markfield, Alan. Pierre Trudeau. United Feature Syndicate (March 27, 1979).

Onuigbo, Wilson I. B. and Twomey, Deirdre. Primary vaginal stone associated with circumcision. *Obstetrics & Gynecology* 44:769–770 (1974).

Park, Ezra E. *Society*. New York: The Free Press, 1955.

Porter, Sylvia. Cost of $3–$5 billion Put on Wife Battering Cases. Springfield Daily News 29 (November 1, 1979).

Russell, Diana E. and Van de Ven, Nicole (eds.). *Crimes Against Women*. California: Les Femmes, 1976.

The Random House Dictionary of the English Language. Jess Stein and Laurence Urdang (eds.). New York: Random House, 1966.

Schulz, Muriel K. The semantic derogation of women, in Barrie Thorne and Nancy Henley (eds.). *Language and Sex: Differences and Dominance.* Rowley, Mass.: Newbury House, 1975.

Shaw, George Bernard. *An Unsocial Socialist.* New York: W. W. Norton, 1972.

Silberman, Charles. *Criminal Violence, Criminal Justice, Criminals, Police, Courts and Prisons in America.* New York: Random House, 1978.

Simpson, George E. and Yinger, J. Milton. *Racial and Cultural Minorities.* New York: Harper & Row, 1965.

Slater, Phillip. *The Pursuit of Loneliness.* Boston: Beacon Press, 1970.

Stromberg, Ann H. and Harkess, Shirley. *Women Working.* Palo Alto, Calif.: Mayfield Publishing, 1978.

Whiting, Beatrice B. Sex identity, conflict and physical violence: a comparative study. *American Anthropologist* **67**:123–140 (1965).

Wirth, Louis. The problem of minority groups, in Ralph Linton (ed.). *The Science of Man in the World Crisis.* New York: Columbia University Press, 1945.

Wylie, Philip. *Generation of Vipers.* New York: Reinhart, 1942.

Contents

WOMEN
AND
VIOLENCE

1. To Be Female: Biological Considerations

"It may be said that a woman is an inferior thing." (Aristotle, *Poetics XIV*)

Aristotle was the widely acclaimed philosopher of the fourth century B.C., whose philosophy is described as empirical and practical rather than metaphysical or idealistic. Women throughout the centuries were considered subordinate and second-rate creatures because of their biologically inherited differences from males. These biological dissimilarities were given a lower status because they indeed did differ from the male organism. It is apparent that the male is used as the yardstick against which what has merit and what is devalued is measured. In intergroup relations the view that one's own group or nation is superior to all others is referred to as ethnocentrism: it is a trait which actively encourages stereotyping, prejudice, and discrimination.

Let us review some of the basic differences between male and female.

A human being is created when a mature ovum is fertilized by a sperm. Each sperm cell contains either an X or Y chromosome. All ova contain an X. Therefore, folklore to the contrary, it is the male who determines the sex of the child. An XX combination is female and an XY male. It is at this time that sex determination is established.

The genetic determination is not final and irrevocable; many external and internal environmental factors may come into operation during the developmental process and modify or completely reverse the genetic constitution of the individual. Germ cells, presumably of identical genetic constitution, may lie close together and differentiate as sperm or ova within the same individual. (Turner, 1966, pp. 376–377).

According to the Old Testament, God made woman out of Adam's rib.

1

So the Lord God caused a deep sleep to fall upon the man, and while he slept took one of his ribs and closed up its place with flesh; and the rib which the Lord God had taken from the man he made into a woman, and brought her to the man. Then the man said,

> "This at last is bone of my bones
> and flesh of my flesh; she shall
> be called Woman, because she was
> taken out of Man. (Genesis II:21).

Scientists have for many years supported the belief that the embryo in its early stages of development is undifferentiated (neither male nor female) and that the female clitoris is really a rudimentary penis. Freud himself believed that the female indeed thought of herself as having been castrated and the young male seeing her without male genitalia developed a fear of emasculation (loss of genitalia)—the myth of Eve evolving out of Adam re-expressed. To accept Freud's belief is to accept the biological inferiority of women and therefore the biological superiority of men (Sherfey, 1973).

Recent scientific data indicate that not only is the beginning embryo differentiated but that it is female. The sex-determining genes influence the fetus during the fifth or sixth week of life. If the removal of the gonads takes place before this time, the fetus will develop as a female without ovaries. This, in spite of genetic determination.

Embryologically speaking, it is correct to say that the penis is an exaggerated clitoris, the scrotum is derived from the labia majora, the original libido is feminine, etc. (Sherfey, 1973, p. 65).

There is even the possibility that the legendary tribe of the Amazons, which according to the Greeks was made up of women only, could have existed and that they could have continued to produce by parthenogenesis (virgin reproduction). This is the process of pricking the ovum with a pin or the use of particular chemicals which activate the development of the ovum into an embryo without impregnation by a sperm cell, a process discovered in 1900 with frogs. The Amazons would in all probability have been weak if they indeed had knowledge of this process because unmixed heredity would tend to intensify any weakness (Swanson, 1974).

Since the ovum contains only X chromosomes and it is fertilized by a sperm carrying a Y the combination is XY (male). In other words the degree of femaleness is lessened and sex-linked inherited weaknesses can occur since they are attributed to genes which are carried only by the sperm cells. These weaknesses or sex-linked defects include hemophilia, color-blindness and hypertrichosis (excessive growth of hair).

There are a greater number of sperm produced than ova and more males conceived than females (we still do not know why). However, the male fetus is more vulnerable and is more often aborted than the female. Twenty-five percent more stillbirths are male than female and the male neonate has a higher mortality rate than the female. Twenty-seven percent more boys than girls die of illness during the first year (Buytendijk, 1968).

The girl baby is on the average somewhat smaller than the boy baby but she is much more developed as an organism, which may very well account for her high rate of survival. The female neonate is about one month to six weeks more mature than the male neonate (Garai and Schienfeld, 1968).

Sex is vital to the differentiation that takes place in the animal world. The big question concerns which is most influential in humans, nature or nurture, inheritance or environment?

The secretion of sex-linked hormones (estrogen in the female, testosterone in the male) affects the fetus as well as the new-born baby. Boy babies are usually less passive in behavior and more aggressive than baby girls and we tend to see this difference continuing (Swanson, 1974). Much of this might very well be reinforced by role expectation since we tend to encourage the motor development of boys more than we do that of girls. But indications that aggression is genetically based result from observations and experiments with monkeys. Male monkeys are less well-behaved and more aggressive than their female counterparts. When a change of the hormonal balance occurs, there is a concomitant change in behavior (Schienfeld, 1965). Swanson (1974) believes that the differential hormones affect moods and that this has fed the commonly held belief that women are changeable creatures. The following chapter will discuss in more detail the research concerning the differences in aggression between males and females and the possible reasons for them.

An article in *Today's Health* (November 1964) states that boys and girls are born different. Support for the continuing nature of this difference is given by citing a study of work roles assigned by sex to men and women in 224 tribes. Professions, waging war, and religious orders were almost exclusively male-assigned roles, while domestic chores and working with pottery were female-assigned roles. Margaret Mead, on the other hand, found that although work roles were linked more commonly with sex, there were societies in which what we would consider role reversal was the norm.

The biologically oriented position of behavior continues to support the concept that woman is "different from man in a bodily way, in her 'nature,' her inborn characteristics and qualities. Besides an anatomical and physiological difference, there is an aboriginal difference in the dynamic structure of all conduct" (Buytendijk, 1968, pp. 7–8).

Differences between males and females become evident early in life, as previously stated. Some researchers believe that males and females have differential interior climates and therefore behave differently. These researchers conclude that males are by nature more dominant than females. "There seems to be a far greater inner pressure, a creative tension, driving males. This is found over and over again: in tests and observations of school children, in comparisons of productivity and 'scope' of male and female professionals, etc." (Ruderman, 1971, p. 50). There are those who believe that males inherently need to be dominant and that female aggressiveness is often associated with male impotence. Here again we have a typical example of what is called "blaming the victim" as well as a complete disregard for the cultural influences which affect infants from birth. The girl is swathed in pink and the boy in blue. Parents tend to play with boy babies in a less gentle manner than girls, and also tend to positively reinforce more aggressive behaviors in boys while negatively reinforcing the same behaviors in girls. How much of the dominance and aggressiveness is nature and how much is nurture?

Florence Ruderman (1971) lists what she believes are some of the basic differences between boys and girls. Girls, she states, are by nature more verbal and passive, have less capacity for thinking conceptually, and boys generally have a greater inner pressure to create than girls. Her thesis is that because anatomical and physiological sex differences have existed from time immemorial, these differences undoubtedly have an influence on how each sex feels as well as how each sex behaves and not only on reproduction in its limited definition. Personality, states Ruderman, has to have been affected in such a manner as to give rise to differences although they may be subtle.

Yes, males and females are physiologically and anatomically different from each other but it is the values placed on these differences and the reaction to them which greatly influence their personality and their behavior. Attempts to distinguish between genetic or culturally conditioned behaviors as determinants of differences in the psychology of men and women are fraught with obstacles (Pengelley, 1974). In most cultures women have been assigned roles which appear to be subordinate to men. This is generally related to the reproductive functions of the female. The characteristic behaviors of men and women are thought by many scientists to be the result of nurture rather than nature. Although men and women are distinguished by their anatomy and physiology, "any genetic differences ascribed to sex in intellectual ability or physiological and behavioral attitudes are insignificant—if they exist at all" (Pengelley, 1974, p. 18).

Males do have more muscle tissue than females and are therefore considered to be stronger. Muscular activity and diet, however, affect strength, and males in our society are encouraged to participate in activities which tend to strengthen their muscles. The Apsorake Indians of the northern plains led such a rigorous life that women in that society tended to be equally as strong as men.

> . . . and women who could carry a quarter of a buffalo apparently without exertion, ride all day and all night with a raiding war-party, or travel afoot two hundred and fifty miles across an unmarked wilderness of mountains, plains, and swollen streams in four days and nights, were not the women to bring forth puny offspring (Curtis, 1909, p. 3).

The proponents of the position that nurture and environment are responsible for the adult human being rather than heredity, believe that humans, unlike mammals in the lower animal kingdom, are greatly influenced by the environment in which they live. These proponents also believe that hereditary characteristics are generally less important in molding human behavior than an individual's life experiences. Biological determinism is challenged, and the concept of social relevancy is upheld. Man is not necessarily determined to be the producer while woman is the reproducer.

Males and females differ in other ways. Males have a greater distribution of body hair, a larger larynx. The sexually mature female has larger breasts, larger hips and smaller shoulders than the sexually mature male. The male who tends to put on weight usually does so from the waist up while the female puts on weight from the waist down (Pengelley, 1974).

Although women are thought of as being the "weaker sex," statistics indicate that they tend to live longer than men. Throughout the years the life expectancy rate of people in the United States has risen and women appear to benefit from this increase more than men (Gove and Hughes, 1979). Women, however, appear to have a higher illness rate than men. Gove and Hughes attempt to explode the myths that women are really not as sick as men but feel freer to complain and have more time to play a sick role. They found that, as they expected, women were indeed sick more often than men, that the illness was generally minor and that their hypothesis is true that mental strain affects physical health and women's role obligations resulted in mental strain, lack of care of self, and as a result, physical illness.

Women become ill more often than men but the male's mortality rate is about 60 percent above that of females (Waldron, 1976). One-third of the difference in mortality rate is attributed to the fact that men more often commit suicide, and suffer from diseases associated with excessive smoking and drinking as well as from vehicular accidents. Waldron believes that these causes of death are associated with masculine behaviors. She points out that a high mortality rate is not universal and appears to be associated with an industrial society.

Twice as many men die from arteriosclerotic heart disease than women and Waldron posits that this is due to their smoking habits as well as their involvement in highly competitive occupations. In fact, men who work exceptionally long hours are more prone to this disease, and as women are entering highly pressured positions in the labor market, the rate of heart attacks among them is expected to increase.

At one time it was accepted that women had inborn safeguards which tended to maintain their longevity over men. Today, we know that cultural factors also have an influence.

Stuttering is twice as common among boys as girls. "Limited vision, deafness, hardness of hearing, infantile autism, the prevalence of idiot savants, and mental defectiveness debilitate far more males than females throughout life" (Garai and Schienfeld, 1968, p. 189).

Women are better able to survive emotional strain and have been proven to be less prone to bomb shock. In London and Kent during World War II, 70 percent more men than women became psychotic (Montagu, 1970).

There is also a belief that girls are more influenced by heredity and boys by their environment. Research has found that there is more intellectual similarity between male identical twins than between female identical twins, although both sets are like their parents to the same degree (Maccoby and Jacklin, 1974).

There is no difference between newborn male and female infants in their visual and auditory abilities, myths to the contrary. Boys appear to have superiority in problem solving requiring visual discrimination but is this inherited? Motivation, ability to manage rote tasks, degree of sociability, suggestibility and self-esteem have not been demonstrated to be different between the sexes (Maccoby and Jacklin, 1974). Garai and Schienfeld (1968) developed a comprehensive list of what they consider sex differences which are supported by the research they reviewed. Included in the list were the following data:

1. Males have more strength and are generally physically bigger than females. They also state that males are more aggressive than females. (The greater pugnacity of the male is discussed in more detail in the next chapter.)

2. Males are more likely to inherit difficulties as a result of genetic aberration than females.

3. Females are more developed at birth, mature at a faster rate than males, reach puberty and mature mentally at an earlier age.

4. Because males mature over a longer period of time than females, they are in a better position to develop their physical and athletic prowess.

5. The female does not act on the environment as does the male but is inherently more reactive; in other words responsive to stimuli.

6. Females are people-oriented while males are more curious about objects and how to handle them, and this difference is seen early in infancy.

7. Females need to relate successfully to people, while males strive to successfully complete goals.

8. Females are motivated from without while males are motivated from within.

9. Males handle spatial problems as well as mathematical problems better than females and are more adept at reasoning. Of course, females are better at linguistics, memorization and "clerical skills."

10. Because men can reason in an abstract manner so much better

than females, they have been able to make great contributions to the fields of science and philosophy.

11. Males contribute more creatively than females in an artistic, musical and scientific manner.

12. For men, masculinity and gratification in life focuses on occupational achievement and success while the female needs to be very close to someone she loves, namely her husband, and it is through this intimacy that she achieves her feminine identity.

Since people are influenced by their environment and by role expectations, what part of these differences are inherited and what part are the effect of nurture?

Attempting to objectively assess the genetic differences between the sexes which affect behavior and psychology is fraught with difficulties. Tavris and Offir (1977) present some of the reasons why reported studies are questionable. They point out that experimenters, although not consciously, and usually nonverbally, tend to influence their subjects so that the expected conclusions of the experimenter are evoked in the behavior of the subjects. A smile and stereotypic beliefs influence results. Tavris and Offir also point out that there is a tendency to publish research that demonstrates sex differences more often than reporting data that do not support these differences, as well as giving more credibility to the former.

Researchers have made giant leaps from findings of differences in inherited divergent hormonal activity to behavioral differences. Others have suggested that the apparent behavioral differences between the sexes are conditioned by culture and learning (Money, 1963). The nature-nurture debate continues. It might be wise to state that with humans environmental influences can mold innate characteristics and that both nature and nurture are significant influences.

Oh yes, another difference which has been greatly emphasized in most cultures is that the sexually mature female menstruates and the sexually mature male does not. Menstruation has been endowed by almost every culture with taboos and myths which imply that women, during the menses, are unclean, untouchable, and imbued with dangerous power. What is menstruation? What are the taboos associated with it and why do they exist?

Menstruation is the periodic (usually monthly) sloughing off of the tissue of the uterus (two layers of the endometrium), by nonpregnant women, discharged through the genital tract. The flow usually lasts about four or five days and normally a discharge of not more than eight ounces of fluid, of which only three ounces are blood, occurs (Pengelley, 1974).

The onset of puberty, according to research, seems to be related to the sex hormones and their influence on the brain (Maccoby, 1966). Puberty is usually defined as the state of development at which one becomes sexually able to reproduce and is marked by menstruation for the girl. It usually has psychological implications but for our purposes we will defer discussion of these until later.

If puberty is defined as the onset of menstruation or the growth spurt which occurs at adolescence, then we find that over the past 100 years, puberty has been occurring at an earlier age. In 1860 the average age of menarche was sixteen to seventeen and by 1960 it had decreased to twelve to thirteen (Maccoby, 1966). The question concerning the effect of environment and/or psychological factors can be raised.

The age of puberty is climactic for the girl and the onset of menstruation is the line that divides girlhood from womanhood. There is no culture that we are aware of that has "ever patterned it out of existence" (Mead, 1949, p. 176). Most primitive societies have a rite of passage from childhood to adulthood. These rites are very specifically related to the onset of menstruation for the female.

Since biblical times, this natural, biological manifestation has been surrounded by superstitions and ignorance. Leviticus fully describes the orthodox Jewish taboos surrounding the menstruating woman.

> When a woman has a discharge of blood which is her regular discharge from her body, she shall be in her impurity for seven days, and whoever touches her shall be unclean until the evening. And everything upon which she lies during her impurity shall be unclean; everything also upon which she sits shall be unclean. And whoever touches her bed shall wash his clothes, and bathe himself in water, and be unclean until evening. (Leviticus 15:19).

Taboos are placed on the man who has intercourse with a menstruating woman. He becomes unclean for seven days. The woman does not "become clean" until seven days after the discharge ends. Male discharge also results in uncleanliness, according to the Old Testament. The Talmud states that if a woman who has just started menstruating walks between two men she will be responsible for the death of one of them. Margaret Mead documented many of the taboos against menstruating women which exist among primitive tribes. In Bali, a woman who is menstruating cannot enter a temple; the Iatmul prohibit her from cooking for her husband unless she wants to harm him. The Arapesh isolate a menstruating woman in an especially built shelter.

> Around each village the ground falls away in these bad places, which are used for pigs and latrines, and on which are built the huts used by menstruating women and women in childbirth, whose dangerous blood would endanger the village, which is level and good and associated with food (Mead, 1963, p. 7).

Menstruating women are often forbidden to touch vessels or clothes. Frazer (1890) relates the story of an Australian tribesman who killed his wife because she had used his blanket to lie on during menstruation and then was himself so frightened that he died a week later of terror. Women in menses cannot touch anything used by men or walk on the same paths.

In Uganda, all pots touched by women during menses and childbirth were destroyed.

The Natural History of Pliny, which is the oldest encyclopedia in existence, lists the dangerous consequences of menstruation discharge. "Contact with it turns new wine sour, crops touched by it become barren, grafts die, seeds in the garden are dried up, the fruit of the trees fall off, the bright surface of mirrors in which it is merely reflected is dimmed, the edge of steel and the gleam of the ivory are dulled, bees die, even bronze and iron are at once seized by rust, and a horrible smell fills the air; to taste it drives dogs mad and infects their bites with an incurable poison" (Pliny, 1961, p. 549). Obviously isolation of menstruating women tended to counteract these dangerous effects.

In the Middle Ages in Europe menstruation was believed to be an indication of the fact that women were wicked and inferior. They were not allowed to enter a church or receive communion during this time. Moslems and Hindus also have taboos concerning menstruating women. Taboos and myths around menstruation still exist today in modern industrial societies. For instance, it is thought that a menstruating woman who bakes a cake will find that it won't rise.

Ashley Montagu (1970) believes that these taboos represent man's jealousy of women, particularly of their childbearing function. He supports his argument by citing the practice of removing the clitoris in primitive societies, and the large numbers of unnecessary hysterectomies and mastectomies which are performed in our society. Australian aborigines performed operations on male adolescents to simulate the female genitalia. The operation consisted of slitting upon the urethra and placing a stone in the opening so that it would not close. Sometimes the penis itself would be incised so that bleeding occurred to imitate menstruation.

Montagu further states that the jealousy of childbearing is evident by the description in the Old Testament of Adam's "giving birth" to Eve from one of his ribs. Some Australian tribes do not connect intercourse with pregnancy. A husband dreams that a spirit has entered his body and then he shares his dream with his wife, thus transferring the spirit to her. Aeschylus (535-456 B.C.) states, "The parent of that which is called her child is not really the mother of it, she is but the nurse of the newly conceived fetus. It is the male who is the author of its being, while she, as a stranger (i.e., no blood relation) preserves the young plant" (Eumenides in Montagu, 1970, pp. 18–19).

Along with taboos around menstruation, women at and after childbirth are also isolated and considered dangerous. Taboos around menstruation may very well represent the jealousy men feel because they are excluded from the childbirth process. The number of taboos around menstruating women in a culture seems to be directly related to the degree of participation by men in childbirth. There has also been noted a positive correlation between high political authoritarianism and the intensity of taboos around contact with menstruating women.

Paula Weideger (1976) contends that the taboos surrounding menstruation are the result of man's jealousy of woman and his attempt to prevent her from gaining status.

The normal biological processes of menstruation and childbirth are interpreted by men to be abnormal and dangerous. The word for menstruation among the Manus is "broken leg" indicating injury. In our society, the psychological effects have been negative. Menstruation is often accompanied by discomfort and supposed mood changes. Dysmenorrhea, painful menstruation, has been an accepted corollary to femaleness. Mead (1964), however, has pointed out that severe menstrual cramps are unheard of in Samoa and it is thought bizarre for a woman to complain of this. Much of the discomfort associated with menstruation appears to be psychological in origin rather than physical.

One psychologist at the University of California found that menstrual problems were related to religious tradition. Jewish women who believed the religious taboo on intercourse during the menstrual period had more difficulty during menstruation than those who did not. The Catholic women who were career-oriented rather than marriage and motherhood-oriented also had less difficulty. Psychologist Karen Paige concludes that there will be a decrease in the degree of acceptance of menstrual taboos as women's role becomes decreasingly that of child producer (*Time*, February 23, 1976, pp. 58–59).

Menstrual discomfort has also been correlated with the nonacceptance of femininity. When we recognize the fact that femininity is culturally defined then the psychological implications of dysmenorrhea become evident. We are in no way implying that menstrual distress may not also be somatic in origin. Dr. Katherina Dalton (1969) has identified two types of somatic dysmenorrhea—spasmodic and congestive. Sometimes, however, expecting menstrual discomfort increases the chances of the discomfort occurring as well as its intensity.

Dr. Edgar Berman, Hubert H. Humphrey's personal physician, created a stir when he said that women were unable to function well in jobs in which there was a great deal of pressure because of the tremendous influence of hormonal change (*Time*, February 23, 1976, p. 58). Dr. Dalton's twenty-year study supports the Berman thesis of the effect of hormonal change on performance. Grades dropped 15 percent when female pupils took exams during the days of "premenstrual tension." The four days before and four days after menstruation was the timespan during which "half of the female job absenteeism, suicides, police arrests, traffic accidents and admissions to mental hospitals occurred . . ." (Dalton, 1969). She concluded that the physical changes which occur during the menstrual cycle do affect the judgments people make.

Some psychologists are quick to point out that stressful conditions can hasten menstruation, and that the fact that an individual is menstruating and does poorly on exams is not a function of the hormones but of the stress. Other psychologists have noted that our culture encourages menstrual irritability by reinforcing it and that attitude towards menstruation is correlated with dysmenorrhea (*Time*, February 23, 1976, p. 58). Some feminists are suggesting that women use the process of period extraction to rid themselves of menstruation as soon as it begins. This is a method, apparently creating high risk of infection, in which a tube attached to a vacuum bottle is inserted into the uterus which, when pumped, acts as a suction device (Frankfort, 1972).

Avoidance of success has been correlated with premenstruation but no such pattern was found for menstruating women. The premenstrual phase has also been linked to loss of self-confidence and self-esteem. This may be related to the negative attitudes and experiences regarding menstruation (Patty and Ferrell, 1974).

Many biologists believe that these hormonally influenced behavior patterns which differ between the sexes at birth are reinforced by the culture.

Differentiating between the influence of hormones and environment on the differences between the males and females is difficult because both hormonal action and societal shaping sometimes result in similar behaviors. Men and women are affected by the two influences. There are those who believe that sex hormones are responsible for the built-in distinctions between males and females and are responsible to a degree for the fact that commonality in courting and sexual relations is found in the different cultures of the world (Swanson, 1974). Biological inheritance and culture (nurture) do interact and affect behavior.

Another area surrounded by myths and misconceptions is the area of female sexuality, particularly the concept that females are less interested in sex than males and that with females the orgasm is unimportant. Masters and Johnson (1966) in their classic work on human sexuality found that in both sexes the physiological processes are closely approximate. In another study of 190 societies around the world and the sexual behavior manifested, it was found that women initiated sexual advances as often as men (Clelland, 1951). Many of the attitudes toward sex as a necessary evil for reproduction and as an activity in which satisfaction for the female was considered unnecessary, which existed until fairly recently in our society, were the result of the Victorian era. In fact, a woman was often not permitted to have a physical exam without the presence of her husband or mother.

Freud was responsible for the focus of the vagina as the locus of female pleasure in spite of the fact that women reported the clitoris to be vital. He said that the clitoris is the focus of eroticism during the period when the girl is going through the phallic stage of development. However, in order to become feminine, the girl must transfer her erotic zone from the clitoris to the vagina where it must remain during her womanhood (Freud, 1946).

He further stated that those women who do not make the transition from clitoris to vagina were neurotic, demonstrating symptoms of frigidity, hysteria, and regression. In fact, Masters and Johnson (1966) found that the same physiological response occurs in orgasm regardless of the method by which stimulation occurs. In addition, they found that when there is sexual dysfunctioning in women it is a direct result of the socio-cultural pressures to deny them satisfaction, the inability of their husbands to control their ejaculations, the concept that in sex, women must satisfy their partners without their partners necessarily satisfying them, as well as the insistence of many men that they are cognizant of a woman's sexual needs, when in reality they are not.

A significant part of the cycle in women is the advent of menopause. This period has been called the "change of life," the "climax," the "climacteric" and the "critical years." All these words imply an alteration in the woman, a dangerous time, a rung in the ladder which results in dramatic change, usually negative. The word *menopause* is derived from the Greek "men" meaning month and "pauein" meaning to cause to cease. Actually, menstruation was thought by the Greeks to be directly related to the changes in the moon and so naturally, according to their thinking, the cessation of menstruation which occurs at menopause was the result of the end of the monthly cycle.

Women throughout the ages have been thought of as reproductive machines.

> As emancipated women, in a wonderfully free land, we may not relish the idea that we are meant chiefly for propagation of the human race. However, that seems to be the niche we are intended to occupy in the universal biologic plan (Levine and Doherty, 1952, p. 197).

If, as it is commonly thought, a woman's usefulness and desirability are associated with her child-bearing function, then menopause becomes a very negative stage in a woman's development.

Menopause actually occurs over a period of several years and heralds the end of a woman's reproductive life. Based on Freud's belief in biologic destiny, Dr. Helene Deutsch in her book, *The Psychology of Women,* states,

> Women go through a "partial" death at the menopause from which they never recover ... they live for the rest of their lives with the dreadful knowledge of already having passed their "natural end" because they cannot have children (Deutsch in Levine and Doherty, 1952, p. 70).

On the other hand Margaret Mead has pointed out that in many primitive societies there is no "hoop-de-la" around menopause and that a woman's status increases when she reaches this stage. In such societies, both girls who have not reached puberty, and postmenopausal women are treated as men (Mead, 1949).

All the reasons as to why menopause occurs are as yet not known; however, it is an accepted belief that there are changes in hormone stimulation from the pituitary gland which gradually cause atrophy of the ovaries, the organs that produce ova. (Apparently menopause has not been recognized among animals.) Eventually there is a cessation of the ovarian as well as the menstrual cycle in humans. Interestingly enough, as the average age of the onset of menstruation has decreased, the average age of the cessation of menstruation (menopause) has increased from thirty-eight to about fifty-one.

Several patterns of the menstrual cycle usually occur during menopause. One is the lessening of the menstrual flow although menstruation continues to be regular. Then there may be irregular periods and sometimes the occasional omission of periods. Sometimes there are both irregular periods and a decrease in flow. Sometimes, too, menstruation can suddenly cease.

Because the secretion of hormones decreases, there are effects on other glands and a concomitant change in their secretions. These changes, which are actually the body's attempt to achieve homeostasis, produce symptoms which vary with each woman.

In addition to the symptoms of change in the menstrual cycle, there may also be the following: insomnia and circulatory symptoms such as hot flashes due to vasomotor instability, headaches, metabolic imbalance caused by glandular changes, aging of the skin, thinning of the hair, and shrinking of the breasts. There is some question as to whether these are directly due to menopause or are the natural symptoms of the aging process in general.

Headaches, nervousness, and depression are also sometimes associated with menopause. These symptoms are often related to woman's role loss at this age and the empty nest syndrome. It is at this time in a woman's life that her children leave the home and she no longer has status as "Mary's mother" or "John's wife." A lack of identity often may lead to psychiatric problems. The myth of menopause and insanity still persists. Actually, women who become emotionally disturbed during menopause usually have demonstrated these difficulties before.

Those women who demonstrate high levels of anxiety, who are extremely tense and depressed, and who have mood swings are considered by Lincoln (1961) to be emotionally disturbed and should be referred for psychiatric help since these are not necessary components of menopause. They coincidentally occur at the same time.

Another myth surrounding menopausal women is that they lose their interest in sex. Sex and reproduction are separate. Sexual organs do atrophy during menopause but interest in sex and the ability to derive pleasure from sexual experiences do not end.

Women have a difficult time in coping with the myth that femininity is lost or diminished at menopause.

> ... femaleness is a fact and femininity is a quality. Femaleness is essentially anatomical and physiological. Femininity is essentially social and cultural (Levine and Doherty, 1952, p. 70).

Because of the concern for the retention of youth among today's women and because of the discomforts associated with menopause (not necessarily distressing for the average woman), hormone therapy is being used for treatment of menopausal symptoms. There is much controversy over their use ranging from the accusation that hormonal therapy increases cancer risks among women as well as the risk of gall bladder troubles, to the other side of the continuum of physicians who insist that the use of hormones not only creates comfort, but also retards the deleterious effects of the aging process.

There is no such dramatic change as menopause in middle-aged men. Men between the ages of forty-five and fifty do, however, have upheavals in affect and in their body which disturb every aspect of their professional and personal lives (Reubsaat and Hall, 1975).

Although these changes do not result in the abrupt cessation of reproduction, physical changes are significant and often do affect the emotional stability of the man. The symptoms include a slow decline in ability, in frequency, achievement, and maintenance of an erection, irregularities in urinary function, hot flashes and liver spots. "Dames" are not the only ones who are dizzy. Men do experience dizziness during this period because of disturbances in the flow of blood. They also may have backaches, headaches, heart symptoms such as heart pounding and irregular heart beat. Middle-aged men have a high rate of peptic ulcer and sometimes present symptoms of hyperventilation. Mental symptoms for men can include loss of sleep, mood swings and depressive states, tiredness, difficulty in concentrating, lack of self-confidence as well as marked changes in behavior.

The male menopause is known as the male climacteric. It, too, occurs because of the fact that men, like women age physically as well as hormonally and this aging process is affected by difficulties in mental as well as social adjustment (Reubsaat and Hall, 1975).

Every woman does go through menopause if she lives long enough. The male climacteric may possibly not be inevitable. Women are also more emotionally prepared for the changes which occur than men in our society and men do experience curtailment of their sexual ability.

So again, contrary to myth, men also go through changes. Their reproductive life, however, does not end.

American society has accepted what Ruebsaat and Hall (1975) have labeled "the Aphrodite Complex" for the man in his middle years. This complex involves a married middle-aged man suddenly seeking out a woman young enough to be his daughter with whom he has a liaison or even marries, much to the distress of his wife of "umteen" years. Like the emotional difficulties of women during the middle years of their life, the Aphrodite Complex is an indication of a flight into youth and an inability to accept the aging process. Ruebsaat and Hall in their excellent book on the male climacteric discussed the reasons for this behavior on the part of men, one of these being the climacteric man who has the idea of a liaison "put into his head by another woman" (Ruebsaat and Hall, 1975, p. 37). This implies the power and evil of women. We know for a fact that a person is responsible for his own behavior and that ideas do not take hold unless there is fertile ground for them.

In this chapter we have tried to discuss women in a biological framework. We also attempted to compare women to men on a biological basis and to demonstrate the controversy that surrounds the differences. It is important to remember that biological differences are reinforced by culture, and the cultural definitions given to them become institutionalized.

References

Anon. Culture and the curse. *Time* 58–59 (February 23, 1976).

————. What's the difference between the boys and girls? *Today's Health* **42**:85 (November, 1964).

Aristotle, *The Poetics*. T. E. Page, E. Capps, W. H. D. Roose, L. A. Post, and E. H. Warmington (eds.). Cambridge: Harvard University Press, 1960.

Bart, Pauline B. Depression in middle aged women, in Vivian Gornick and Barbara K. Moran. *Woman in Sexist Society*. New York: Basic Books, 1971.

Buck, Pearl S. *Of Men and Women*. New York: John Day Co., 1941.

Buytendijk, F. J. *Woman: A Contemporary View*. New York: Newman Press and Association Press, 1968.

Clelland, Ford S. and Beach, Frank A. *Patterns of Sexual Behavior*. New York: Harper & Row, 1951.

Cooper, Wendy. *Don't Change: A Biological Revolution for Women*. New York: Stein & Day, 1975.

Coppen, A. and Kessel, W. Menstruation and personality. *British Journal of Psychiatry* **109**:711–721 (1963).

Curtis, Edward S. *The North American Indian,* 20 Vols. Cambridge, Mass.: University Press IV:3 (1909).

Dalton, Katherina. *The Menstrual Cycle*. New York: Pantheon, 1969.

Frankfort, Ellen. *Vaginal Politics*. New York: Bantam Books, 1972.

Frazer, Sir James. *The Golden Bough*. New York: The Macmillan Co., 1890.

Freud, Sigmund. Transformations of puberty, in *The Complete Works of Sigmund Freud,* James Strachey (ed.). London: The Hogarth Press and the Institute of Psycho-analysis, Vol VII 1953, pp. 207–230.

Epstein, W., Fuchs, Cynthia and Goode, William J. *The Other Half: Roads to Women's Equality*. Englewood Cliffs, N.J.: Prentice-Hall, 1971.

Garai, Josef and Schienfeld, Amram. Sex differences in mental and behavioral traits, Genetic Psychology, Monographs, child behavior, animal behavior and problems of aging. *Journal Press* **77**:169–299 (May, 1968) Provincetown, Mass.

Glazer-Malbin, Nona and Waehrer, Helen Youngelson (eds.). *Woman in a Man-Made World*. Chicago: Rand McNally, 1973.

Goldberg, S. and Lewis, M. Play behavior in the year-old infant: early sex differences. *Child Development* **40**:21–31 (1969).

Gornick, Vivian and Moran, Barbara K. *Woman in Sexist Society*. New York: Basic Books, 1971.

Gove, Walter R. and Hughes, Michael. Causes of sex differences in physical health. *American Sociological Review* **44**:126–146 (February, 1979).

Greer, Germaine. *The Female Eunuch.* New York: McGraw-Hill Book Co., 1971.

The Holy Bible. Revised Standard Edition, Toronto: Thomas Nelson & Sons, 1952.

Levine, Lena, M.D., and Doherty, Beka. *The Menopause.* New York: Random House, 1952.

Lincoln, Miriam. *You'll Live Through It: Facts About Menopause.* New York: Harper & Brothers, Publishers, 1961.

Linton, Ralph. *The Study of Man.* New York: D. Appleton Century, 1936.

Maccoby, Eleanor (ed.). *The Development of Sex Differences.* Stanford, California: Stanford University Press, 1966.

Maccoby, Eleanor Emmons and Jacklin, Carol Nagg. Myth, reality and shades of gray: what we know and don't know about sex differences. *Psychology Today* **8:**109–112 (December, 1974).

Masters, William H. and Johnson, Virginia E. *Human Sexual Inadequacy.* Boston: Little, Brown, 1970.

―――. *Human Sexual Response.* Boston: Little, Brown, 1966.

Mead, Margaret. *Coming of Age in Samoa.* New York: William Morrow, 1964.

―――. *Male & Female.* New York: William Morrow, 1949.

―――. *Sex and Temperament in Three Primitive Societies.* New York: William Morrow, 1963.

Money, John. Developmental differentiations of femininity and masculinity compared, in Seymour Morgan Farber and R. H. L. Wilson (eds.). *Man and Civilization: The Potential of Women.* New York: McGraw-Hill Book Co., 1963.

Montagu, Ashley. *The Natural Superiority of Woman.* London: The Macmillan Co., 1970.

Parker, Elizabeth, M.D. and Evelyn Breck (eds.). *The Seven Ages of Woman.* Baltimore and London: The Johns Hopkins Press, 1960.

Patty, Rosemarie Anderson and Ferrell, Marcia M. A preliminary note on the motive to avoid success and the menstrual cycle. *Journal of Psychology* **86:**173–177 (January, 1974).

Pengelley, Eric T. *Sex and Human Life.* Reading, Mass.: Addison-Wesley, 1974.

Pliny, *Natural History,* Vol 11. H. Rackham (ed.). Cambridge: Harvard University Press, 1961.

Reeves, Nancy. *Womankind Beyond the Stereotypes.* Chicago, New York: Aldine-Atherton, 1971.

Ruderman, Florence A. Sex differences: biological, cultural, societal implications, in Cynthia Fuchs Epstein and William J. Goode (eds.). *The Other Half.* Englewood Cliffs, N.J.: Prentice-Hall, 1971.

Ruebsaat, Helmut, J., M.D., and Hall, Raymond. *The Male Climacteric.* New York: Hawthorne Books, 1975.

Schienfeld, Amram. *Your Heredity and Environment.* Philadelphia: J. B. Lippincott, 1965.

Sears, R., Maccoby, E., and Levine, H. *Patterns of Child Rearing.* New York: Harper & Row, 1957.

Sears, Robert R. Development of Gender Role, in F. A. Beach (ed.). *Sex and Behavior.* New York: John Wiley, 1965, pp. 234–265.

Shaines, W. A re-evaluation of some aspects of femininity through a study of menstruation: a preliminary report. *Comparative Psychiatry* **2**:20–26 (1961).

Sherfey, Mary Jane. Female sexuality and psychoanalytic theory, in Nona Glazer-Malbin and Helen Youngelson Waehrer (eds.). *Woman in a Man-Made World.* Chicago: Rand, McNally, 1973.

Slater, Phillip. *Pursuit of Loneliness.* Boston: Beacon Press, 1970.

Solomon, Jean. Menopause: a rite of passage. *Ms* (December, 1972).

Swanson, Harold D. *Human Reproduction: Biology and Social Change.* London, Toronto: Oxford University Press, 1974.

Tanner, J. M. *Growth and Adolescence* (2nd ed.). Oxford: Blackwell Scientific Publications, 1962.

Tavris, Carol and Offir, Carole. *The Longest War.* New York: Harcourt, Brace, Jovanovich, 1977.

Turner, Donnell C. *General Endocrinology.* Philadelphia: W. B. Saunders, 1966.

VanGennep, Arnold. *The Rites of Passage.* Chicago: The University of Chicago Press, 1960.

Veblen, T. *The Theory of the Leisure Class.* New York: Viking Press, 1931.

Waldron, Ingrid. Why do women live longer than men? *Journal of Human Stress* **2**:2–13 (March, 1976).

Weideger, Paula. *Menstruation and Menopause.* New York: Alfred A. Knopf, 1976.

Young, F. W., and Bacdayan, Albert A. Menstrual taboo and social rigidity. *Ethnology* **4**:225–240 (April, 1965).

2. Aggression and Violence

To be called assertive is a compliment. To be told one is aggressive is viewed as a criticism, and to be considered violent is to be condemned. What are the differences between the three? *The Random House Dictionary* (1966) defines assertive as "positive; aggressive; and dogmatic" (p. 90). Aggression is defined as "an unprovoked offensive attack, invasion, or the like" (p. 28) and violence as "rough or injurious physical force, action, or treatment; an unjust or unwarranted exertion of force or power . . ." (p. 1594). It is obvious that the dictionary definition of assertiveness does not coincide with the concept of assertiveness held by psychologists, social workers, psychiatrists, and others in the helping professions.

Lange and Jakubowski in their book, *Responsible Assertive Behavior* (1976) define assertion as "standing up for personal rights and expressing thoughts, feelings, and beliefs in direct, honest, and appropriate ways which do not violate another person's rights" (p. 7).

Assertiveness, therefore, does not involve attack. The object of being assertive is to prevent oneself from having one's needs unmet and not, as the dictionary definition would imply, to hurt someone else. Self-respect as well as regard for others is implicit in assertive behavior.

Aggression involves complete lack of concern for the other person and major emphasis on the "gimme" syndrome without consideration for the others involved.

Assertiveness helps a person become self-actualizing; that is, to fully realize his/her potential, to be fulfilled rather than frustrated. But women who are assertive are often labeled aggressive. Influencing this attitude is the concept that women are innately less aggressive than men, and therefore any demonstration of definitive behavior is perceived negatively, since it is unexpected.

Let us look at the research on aggression as it attempts to explain human behavior, and as it attempts to establish whether or not females are biologically less aggressive than males.

Finding an all-inclusive definition of aggression is very difficult. Goldstein defines aggression as "behavior whose intent is the physical injury of another person," (Goldstein, 1975, p. x). This is synonymous with the dictionary's definition of violence. This definition means that verbal abuse as well as physical assault can be considered aggressive behavior. The purposeful act of hurting someone in some way is aggressive while causing an accidental injury to someone is not. What Goldstein does not address himself to in any great detail is whether the intent has to be conscious. Can unconscious intent be construed as aggression?

For example, as a young girl I spent many summer vacations on my aunt and uncle's dairy farm in New Jersey. Since they did not have a machine to wash bottles, water was boiled, and the milk bottles were cleaned manually. In the process of helping my cousin carry a large tub of boiling water to the sink, I accidentally jolted the tub, splashing a small amount of hot water on my hand. As a self-protective impulse, I dropped the handle of the tub, thereby causing boiling water to spill on my cousin's feet and to burn her. My conscious intent was not to hurt my cousin. Would psychoanalytically oriented psychiatrists say that I felt some unconscious hostility, and if so, would the "accidental" burning of my cousin be considered aggression? Actually, Goldstein does state that aggression can be viewed on a continuum, and that behavior of any kind may have elements of aggressiveness. Accidental hurting would be placed on one end of the continuum, while a deliberate attempt to annihilate someone would be on the other end.

Moyer, in his book, *The Psychobiology of Aggression* (1976), states that aggression is " . . . overt behavior involving intent to inflict noxious stimulation or to behave destructively toward another organism" (p. 2). He views intent as purposeful, and not some act which occurs unintentionally, but does state that aggression may be direct or indirect, successful or unsuccessful. The person who attempts unsuccessfully to stab another person is demonstrating aggressive behavior. Assertive behavior, he argues, is not aggressive behavior because the intent is not to hurt another but to stand up for one's rights. Hostility and aggression are synonymous to Moyer, although hostility is often defined as a learned negative attitude.

Although the word *intent* was not used in one of the early definitions of aggression, that proposed by Dollard and his colleagues in 1939, it seems to be implied. They defined aggression as " . . . an act whose goal-response is injury to an organism (or organism-surrogate)" (Dollard et al., 1939, p. 11).

Aggression to Buss is "a response that delivers noxious stimuli to another organism" (Buss, 1961, p. 1) and is synonymous with attack. He states that intent refers to future orientation which cannot be measured behaviorally, and that it is more important to look at those consequences of aggressive behavior which reinforce it.

Bandura, a proponent of the social learning school of behavior, states that aggression is ". . . behavior that results in personal injury and destruction of property. The injury may be psychological (in the form of devaluation or degradation) as well as physical" (Bandura, 1973, p. 5). However, the way society labels the behavior is germane to whether or not it is seen as aggressive; in other words a parent's spanking of a child or a doctor's injecting a needle into a patient, although treating pain would be excluded from the definition of aggression. Therefore, aggression is *"injurious and destructive behavior that is socially defined as aggressive on the basis of a variety of factors, some of which reside in the evaluator rather than in the performer"* (Bandura, 1973, p. 8). People judge acts as aggressive based on several factors, one of which is the type of behavior whose consequences are generally repugnant, such as physical attacks as well as the demolition of property. "Intensity of responses" affects the judgment made on the behavior. Loud, impulsive responses are more apt to be labeled as aggressive. If the receivers of the act express pain or demonstrate injury, the behavior will have a greater chance of being labeled aggressive. The characteristics of the labelers, as well as the way the labelers perceive the intent of the person performing the behavior, affect judgment. In summary, aggression, according to Bandura, cannot be labeled as such in isolation.

What permeates all the definitions is the concept that aggressiveness is negative. Therefore, when an assertive act by a woman is labeled as aggressive, it gives the woman the message that the act of standing up for her rights is unacceptable. Buss (1961) classifies aggression into "angry aggression" and "instrumental aggression." Angry aggression for Buss is set off by stimuli which produce anger such as verbal or physical abuse. Instrumental aggression is aggression which is performed in order to achieve a goal. In this situation, hurting or destroying is not an end in itself but rather a means to an end. It is believed that most aggressive behavior falls into this category.

Megargee (1969) further differentiated the angry aggression into violent acts resulting from inability to control aggressive impulses and the expression of anger that results from overly controlling angry feelings. "Like steam in a kettle, the anger builds up until it explodes."

Defining violence is a difficult task. Everyone has a different idea concerning what constitutes violence, and many articles and books written on that topic don't even bother to define what is meant by the word. If violence is correlated with destruction, then aggression at times is correlated with it, and violence can be viewed as an extreme form of aggression. Steinmetz uses in her book, *The Cycle of Violence* (1977), the definition that violence is "the unsanctioned use of force" (p. 31). She states that force can be used in a legitimate manner in order to achieve an end which is considered beneficial. Using force to subdue an uncontrolled, acting-out mental patient would therefore not be considered violence. The use of force on a passive, withdrawn patient would be a violent act. The use of force by parents and policemen is socially sanctioned unless the degree of force used is considered to be excessive and unless the forceful reaction is not warranted by the situation.

What is the origin of aggression in humans? The controversy over whether aggression is instinctual, learned, or a combination of both has been raging for decades.

Sigmund Freud was a proponent of the theory that there are such things as instincts in humans and that these instincts are very important in shaping behavior. Early in his career, Freud developed the theory that people were influenced by two basic instincts, one the sexual instinct (libido), and the other the ego instinct. The ego, he theorized, was involved with reality, while the sexual instinct was pleasure based, and therefore a conflict existed between the two. Neurosis occurs when the individual represses earlier sexual wishes. The goal of the ego instincts is preservation of the organism, and aggression manifests itself when the ego is thwarted. Later, Freud revised his theory to include two basic instincts: Eros, the life instinct and Thanatos, the death instinct. Aggression became to Freud, a basic instinctual force which vied with the life instinct for control. The death instinct strives to bring the individual to a state of complete lack of tension. Since life itself is tension producing, the death instinct is opposed by Eros (life instinct) which permits only sexual tension to be discharged (Buss, 1961). If as Freud posited, aggression is a basic instinctual drive, then it is always striving for discharge. Discharge need not be direct in terms of destructive behavior but can occur through the process of catharsis through which aggressive impulses can be dissipated vicariously by viewing violence or through the use of one of the ego defense mechanisms such as sublimation, etc. If the death instinct is not dissipated, it can be turned inward and result in some form of self-destruction. The greater the energy of the death instinct, the more the individual needs to siphon aggression off by discharging it to objects or other people.

The death instinct is therefore self-destructive when focused on self or destructive to others when it is expressed outwardly. In sadism and masochism, sexuality merges with the death instinct. Aggression in man is an ever-present biologically rooted impulse.

Freud's concept of a death instinct is not accepted by all psychoanalysts. Some uphold the concept of an aggression instinct, while others believe that Freud's original thesis was correct; i.e., frustration produces aggression and that aggression itself is not biologically based (Buss, 1961).

Criticism of Freud's theory of aggression as an instinctual force abounds. Berkowitz (1962) criticizes Freud's theory of aggression by pointing to a number of studies which demonstrate that organisms are not always attempting to reduce tension, but at times seem to need increased stimulation and that achieving quiescence through death is not basic to all life. Other researchers like Buss (1961) point out that aggression is thought to be instinctual because it appears to be unlearned. However, says Buss, in humans it is very difficult to differentiate between learned and unlearned behaviors.

Karen Horney (1937), a neo-Freudian, made a major contribution to the psychoanalytic theory of aggression. She did not accept either the death instinct or aggression as instinctual, but stated that hostility and aggression occur because of the individual's need to work through what she called "basic anxiety," the apprehension a child feels in the world, which is perceived as hostile and in which the child feels alone. The child may respond to this feeling by movement toward, against or away from others. The aggressive individual is one who sees the world as a hostile place and who needs to strike out against it. Buss (1961) criticizes that portion of her theory which does not explain the causes of the various tendencies in each individual. Why does one person reach out whereas another aggresses? Childhood experiences seem to play an important role in determining how aggression is handled.

There is also a human development theory of violence that posits the following. All children have aggressive tendencies which are usually fused with what Anna Freud called "loving urges" unless something happens which makes it difficult for a child to achieve this fusion. Rejection by parents or excessive punishment neutralizes the child's desire to give up destructive behavior for love.

> ... violent people are the products of human development ... Violence appears in the life of the individual whose parents showed him no love, whose parents portrayed life and the world as violent, and whose parents reinforced violence as desired behavior, rationalizing it as reasonable, and natural, rather than monstrous in quality. Life experiences reinforce those from infancy and childhood, and increase the likelihood that intense anger will become coupled with poor control and result in violence (summary of E. McNeil's concept of violence as discussed in Chodorkoff and Baxter, 1969, p. 1132).

Konrad Lorenz made headlines with his book, *On Aggression,* published in 1964. In it he proposed that aggression was indeed an instinct made up of energy which was ever present. If the energy is not released, he argued, it accumulates until it explodes. Animals and people usually find ways of releasing this energy before it becomes explosive and very often actively look for stimuli in order to achieve this release. "Appetite behavior" is those actions whose goal is to seek out stimuli in order to achieve release of this aggressive energy. Outside stimuli, according to Lorenz, are not essential to aggression, which will be expressed anyway. Lorenz posits that the aggression instinct has been instrumental in the survival of animals (Fromm, 1973). It has created problems for humans because man does not have a specialized mechanism for killing and therefore had no need to evolve with inhibitions in this area. But man is dangerous because while having no inhibitions, he has *developed* mechanisms to inflict death.

Although Lorenz studied aggressiveness in animals, he generalized his findings onto man. He suggests that aggression is an unlearned biological drive and is a destructive force in man but was an adaptive force in animals functioning to help them to survive.

Lorenz has been criticized for not relying on adequate data on aggression in animals, for assuming that because some men murder there is no inhibition against killing (Johnson, 1972), as well as assuming that what holds true for animals is true for man (Fromm, 1973). Fighting and killing intraspecies is not only a characteristic of man, as Lorenz would have us believe. Man, however, will fight for emotional reasons such as patriotism, the defense of honor, or religious beliefs; while other animals, so far as we know, seem to fight only for survival. In addition, Johnson maintains that fighting is not the only survival mechanism for animals. He cites behaviors such as flight, as well as "playing possum" or the lizard's shedding of parts of its body as examples of survival-aiding mechanisms. In some primates cooperation leads to survival. This is the case with the baboons, in which a one-to-one contest with a lion would meet with the ultimate defeat, death. Johnson therefore concludes that fighting behavior was only one of the methods animals used for survival.

Johnson also points out that although some animals are equipped with deadly weapons, such as claws, horns or fangs, they do not always make use of them, especially when fighting with animals of the same species.

Ardrey (1966), another proponent of the instinct theory, postulates that, like animals, man has a territorial instinct and aggression is directly related to it. "We defend our space, our home, our village, our nation, not because we choose but because we must" (Ardrey, 1976).

Actually, man is the only animal in which aggression is not always instrumental; that is, for the purpose of achieving a goal such as food, shelter, a mate or a nesting site. Most animals do not fight for the sake of fighting and do not demonstrate the need to injure their foe (Johnson, 1972). Although defense of territory is fairly common among most animals, there are some who do not manifest this behavior, such as the zebra and many of the primates. Johnson raises the question of the danger of generalizing from animals to humans. He does state that defense of territory and concern for ownership is prevalent in human beings but that there are some cultures in which private property is nonexistent. To assume that defense of territory is an inherited characteristic in humans is a questionable assumption (Johnson, 1972). To conclude that it is the basis of aggression is even more suspect. Scientists are still unsure of how territoriality evolved but they do know that many species manifest territorial behavior.

There is an increasing interest in the concept of space relating to human behavior. Territoriality means defining one's physical space and defending it against the intrusion of others. We defend our homes from robbers and our country from invaders, but so far there has not been any hard data which supports Ardrey's concept that these behaviors are instinctive rather than learned.

Experiments have shown that people do define their personal space and do not like having it violated. In one experiment mental patients tended to sit on unoccupied benches and to move away from the bench when someone else sat down next to them by the time twenty minutes had elapsed. College students manifested the same behavior (Felipe and Sommer, 1966).

In 1939 John Dollard and his associates at Yale published a theory of aggression which was widely accepted and is still being tested as well as debated today. Basically, they proposed that aggressive behavior indicates that frustration has occurred. They defined frustration as *"that condition which exists when a goal-response suffers interference"* (Dollard et al., 1939, p. 11). In simple words, the interrupted goal-directed behavior results in aggression, an unlearned response. A motivating force is created and is usually directed to the person who becomes the object of aggression and who is usually the thwarter. Frustration leads to aggression. Several years later some of the members of the Yale group who had been instrumental in developing the frustration-aggression theory with Dollard modified the hypothesis to include the occurrence of behaviors other than aggression as a reaction to frustration. These behaviors emerged because aggressive behavior was not reinforced (Bandura, 1973).

The frustration-aggression theory also assumed that the intensity of aggressive behavior was directly related to the degree of frustration.

Dollard et al., posited that the aggressive behavior could be covert as in thinking or fantasizing, as well as overt towards people or objects directly or symbolically.

Berkowitz (1962) presents a modified version of the Dollard et al., theory. He agrees with the basic frustration-aggression hypothesis and posits that each frustration produces the emotion of anger, which is the instigating force for aggressive behavior. The determining factor as to whether or not the aggression is expressed is the stimulus or cue linked with the "anger instigator."

Berkowitz discusses the effect that previous experience has on the manner in which the person responds to the frustration. He points out that an individual defines what is occurring based on what she/he has been exposed to in the past and that the manner in which she/he interprets the obstruction is determined by his perception of the frustration.

Past experiences also influence whether an aggressive or nonaggressive response will be elicited as well as its intensity. Berkowitz also supports the concept that the degree of anticipated punishment (physical or social) and the degree to which an individual feels his/her behavior will contradict his/her desired standards, will have an inhibitory effect on aggressive behavior. Punishment is a deterrent only if the act to be committed has the potential of being discovered by the punisher. Berkowitz also presented the following hypothesis concerning the chosen target for aggressiveness after a frustration had occurred: (1) The perceived source of the frustration usually receives the aggressive response; (2) the objects which are perceived to be like the frustrating agent become to a degree the focus of the aggressiveness. This latter hypothesis has relevance in terms of the hostility that men who rape express towards their victims.

It has been theorized that some men rape as an expression of hostility towards the significant woman or women in their lives. The concept of displacement enters into the picture here, and Berkowitz addresses himself to that particular mechanism and its relationship to frustration. Displacement is the process of releasing energy towards one object which was unable to be released toward the original source. A student who is angry with the teacher because he has been kept in after school may not feel that he can express his anger towards the teacher because he may be further punished. In the hydraulic theory of aggression, the energy needs to be dissipated and so the child yells at a friend with minimal provocation. It is also theorized that the substitute object who is chosen for expression of the hostility (the scapegoat) is usually one who is perceived as nonretaliatory (Williams, 1947).

In an attempt to summarize the conflicting literature on catharsis in the report by the National Commission on the Causes and Prevention of Violence (1969), Megargee concludes that

> counteraggression undoubtedly can reduce instigation to aggression. However, this is not inevitable, nor is counteraggression necessarily the most effective way of reducing instigation. Over a long period of time, the problem is complicated by the fact that: (a) subsequent stimuli, or the individual's own reminiscences, can rearouse the instigation despite catharsis; and (b) while the catharsis may lower instigation, it may also lower inhibitions even more, so that the individual will have an even greater propensity for aggressive behavior after the catharsis than he did prior to it. (Megargee, 1969, p. 1074).

Bandura (1973), a proponent of the social learning theory, believes that all behavior among humans is mainly socially transmitted and that aggressive behavior, as one form, is basically learned. Humans have the neurological and physiological potential to behaviorally express aggression but whether or not a person does so depends on what type of stimulus the individual receives as well as the exercise of control from the brain. Past experiences, therefore, he argues, determine how, if, when, and how often aggression is manifested, as well as who or what the object of aggression will be. Because behavior is learned, aggressive behavior can be transmitted. Children tend to learn how to behave from the actions they see around them. Significant adults provide them with role models. One study demonstrated that there was a correlation between fathers' criminality and the tendency of sons to become involved in crime (McCord et al., 1959). The behavior of one or both parents of delinquent boys was found to be more aggressive than that of nondelinquent boys (Glueck and Glueck, 1950).

There are those researchers who have stressed the role of the brain in aggression (Delgado, 1967, and Heath, 1962). Delgado demonstrated that by placing electrodes in the brain and by stimulating the hypothalamus, the aggressive behavior of cats and other animals could be controlled.

Among many animals, aggressive behavior increases during the mating season. Camels become violent during this time and in order to avoid having to cope with this destructive behavior, in the Sahara only one male is allowed to remain with a group of females. Brain damage can also affect both sexual and aggressive acts in humans. One woman who demonstrated severe violent behavior culminated by razor-blade and broken-glass assaults indicated that in addition to participation in a number of sex orgies she also masturbated as much as 20 times daily (Mark and Ervin, 1970). She was found to have a brain abnormality.

Tumors in the brain have been known to cause personality changes which include irritability and violent outbursts. Moyer (1976) cites the case of Charles Whitman, who felt that his compulsion to commit violent acts was becoming uncontrollable. In the note he wrote prior to his death in 1966, he described himself as having severe headaches, and requested that an autopsy be performed to investigate the possibility of a physical cause for his difficulty. After killing his wife and his mother, he took a rifle to the tower at the University of Texas and indiscriminately fired at people below. Fourteen murders and 24 wounded people later, he was shot by the police. A post-mortem examination revealed the possibility of a tumor in his bullet-shattered brain. People were shocked by the killings.

Periodically, a headline hits the front pages of the newspapers about a quiet, nonviolent, low-key person who suddenly commits murder. These sudden murderers usually have some elements of their background in common. They come from fairly conforming families who are a cohesive unit. Because of personality difficulties, these murderers were not able to achieve the conformity expected of them, projected their difficulties on to others and felt alone. They become increasingly angered and enraged because people they are relating to have expectations of them which they cannot meet. Extreme anger is triggered off at the slightest provocation, and violence in the form of homicide results (Lamberti et al., 1967).

Epilepsy and behavior disorders are also companions. Abnormal EEG's are frequently found in violent habitual criminals. Sixty-five percent of the criminally violent in a study in London were found to have abnormal EEG's as compared with 24 percent of those who were sentenced for only one violent criminal act (Williams, 1969).

Surgically induced lesions in certain areas of the brain tend to reduce aggressiveness, and this technique was used with some frequency in the past before the use of drug therapy to control the violent behavior of mentally disturbed patients. Implantation of electrodes to reduce pain is at present being experimented with. Moyer concludes that human hostility and aggressiveness are neurologically based and become operative as a reaction to particular stimuli. The hostility and aggressive feelings may be translated into behavior. He does not accept the concept of energy associated with aggression which needs to be released but does state that learning to inhibit aggression is impossible (Moyer, 1976).

There are also those who believe that violence is genetically determined. In 1965 Jacobs, Brunton, and Melville's research led them to the finding that there were a larger number of mentally "sub-normal" men with the XYY combination in criminal institutions than there were in the general population. The sample they used, however, was biased since they selected as their subjects tall men rather than testing the total population or random sampling. (Excessive height is believed to also be associated with the "XYY Syndrome.") Again in 1967

Court-Brown found that the prisoners he investigated, who were labeled as criminally insane, had an extra Y chromosome 20 times more often than the normal population. These studies were used as evidence that aggressiveness, and therefore criminal behavior was genetically determined.

What was overlooked was the fact that, in some of the research, the criminal population used had most often committed crimes against property rather than against people (Bandura, 1973). Price and Whatmore (1967) refuted the conclusion that an extra Y chromosome predisposed a man to violent acts by demonstrating the prisoners with the XYY anomaly actually had committed fewer sexual and physical attacks on people than a comparable group with the Y. There have been court cases in the United States and in other countries in which the extra Y chromosome was used as a defense to absolve a client from guilt of having committed a crime. It is argued that if a person is born to be a criminal, then that person does not have control over his behavior.

It is also possible that genetic brain abnormalities may result in aggressive behavior; however, researchers question whether pathological conditions in the brain alone create violent attacks or whether these conditions combined with influential environmental factors result in violent behavior (Mulvihill and Tumin, 1969).

Studies have effectively demonstrated the relationship between alcohol consumption and violence (Wolfgang, 1958, Blum, 1969. Report of the President's Commission on Crime in the District of Columbia, 1966). They indicate that a large number of murders, rapes and assaults involve at least one person who has been drinking, either the attacker or the victim. In one study in which the Thematic Apperception Test was used, hostile feelings appeared to increase as drinking increased. The TAT is a projective test in which the subject is asked to tell a story about an ambiguous picture she/he is shown. The researchers found that after about four or five drinks, the subjects, college men, presented themes which were less physically violent and increasingly physically sexual in form. Heavy drinking resulted in a return of the physically violent theme (Kalin et al., 1965). What is still not apparent is whether people who are basically nonviolent become violent with alcohol consumption; whether the same people who committed violent acts during an alcoholic bout were previously passive during other occasions of excessive consumption of alcohol.

Studies currently available do not indicate what the chances of killing or being killed while drinking are, relative to the chances of the same hazard while not drinking . . . One must keep in mind that even if alcohol appears to be a necessary element in some instances of homicide, it is clearly not necessary for all of them. Further, it is important to bear in mind that alcohol use does not automatically or necessarily lead to violence (Mulvihill and Tumin, 1969, pp. 648–649)

A disease like rabies which is not only contracted by animals but also by humans causes a surge of hostile and aggressive behavior in both, apparently by irritating and damaging nerve cells in the brain.

Impulsive aggressive behavior is also commonly found in patients suffering from encephalitis which causes an inflammation of the brain. The resultant behavior may often be misdiagnosed as psychotic although it is the result of a neural viral infection.

In many societies the behavior of women is less aggressive than that of the men. Can we then conclude that women are born to be passive? Sex hormones are apparently important influencers of behavior, more so in animals than in humans. Castrating a stallion or a bull dramatically changes the animal's behavior from pugnaciousness to tameness. Androgens (male sex hormones) are associated with aggressive behavior in animals (Lagerspetz, 1969). As animals become sexually mature, there is an apparent increase in aggressiveness (Johnson, 1972). Although there are several sex hormones in both males and females, the androgen testosterone is considered to have the greatest effect on aggressiveness. This hormone is responsible for triggering puberty in males. In studying the behavior of rats, one finds that there is no excessively combative behavior until puberty is reached. Levy and King (1953) found that if prepubertal rats receive testosterone injections, fighting increased.

Testosterone-injected hens will develop male secondary sex characteristics such as a rooster-like comb as well as demonstrate increased aggressive behavior. Their status in the pecking order also changes. A loss of status in the pecking order is associated with castration and injection with female hormones (Johnson, 1972). Replication of this experiment in primates produced the same results.

The effect of the hormonal change is not always that direct. If male rats are castrated before birth, their behavior at maturity closely resembles that of the female (Conner and Levine, 1969). However, Denenburg (1971) found that when male rats who killed young rats were castrated they continued to manifest this behavior, but that castration before birth resulted in non-pup-killing behavior. Injection of androgen in female rats immediately following birth increased aggressive behavior, especially during courting attempts (Bronson and Desjardins, 1968).

Evidence of greater aggressive behavior in males has also been obtained from experiments on primates. Play in monkeys is considered functional as preparation for their roles as adults. Male monkeys appear to engage in more physically aggressive play than females as a way of preparing them for their adult role of seeking dominance and protection (Devore, 1965). In many of the animal species, males generally display more fighting behavior than females. Female monkeys who are injected with androgens display increased aggressive behavior (Joslyn, 1973).

Evidence supports the concept that female and male hormones have an effect on behavior and that in primates other than man, males are more aggressive than females. Evidence also supports the thesis that females injected with male hormones demonstrate increased aggressive behavior and that castrated males become less aggressive. Although males are more often the fighters in the animal kingdom, how the species is socially organized affects who aggresses more (Johnson, 1972).

What about humans? Can we conclude that because sex hormones are important influencers on the behavior of animals that this holds true for the human species?

It is very difficult to experiment with humans in the same manner as with animals. Very often we study people who already demonstrate the symptom or behavior that we are interested in rather than setting up an experimental design because this might be detrimental to the health of the subject. Studies of hermaphrodites have elicited information on the effects of sex hormones, particularly on the fetus. Hermaphrodites are individuals who, because of hormonal imbalance, are not clearly differentiated sexually. The genetic transmission of the Adrenogenital Syndrome (AGS) results in a malfunctioning of the fetal adrenal glands. Androgens are secreted in overabundance, thus resulting in the development of ambiguous genitalia in the female. Surgery plus lifelong cortisone treatment is used to remedy the difficulty. Although these females have not been experimentally injected with androgens, the excessive secretion of male hormones in the fetal state is similar to the experimentally induced situation in which female mice were treated with androgens to test their effect. Several studies on girls with AGS have been done to determine whether, because of the excessive amounts of secreted male hormones, they displayed excessive masculine behaviors or in other ways were more masculine than girls who were not so affected. In 1967, interviews with the girls and their mothers revealed that the androgenized girls viewed themselves as tomboys, were more interested in sports and tended to shy away from frilly clothes and did not place a great deal of emphasis on marriage as a primary goal compared with the control group. Both the control group and the research subjects show equal aggressiveness (Money and Ehrhardt, 1972).

But boys with AGS do not differ from normal boys in appearance but need to be treated with cortisone to prevent early onset of puberty. With these boys, increase in feminine characteristics, as well as bleeding through the urethra may occur if untreated. In their 1974 research Ehrhardt and Baker found that androgenized girls on the average were more physically oriented in their play during childhood, and although they were not too concerned with cosmetics and hairstyling, they had an evident identification with being female. The researchers conclude that fetal hormones may have a contributory influence on behavior, but that in human beings the influences are not conspicuous, and in no way should be used to determine feminine and masculine roles. There are great variations in hormonal secretions in each person and not all females, nor all males, are alike.

During the Middle Ages, boys were castrated so that they could become court jesters and not in any way pose a sexual threat to the women in court. Eunuchs stood guard in harems in some countries.

A State Training School in Kansas had the dubious honor of being the first to castrate a young man in the United States in order to control his sexual perversions. In Germany and Switzerland castration of criminals was legal but seldom used. In Denmark, a prisoner committed for a sex crime can obtain an early release from prison if he voluntarily submits to being castrated. A correlation between a decrease in recidivism and castration has been found (Johnson, 1972). The view that sex criminals, most of whom are men, should be castrated still exists today. As recently as April, 1979 the Maine legislature had before it a bill which would have provided for the castration of anyone who was convicted more than once of molesting a child under the age of fourteen. John Money, a sex researcher, testified before the lawmakers and urged them to use hormone therapy to decrease the offender's sex drive as opposed to permanently desexualizing him. The bill was defeated.

Generally, however, castration is not practiced in our society. There was, however, a reported case of an accidental destruction of the penis of a seven-month-old boy during circumcision. The parents faced a terrible dilemma. Should the child be raised as a girl in contrast to his identical twin, who was being reared as a boy? Reconstruction surgery to approximate the female genitalia was done and the child's name changed to a feminine one when the youngster was almost one and one-half years old. Later, in comparing each twin to the other, Money and Ehrhardt (1972) found that the twin whose sex identity had been reassigned, had many of the attributes considered feminine in our society, such as an interest in frilly clothes, concern with hair style and a strong preference for play with dolls. The other twin, on the other hand, was more rough in play and identified with the father and his interests. It is apparent from this research that gender identity is not solely a function of physiology but develops after we are born. Although aggressiveness is closely associated with masculinity in humans, gender role (the degree to which one is masculine or feminine) is believed by many researchers, including Money and Ehrhardt, to be influenced by hormones in utero but most importantly to be influenced by postnatal experiences.

The menstrual cycle in women is associated with cyclic changes. The secretions of hormones, some researchers have suggested, can create changes in mood. These mood fluctuations range from minimal hostile feelings or anxiety during ovulation (Gottschalk, 1969), to irritability, hostility, aggressiveness and mood swings in the premenstrual phase. These symptoms also manifest themselves during the actual menstrual flow. Attempts at suicide increase dramatically during the premenstrual phase (Dalton, 1959). The premenstrual and menstrual phases, according to research, are fraught with negative behaviors and symptoms of difficulty. Women tend to actively initiate psychiatric help during the premenstrual cycle (Jacobs and Charles, 1970). Among women, admissions to psychiatric hospitals, commission of crimes, and accidents have been found to significantly increase during this period (Dalton, 1964).

A little over half the wives of graduate students studied at one university stated that irritability increased during a number of their premenstrual experiences and was the emotion felt to a greater degree than that of depression (Hamburg, 1971). In one study of women in prison, 62 percent of crimes considered violent were found to have been perpetrated during the week prior to the onset of the menses (Morton et al., 1953).

In an article entitled, "The Premenstrual Syndrome" (1973), Parlee reviews the research in the area of premenstrual effects on mood and behavior and discusses the problems surrounding methodology. One approach used by researchers was to analyze behavior occurring during the premenstrual cycle in order to see whether or not there were some consistent patterns. Some correlational studies, states Parlee, may actually demonstrate that there is an association between the menstrual cycle and behaviors, such as commission of crimes, suicides, etc. The research, however, does not actually show that hormonal change was the causal factor and that a wider range of correlational studies on other populations, including men, needs to be done before accurate conclusions can be reached. Observing behavior of males and interviewing them, one researcher found that men also have fluctuations in mood and that these mood changes are cyclic. In addition, the cycles of the moon have been found to have an influential effect on the commission of violent crimes by males and females (Lieber and Sherin, 1972). Parlee also critically analyzed those research projects which relied on the use of retrospective questionnaires. In this method, women are asked to respond to questions relating to the memory of their moods during a particular phase of the cycle. Parlee questions the reliability and validity of the questionnaires used since the methodology did not ensure objectivity and reliability.

The use of "daily self-reports or observations" is one of the more reliable approaches according to Parlee. Most of the individual reports did not support the concept of individual definitive cycles occurring during the studied time span. When all individual reports were consolidated, distinct menstrually related cycles were evident in terms of increase of irritability, depression, sensitivity and physical symptoms, such as changes in the breast, pains in the head as well as in the back. More studies, Parlee suggests, need to be done using women who are not menstruating as control groups.

Another approach to studying the effects of the menstrual cycle is one called the "thematic analysis of unstructured verbal material," a technique commonly referred to as the Gottschalk technique. In this method, women are asked to talk into a tape recorder for a five-minute period on anything they wish which revolved around some life experience. Gottschalk (1969) and his group developed a scoring method in which what was said, if hostile, could be identified as hostility, both directed inwards and outwards, as well as identifying anxiety. Parlee does state that studies done using the Gottschalk technique have noted that changes in anxiety and hostility do occur during the menstrual cycle.

Parlee's main criticism of most of the studies done with the premenstrual syndrome is the lack of standardized definition of its meaning as well as the lack of the use of adequate control groups.

Johnson (1972) accepts the conclusion that low emotional trigger points are cyclic in women and that the rhythm of hormonal secretions during the menstrual cycle has an effect on this. However, Johnson believes that the exact reason for these changes occurring is still not clear. There is evidence that the increase in hostility is associated with the increase in the secretion of estrogen. Progesterone treatment reduces these symptoms, and women who are taking oral contraceptives tend to be less irritable than those who are not on the pill. Hypoglycemia, according to Johnson, may also be related to the premenstrual syndrome, which he defines as consisting of physical symptoms, such as headaches, swelling of some parts of the body, gaining of weight as well as increase in energy. Irritability was found to be associated with hypoglycemia in several studies, and there is evidence that blood sugar decreases prior to menstruation (Billig and Spalding, 1947). Hypoglycemic murderers have on occasion been absolved of responsibility for the crime they committed because they were judged temporarily insane as a result of the hypoglycemia. If, indeed, women feel particularly irritable, hostile and aggressive premenstrually, feeling and acting on one's feelings are different. Since anthropologically and sociologically menstruation does not exist in physiological isolation but is influenced by societal definition and cultural expectations, would it not be more accurate to say that hormonal changes alone are not sufficient to explain behavior, and that the feelings people have and the behavior they manifest are influenced by their environmental and cultural milieu?

Bandura (1973) suggests that a person learns how to react to particular stimuli (menstruation can be included in this category) and that the behavior the stimuli elicits is influenced to a large degree by experience. We again ask the question, are boys more aggressive than girls?

Bandura (1973) did an experiment in which girls and boys watched violence on a film. In one situation the aggressor was punished, in another given praise and a reward, and in the third situation nothing happened to the model. There was a sex difference in the reproduction of the modeled behavior between boys and girls. Boys tended to readily produce the modeled aggressive behavior, particularly those boys who had not seen the model punished or those who had seen the model rewarded. Girls, on the other hand, refrained from demonstrating aggressive behavior until reassured that it was okay. The consequence of the behavior of the model did not influence the behavior of the girls. Bandura concluded that girls very often learn aggressiveness but refrain from performing aggressive acts. They learn that aggressing physically is not appropriate for females.

Bandura also posits that learning takes place through observations of role models, especially those who resemble oneself (Mischel, 1970). Many of the role models that girls are exposed to are nonaggressive women; women who themselves have been molded by the role expectations of women in our society. If physical acting out or an expression of verbal aggression is not positively associated with the proper way females are expected to behave, little girls are influenced by nonaggressive role-models. Learning, according to Bandura, also occurs through the opportunity to practice behaviors and the response these behaviors elicit. Girls are less apt to be permitted to repeat aggressive acts.

"Men probably have stronger aggressiveness habits than do women and thus generally make stronger hostile responses to the evoking cue. . . . Those presumably strong aggressiveness habits would be an outgrowth of the greater parental reinforcement of aggression by boys and girls" (Berkowitz, 1962, p. 269).

Berkowitz and his colleagues found that women find difficulty in directly expressing aggression. He believes that one reason for this inhibition is the fact that women in our society are more oriented towards conformity towards the sex-role expectation. He cites a study of 379 children in the Boston area who came from middle- and lower-class environments, a study made by Sears and his colleagues. Aggressive behavior, they concluded, was expected and considered normal for boys by their parents, but direct expression of aggression was discouraged for girls.

A woman tends to express her aggression in a less direct manner. Berkowitz also posits that girls, in some cases, do not copy the aggressive behavior of role models because this behavior is considered to be sex inappropriate in our culture.

The ability to perceive violence differs in males and females and is positively related to age (Moore, 1966). Johnson (1972) presents this as an indication that differential experiences as indicated by the differences in the sex of the individuals, as well as the degree of experience, as indicated by age, influence one's perception. Remember, too, that perception, according to Berkowitz, is an influencing factor in determining the object of aggressive acts.

The question is, are men innately, hormonally or environmentally more aggressive than women or a combination of any or all three? If the tendency to behave aggressively differs, what determines who, when and if one does aggress?

Another question that might be raised is whether sex and aggression are related in some way. Researchers seem to have found significant correlations between the two. A diminution of sexual and aggressive behavior took place in rats which were castrated. Aggressiveness and sexual behavior increased when these same rats were injected with testosterone (Beach, 1945). Berkowitz (1962) feels that there is inadequate evidence to support the existence of an aggressive drive.

The debate rages as to whether or not violence on television influences the commission of violent acts. The movie, *The Warriors,* a movie about teen-age violence apparently triggered off a number of assaults in the area in which it was shown. Olivia Niemi, a nine-year-old girl was sexually assaulted by three girls after seeing the movie, *Born Innocent* on television in which a similar act took place. Her parents filed an $11 million suit against NBC and Kron-TV. As early as 1961 Senator Thomas Dodd, Chairman of the Senate Subcommittee to Investigate Juvenile Delinquency, strongly supported the concept that viewing violent acts on TV is detrimental to children. He pointed out that half of the programs presented during prime time contained excessive violence, and that a large number of children exposed to these programs were twelve years old or younger. Even when the main characters in a program use violence in order to save someone or in order to prevent or stop a criminal act, children are being taught that violence is an appropriate behavior.

There are those, such as Feshbach (1955) and Levine (1968) who propose that watching violent programs on television has a cathartic effect and that people, in general, need to have this outlet available to them. The frustration hypothesis, first proposed by Dollard and his associates at Yale (Dollard et al., 1939), basically posits that the blocking of a goal results in aggression which must be released. Aggressive drives once activated must be released in some way. If this cannot be directed toward the original source of frustration, they will be directed toward a substitute. Vicarious viewing of violent acts would act as siphoning of the aggression (catharsis). Singer (1971) argues that people who are mildly aroused are able to achieve catharsis through watching violence while those who might be very frustrated will feel increased frustration and perhaps behave in an increased aggressive manner.

Bandura (1973) suggests that media violence has a negative effect since it results in children imitating the behavior of the people on the tube. Television-learning has proved to be as good as learning from people in some cases (Chu and Schramm, 1967). Many schools are using teaching machines to aid the teachers. Aggressiveness towards others appears to increase with viewing violence on television (Stein et al., 1972). Goldstein (1975) and his colleagues interviewed adult men in various countries in the world prior to and following the viewing of films portraying aggression. Although films with a high sex content did not appear to influence significantly the degree of punitiveness (the measure used) expressed, viewing an aggressive film did. The Bandura experiment, cited earlier, in which children viewed an aggressive TV model in three situations in which the consequences differed, demonstrated that males are more apt to imitate agressive behavior than females.

Singer attempted to summarize the many studies done on the effects of the portrayal of violence and came up with the following conclusions. He states that there may very probably be children or adults who, after watching violence on TV, and being immediately frustrated, would tend to imitate the violent behavior just viewed. He adds that there may also be an uninhibiting effect on aggression by viewing violence on TV even if the violence is justified. And finally, those portrayals of violence which are not closely related to the person's life are less likely to be imitated (Singer, 1971).

The degree of influence of violent portrayals on children varies with the type of parental role models. Children whose parents are fairly nonaggressive will be less influenced than those whose parents present aggressive role models or encourage the expression of aggressive behavior (Chaffee and McLeod, 1971).

The viewing of a film which displays aggressive acts has been found to be correlated with subsequent aggressive play in children (Lovaas, 1961, and Siegel, 1956). There also seems to be a long-term effect of the viewing of aggressive acts by children (Hicks, 1968b) but how long the effect lasts has as yet not been determined.

Eleanor E. Maccoby (1968) cautions that to state that violence on television is bad is an oversimplification. She suggests that children react differently to viewing violent acts depending on the type of children they are.

One study of violence in television concluded that when violence occurs on television, the female is most often the object of the violence rather than the perpetrator (Gerbner et al., 1977). Looking at another study which compared the reactions of males to seeing people of different sexes victimized might create concern. When college students witnessed a realistic fight between two males or between a male and a female, there was a significant behavioral difference in the actions taken by males dependent upon who was fighting. More males tried to intervene when a male was physically attacking another male but did not attempt to break up the fight when a male was assaulting a female. The experimenters concluded that the males appeared to receive gratification from watching a male harming a female and that this gratification had either hostile or sexual overtones or a combination of the two (Borofsky et al., 1971).

Perhaps we need to ask the question whether increasingly violent television is not dangerous to a woman's health.

References

Anon. *Report of the President's Commission on Crime in the District of Columbia.* Washington, D.C.: U.S. Government Printing Office, 1966.

Ardrey, Robert. *The Hunting Hypothesis.* New York: Atheneum, 1976.

_____. *The Territorial Imperative.* New York: Atheneum, 1966.

Bandura, Albert. *Aggression: A Social Learning Analysis.* Englewood Cliffs, N.J.: Prentice-Hall, 1973.

Beach, F. A. Bisexual mating behavior in the male rat: effect of castration and hormone administration. *Physiological Zoology* **18**:390–402 (1945).

Berkowitz, Leonard. *Aggression: A Social Psychological Analysis.* New York: McGraw-Hill Co., 1962.

Billig. H. E., Jr. and Spaulding, C. A. Hyperinsulinism of menses. *Industrial Medicine* **16**:336–339 (1947).

Blum, R. H. Drugs and violence, in D. J. Mulvihill, and M. M. Tumin (eds.). *Crimes of Violence,* Vol. 13. Washington, D.C.: U.S. Government Printing Office, 1969.

Borofsky, G. L., Stollak, G. E. and Messe, L. A. Sex differences in bystander reactions to physical assault. *Journal of Experimental and Social Psychology* **7**:313–318 (1971).

Bronson, F. H. and Desjardins, C. Aggression in adult mice: modification by neonatal injections of gonadal hormone. *Science* **161**:705–706 (1968).

Buss, Arnold H. *The Psychology of Aggression.* New York: John Wiley, 1961.

Chaffee, S. and McLeod, J. Adolescents, parents, and television violence. Paper presented at American Psychological Association. Washington, D.C. (1971).

Chodorkoff, Bernard and Baxter, Seymour. Psychiatric and psychoanalytic theories of violence, in David J. Mulvihill and Melvin M. Tumin. *Crimes of Violence,* Vol. 3. Washington, D.C.: U.S. Government Printing Office, 1969.

Chu, G. C. and Schramm, W. *Learning from Television.* Stanford University: Institute for Communication Research, 1967.

Conner, R. L. and Levine, S. Hormonal influences on aggressive behaviour, in S. Garattini and E. B. Sigg (eds.). *Aggressive Behaviour.* New York: John Wiley, 1969.

Court-Brown, W. M. *Human Population Cytogenetics.* New York: Wiley, 1967.

Dalton, K. Menstruation and acute psychiatric illness. *British Medical Journal* **1**:148–149 (1959).

_____. *The Premenstrual Syndrome.* Springfield, Ill.: Charles C. Thomas, 1964.

Delgado, J. M. R. Aggression and defense under cerebral radio control, in *Aggression and Defense: Neural Mechanisms and Social Patterns.* Berkeley: University of California Press, 1967.

Denenburg, V. H. *Developmental Factors in Aggression.* Paper presented at a symposium at the State University of Iowa, May, 1971.

DeVore, I. (ed.). *Primate Behavior: Field Studies of Monkeys and Apes.* New York: Holt, Rinehart & Winston, 1965.

Dollard, J., Doob, L. W., Miller, N. E., Mowrer, O. H. and Sears, R. R. *Frustration and Aggression.* New Haven, Conn.: Yale University Press, 1939.

Ehrhardt, A. A. and Baker, S. W. Fetal androgens, human central nervous system differentiation and behavior sex differences, in R. C. Friedman, R. M. Richart and R. L. Vandewiele (eds.). *Sex Differences in Behavior.* New York: John Wiley, 1974.

Felipe, Nancy Jo and Sommer, Robert. Invasions of personal space. *Social Problems* **14**:206–214 (1966).

Feshbach, S. The drive-reducing function of fantasy behavior. *Journal of Abnormal and Social Psychology* **50**:3–11 (1955).

Fromm, Erich. *The Anatomy of Human Destructiveness*. New York: Holt, Rinehart & Winston, 1973.

Gerbner, G., Gross, L., Eleey, M. F., Jackson-Beeck, M., Jeffries-Fox, S. and Signorell, N. T.V. violence profile no. 8: the highlights. *Journal of Communication* **27**:171–180 (1977).

Glueck, Sheldon and Glueck, Eleanor. *Unraveling Juvenile Delinquency*. Cambridge: Harvard University Press, 1950.

Goldstein, Jeffrey. *Aggression and Crimes of Violence*. New York: Oxford University Press, 1975.

Gottschalk, L. A. Phasic circulating biochemical reflections of transient mental content, in A. J. Mandell and M. P. Mandell (eds.). *Psychochemical Research in Man*. New York: Academic Press, pp. 357–378, 1969.

Hamburg, D. A. Recent research on hormonal factors relevant to human aggressiveness. *International Social Science Journal* **23**:36–47 (1971).

Heath, R. G. (ed.). *Psychosomatic Medicine*. Philadelphia: Lea & Fabiger, 1962.

Hicks, D. J. Short- and long-term retention of affectively modeled behavior. *Psychonomic Science* **11**:369–370 (1968 b).

Horney, Karen. *The Neurotic Personality of Our Time*. New York: W. W. Norton, 1937.

Jacobs, T. J. and Charles, E. Correlation of psychiatric symptomatology and the menstrual cycle in an outpatient population. *American Journal of Psychiatry* **126**:148–152 (1970).

Jacobs, P. A., Brunton, M. and Melville, M. M. Aggressive behavior, mental subnormality and the XYY male. *Nature* **208**:1351–52 (1965).

Johnson, Roger N. *Aggression in Man and Animals*. Philadelphia: W. B. Saunders, 1972.

Joslyn, W. D. Androgen-induced social dominance in infant female rhesus monkeys. *Journal of Child Psychology and Psychiatry* **14**:137–145 (1973).

Kalin, R., McClelland, D. C. and Kahn, M. The effects of male social drinking on fantasy. *Journal of Personality and Social Psychology* **1**:441–452 (1965).

Lagerspetz, K. M. J. Aggression and aggressiveness in laboratory mice, in S. Garattini and E. B. Sigg (eds.). *Aggressive Behaviour*. New York: John Wiley, pp. 77–85, 1969.

Lamberti, Joseph W., Blackman, Nathan and Weiss, James M. A. The sudden murderer, in Marvin Wolfgang (ed.). *Studies in Homicide*. New York: Harper & Row, 1967.

Lange, Arthur J. and Jakubowski, Patricia. *Responsible Assertive Behavior*. Champaign, Illinois: Research Press, 1976.

Levine, S. *Motivation in Humor*. New York: Atherton, 1968.

Levy, I. V. and King, I. A. The effects of testosterone propionate on fighting behavior in young C57BL/10 mice. *Anatomical Record* **117**:562 (1953).

Lieber, A. and Sherin, C. The case of the full moon. *Human Behavior* **1**:29 (1972).

Lorenz, Konrad. *On Aggression.* New York: Academic Press, 1964.

Lovaas, O. I. Effect of exposure to symbolic aggression on aggressive behavior. *Child Development* **32**:37–44 (1961).

Maccoby, Eleanor. Effects of the mass media, in Otto N. Larsen. *Violence and the Mass Media.* New York: Harper & Row, 1968.

Mark, V. H. and Ervin, F. R. *Violence and the Brain.* New York: Harper & Row, 1970.

McCord, W., McCord, J. and Zola, I. K. *Origins of Crime: A New Evaluation of the Cambridge-Somerville Youth Study.* New York: Columbia University Press, 1959.

Mead, Margaret. *Sex and Temperament in Three Primitive Societies.* New York: William Morrow, 1963.

Megargee, Edwin. A critical review of theories of violence, in Donald J. Mulvihill and Melvin M. Tumin (eds.). *Crimes of Violence* 13. Washington, D.C.: U.S. Government Printing Office, 1969.

Mischel, W. Sex-typing and socialization, in P. H. Mussen (ed.). *Charmichael's Manual of Child Psychology.* New York: John Wiley, 1970.

Money, John. Development differentiation of femininity and masculinity compared, in Seymour Morgan Farber and R. H. L. Wilson (eds.). *Man and Civilization.* New York: McGraw-Hill Book Co., 1963.

Money, J. and Ehrhardt, A. A. *Man and Woman, Boy and Girl.* Baltimore: The Johns Hopkins University Press, 1972.

Moore, M. Aggression themes in a binocular rivalry situation. *Journal of Personality and Social Psychology* **3**:685–688 (1966).

Morton, J. H., Addition, H., Addison, R. G., Hunt, L. and Sullivan, J. J. A clinical study of premenstrual tension. *American Journal of Obstetrics and Gynecology* **651**:1182–1191 (1953).

Moyer, K. E. *The Psychobiology of Aggression.* New York: Harper & Row, Publishers, 1976.

Mulvihill, Donald J. and Tumin, Melvin M. (eds.). *Crimes of Violence* 12. Washington, D.C.: U.S. Government Printing Office, 1969.

Parlee, M. B. The premenstrual syndrome. *Psychological Bulletin* **80**:454–465 (1973).

Price, W. H. and Whatmore, P. B. Behaviour disorders and pattern crime among XYY males identified at a maximum security hospital. *British Medical Journal* **I**:533–536 (1967).

The Random House Dictionary of The English Language. Jess Stein and Laurence Urdang (eds.). New York: Random House, 1966.

Siegel, A. E. Film-mediated fantasy: aggression and strength of aggressive drive. *Child Development* **27**:365–378 (1956).

Singer, Jerome L. (ed.). *The Control of Aggression and Violence.* New York and London: Academic Press, 1971.

Stein, A. H., Friedrich, L. K. and Vondracek, F. Television content and your children's behavior, in J. P. Murray, E. A. Rubenstein, and G. A. Comstock (eds.). *Television and Social Behavior* 2, *Television and Social Learning.* Washington, D.C.: U.S. Government Printing Office, pp. 202–317, 1972.

Steinmetz, Suzanne K. *The Cycle of Violence*. New York: Praeger Publishers, 1977.

Williams, Denis. Neural factors related to habitual aggression: consideration of differences between those habitual aggressives and others who have committed crimes of violence. *Brain* **92**:503–520 (1969).

Williams, R. M., Jr. The reduction of intergroup tension. *SSRC Bull. No. 57.* New York: Social Science Research Council, 1947.

Wolfgang, Marvin E. *Patterns in Criminal Homicide*. New York: John Wiley, 1958.

3 Sisters Under the Skin

Tis the strumpet's plague
To beguile many, and be beguil'd by one.

Prostitution is often referred to as the "oldest profession," thus giving the sale of a woman's body legitimacy. A profession has a method, a body of knowledge, and a code of ethics. Prostitution has all of these. How is prostitution defined? To define prostitution as the use of sex for "non-sexual" purposes is too general a definition and according to Kingsley Davis it would incorporate all behavior involving sex characteristics of the basic institutions of our society, such as courtship and marriage as well as concubinage (Davis, 1937). Degrees of sexual intimacy are involved in the courtship process and defined by societal norms. For many women, marriage today is still the exchange of sexual favors for emotional and financial support. Note that in only four states, Oregon, Iowa, Delaware and New Jersey, can a husband be charged with raping his wife. In the other 46 states, sexual access is the established right of a husband. There are jokes about "holding out" on sex in order to get money or some expensive material object in return. Yet this type of interchange between husband and wife is not defined as prostitution. Sex within marriage, regardless of the so-called strings attached, is socially sanctioned and considered legitimate. Yet, as Goode and Troiden (1974) said, "There is an element of prostitution in all heterosexual sex" (p. 102).

What they seem to be saying is that in every sexual relationship each person is generally not solely participating for sexual gratification but also for some secondary gains such as a feeling of being wanted etc. Kinsey (1948) pointed out that "If the term prostitution were to be applied to all sexual acts for which either participant received some valuable consideration, it would be impossible to draw a line between the most obvious sort of commercialized prostitution and the relationship of every husband and wife" (p. 595).

Sex between a woman whose sole purpose is financial return, and a man whose sole purpose is his own pleasure for which he pays is considered to be prostitution. This definition eliminates the problem of loosely defining prostitution as sexual permissiveness. Although prostitutes are sexually permissive, since they generally have intercourse with large numbers of men, a promiscuous woman is not necessarily a prostitute since she may not be paid for the sexual act.

How about the mistress who is "kept" by a man and given many luxuries in exchange for sexual favors and companionship? Some people would call her a prostitute, even though her sexual favors are shared with one man and for a sustained period of time. Then, too, does the woman herself have to be the recipient of the monetary reward for the sexual act of prostitution? During the American slave era, women were openly sold for sex, particularly in New Orleans. In 1850 Frederick Douglass said that those who owned slaves were also involved in prostituting them (Douglass, 1851).

How do we then classify partner surrogates used by Masters and Johnson (1970) in sex therapy for the unmarried men? They state that in order to be successful in treating male sexual inadequacy it was necessary to find women whose function would be to present a sense of care regarding the achievement of a solution to the sexual problem. The female surrogate needs to be cooperative with the client in carrying out the advice given by the sex therapist and to be able to demonstrate to the client the range of female responsiveness.

They proposed that most of the women who were accepted for the role of partner surrogate had volunteered to do so because of their own interest in being of help to others. Today, however, many sex therapists do offer some monetary remuneration for their services. However, according to Masters and Johnson, these women cannot be considered prostitutes. They never considered using prostitutes because "so much more is needed and demanded from a substitute partner than effectiveness of purely physical sexual performance that to use prostitutes would have been at best clinically unsuccessful and at worst psychologically disastrous" (Masters and Johnson, 1970, p. 148).

There are specific characteristics of the relationship between prostitute and client which differentiate it from other relationships, and one of these is the number of men involved. In prostitution there are many; the woman receives payment for each sex act she performs as opposed to the wife or mistress, who receives ongoing compensation. The relationship in prostitution is fleeting and there is little if any personal involvement between the parties (Benjamin and Masters, 1965).

The *Random House Dictionary of the English Language* (1966) defined a prostitute as "a person, usually a woman, who engages in sexual intercourse for money" (p. 1155). Yet, is not a man who does the same committing prostitution? The definition of a prostitute offered in the *American Criminal Law Review* proposes that prostitution is "the practices of a female offering her body to an indiscriminate intercourse with men usually for hire" (Rosenbleet and Pariente, 1973, p. 373).

Actually, an increasing number of states have changed the definition of prostitution to include men, especially since there is an increase in males offering their sexual services to other males for a price. This chapter will focus mainly on women and prostitution. As stated earlier, prostitution has a method, a body of given knowledge and a code of ethics. What are they? The method and body of knowledge involve how to attract a customer, how to negotiate for a fee, and various techniques of satisfying the buyer, and how to protect oneself from such difficulties as becoming pregnant, getting V.D., being picked up by the police and being hurt by the customer. A study of thirty-three call girls in Los Angeles produced the following information regarding their apprenticeship. Pimps are the trainers, often leaving the training of a new woman to another prostitute or sometimes to a madam who runs a training program for "new girls" as well as running her regular brothel. The prostitutes interviewed were able to name at least one person from whom they received formal or informal training for their job. Most of the focus in the apprenticeship consisted of learning how to find customers as opposed to being taught the actual techniques of the trade (Byran, 1965). Because teaching a new recruit is time-consuming and costly, madams prefer not to have to do this. Barbara Heyl (1977) studied one training brothel operated by a forty-one-year-old madam who had been part of the prostitution scene for twenty-three years. For her training house, most of the "girls" were referred by their pimps. The purchasers of services were mostly working-class men who paid a discounted fee since they were being serviced by novices. Twenty prostitutes had been trained by this madam in the six years that the "program" had existed. The trainees were housed in living quarters within close physical proximity to the "house" and remained in training for a two- to three-month period. They learned fellatio, genital intercourse, and a combination of the two known in the "life" as "half and half." They were taught to examine a client for V.D. and the techniques of setting fees and time limits (Heyl, 1977).

Byran (1965) found that prostitutes are taught values particularly identified with the subculture of prostitution. They are encouraged to believe that the relationships between themselves, their pimps, and other prostitutes are better than those between people of the straight world, which are said to be cold and fake. Although these attitudes are taught to "new girls," there is evidence to support the thesis that in reality there is competition and distrust of other women in the "life." Recruits are also often taught that married women are prostituting themselves but are not being honest about it. They are taught that their "trade" is especially important because it saves other women from men who want "kinky" sex, helps marriages, and serves a therapeutic function.

So our so-called oldest "profession" may very well be seen by the participants as a profession. But it certainly isn't what most mothers would want their daughter to be. Recently, a mother in Vermont killed her 19-year-old daughter as a last ditch effort to save her from the life of prostitution the daughter was determined to resume (Associated Press, November 14, 1978).

Prostitution has its own subculture, which includes a way of dressing, a lingo, as well as its own value system. Prostitutes have to dress in a fairly seductive manner in order to attract their customers, or in the case of the call girl, to retain the interest of the clients. In different periods of history prostitutes were forced by law to color their hair, usually blonde, and to wear certain types of clothes of a special color so that they could be identified as ladies of the night.

In the 1930s prostitutes tended to dye their hair blonde, but then blonde hair became the fashion. In the 1940s streaking the front of the hair was fashionable among some prostitutes, and soon became the fad among many women. The same thing happened with colored stockings. Today, it is difficult to distinguish a prostitute from the rest of womanhood.

Clifton Bryant (1977) in his research found that where the prostitute will be working, whom she is trying to attract, and how she wishes her potential client to view her, will determine what she decides to wear on a given occasion. A street walker has to project her image in an open way as opposed to a prostitute working the bars. The bar prostitute needs to project semirespectability as well as seductivity. Today appearance alone is not enough to identify a prostitute from a woman of the straight world.

The world's oldest "profession" probably existed at least since recorded history. Restrictions on premarital behavior and the increasing stress on the importance of property affected the emergence of prostitution, Will Durant suggests (1954). In primitive societies prostitution was practically unknown, and in those cases where young women exchanged sexual favors for their dowry, society gave its stamp of approval.

Prostitution associated with religion may have been the original beginning of prostitution (Benjamin and Masters, 1965). Two types of sacred prostitution have been identified. One type occurred when a woman was expected to participate in an indiscriminate sexual act before being eligible for marriage. The other type of prostitution was one in which women become associated with the temple for life, and prostitution was considered a part of their sacred duty (Henriques, 1959). One of the early types of sacred prostitution was described by Herodotus as having occurred in Babylonia.

> Every woman born in the country must once in her life go and sit down in the precinct of Venus, and there consort with a stranger. Many of the wealthier sort, who are too proud to mix with the others, drive in covered carriages to the precinct, followed by a goodly train of attendants, and there take their station. But the larger number seat themselves within the holy enclosure with wreaths of string about their heads,—and here there is always a great crowd, some coming and others going; lines of cord mark out paths in all directions among the women, and the strangers pass along them to make their choice. A woman who has once taken her seat is not allowed to return home till one of the strangers throws a silver coin into her lap, and takes her with him beyond the holy ground. When he throws the coin he says these words—'The goddess Mylitta prosper thee.' (Venus is called Mylitta by the Assyrians.) The silver coin may be of any size; it cannot be refused, for this is forbidden by the law, since once thrown it is sacred. The woman goes with the first man who throws her money, and rejects no one. When she has gone with him, and so satisfied the goddess, she returns home, and from that time forth no gifter however great will prevail with her. Such of the women as are tall and beautiful are soon released, but others who are ugly have to stay a long time before they can fulfil the law. Some have waited three or four years in the precinct. A

custom very much like this is found also in certain parts of the island of Cyprus (*The History of Herodotus,* trans. by Rawlinson, pp. 264–266, 1880).

Virgins in Phoenicia had to submit to losing their virginity by a stranger before they were eligible for marriage. Babylonian women had to accept the first offer they received. On the other hand, it seems that an Armenian woman of class could refuse someone who was not of equal status (Henriques, 1959). Durant raises various questions around the reasons for ritualized defloration. He proposes that perhaps this act reflected the first night right of the community, the fear of being the one to cause bleeding, or perhaps was a sacrificial giving to the goddess (Durant, 1954). The custom among the Marquesans was to have all the men who were present at a wedding have intercourse with the bride that night as she lay beside her husband. After all the men had taken their turn, the husband's opportunity occurred (Henriques, 1959).

The second type of sexual prostitution was known in Sumeria where women were associated with the temples to be sexually used by the gods or those men through whom the gods functioned (Durant, 1954). Perhaps the change from religious to ancient prostitution as a profession took place when the women began to be paid for their services.

Prostitution in Egypt was secular as well as temporal. It is said that part of the pyramid was paid for with money obtained from the prostitution of the daughters of upper-class families (Durant, 1954).

In ancient Athens, religious prostitution prevailed although lay prostitution also received approval when brothels for slaves were established by the state and taxes were levied on them. These prostitutes had to wear special dresses and were not permitted to participate in religious services or to enter a temple. On the other hand, the Spartans did not maintain legal control over prostitution. The sole purpose of women was to bear children, and although not considered prostitution, it was customary for a husband to allow another man to have sexual relations with his wife so that she could become pregnant (Sanger, 1937).

The prostitutes in Athens were divided into various classes, each having a different status. The Pornai were on the lowest rung of the status ladder, and worked in a common brothel. Poorly dressed and of oriental parentage, they were perused as one would look over cattle for purchase before their services were bought (Durant, 1939). The Flute Players or Ayletrides had higher status, entertaining guests with music as well as sexual ways. The Hetairae occupied a high position in Athenian society and had privileges which far surpassed those of the ordinary Athenian woman citizen who was uneducated, forbidden to attend games, and had to have her face covered in public (Sanger, 1937). Some Hetairae wielded a great deal of power through the men they entertained. They could amass great wealth and were sometimes held in high esteem. Interestingly, many Hetairae dyed their hair blonde in the belief that Athenians preferred blondes. Perhaps that's where our folklore that blondes have more fun comes from.

The early Romans were fairly strict in their moral code until the Christian period. The Julian laws forbade marriages between Roman citizens and the offspring of prostitutes. Registration of prostitutes was required. Women who were "in the profession" were required by law to dress in a specific fashion and to color their hair (Sanger, 1937).

Sacred prostitutes apparently existed among the ancient Jews until about the 5th century B.C., but following this time, prostitution of Jewish women was prohibited. However, prostitution continued to exist, and women selling their sexual wares, although banned from Jerusalem and the Temples, were to be found outside the city (Benjamin and Masters, 1965).

The Book of Moses contains passages relevant to prostitution. "Do not prostitute thy daughter, lest the land fall to whoredom . . . There will be no whore of the daughters of Israel" (Exodus XXII, 19, Leviticus XVII, 23). Solomon, who is said to have had many concubines, allowed prostitutes to practice their trade in Jerusalem. Until the Temple was destroyed, prostitution was a part of the fabric of Jewish society (Sanger, 1937).

During the early Christian era, the Romans forced Christian women to make sacrifices to their Roman gods. Those who refused were sent to houses of prostitution. The Christians themselves focused on the conversion of prostitutes whom they considered fallen women. During the early part of the Christian era Saint Augustine himself viewed prostitution as necessary in order to prevent lust from running rampant and destroying society (Sanger, 1937).

During the Crusades many women prostituted themselves as they traveled in order to pay for their pilgrimage. The story is told that at Acre in 1189 the French soldiers refused to fight until they were provided with women; and so they were—300 of them (Durant, 1950).

Attitudes toward prostitution vacillated between acceptance and strict regulation; for example under Charlemagne there were laws punishing prostitution with death, removal of noses or ears, decapitation, or burning at the stake (Benjamin and Masters, 1965). In 13th century France banishment of all prostitutes was decreed, and stringent measures to curb prostitution emerged again with the increase in the rate of V.D. in the 16th century. Prostitution continued to exist despite the attacks. In the 18th century in France and England, prostitution ran rampant and child prostitution became a problem; young girls were kidnapped and forced into brothels as captives (Benjamin and Masters, 1965).

In the mid-1700s the English were particularly hard on prostitutes. The *Grub Street Journal* of May 6, 1731 published the following tale. "Yesterday the noted Mother Needham stood in the pillory in Park Place near St. James's Street, and was severely handled by the populace. She was so very ill that she lay along the pillory, notwithstanding which she was severely pelted, and is thought she will die in a day or two" (Durant and Durant, 1965, p. 64). But it was only the poorest prostitute who could not afford to bribe her way to freedom, who found herself in the pillory.

In the late 18th and early 19th centuries a number of medical men and political figures in Europe began to express concern about prostitution and what they saw as the resultant rampage of V.D., and *réglementation* emerged. Réglementation involved the separating of sufferers of V.D. from the rest of society, and in order to prevent its spread, regular medical inspection of prostitutes. Réglementation, in some form, was also tried periodically in the United States (Pivar, 1973).

Professional prostitutes were not found in abundance in the early colonial days except for seaports like Boston, which had a large number of prostitutes by the late 1600s. In the 1730s several brothels were destroyed by mob action in Boston. Much of the prostitution in the seaports of the South during the era of slavery involved black women who were sold to brothels. Light-skinned black women (as young as twelve years of age) were sold to houses of ill repute for sizable sums of money. In the colonies female indentured servants were not permitted to marry without their masters' consent and had to be sexually accessible to them at all times (Benjamin and Masters, 1965).

The government of the thirteen colonies was opposed to prostitution and expressed this opposition with repressive measures and later with attempts to save the "fallen" women. Prostitution, however, persisted and grew to such large dimensions just prior to the beginning of the Civil War, that printed literature on the locations of bordellos in the larger cities was available. (Recently Pan American World Airways' guidebook to New York City became a best seller when the Associated Press described its contents as supposedly including a guide to the city's prostitutes.)

In the mid-1860s in the United States a partnership was cemented between the Women's Christian Temperance Union and the General Federation of Women's Clubs for the purpose of eradicating prostitution. Women continued to oppose prostitution and particularly to oppose its legalization. Susan B. Anthony actively campaigned to prevent prostitution from being legalized and was unaccepting of the contentions of the supporters of réglementation that men needed sex to remain mentally and physically healthy and that therefore prostitution was necessary (Pivar, 1973). Former abolitionists, both men and women, took up the banner against prostitution.

Women reformers attacked inequities in laws which affected prostitution. The age at which a girl could legally "agree" to sexual intercourse varied from state to state, from the age of seven in Delaware, which meant that at seven years of age a girl could be legally seduced or enticed to brothels. The reformers stressed that a woman had the right of control over her own body and fought to block attempts to legalize prostitution which they felt to be degrading to women.

In spite of the valiant efforts to erase prostitution from the face of the United States, by 1910 red-light districts could be found in almost all cities. Within eight years, however, many of these districts were shut down as a result of a strong crusade against vice which had its origin in Chicago, the first city to establish municipally supported investigations of vice and one of the first cities to begin an all-out attack on bordellos (Anderson, 1974).

In 1910, the Federal White Slave Act, which prohibited the transportation of girls and women across state lines for the purpose of prostitution was passed. By then almost all of the states had legislation regarding houses of prostitution and prostitution itself, and a large number of cities had established vice commissions. Laws declaring brothels to be public nuisances and allowing citizens to file complaints against brothels (abatement laws), as well as laws forbidding the peddling of sex on the streets or procuring, were in effect in many states. Despite these attempts, prostitution refused to be stamped out, and as military bases increased in number just prior to the beginning of World War II, so did the numbers of prostitutes surrounding them. Distressed by this and the increase in the V.D., the May Act was passed by Congress designating certain areas near army and navy installations out of bounds to prostitutes. The individual states also acted to outlaw brothels. Men in the armed forces were lectured on how to avoid V.D. They were shown training films, one of which was entitled "V.D. Mary" and given prophylactics to be used as protection from the disease. Although V.D. had increased to serious proportions, most of the women who infected the men were not professionals but were what was commonly called "Victory Girls." About 85 to 90 percent of V.D. cases originated from these nonprofessionals who were attracted to the bases because of job opportunities. In writing about the crusades against V.D., one authority stated that methods of finding the originators of V.D. as well as also identifying how often a Victory Girl was able to infect her partner were highly developed. However, no effort was made to indict their partners. "Girls must be chased, arrested, sentenced and reformed. Men simply have to be cured, warned, handed a prophylactic kit or a sermon" (Carter, 1946, p. 91).

After the end of World War II prostitution suddenly increased. Commercialized prostitution reappeared in force until a decline in the 1950s resulting from better law enforcement. During the Vietnam incursion, special brothels were set up in that country especially designed to cater to American military men and sanctioned by the military itself.

In the 1940s Kinsey (1948) found that about 69 percent of white men in the United States had some contact with prostitutes and that for 15 to 20 percent of them these contacts had extended over a five-year period. In 1975 it was estimated that there were about 250,000 full-time prostitutes in the United States (*The Decriminalization of Prostitution*, 1975).

In spite of the attempts throughout the ages to eradicate prostitution in all forms, women as well as men are still in the profession and are still being plagued by citizen groups and law enforcement representatives. Prostitution still persists. It is found in the streets of the larger cities, in the houses of prostitution with esoteric titles, and in massage parlors. One bordello in New York called itself the Temple of Fellowship for Human Happiness and listed itself as a nonprofit organization, thereby gaining exemption from paying taxes.

What types of prostitutes are there in the United States? Benjamin and Masters (1965) attempted to classify prostitutes according to their modus operandi and the location of their practice. The call girl is considered to be the crème de la crème of hustlers. The term itself may have derived from the 1920s when women were summoned by the madam to meet men for sexual liaisons. The madam who arranged the meeting would receive half the fee.

Why is a call girl on the top of the status ladder? She is generally fairly well educated, lives in expensive housing, wears expensive clothes, and caters to men who are well-endowed financially and who have expensive tastes. Her fees are high, and she can be selective in choosing with whom she will have a liaison (Benjamin and Masters, 1965). She is generally a single woman but can also be a married housewife who is earning extra money with or without her husband's consent and encouragement. She may have another job as a receptionist or model and sometimes goes out with her boss or other executives she meets at work, thus supplementing her income. She may also be an aspiring actress. Her demeanor is one of refinement and her clothes in good taste so that she makes a respectable looking companion. Her customers are referred to her by her pimp or other women in the business. Often she is trained for the "life" by either one of the aforementioned people, usually another call girl. Her initial contact with her customer is by phone. Completion of the tryst most often does not take place in her apartment but in the customer's hotel room, yacht, or in someone else's apartment, and she has only one date each evening. Call girls have a high level of anxiety, strong dependency needs, difficulty in establishing inner "controls," and have demonstrated overtones of masochistic traits (Byran, 1965). The call girl often has an unstable temperament with rapid mood swings. Her native intelligence and her rearing in at least a middle-class socio-economic environment result in a greater alienation from her family and therefore a tendency toward neuroses (Benjamin and Masters, 1965).

Attempts at suicide are numerous, but actual success is infrequent (Benjamin and Masters, 1965). Medical expenses are high. She receives medication for the cure of V.D., aborts when she becomes pregnant, and uses a physician whose specialty is "call girl" medicine and who therefore charges higher than average fees. The characteristics which determine the call girl's status in her community include her ability to dress well, her beauty, and the powerful people she knows. She views herself as different from the common prostitute (Greenwald, 1958).

The street walker is in a more dangerous position than the call girl. Her territory is the outdoors, usually in a fair-sized city. Weather conditions and harassment from the police are her constant enemies as is also abuse by sex deviates and infection with V.D. She is less neurotic than the call girl, and usually comes from a family which is less well placed than that of the call girl.

Runaway teens commonly use street walking to support themselves. Sometimes the teen is enticed into prostitution by a pimp who lives off the profits she earns.

Running away from home has now become an epidemic among young girls. In 1973 the FBI reported that there were 256,000 arrests of runaways. It estimates that in any given year at least 600,000 to 1 million youngsters run away from home (Morgan, 1975).

As many as 3000 girls and boys who are under the age of fourteen are estimated to be involved in prostitution in Los Angeles. Although the majority of the youngsters hustling have run away from home, a small number earn their pocket money by trading their bodies while still living with their families. In New York City alone there are about 20,000 youngsters under sixteen fending for themselves on the streets and providing easy prey for the pimps (*Time,* November 28, 1977, p. 23). Children as young as nine years old enter the profession in New York City after running away from home. In August, 1973, the Runaway Youth Act was passed by Congress in response to the horror at the unearthing of twenty-seven graves of young runaway boys in Houston, Texas. Money was appropriated for the establishment of the national toll-free switchboard so that runaways or their parents could call to leave messages for each other. One thousand calls were received each month during the first year of operation, some from youngsters as young as eight. Thirty-six percent of the callers were males compared with 64 percent who were female (Morgan, 1975).

Many of the young women prostitutes are brought to New York City from Minneapolis to what is now commonly called the "Minnesota Strip" at a rate of about 400 each year. The pimps who control these youngsters usually have several girls in their stable, and behavior is controlled by the enticement of possibly becoming number one in the hierarchy with all the privileges commensurate with this, including furs, attractive clothes, etc. Negative reinforcement, such as beatings, burnings with heated metal coat hangers, and forcing the girl to commit degrading acts in the presence of the other girls or another pimp are also used. Girls have been brutally punished for attempting to run away. *Time* Magazine in its November 28, 1977 (p. 23) issue related the sad tale of Karen, who after having an argument with her parents, began working the streets for her pimp in Minnesota until she and her pimp both moved to Chicago, where the sale of her body brought him $800. On to New York, where the pimp received $4000 in a period of ten weeks for Karen's hustling on the streets. During that time Karen's attempt to leave the "life" earned her hospitalization for a broken nose and a broken jaw. She went back to the streets again, and after an unsuccessful attempt to kill herself she made a desperate phone call to her parents and went home.

Karen's story is not unusual. Many of the girls like her who become street walkers come from homes that have been broken by divorce, separation or death of a parent. If the home is intact, it is usually unstable and the pimp provides a structure of do's and don'ts and therefore a feeling of security.

Of course, all girls who run away from home do not necessarily become prostitutes. One study of the differences between runaways in prostitution and runaways who did not "turn out" found that those who became prostitutes had had more frequent involvement in previous sexual activities, more absenteeism from school, as well as truancy. Drug abuse involving pills, pot, and alcohol was greater, too. When the young girls who turned to prostitution ran away, they generally avoided staying with friends or relatives and stayed away from home for longer periods of time (Crowley, 1977).

The bar prostitutes are those who confine themselves mainly to the bar scene, usually those bars which cater to the working class and which are located in decaying areas of a city. Many of the women who become bar prostitutes are between the ages of seventeen and twenty-five and come from families which are of the low socio-economic level. More than three-quarters of the bar "girls" have not graduated from high school, and many of them have another job in addition to that of prostitute. If married, their marriages are unstable, and a significant number of these women have placed at least one child up for adoption. Their standards of hygiene are not high, since they soon become disinterested in their health and appearance. Their excessive drinking often results in a decrease in sexual response (Benjamin and Masters, 1965).

The brothel prostitutes work for a madam who is responsible for finding customers for them, and to a certain extent is also responsible for the prostitutes themselves. There are rules and guidelines set up by the madam to which the brothel prostitute must adhere, often including avoidance of alcohol and drugs, practicing good hygiene, and learning how to dress well. Because the madam is an authority figure, she offers the prostitute someone on whom to lean as well as protection from abuse. She is, however, characterized by below average intelligence, little formal education, and her earnings are minimal (Benjamin and Masters, 1965).

And then there are the massage parlors, which cater to a man wanting sexual activity, such as masturbation or coitus or whatever his tastes may be. Illegitimate massage parlors have sprung up all over the country with a high concentration in the decaying area of cities. In the seventies New York had such a tremendous proliferation of massage parlors in the Times Square area that legal attempts were made and are still being made to eliminate the operations that are camouflaged prostitution dens. These laws include the licensing of legitimate masseurs as well as laws to regulate their activities. On June 14, 1973, the New York City law to regulate massage parlors was declared unconstitutional. Superior Court Justice M. B. Stecher stated that because the law was nonspecific "any human contact more intimate than a handshake" would be considered illegal, including a scalp massage given by a barber or whatever touching occurs when a manicurist does her job. To protect themselves from being shut down, massage parlors began to portray themselves as offering body painting or rap sessions. For $40 an hour in Los Angeles, a person could have a nude encounter with a female who while naked would sit and presumably listen to the client's problems.

There appears to be an easy transition from masseuse to prostitute. Albert Velarde interviewed fifteen American women masseuses. He found that these women, who had responded to advertisements in the newspaper, were in financial difficulty, needed to find work and assumed that masseuses would be doing some type of physical therapy. When they were first asked to masturbate the customer they did so, they said, without thinking it through because they were so shocked by the request. Because the first day's work was successful financially (usually prearranged by the owner of the parlor), the women returned. Some of the masseuses interviewed refused to view their activity as prostitution. These women perceived themselves as "touchy feely" people who liked to gratify others. Those who admitted to being prostitutes, placed themselves on the top rung of the ladder, even above the call girl. The high status was rationalized with the fact that they operated from their own "offices." The women who felt the worst about themselves were the closet masseuses, those whose families and friends were unaware of their activities (Velarde, 1975).

Other types of prostitutes are those found near military bases, in dance halls, and the most pathetic, older women sometimes in their sixties and seventies, riddled with V.D., ravaged by alcoholism, whose customers are the skid row crowd and who are released from their degrading life by institutionalization or death (Benjamin and Masters, 1965).

Now we raise the question which has been asked of prostitutes for eons. "What is a nice girl like you doing in a place like this?"

To this question Sanger's 2000 interviewees gave the following reply: 513 said that they were so inclined, 525 gave "destitution" as a reason, 250 had entered the profession after being "seduced and abandoned." "Drink, and desire to drink" accounted for 258, treatment of parents, relatives, or husbands accounted for 164, and "an easy life" for one hundred twenty-four. "Bad company," 84, "persuaded by other prostitutes," 71, "too idle to work," 29, "violated," 27, while 24 had been seduced on the immigrating ship or in boarding houses where they had been living (Sanger, 1937, p. 489).

Every society, including that of the United States, has developed behaviors which are considered appropriate in different situations. Prostitution is considered deviant behavior in our society, that is to say behavior which differs from the norm and which breaks rules sanctioned by society. Such rules are broken for a variety of reasons. A person may never have learned the rules because of lack of understanding of what they are all about. Sometimes the person breaks the rules because intellectually she is unable to perform in the expected manner. Sometimes the rules seem to make no sense or to contradict a basic belief held by an individual (Birenbaum, 1976).

Many prostitutes find it difficult to conform to the norms that society has established. They find it difficult to distinguish between deviant and nondeviant sex behavior for females, since the line between the two is unclear. Female attributes, such as seductiveness, are the same wiles that are used by prostitutes to attract the "John." The prostitute portrays an exaggeration of the acceptable sex-appropriate behavior and uses it for financial gain as opposed to wedlock (Rosenblum, 1975).

A number of prostitutes come from a subculture in which prostitution is tolerated as a way of life and is an escape from poverty. The degree of isolation a woman feels from the greater society determines the degree to which her behavior will conform or deviate from the behavioral expectation of that society. The individual who is isolated rationalizes her nonconformance. The prostitute feels that everyone in the society violates the expected codes but the prostitute is more open about it and prostitutes are really not disdained, anyhow (Holmes, 1971).

Women in our society are valued as sex objects. Their own personal identities are affected by this view, since their value as people and their value as sex objects is indivisible. They are often defined in terms of their sexual value while occupation generally defines the male (Gagnon, 1965). Some women, then, use sex in order to gain attention and status. Prostitution for the myopic appears to be a way of achieving these goals.

Children who have been sexually abused, and children and women who have been raped have their concepts of themselves as sex objects strengthened. Sixty-five percent of the adolescent prostitutes in one study were forced into sexual activities as children; 57 percent had been raped and one-third of those had been raped more than once (James and Myerding, 1977). We know that in most of the cases of sexual abuse with girls the father or a male relative is the aggressor. In the 1940s Sloane and Karpinsky did a follow-up study of three girls who had incestuous activity with their fathers. One of the three had later acted out sexually by becoming a prostitute for several years (Sloane and Karpinsky, 1949). Other studies have corroborated the finding that a number of girls involved in father-daughter incest during childhood had become prostitutes during adolescence. A study of call girls by Greenwald uncovered the fact that many of the women had been rewarded for sexual activity when they were little by a male relative or friend.

It is safe to conclude that rape and incest have an emotionally negative effect on girls. James and Myerding (1977) suggest that a pattern of poor parenting with resultant introduction into early sexual activity, learning that social status can be obtained through sex, as well as the trauma of sexual abuse, are important patterns which can lead a young girl into prostitution.

Although all poor women do not become prostitutes, and all prostitutes are not necessarily poor, economic necessity has been espoused as one of the contributing factors in prostitution. Sanger (1937) in his study of 2000 prostitutes in New York City in the late 1800s found that a large number of immigrants in prostitution were devoid of other income.

Many of the prostitutes today also come from poverty areas, but then there are the call girls, most of whom are in the middle or upper socio-economic class. It has been proposed by Goode and Troiden (1974) that the pattern of sexuality among the working class influences the manner in which women are recruited to prostitution. A small number of women among the working class have sexual relations without pay with a large number of men at an early age, starting at about twelve to fifteen years of age. Because of this early entry into sexual activity, the girls are viewed as tainted. Many of these adolescents want to be accepted and are seeking social status, which unfortunately they do not achieve. The majority of prostitutes are recruited from this group.

Those young women who are more sexually active and perhaps also more obvious in their sexual behavior than their peers are negatively labeled by the community, resulting in an identity crisis. They identify themselves as deviants, tend to seek out other deviants and become involved in deviant behavior (Davis, 1971).

Almost half of the prostitutes in one study had been identified as having been juvenile "sexual-actor-outers" in the past (James and Myerding, 1977).

The prostitute's family is usually one which is characterized by exploitation of others. In one way, the prostitute herself is feeding on the sexual needs of men while she herself allows them to use her as a sex object, just as she is being exploited financially by her pimp.

There is little evidence to support the contention that women become prostitutes because they have strong sexual desires. Sanger (1937) believed that ". . . man is the aggressive animal so far as sexual desire is involved. Were it otherwise, and the passions in both sexes equal, illegitimacy and prostitution would be far more rife in our midst than at present" (p. 489). Most often, the hustler today does not have an orgasm with her client, which may help ease her guilt. Sex for pleasure is generally reserved for her boyfriend or pimp. Some prostitutes may have a lesbian lover and even a lesbian pimp. Benjamin and Masters (1965) estimate that about 10 percent of the pimps in New York City are lesbians and the number is increasing steadily.

Psychoanalytically, the prostitute is viewed as a woman who had either a passive, nonaggressive father or most often a father who brutalized her. She is immature emotionally, and translates her need for love by sexual involvement with many men. She has a poor self-image, and reinforces this view of herself by disallowing herself the striving for a "normal" love relationship. Masochistically, she repeatedly places herself in a degrading position (Winick and Kinsie, 1971).

Women also become prostitutes in order to support an expensive drug habit, and then there are those women who become drug-addicted after entering the profession. A study of drug addiction of women who were arrested in New York City because of prostitution found that there was a positive relationship between the number of arrests and drug addiction. The more times the woman had been arrested, the greater the possibility that she was addicted. One-quarter of the women who had been arrested five times, half of those who had been arrested eleven to fifteen times and a little over 70 percent of those who had been arrested at least twenty times were found to be drug addicted (Winick and Kinsie, 1971). Today, then, drug addiction and prostitution appear to be close companions.

Prostitutes come in all ages, as young as nine and as old as sixty or seventy, in all shapes and forms and from all ethnic groups. Although blacks comprise about 11 percent of the general population, 53 percent of the prostitutes arrested in urban areas are black (Winick and Kinsie, 1971). Perhaps blacks tend to be picked up more often by the police than whites.

Benjamin and Masters (1965) seem to think that the disproportionate number of black women arrested for prostitution reflects the actual ratio of blacks and whites on the street.

Contrary to the popular belief in the past, prostitutes are generally of average intelligence, and those who entered the profession after adolescence have held a variety of jobs, many of them straight. One interviewer found that a number of prostitutes he spoke with liked the money they earned, felt that they had more freedom in prostitution, and gave prostitution as an alternative profession, one which would entail helping people (James, 1973).

A pimp rises out of poverty, is usually black or Hispanic, not very intelligent and is in some ways a "kept man." His women work for him while he spends his time wearing flashy clothes and driving flashy cars. He is often into other "shady" enterprises, such as gambling and narcotics, and uses the drugs to keep his women working and loyal. He is generally drug-addicted, thus using the prostitutes to support his own habit. He tells his women where to work, sometimes gives them some tips on how to pick up clients, provides bail if they are picked up, and protection against being robbed. They bring back the loot to the pimp, who is usually also their lover, their protector, and the one from whom they seek affection. They get "hooked" on him, and he in turn then continues to exploit them while he enhances their self-esteem, sets limitations which in turn give them a feeling of security, and beats them savagely if they digress.

Psychoanalytically, the pimp is seen as a regressed individual who has a strong need for a mother figure, someone to take care of most of his needs. He is anxious about his sexual potency, and, in fact, most often indulges mainly in cunnilingus with his women. In this manner his oral, passive needs are satisfied while he can sexually service a number of women in a short time-span (Winick and Kinsie, 1971).

Pimps recruit women by becoming sexually intimate with them. A typical encounter might be similar to that experienced by a thirteen-year-old runaway who filed a complaint against a pimp, whom she and her friends met in the Port of Authority Bus Station in New York. He raped her and the other girls in an effort to get them to join his stable. She ran to the police while the other two girls agreed to "turn out."

Ethnicity also seems to play a role in who becomes a pimp during a particular time in history. In the 1920s and 1930s a large number of pimps were of Jewish or Italian heritage. This was a time when Italians and Jews, newly immigrated, were attempting to find a place for themselves in American society in the face of prejudice against "greenhorns." Today the blacks and the Hispanics are in the same situation, and it is they who comprise the majority of pimps. The pimp has a low status in our society, and he is aware of this. Calling someone a pimp is an attempt to degrade him. It connotes exploitation and actually that is exactly what it is.

Pimps have declined in number with the decline of the brothel. Most prostitutes today are not full-time professionals; they are mainly free agents, and hold other jobs as well.

Why does a man pay for sex? At one time it was thought to be advantageous for a young man to gain some sexual experience. Since "good" girls were not usually sexually active, the prostitute became the most logical source of initiation into sex. Besides which, sex was supposed to cure pimples, so why be pimpled until marriage? Many famous people frequented houses of prostitution including the great composer, Brahms. The story has it that when he was a child Brahms lived near an inn inhabited by ladies of the night who would sexually stimulate him. When he grew up it was natural for him to relate to them for sex (Winick and Kinsie, 1971).

A man who receives his sexual satisfaction only from prostitutes may be suffering from a "madonna-prostitute complex." This man distinguishes between those women who are to be respected and therefore not sexually used, and those women whom one can debase by having a sexual relationship with them. The respected woman represents the mother, and sex with this woman would create too much anxiety because of its incestuous overtones.

Men may seek out prostitutes because of the unavailability of other sexual partners. Military establishments with their skewed ratio of men to women provide a market for the women and the trade. Gang initiation rituals sometimes prescribe a visit to a prostitute. Benjamin and Masters propose that some men fear the possibility of impregnating a woman or fear an emotional attachment that might develop in other kinds of sexual unions. A visit to the prostitute, therefore, is viewed as less dangerous and less costly. They also propose that an insecure man, or one physically or mentally impaired in some way, and therefore unable to become involved in "normal" relationships with the opposite sex, would find sexual activity with a prostitute less anxiety producing, since it is a business arrangement (Benjamin and Masters, 1965).

And then there are those men with fetishes or sexual needs which are considered deviant. Paying for these activities might be the only way to get them. A case in point is a man who could not have sexual intercourse or become sexually stimulated unless his sex partner stepped on and squashed a frog as part of the sex play. Prostitutes usually charge an increased fee for such "kinky" sex.

Clients are older than they were in the 1940s and early 1950s. About one-quarter of college students in the United States during that period were initiated into sex by a prostitute as compared with 2 to 7 percent in 1967 (Winick and Kinsie, 1971). College men usually went to visit a prostitute with other buddies during a drinking escapade to satisfy their curiosity (Kronhausen and Kronhausen, 1960).

Gebhard, et al. (1965), found that a large number of men in the Kinsey Institute Study of Sex Offenders had their first coitus with prostitutes. There was also a direct correlation between nonpaid first coitus and future sexual success. "Putting it another way, subsequent heterosexual 'success' (in terms of both coital frequency and numbers of premarital coital companions) is foreshadowed by the first coitus being with a companion rather than with a prostitute" (p. 555).

It has been suggested that women are perceived as erotic toys by some men and that prostitutes epitomize this view (Katchadourian and Lunde, 1972). Men who engage prostitutes may very well perceive them as playthings. Conventions and conferences largely populated by men make lucrative territory for hookers.

The United States has vacillated between attempting to control prostitution and allowing it to exist without much interference. It is only after public outcry that laws which are already on the books are enforced, and these laws place a heavy burden on the prostitute with little if any responsibility on the client. Prostitution is viewed as immoral, and the prostitute herself is viewed as a worthless tainted woman. Yet what are our attitudes towards the customer, the purchaser of the service? Without the clients, prostitution would not exist.

Every state has laws which in some way covertly or overtly punish prostitution. In the majority of the states the customer is also guilty of breaking the law, but many of them are not arrested. In 1971 in Oakland, California 3,663 prostitutes were arrested while only 21 clients were apprehended (Shiels et al., 1976). A woman judge, in an attempt to focus on the inequities of selective enforcement, dismissed the charges against 37 women in one community basically because their clients went scot free. In 1974 in Oakland, California, there were 663 prostitutes arrested and 21 Johns. In 1972 in San Francisco 904 women were convicted out of 917 arrests for prostitution (Jennings, 1976). After the ruling on equal enforcement of the law in California, Oakland police in 1975 arrested 651 women and 461 men in a given year. The names of men arrested for contracting for the services of a prostitute were published in the *Oakland Tribune* as a deterring mechanism (Shiels, et al., 1976).

We accept the fact that men want women sexually, and that if they cannot find a legitimate sex partner, they will accept one who is not, and we accept the fact that women are viewed in our society as sex-objects and are identified in terms of their ability to gratify a man's sexual appetite instead of the other kinds of factors which give men their identity, such as their profession or their personal qualities. And if we also accept the fact that sex between two consenting adults is their personal choice, and that because of discrimination against women in the labor market and elsewhere, a woman's body becomes her one and only salable commodity, then we can't help but conclude that prostitution always will be with us.

Laws that are enacted to control prostitution reflect judgments concerning the degree of the injurious effects of prostitution on a society. They also reflect an attempt to obtain a balance between individual interests and those of the public. The cost of enforcement compared with the advantages of enforcement are also considered (Jennings, 1976).

In the United States, most laws geared toward attempting to control prostitution address themselves to controlling the activities of the prostitutes themselves, their pimps, their clients, and the owners of brothels and massage parlors in which they work. Enforcement of these laws is extremely costly and they have not eradicated prostitution or drastically affected any woman's decision to become or remain a prostitute. In 1971, San Francisco spent $375,000 to arrest about 2116 people for prostitution (Wade, 1975). In some cities as many as 50 percent of the inmates in jails are there because of prostitution convictions. The prostitution laws now on the books in most states are not only costly but are also unenforceable, as are most laws regulating consensual activity between two adults. These laws tend to decrease respect for the law in general and tend to discriminate against women.

In some states the laws against prostitution apply only to women and not to men. Alaska's prostitution law was declared unconstitutional because only women were charged for soliciting with prostitution as the motive. This violates the equal protection clause of the 14th Amendment to the Constitution. The court concluded that "If control of solicitation is the goal, then the buyer, as well as the seller, is contributing to the act through exchange of negotiations" (Wade, 1975). The need for laws against clients was recognized as early as 1922 by the United States Surgeon-General, Claude Connor Pierce. He stated that agencies concerned with abolishing prostitution recognized the buyer of the service as contributing equally to blame (Winick and Kinsie, 1971).

Entrapment, a method of using male decoys in order to arrest women for prostituting themselves, appears to be a violation of federal laws which make it illegal for law enforcement agencies to entice someone into criminal activity (Shiels et al., 1976).

Many prostitution laws are now being questioned in the courts for their possible violation of the right to privacy, which was established by the United States Supreme Court in Griswald v. Connecticut (381 U.S. 479) (1965). The decision in this case struck down Connecticut's law against the use of contraception. Increasingly, people's private concerns have been included in the right of privacy which is protected by the Constitution of the United States.

> Prostitution, both in the preliminary solicitation and negotiations and in the act itself, is overwhelmingly a private, consensual affair between individuals who wish to make their own decisions as how to control their sexual lives and use their bodies (Rosenbleet and Pariente, 1973).

Antiloitering laws whose objectives are control of solicitation are sometimes too vague and all-encompassing, thereby violating constitutional protection. Chicago's loitering law was declared unconstitutional and in New York City, the law which allows police to arrest individuals for "repeated beckoning" was labeled as violating constitutional rights by the New York Civil Liberties Union. Police, in making their sweeps on the streets of downtown New York, have picked up a young college student who had just left a movie, a young woman counselor as well as some prostitutes.

Present laws on prostitution are also being questioned concerning the possible violation of the constitutional right of freedom of speech. The question that needs to be resolved is does a prostitute have the right to ask a man whether he wants sex? What laws are there which make it illegal for a man to whistle at a woman or make sexually explicit remarks to her as she walks along the street?

Legalization of prostitution and the resultant licensing of brothels is now being debated. The proponents of legalization contend that V.D. would be better controlled, that crimes that are generally associated with prostitution, such as robberies, drug abuse, etc., and the intervention of organized crime would be limited, and that legalization would protect minorities and young girls from being lured into becoming hookers (Jennings, 1976).

V.D. was closely associated with prostitution in the 1930s when it was estimated that prostitutes were responsible for about 75 percent of its spread. Although about 90 percent of the hookers have had V.D. at one time or another, only 5 percent of the cases in the United States can be attributed to them today (Winick and Kinsie, 1971). Adolescents have been increasingly sexually active in the past decade, and because of their limited information on venereal disease are considered to be the group most responsible for its spread. V.D. is at present lower in those groups which would most often tend to visit a prostitute, the man who is middle-aged. In 1970, 84 percent of the reported cases of gonorrhea in Washington D.C. were fifteen to thirty-year-olds (Jennings, 1976). With legalization would come regular exams of women for signs of V.D. Unfortunately, early detection is difficult and a large number of customers could contract diseases before a prostitute with V.D. was identified.

Let us now look at the argument that if prostitution were legalized there would be less crime associated with it. The laws being proposed to legalize prostitution involve licensing of brothels but would still make street soliciting a crime since it is a nuisance to others. Those prostitutes who were not associated with a house of prostitution, for one reason or another, would still be prey to the same criminal "elements" as today. Prostitutes might still be at the mercy of the "protectors" and the police whom they might have to attempt to bribe in order to continue their work (*Women Endorsing Decriminalization,* 1973). For those women associated with a house of prostitution, the pimp's importance would be minimized. He would no longer be the protector, the procurer, and would have less of a hold on them for exploitation purposes.

The prostitute is often the victim of assaults, as well as robberies, and even homicides on the street. Each year a number of prostitutes are murdered by their clients. Since there is no emotional attachment between the prostitute and her John, the prostitute can easily represent whatever the John wants her to be: for example the hated sex object, his wife or lover, and he therefore projects on to her all his hostile feelings toward the important women in his life, sometimes acting out his hostility to the extent of murder.

Hotel owners and police departments have often stated that prostitutes are responsible for a large number of robberies in hotels. Legalization might decrease the incidence of this type of crime.

Gambling and prostitution are often related according to Winick and Kinsie (1971), and organized crime was associated with prostitution until the 1930s when it found loan sharking and traffic in drugs more profitable. Signs of mobster control of the massage parlors, some of the bars featuring half-naked women, and the "shady" hotels are evident today. In December, 1977, a booby-trapped letter was sent to a massage parlor in Pittsburgh. Its explosion resulted in the death of one woman and the injury of three other persons. The bombing was believed to be the result of a power struggle between two groups attempting to gain control of the massage parlors in that city.

Although it is argued that organized crime has a strong hold on the prostitution industry, the President's Commission on Law Enforcement and Administration of Justice (1967) does not give support to this argument. The Commission found that prostitution is not easy to organize, in part because the participants are not disciplined people.

Many feminists today are in favor of decriminalizing prostitution, but are adamantly opposed to its legalization. They feel that legalizing prostitution is tantamount to supporting its concept and sanctioning it, so that it becomes a legitimate profession for women. Because of its focus on the exploitation of the female body, because of its degrading qualities, and because it can never attain status as a coveted "profession," feminists feel that legalizing prostitution would increase the number of women who might choose this avenue of escape from difficult environmental and emotional circumstances. They also feel that:

> Legalizing prostitution would permit pimps to become legitimate brothel owners, glorified and revered for their industriousness in our "free enterprise" system. The independent prostitutes would be forced to join a brothel by being physically coerced or by other types of pressure. Brothel owners, having a greater concentration of power than the individual prostitute, could lower the brothel prices and lobby to make independent prostitution illegal. Brothel owners would be more powerful pimps than those which exist today—with more power to manipulate and exploit women (Women Endorsing Decriminalization, 1973).

Although most feminists are openly opposed to legalizing prostitution, prostitutes are in favor of it. One study in Washington, D.C., which involved interviewing prostitutes found that twenty out of the twenty-seven prostitutes contacted were in favor of legalization because it would benefit their health, give them protection, and ensure them a steady income. Six preferred decriminalization so that competition could still exist, but they would be eligible for a tax exemption. The one who preferred the status quo felt that legalizing or decriminalizing prostitution would take the excitement out of it (Saffold, 1977). Of course this sample was very small and therefore not reliable. However, large numbers of prostitutes have formed an organization called COYOTE (Cast Off Your Old Tired Ethics). They claim to have a membership of at least 9000 and have chapters in cities such as New York, Seattle and Chicago. Their first national convention was held in San Francisco in 1974. The organization's main focus is an attack on the present antiprostitution laws, which they feel discriminate against them because they are women, invade their right to privacy, result in cruel and unusual punishment, and violate due process under the law (Williams, 1974). Many legal experts support the organization's contentions.

Decriminalization of prostitution has been gaining popularity because of the increasing self-awareness of women, the increasing lobbying of women's groups, as well as the organization of groups of prostitutes and the emphasis on civil rights. Decriminalization would mean the repealing of all laws which make prostitution illegal so that there would not be any punishment for those who participate in it. Decriminalization does not sanction prostitution, but it does diminish the harassment of prostitutes by the police. It would also afford prostitutes the avenue of filing a complaint to the police for crimes to which they are subjected, such as rape and robbery, which they are now reluctant to report. Decriminalization would remove this differential treatment of prostitutes because they would no longer be viewed as criminals. It has been suggested that in addition to decriminalizing prostitution, society must address itself to its many causes, which include economic and social conditions, which discriminate against women.

The world that the prostitute lives in is an exaggeration of the man's world of our greater society. A thirty-five-year-old prostitute says it very well. "It's a gentleman's trip. A man propositions you, a man busts you and a man bails you out" (*Newsweek,* July 8, 1974, p. 65).

References

Anon. Call me madam. *Newsweek* **84**:65 (July 8, 1974).
_____. *The Decriminalization of Prostitution.* Pennsylvania Program for Women and Girl Offenders, Inc., Philadelphia, Pa., 1975.
_____. Mother Kills Daughter to Save the Girl's Life. Associated Press. November 14, 1978.

_____. *President's Commission on Law Enforcement and Administration of Justice: The Challenge of Crime in a Free Society*, 1967.

_____. Women Endorsing Decriminalization. Prostitution: a non-victim crime? *Issues in Criminology* **8**:137–162 (Fall 1973).

_____. Youth for sale on the streets. *Time* **110**:23 (November 28, 1977).

Anderson, Eric. Prostitution and social justice: Chicago; 1910–1915. *Social Service Review* **48**:203–228 (1974).

Benjamin, Harry and Masters, R. E. L. *Prostitution and Morality*. London: Souvenir Press, 1965.

Birenbaum, Arnold and Sagarin, Edward. *Norms and Human Behavior*. New York: Praeger Publications, 1976.

Bryant, Clifton D. (ed.). *Sexual Deviance in Social Context*. New York: New Viewpoint, 1977.

Byran, James H. Apprenticeship in prostitution. *Social Problems* **12**:287–97 (Winter 1965).

_____. Occupational ideologies and individual attitudes of call girls. *Social Problems* **13**:441–450 (Spring 1966).

Carter, Herbert D. *Sin and Science*. New York: Heck-Cattell Publishing, 1946.

Crowley, Maura G. *Female Runaway Behavior and its Relationship to Prostitution*. Sam Houston State University, Institute of Contemporary Corrections and Behavioral Sciences, 1977. Master's Thesis.

Davis, Kingsley. The sociology of prostitution. *American Sociological Review* **2**:744–755 (October 1937).

Davis, W. J. The prostitute developing a deviant identity, in *Studies in the Sociology of Sex*. Edited by J. Henslin. New York: Appleton-Century Crofts, 1971.

Douglass, Frederick. *Lectures on American Slavery*. Buffalo: G. Reese, 1851.

Durant, Will. *Our Oriental Heritage*. New York: Simon & Schuster, 1954.

_____. *The Age of Faith*. New York: Simon & Schuster, 1950.

_____. *The Life of Greece*. New York: Simon & Schuster, 1939.

Durant, Will and Durant, Ariel. *The Age of Voltaire*. New York: Simon & Schuster, 1965.

Gagnon, J. Female child victims of sex offenses. *Social Problems* **13**:176–192 (1965).

Gebhard, Paul H., Gagnon, John H., Pomeroy, Wardell B., Christenson, Cornelia V. *Sex Offenders*. New York: Harper & Row, Publishers and Paul B. Hoeber, Inc., Medical Books, 1965.

Goode, Erich and Troiden, Richard (eds.). *Sexual Deviance and Sexual Deviants*. New York: William Morrow, 1974.

Greenwald, H. *The Call Girl: A Social and Psychoanalytic Study*. New York: Ballantine, 1958.

Henriques, Fernando. *Prostitution and Society*. New York: The Citadel Press, 1959.

Heyl, Barbara Sherman. The madam as teacher: the training of house prostitutes. *Social Problems* **24**:5:545–558 (June 1977).

Holmes, Ronald M. *Sexual Behavior*. Berkeley, California: McCutchan Publishing, 1971.

James, Jennifer and Myerding, Jane. Early sexual experiences and prostitution. *American Journal of Psychiatry* **134**:1381–1385 (December 1977).

James, Lionel. On the game. *New Society* **24**:426–429 (May 24, 1973).

Jennings, M. Anne. The victim as criminal: a consideration of California's prostitution law. *California Law Review* **64**:1235–1284 (September 1976).

Katchadourian, Herant and Lunde, Donald T. *Fundamentals of Human Sexuality.* New York: Holt, Rinehart and Winston, 1972.

Kinsey, Alfred C., Pomeroy, Wardell B. and Martin, Clyde E. *Sexual Behavior in the Human Male.* Philadelphia and London: W. B. Saunders, 1948.

Kronhausen, Phyllis and Kronhausen, Eberhard. *Sex Histories of American College Men.* New York: Ballantine, 1960.

Masters, William H. and Johnson, Virginia E. *Human Sexual Inadequacy.* Boston: Little, Brown, 1970.

Morgan, Ted. Little ladies of the night. *New York Times Magazine* 34–38 (November 16, 1975).

Pivar, David J. *Purity Crusade.* Westport, Conn.: Greenwood Press, 1973.

The Random House Dictionary of the English Language. Jess Stein and Laurence Urdang (eds.). New York: Random House, 1966.

Rawlinson, George. trans. *The History of Herodotus.* New York: D. Appleton, 1880.

Rosenbleet, Charles and Pariente, Barbara J. The prostitution of the criminal law. *American Criminal Law Review* **11**:373 (Winter 1973).

Rosenblum, Karen. Female deviance and the female sex role: a preliminary investigation. *British Journal of Sociology* **26**:169–185 (June 1975).

Saffold, Carolyn R. *A Street Perspective of Prostitution, Police, Prostitutes and the Public.* National Council on Crime and Delinquency. Washington, D.C.: AFL-CIO Labor Participation Department, 1977.

Sanger, William W. *The History of Prostitution.* New York: Eugenics Publishing, 1937.

Shiels, M., et al. Flatfoot floozies. *Newsweek* **87**:27–28 (June 28, 1976).

Sloane, P. and Karpinski, E. Effects of incest on the participants. *American Journal of Orthopsychiatry* **12**:666–673 (1949).

Velarde, Albert J. Becoming Prostituted. *British Journal of Criminology* **15**:251–263 (1975).

Wade, Daniel E. Prostitution and the law: emerging attacks on the women's crime. *University of Missouri—Kansas City Law Review* **43**:413–28 (1975).

Williams, Roger M. The oldest profession in Nevada—and elsewhere. *Saturday Review* **1**:9 (September 7, 1974).

Winick, Charles and Kinsie, Paul M. *The Lively Commerce.* Chicago: Quadrangle Books, 1971.

4. My Body is My Own

Rape has existed ever since the arrival of man on the earth. Woman was the victim and man the victimizer. Simply defined, rape is the act of forcibly having sexual intercourse with a person without his/her consent. In this chapter we will, however, only discuss rape as it relates to women. There are many cartoons picturing an early caveman with a club in one hand dragging a woman by the hair. His purpose, sexual intercourse, may be inferred from this picture. Since she is being dragged by her hair, one can also infer that the sexual intercourse will occur against her will. Susan Brownmiller (1975) in her book, *Against Our Will* conjectures that women allowed themselves to become the property of one man to protect themselves from sexual abuse from many men. A man became a woman's protector since she, because of her lesser physical strength, was unable to ward off attacks by men who wished to violate her.

Marriage by capture was a common custom at various periods. A man would carry off an unwilling maiden and then rape her, thus branding her as his property. The founders of Rome, Romulus and Remus, were guilty of this type of action. When they founded the settlement in 753 B.C. it is said that they neglected to bring women with them. Their Sabine neighbors refused to give their daughters in marriage, so Romulus and Remus invited them to dine, and at a given time carried off the youngest and most beautiful of the daughters, killing some of their defenders in the process. Shortly thereafter, they took these women for their wives. This is the episode known as "The Rape of the Sabine Women." An interesting epilogue to the story is that the Sabines were prevented by their own daughters from taking revenge on Romulus and Remus because the young women became pregnant (Bullough, 1974).

Historically, women were and still are victims of rape during war. Conquering armies move in to reap the harvest of their triumph—sexual abuse of women. The Ottomans were guilty of rape in 1453 after the fall of Constantinople, the Japanese in China in the late 1930s, as were the Germans, the Russians, and the Americans during World War II. Rape is universal, and women are part of the spoils of war. In Bangladesh an estimated 200,000 or more women were raped. They were later rejected by their husbands and other men because they had been defiled (Brownmiller, 1975).

If rape is common during war, it is also thought to be "normal" during peacetime. An example of this type of attitude was expressed in the case of *State* v. *Chaney* heard in the Alaska Supreme Court (LeGrand, 1973). The victim joined the accused and his accomplice in his car. The victim was then forced to perform fellatio on the accused. She was beaten, raped four times and, to add insult to injury, her money was taken. The Supreme Court of Alaska heard an appeal by the defendant, who claimed that his sentence of two concurrent years in prison was excessive. The defendant's lawyer in recommending immediate parole stated that the encounter was a common one in our society, and that the defendant had a bad stroke of luck because the young woman told on him.

In the summer of 197t a Madison, Wisconsin judge, Archie Simonson, heard the case of a fifteen-year-old boy who raped a sixteen-year-old Madison High School girl in a stairwell. Before sentencing the offender, who was found guilty of delinquency, the judge remarked that the braless fashion on the campus of the University of Wisconsin and pornography, and the nude dancing at nightclubs affect young men. "Are we supposed to take an impressionable person 15 or 16 years of age who can respond to something like that and punish that person severely because they react to it normally?" (Harper, 1978, January 3, 1978). He then placed the offender on probation. Women's groups were in an uproar, a recall petition forced an election, and the judge was defeated by a large margin.

In Colorado, District Judge Dean Mabrey heard the case of a man who was accused of forced entry into the home of a woman whom he proceeded to attempt to rape by throwing her on the floor and placing his hands inside her pants after breaking the zipper. The judge called these events an attempt at seduction and summarily dismissed the case (Harper, 1978).

Rape is viewed by some as the culmination of an uncontrollable desire which is exacerbated by a woman who entices in some way. Women are characterized as being basically manipulative, evil, and seductive. Was it not Potiphar's wife who attempted to seduce Joseph (Genesis 39:7–18)? And Delilah, didn't she emasculate Samson (Judges 16:4–20)? Oh, yes, we forgot that Eve made Adam eat the apple and is therefore responsible for the ills of the world. It seems no one asks why Adam was stupid enough to eat it.

The myth of women as seductresses is often accompanied by the myth that women enjoy being raped. The dating game functions to encourage this. Men are the aggressors and the pursuers and women the pursued. It becomes difficult for some men to know when enough is enough.

The concept of women as inherently masochistic, one that was formulated by Freud, and given much weight as a result, continues to foster the false idea that women like to be raped. A group of eminent people from the Institute of Sex Research founded by Kinsey (Gebhard et al., 1965) stated that women are somewhat masochistic and like to be man-handled at times. They feel that it is ego-bolstering to have a man lose control of himself and begin to treat them in the rough manner in which cavemen were supposed to have treated their women. Some women, state the Kinsey researchers, want to be "taken" rather than asked if they wish to indulge in sex. They then go on to state that there is biological support for the belief that women are supposed to respond positively to being roughed up by men, citing the behavior of *mink* to support their contention.

Clifton D. Bryant (1977) in his study of sexual deviancy refers to a woman's "normal 'masochistic' tendencies."

Some feminists like Diana E. H. Russell (1975) discuss rape as a class crime. They see rape as a crime by men against women as a group. Susan Brownmiller (1975) views rape as an attempt by men to control women and keep them in their "place."

Women all over the world live in fear of the violation of their bodies. They are taught from childhood onward about the dangers lurking to envelop them, dangers over which they have little or no control. Walking down a dimly lit street and hearing a slight noise can precipitate at the least a quickened heart beat and sometimes panic. An unescorted female feels herself to be a potential victim. It would seem that living with the fear of victimization would hamper an individual from becoming a mature, self-sufficient adult and would also lend itself to compulsive pairing and/or marriage for protection.

A classic example of the dangers of being alone is the short story related in a book written in 1855 by Rev. Daniel Smith and called, *The Ladies Book of Anecdotes*. The story is entitled, "The Danger of Trusting Young Females Alone," and relates the tale of a young woman who goes to the city to visit an uncle. She is met by a cunning woman who takes her to her own home instead of her uncle's, and allows a gentleman to enter the young lady's room for the night. When dawn breaks, the wretched young woman attempts to kill herself with poison, only to be rescued by the pharmacist from whom she bought the lethal dose. The moral of the story is, "Young ladies, beware of visiting the city alone" (Smith, 1855, p. 423).

Actually, the realities of the possibility of being raped are supported by recent statistics. The FBI *Uniform Crime Reports for the United States* (1975) indicate that of the indexed crimes against the person, rape cases increased from 23,330 or 12.1 per 100,000 inhabitants to 55,210 or 26.1 per 100,000 inhabitants in 1974. It is estimated that a rape occurs every 31 seconds and that two out of three victims do not report the crime. The more recent FBI statistics for 1977 indicate that there was an 11 percent increase in the number of reported rapes (*Uniform Crime Reports for the United States,* 1978).

If some feminists view rape as a method of controlling and subjugating women, the legal system generally defines rape as the actual penetration of the female genitalia by the penis with the use of force and without the consent of the woman victim to whom the man is not married. Because penetration is part of the legal definition, sexual abuse of a woman that does not result in actual penetration can therefore not be considered rape. The definition also implies that rape is mainly a sexual act; whereas we will see in later discussions that research indicates that sex is very often a minor motive on the part of the rapist.

If rape is viewed as a sexual act, then legal evidence to affirm the fact that a rape has taken place, such as evidence of sperm, is important although not necessarily essential.

Between 1972 and 1973 Groth and Burgess (1977) collected data on 133 offenders and 92 victims and found that in 15 percent of the cases the rapists experienced an inadequate erection or inability to ejaculate, and in another 16 percent temporary impotency. In these types of situations then, there would not be any evidence of sperm, but rape did take place.

The second important aspect of the legal definition of rape is that the act was one which was forced on the woman without her consent. Because of this, for many years, and in a large number of states today, evidence of resistance played and still plays an important role in the conviction or acquittal of rapists.

Use of force could include verbal threats, or the use of physical force to make the woman submit. Evidence would consist of scratches, bruises, lacerations, torn clothing, etc. One of the many false ideas about rape is that it is impossible to rape a woman unless she is under the influence of drugs or alcohol or is not emotionally or mentally sound. With this kind of attitude, dramatic evidence of resistance is expected. Compliance as a result of threats of bodily harm or threats to harm others would not be clear evidence of resistance, and therefore compliance could be construed legally as consent unless the rapist held a weapon such as a knife or gun.

The question of how much resistance is legally enough is a very difficult one to answer. Hilberman (1976) points out that there is an expectation that a "good" woman will allow herself to be severely abused before allowing herself to be sexually assaulted. She also states that women are viewed as people in whom the truth is not always present, and that therefore, a woman's word is not automatically accepted. Did not John Home write, "He seldom errs who thinks the worst he can of womankind" (Home, 1756, p. 663)?

In 1974 the National Institute of Law Enforcement and Criminal Justice provided funds for extensive study of the methods used by criminal justice systems throughout the country to investigate cases of forcible rape. The most common weapon used in rape was found to be a gun, and the most common form of resistance used by the victim was verbal. The study also found that there was an increased likelihood of the victim being injured if she resisted and that those individuals who did put up a struggle were twice as likely to be hurt badly enough to require hospitalization (Brodyaga et al., 1975).

The following is the testimony of a twenty-year-old rape victim and her efforts to resist the attack:

I went to visit a friend at her apartment and when I arrived at 7:30 P.M., I found three males and two females, all of whom I knew. There was one male I did not know. The people in the room were listening to music. I began to talk to the male I had not known. He said that he knew my brother, and he invited me up to his apartment to listen to more music since the other four people had paired off. When we got to his apartment in the same complex, we sat down to listen to the music. He kissed me once and I told him that I wasn't in the mood. He tried to kiss me a second time, but I pulled away and refused to kiss him. He then started to read poetry to me.

Suddenly, he picked up a pronged stick, pulled a white scarf out of his pocket and put it around my neck. I screamed but he told me it was no use since he had done this before. He pulled up my skirt and tried to pull my panties down as he tried to choke me with the pronged stick which he held at my throat applying pressure. He then removed the stick from my throat and clawed at my neck.

During this time I kept telling him that I wanted to leave. With the stick in his hand he said that he was going to kill me. He began to jab at my eyes and hitting me on the mouth with the stick. He then pushed me on the bed, opened his fly and stuck his penis into my mouth. I bit hard on his penis and hurt him. He started to cry, and told me that I almost bit his penis off; and still crying said that he was going to kill me and called me a white bitch. He tried to have intercourse with me.

He had taken his pants off and had pushed my skirt and blouse up and was trying to get my pantyhose down, when I elbowed him in the groin. He grabbed me again and this time wrapped his legs around my head and made me have oral sex. He still had the stick in his hand, so I grabbed hold of it and hit him with it. He pushed me backwards against the head-board of the bed so that I was leaning over the bed. We both landed on the floor and he was sitting on me and beating my head. He told me that he was going to gouge my eyes out and kept hitting me with his hands and with the stick on my head. He asked me which eye I wanted to save since he would only take one out. He then stood up and put his pants on. While he was standing over me he put his foot on my face and ground his foot into it. He then told me to get up and sit in the chair. When I didn't move he said "Sit or I'll kill you."

The victim stated that she escaped when someone knocked on the door and the defendant went to open it. In the process of escaping, the victim dropped her keys and had also lost a pair of earrings in the scuffle.

The victim arrived at the hospital emergency room with a swollen face, two black and blue eyes and numerous cuts and scratches on her face and neck. At the time of his arrest at 5:00 A.M. in the morning, the defendant was found in his apartment with his penis wrapped in a white cloth. The key that the victim had lost was found on the floor. Also found was a blood-stained tree branch, three feet, four inches long and about one and one-half inches thick at the base. The stick was forked at the top. The defendant was charged with assault with intent to rape, assault and battery, assault and battery by means of a dangerous weapon, and with committing unnatural and lascivious acts. He pled not guilty to all charges, and was held in $20,000 cash bail. He was eventually convicted of the charges and given an indeterminate sentence.

In spite of the fact that there appears to be a direct correlation between resisting rape and the amount of injury, the victim, the raped woman, is expected to establish proof of her innocence by demonstrating that she fought hard to stop the sexual attack.

In 1960 *Farrar* v. *U.S.* (275 F2d) the convicted rapist appealed his conviction. The victim had stated that although she had not actually seen a knife, she believed that the defendant held a knife at her throat. The Appellate Court reversed the conviction, stating that "the law may permit conviction of rape upon the basis of a concealed knife, but it does not permit conviction premised upon an invisible knife. The rape penalty does not rest upon imaginary forces" (Gager and Schurr, 1976, p. 142).

In 1969, the report of the National Commission on the Causes of Violence (Mulvihill and Tumin, 1969) did not include the act of rape itself in its definition of injury. Injury was defined as physical damage that occured besides the act of sex itself. Using this guideline, the Commission found that in three-quarters of the reported rapes, there was no injury. Age was a factor in the chances of being hurt. The older the victim, the greater the chances of being injured. The age of the offender was also seen as significant in increasing the probability of inflicting harm. Offenders between the ages of twenty-one and thirty used violence more often than those of other ages, while racially, whites tended to cause more bodily injury than blacks (Mulvihill et al., 1969).

Absence of consent was also determined by the victim's previous sexual conduct. Her previous sexual history served to discredit her testimony. Besides putting the victim in a position of having her past sexual behavior publicly aired, the severity of the assault was minimized and the victim, rather than the accused, became the focal point of the trial.

In 1949 the Nebraska Court in *Frank* v. *State* (35 NW2d) ruled that "in cases where a woman charges a man with a sex offense, immorality has a direct connection with veracity . . . and direct evidence of the general reputation of the prosecutrix for sexual morality may be shown by defendant . . ." (Gager and Schurr, 1976, p. 1).

In spite of the fact that a rape victim's past sexual history almost automatically became part of the defense, accused rapists were protected. In one case a man was tried and convicted for raping a woman, let us call her Mrs. A., using force and threats to do so. A witness for the prosecution, Mrs. C. testified that she was also raped by force by the same defendant seventeen months earlier. At this time the defendant used the same mode of operation, raping Mrs. C. on the day they met. The defendant had been tried and convicted for assault and not rape of Mrs. C. The court therefore in *Jackel* v. *State* (App. 506 SW2d, 1974) in Texas reversed the conviction of rape in Mrs. A.'s case on the grounds that Mrs. C.'s testimony for the prosecution was inadmissible since the issue in question was whether or not the sexual act took place with consent (Kattner, 1977). The fact that one woman had been raped had no bearing on whether or not the other woman had consented.

Recent reform has focused on setting guidelines for admitting past sexual history of the victim as evidence. The future rape victim will thus be better protected from a violation of privacy, thereby increasing the possibility of the victim stepping forward to press charges against the rapist.

The statutory reforms in submission of evidence in rape cases take the form of requiring establishment of the pertinence of the information as well as in some states a balancing test which weighs the value of the testimony to the case with the effect of publicly airing the past sexual behavior. Some statutes specifically itemize those situations in which evidence of past sexual history may be admitted.

In Texas and New Mexico the judge is given the power of using discretion to determine the relevancy of the evidence and to make a decision regarding the balance of public disclosure versus the probative value. In New Mexico the criminal law of sexual assault has been broadened so that it is now a sex-neutral crime, whereas in Texas, exclusion of prior sexual evidence is the judge's decision. In Texas, therefore, a judge with traditional attitudes towards the role of women may readily agree to the admission of previous sexual behavior on the basis of relevancy (Ireland, 1978).

Some states admit evidence of past sexual behavior only in cases where it is important to demonstrate that the victim consented or did not resist. These new evidentiary rules still seem to be sex-biased. Progressive legislation allows admission of past sex history of the rapist and his victim only in those cases where the two have had previous sexual relations. The assumption is that if they have been sexually intimate previously, there is a greater probability that consent was given.

In 1977, Representative James R. Mann, a Democrat representing the 2nd District in North Carolina, arose before his fellow congressmen and said, "Mr. Speaker, I move to suspend the rules and pass the bill (H.R. 4727) to amend the Federal Rules of Evidence to provide for the protection of the privacy of rape victims as amended" (*Congressional Record*—House, October 10, 1978, H 11944). This bill disallowed evidence of a rape victim's past sexual behavior except under very specific circumstances, for example if the sexual history involved the defendant. Before being admissible as evidence, the information must be accompanied by written evidence of proof and submitted at least fourteen days before the trial begins so that the relevancy of the material can be determined. The bill was passed, and perhaps it will establish a pattern of enlightenment for future rape legislation.

Corroboration of the victim's testimony is one of the discriminatory practices in rape cases. Basically, corroboration means getting testimony either from other witnesses, or circumstantial evidence to support the prosecution's case. In *Allison* v. *U.S.* (409, F2d, 1969), the United States Court of Appeals for the District of Columbia listed the facts which courts usually accept as circumstantial evidence in rape cases. These include:

1. Evidence presented orally or in writing by medical personnel.
2. Proof that the accused had entered the victim's apartment forcefully.
3. Evidence of physical wounds.
4. The state of disarray, etc., of the victim's apparel.
5. The degree of elapsed time between the actual rape and the time it was shared with others.
6. The victim's mental state; whether she was calm, hysterical, etc.

7. Whether or not the victim had a motive to misrepresent what had happened.
8. Blood and especially semen on the person who was raped as well as on the man or men who raped her.
9. The way the suspected rapist behaved when arrested.
10. Whether or not the accused was in a position to have committed the crime (Gager and Schurr, 1976).

The person who was the accuser in this case was an eleven-year-old girl called Mary. Accompanied by her brother, Joseph, aged ten and her cousin, Edward, aged five, she and the two boys were hailed by Allison as they walked along a street. He then took Mary's brother into his house with Mary, and her cousin followed. Allison sent the two boys out to the store with some money, and as Mary attempted to leave with them, Allison pulled her back into the house, slamming the door behind them. According to Mary, he attempted to kiss her and then flung her on the couch, while Mary screamed and attempted to extricate herself from his grasp. Allison threatened to cut her head off if she continued her battle, following which he exposed himself and attempted to take her panties off. When Joseph and his cousin returned to the house, they found the door locked, heard Mary screaming, and looking through the keyhole saw Allison on top of Mary. As Joseph attacked the door with his feet, Mary was able to wrest herself from her assailant and open the locked door with Joseph's instructions. A woman spoke to Mary at her home in order to ascertain why the young girl was crying, and she later testified that Mary appeared in hysterics.

What is especially interesting about this case is that Allison was tried and convicted for assault with an attempt to commit carnal knowledge. In the United States Court of Appeals, the judge ruled that the assault with the intent to commit carnal knowledge conviction did not have enough corroborative evidence to uphold this conviction. He specifically stated that although there was some corroborative evidence of taking indecent liberties, there was no corroborative evidence to support Mary's statements that Allison had exposed himself, had flung her on the couch, and had tried to remove her panties. The evidence suggests that, minimally, Allison was attempting to arouse and/or gain satisfaction for his sexual desires.

The Appellate Court judge made note of the fact that the jury had originally been confused by their charge that if they found Allison "guilty of assault with intent to commit carnal knowledge, they were not to consider the taking indecent liberties count" (*Federal Reporter*, 1969, p. 452). The Appellate Court judge ruled that the conviction be upheld since "Appellate stands in the same legal position as one who had been found guilty only of carnal knowledge" (*Federal Reporter*, 1969, p. 452).

It is evident that instead of focusing on the victimizer, many of the requirements of circumstantial evidence are concerned with the victim. If she does not struggle, if because of the tremendous trauma she is experiencing she is unable to call the police or tell her friends, if because of shock she is not hysterical, she may have her testimony held in question.

A 24-year-old woman was raped by two unknown assailants at 8:00 P.M. one evening. As she approached her car in a dimly lit parking lot of a university, she was suddenly seized from behind and forced into her car where the double rape took place. Feeling stunned, overwhelmed, and degraded, she drove around in her car for two hours after the incident, unable to return to the apartment she shared with several other women. When she finally arrived home, she talked to no one, quickly showered and went to bed. It was not until the next morning that she was able to share what had happened to her. In this situation, the victim destroyed corroborative evidence of the rape and also delayed in telling anyone about it, thus making it more difficult for a conviction to take place, if indeed she did decide to file a complaint, and if her violators were found. In spite of urging and support from a number of people, the young woman did not file a complaint, never told her family about her experience, and after several weeks quietly dropped out of the Master's Degree program in which she had been enrolled, and in which she was excelling.

As recent as 1969 in *Coltrane* v. *U.S.* (135 U.S. App. DC), the U.S. Court of Appeals for the District of Columbia supported the concept of corroboration (validating the victim's testimony). The court stated that past experience demonstrates that "all too frequently such complaints have an urge to fantasize or even as a motive to fabricate. . . ." In the State of Florida a polygraph test was given as standard operating procedure to every victim of reported rape. Convictions of rape in Florida resulted in the death penalty so that every effort is made to test the veracity of the complaint.

Corroboration of witness testimony is not required in other crimes. Implied, then, is the concept that the victim of rape is less credible than the victim of other crimes, that sexual purity is related to honesty, and that therefore the rape victim's testimony is more suspect than that of other witnesses (Ireland, 1978). We owe the questioning of the credibility of rape victims to Lord Hale, who in 1680 stated in his Pleas of the Crown that juries should be instructed in rape cases that "Rape is a crime easy to accuse of and difficult to defend against" (Pleas of the Crown, 635). The focal point of the rape trial becomes the victim rather than the victimizer. Those instructions to jurors have been given in many states throughout the United States ever since. It is only recently that rape law reform in some states included prohibition of the Hale plea from automatically being given to jurors.

It is interesting to note that corroboration was not required by common law. In *Lyles* v. *U.S.* (20th App. D.D.), in 1902 the court warned that basing a conviction on the testimony of one witness was dangerous, and that evidence needed to be introduced to corroborate the testimony of the witness (Hill, 1976). The government began to use corroborative evidence in order to validate witnesses' complaints of rape. This practice continued.

One of the early moves away from corroboration of witness testimony occurred in *Arnold* v. *U.S.* (358 A.2d D.C. Ct. App. 1976). The presiding judge disregarded the District of Columbia's corroboration rule and did not instruct the jury that corroboration of the victim's testimony would be required in order to convict the defendant. On May 30, 1973, Eugenia Dickerson was raped. Portia Mills was raped two weeks later, and both victims identified James Arnold as the perpetrator. Arnold appealed the sentence he received as a result of his having been found guilty by the court because the jurors had not been charged with the necessity of having the victim's testimony corroborated. This case resulted in a review of the law requiring corroboration. The court rejected the concept that a rape victim's testimony needed to have its credibility established. Arnold's conviction and sentence was upheld (Hill, 1976).

In California the judge was required to read the following:

Evidence was received for the purpose of showing that the female person named in the information was a woman of unchaste character.

A woman of unchaste character can be the victim of forcible rape, but it may be inferred that a woman who has previously consented to sexual intercourse would be more likely to consent again.

Such evidence may be considered by you only for such bearing as it may have on the question of whether or not she gave her consent to the alleged sexual act and in judging her credibility (CALJIC 10.06 (1970 Rev.).

Finally in 1975 in *People* v. *Rincon-Pineda,* the California Supreme Court supported eliminating the cautioning of jurors in regard to the testimony of rape victims. The court pointed out that the defendant's constitutional rights were protected by the usual guidelines; he would be presumed innocent until proven guilty and the proof of his guilt would have to be beyond a reasonable doubt; he would also have the right to witness support in his defense and the right to retain legal help (Hill, 1976).

Many states such as Connecticut, Iowa, Pennsylvania, Texas, and Washington have since 1974 revoked statutory corroboration requirements. States such as New York, Minnesota, New Mexico, Pennsylvania and Texas have passed statutory requirements which specifically state that no corroboration is required in cases of rape. New York has recently passed a law stating that in cases where the victim is a minor or mentally incompetent, corroboration of witness testimony would be required in a rape case. These changes in the corroboration rules recognize that a rape victim's testimony is not less believable than the testimony of victims of other types of crimes.

Reform is also seen in the repeal of Lord Hale's instructions to the jury. States such as Iowa, Minnesota and Nevada forbid Lord Hale's instructions, while other states have established firm rules under which special instructions to the jury in a rape case may be given (Ireland, 1978). Lord Hale's sex bias is finally being expunged from the law after almost 300 years of practice.

Concern for false accusation of rape has always existed. Is this in reality a factor? Do women consent to sexual intercourse and then cry rape? The FBI *Uniform Crime Reports for the United States* (1978) estimated that in 1971 in California one-fifth of the rape complaints were labeled unfounded. The criteria for labeling the case unfounded included the fact that the case was not reported immediately, lack of corroboration involving the physical status of the alleged victim, alcoholism, and the victim's refusal to submit to a physical examination.

What kind of situations create crying rape when rape has not taken place? Occasionally, a young woman who suddenly realizes that she may have contracted a venereal disease or is pregnant may make an accusation. A woman who has not been able to hide the evidence of sexual intercourse from her husband or boyfriend may accuse her recent sexual partner of rape to avoid the consequences of her actions. Such a situation recently occurred.

A young college student consistently handled her relationship with her boyfriend by sexually seducing another male each time she and her boyfriend had an argument. It was almost as if she were saying, "See, you may be angry with me but I am desirable to another." One night she and her boyfriend had a quarrel, after which he proceeded to go to his room in the dormitory to sleep. She went out for a walk on campus, met a young man with whom she had had relations before and began to play with his genitals. They then proceeded to find a dark secluded spot on campus where sexual intercourse took place. After the encounter, the young woman returned to her room to find her boyfriend waiting for her return. Her response to the questions concerning her disheveled clothes and the grass stains on her clothes was that she had been raped by an unseen, unknown assailant. He immediately called the women in the next room, who coerced the young woman to report the rape to the campus police. Investigations of the incident and statements by the alleged victim, her boyfriend, and her recent sexual partner, who had been the person identified as the first person she had seen after the alleged rape, were contradictory. The young woman refused to talk further to the investigating officer, and it was evident from the facts culled that rape had not taken place. The case was labeled unfounded.

Similarly, a woman who had had consensual sex and then was degraded by her partner, a young woman who was "found out" by her parents, might also cry wolf. As we see, however, from statistics available, unfounded rapes constitute a small percentage of all rapes reported. Interestingly, forcible rape is the only crime for which an "unfounded" crime is calculated. The National Institute of Law Enforcement in its national survey of more than 50 police departments in 1974 found that reports of rape which were labeled unfounded varied from 1 percent to 25 percent of the total of all reported forcible rapes and averaged 10 percent (Brodyaga et al., 1975).

According to the Uniform Crime Report, rape is one of the crimes that is under-reported (*Uniform Crime Reports for the United States* 1976). Studies have estimated that 20 percent of forcible rapes are not officially reported. Why, then, is there so much suspicion of a woman who claims she has been raped?

Another area of reform in rape laws is in the area of the emphasis on the degree of force. Michigan's new law on rape, which was passed in 1975, was a model for future reform. The old rape statute was replaced with a sexual assault statute that established culpability of the crime on the degree of sexual invasion and the extent of force used. The type of sexual involvement is the focus rather than the amount of force used. Purposefully touching a female's body with the goal of sexual gratification is considered a crime if it is done without mutual consent. Use of force which injures the victim or using weapons meets the requirement for a first-degree offense. Sexual activity such as fellatio, cunnilingus, intercourse vaginally or anally, as well as use of an inanimate object are acts which meet the first-degree violation definition.

Michigan's law moves away from stressing penetration, which implies protection and concern for chastity, to stressing force. Consent does not become an issue.

> ... other first-degree violations include sexual intercourse with a minor under thirteen, incest with one under sixteen, and penetration during the commission of a felony, or on an incapacitated victim or with the aid of an accomplice. A second-degree violation involves only sexual contact. A third-degree violation occurs whenever force or coercion is used to achieve penetration. Any sexual contact achieved by force or on an incapacitated victim is fourth-degree criminal sexual conduct. The penalty varies with the degree of the crime and a mandatory sentence is imposed on recidivists (Ireland, 1978, pp. 194–195).

Penalties for rape have varied throughout the years. In some states, rape was considered an offense which warranted the death penalty. When men took the law into their own hands, death by lynching was meted out to accused rapists, especially if they were black and their victims white. In general, blacks comprised 90 percent of the victims of mob lynchings between 1862 and 1941. Of those blacks lynched, 20 percent had been accused of rape. Legally, too, a disproportionate number of blacks were executed for rape. Since 1930, of the 455 men who were legally executed in the United States for a rape conviction, 89 percent were black. In a majority of these cases, the women rape victims were white (Sagarian, 1977). In North Carolina between 1909 and 1954 blacks comprised 56 percent of the men who were executed for rape in contrast to the 43 percent white men who were executed for similar convictions. In Florida, between 1940 and 1964 six white men who raped white females were executed in comparison to 45 of 84 (54 percent) blacks who were executed for raping white women. No offender, white or black, who raped black females received the death penalty (Wolfgang and Riedel, 1974).

In 1972 the Supreme Court in a 5 to 4 decision ruled that the death penalty was unconstitutional. Three of the petitioners in this case were black, one of whom had been convicted of a felony and the other two had been convicted of rape. The court stated that ". . . the imposition and carrying out of the death penalty in these cases constitutes cruel and unusual punishment in violation of the Eighth and Fourteenth Amendments" (*Furman* v. *Georgia*) 408 U.S. 238 (1972). In essence, the text of the decision implied that the imposition of the death penalty in states where specific standards are not outlined for jurors and judges did not comply with the safeguards of the Constitution. In response to this decision some states have passed legislation making the death penalty mandatory for the commission of specific crimes. In Georgia, the death penalty is automatically given to a convicted rapist, murderer, armed robber, or one who has been convicted of kidnapping, if there has been evidence of an additional aggravating circumstance such as previous convictions of a crime or a record of sexual assaults (Wolfgang and Riedel, 1975).

The death penalty for rape may have been one of the factors instrumental in the low conviction rate of rapists in this country. Forty-nine percent of the men who were prosecuted for rape in 1976 were acquitted or had their cases dismissed (*Uniform Crime Reports for the United States,* 1977).

Rape, like other crimes, has been increasing on college campuses. According to research done by the Center for Women's Policy Studies for the National Institute of Law Enforcement and Criminal Justice, there are about one to twelve forcible rapes each year on every campus (*The Problem of Rape on Campus,* n.d.).

It wasn't until 1971 that concern for the increasing incidences of rape on college campuses led the FBI to report campus rapes as a separate statistic from forcible rapes in general. It is believed that unreported campus rapes may be from three-and-a-half times to nine times that of reported rapes.

Although the exact national incidence rate of rape on campus remains unknown, various surveys have approximated the extent of rape on campus. In 1968, a sample of 261 college women showed that 3.4% had been raped,

31% had experienced sexual violence short of rape (and 3.7% of the college males interviewed admitted to being rapists). An article appearing in the December, 1973 issue of *College Management* calculated 8,952 'sex crimes' in 1972 for all campuses. Of a sample of 55 college students in 1975, 26% reported being raped or experiencing an attempted rape (although not necessarily on campus) from one to six times over a three-year period (*The Problem of Rape on Campus*, n.d., p. 2).

In 1976, the FBI *Uniform Crime Reports* indicated that in 1975 157 rapes were reported on 168 campuses researched (*The Problem of Rape on Campus*, n.d.).

Actually, college campuses with their concentration of women in dorms have become the ideal target for rapists. Because women tend to feel that the campus is like their own home and regard it as a haven, they walk the campus alone. Most often, rape on the college campus, as is the case with rape in general, is committed by an unknown assailant. Rapes which occur on dates are often reported less frequently, mainly because the victim fears that she will be accused of having enticed the man and therefore of sharing responsibility for the act.

The brazenness of campus rapists is demonstrated by the following attack which took place on a large northeastern university campus in a dorm room.

I was awakened (around 1:00 A.M.) by a male who jumped on the bed attempting to cover my mouth with his hand. He told me not to scream (as I had started to do), that he had a knife—that all he wanted was "a piece of ass." I told him that I wouldn't scream and asked him who he was. He didn't answer that, just told me to do as he asked and I wouldn't get hurt.

He started to pull back the bed covers telling me to take off my nightgown. All the while, I kept talking, pleading that he promise to leave when he was done, asking him to see my position. He kept agreeing, assuring me that no harm would come to me. I asked him how he got in? "The door was unlocked." By this time, he had taken his pants off and had pulled my nightgown off. Then he started oral sex. This lasted for less than a minute.

I heard (at this time) my roommate run out of her bed and out the door. Actually, just before this moment, the male had started having intercourse. I begged him to let her go. In a few seconds, I heard another male voice from outside. The first male got up abruptly, grabbed his pants and placed what appeared to be a knife enclosed in a case on the edge of the bed. It seems as though he placed the knife on the bed after picking it up from the floor. Before I let him do anything I told him that I wanted to see him put the knife on the floor. He did this (or at least made a motion of doing this). He hastily pulled on his pants and made a motion to get me out of bed as if he wanted me to come with him. I told him I wasn't going anywhere until I got some clothes on.

Meanwhile, I was yelling out the door to my roommate and the neighbor to let him go. I yelled this two or three times until I saw the man go out the door.

Due to the fact that all the lights were out I never really got a good look at him except that he had short wavy or curly hair and was medium build, not thin.

The victim's roommate related the following:

I was sleeping and heard a guy talking in a low voice to my roommate in the next bed. As you walk into the bedroom my bed is on the right set back in an alcove and my roommate's bed is near the window and you would tend to see that bed first. I don't think he realized I was there. I heard Jane say something about a knife and kept asking him who he was. I realized he was going to try and rape her. He said he wouldn't hurt her if she gave him a "piece of her ass." She asked him if I was okay and not to hurt me. She was scared but very calm and tried to stall him sort of by asking that he put the knife down on the floor which I thought I heard him do. Then he told her to take her nightgown off—he was on the bed leaning over her the whole time. He took his pants off and got on top of her. I could hear someone's hair being pulled and he was raping her. My roommate called my name to see if I was awake and asked him to leave me alone.

I heard my roommate sort of choking and it sounded like she was struggling not to scream—she kept asking him to leave, but he wouldn't stop. As soon as I thought he wouldn't hear me, I got out of bed and ran out the front door into the street. I heard someone walking and called out for help. He asked me what was wrong and I told him my roommate was being raped. He ran toward the house and turned on the lights. My roommate yelled out to turn out the lights and that he had a knife and to leave him alone. She turned out the lights and went outside while he slowly came out of the house.

He was about 5'10" and had very short light brown or blond curly hair—like he was in the service. He had a navy peacoat on. He headed for the street and for the front of the building—I then went inside.

Many people wonder about the type of man who would commit rape. People often think of the rapist as being mentally ill. What do we know about the men who commit this vicious crime?

Contrary to popular belief the rapist is generally not mentally ill. Groth and Burgess (1977) found that only 10 percent of the 133 offenders they studied manifested psychotic processes. Psychiatric normality is one of the characteristics of the rapist according to psychiatric classification. The man who commits a rape is unable to restrain his sexual-aggressive needs and has poor impulse control. He usually has been charged previously with crimes against the person, and when he commits a rape, he may do so in a brutal manner (Amir, 1971). Actually, there is a great deal of diversity among rapists. The following is a case illustration of a man who was found innocent of forcible rape charges by reason of mental illness, and who demonstrated obvious symptoms of emotional disorder.

> Victim was taking a sunbath in her backyard when the defendant suddenly grabbed her, put a pen knife to her throat and forced her to go with him to the nearby woods. There they undressed and he got on top of her and forced her to have intercourse with him. For three hours, he forced the victim to sit on his lap with her legs around his body while he periodically made growling noises. The victim did not try to escape because of fear. She recognized the fact that he seemed to be out of touch with reality.

This type of rapist belongs to one of two categories defined by Gager and Schurr and would be considered the social psychopath or sociopath who is not mentally responsible for his acts and is therefore committed to a hospital instead of to jail (Gager and Schurr, 1976). The other type of rapist according to Gager and Schurr is the so-called "normal" rapist who has been environmentally conditioned to rape or whose act of rape is a result of a particular circumstance, such as being seduced but not being able to complete the sexual act because of refusal of the partner. He therefore takes what he believes is coming to him. This type is very often not charged, and when he is charged does not receive a sentence of commitment to jail or hospital.

In May of 1978 the Colorado Supreme Court censured District Court Judge Dean Mabry for preventing a case of sexual assault from going to a jury. He had expressed disbelief in a woman's claims that she had been sexually assaulted and stated that her story resembled one of attempted seduction rather than attempted rape although ". . . a little bit rough . . . that's the way things are sometimes."

Groth and Burgess (1977) found that rapists could be categorized into two types according to the motivational force; the anger rapists and the power rapists. The anger rapist feels extremely hostile to and contemptuous of his victim and is attempting to make up for what he perceives as the many hurtful acts which women in his life have committed against him. He retaliates, using as his victims women with whom he is not acquainted. The act of rape itself, therefore, involves more force than necessary, use of profane language and forcing the victim to perform acts which are degrading, and so additionally abusive. The rapist receives little sexual gratification from the sex act itself. His motive, pure and simple, is to express his hate, and it is women whom he hates (Groth and Burgess, 1977). One-quarter to one-third of sexual offenses are estimated to be the assault type (Gebhard et al., 1965).

The ultimate expression of hate against women is murder, but many violent acts are committed in addition to the act short of murder.

A fifty-one-year-old merchant seaman, Larry Singleton, perceived by a neighbor as a "peach of a fellow," was arrested in Sparks, Nevada in September, 1978 and charged with the rape and mutilation of a young girl. The girl, Mary, was a runaway who lived with her boyfriend in Sausalito, California, using a car as their domicile. She stated that she had been given a ride by the suspect who raped her, hacked off both her arms, and then abandoned her, thinking she was dead. Mary was found on a California freeway as she staggered about naked. The suspect stated that he remembered having sexual intercourse with the victim with her consent and cannot remember much else because he was in an alcoholic stupor (Associated Press, October 10, 1978).

The purpose of rape is to hurt according to inmates at the Bridgewater Treatment Center who were convicted of rape. Anger toward women is what the offenders stated they felt. Women may be brutalized by insertion of objects in orifices of the body, biting, clawing or using a knife on breasts, vagina or other parts of the body. Aggression serves to help fulfill sexual desire (Cohen et al., 1974).

The concept of rape as an act of hostility toward women is not a new one and is held by a number of people. Feminists believe that it is man's hatred and contempt for women that allows rape to occur and to often go unpunished.

Groth and Burgess's (1977) second type of rapist, the power rapist, rapes in order to feel dominant and to conquer. Sixty-five percent of their sample fit this category. Power rapists are those who gain pleasure from their control of another human being. They fantasize that the woman will willingly submit and enjoy the act, even if she tries to fight him off initially. This type of rapist sees himself as God's gift to women and in essence feels that he is doing the victim a favor by having sexual relations with her. This type will often use a weapon, usually a knife. The power rapist can be divided into two kinds. The "power assertive" rapist who views the sex act as a means of demonstrating his masculinity as well as power. He feels that women are there to satisfy the needs of men. The second kind of power rapist is the "power-assurance" rapist, who feels more worthy when he places women in a position of powerlessness, and also rapes to reassure himself that indeed he is a male (Groth and Burgess, 1977).

Selkin (1975) classified rapists as either those with ego splits or those who are predators. The ego-split variety is one who is usually married, working, and considered normal. His difficulties with women in his family are acted out in his attacks on unknown women. The predator, on the other hand, is motivated to rape as a second thought while in the act of committing another crime such as robbery.

Whether the rapist is considered normal or mentally ill, no matter how one attempts to categorize him, the fact remains that women are the objects of his violence and the victims of it.

In addition to being considered normal mentally, our average rapist is fairly young, twenty-four or younger. Arrest for rape seems to decline at the age of twenty-five and after. The highest rate for rape offenders is in the fifteen- to nineteen-year-old bracket (Amir, 1971). Sixty percent of the rapists Gebhard (1965) studied came from broken homes.

Groth and Burgess (1977) found that one-third of the offenders they studied were married and sexually active with their wives. The single, divorced, separated, or widowed rapist was sexually active with women or homosexual partners. This figure is the same as Gebhard's. Amir (1971), however, found that singlehood is the status of most rapists. Rapists generally work in low-status positions, very often in jobs which are associated with masculinity, and will tend to be black, according to Amir, although contrary to popular thinking, these blacks will tend to choose black victims, since most rapes are intraracial. The rapist will look for a victim who is vulnerable, either by virtue of being unattended, under the influence of alcohol, asleep, old or incapacitated emotionally or mentally. What woman is therefore safe from possible attack?

Amir's (1971) study found that weekends, and particularly 8:00 P.M. to 2:00 A.M., were the times when rape was most likely to take place. A group of women in Amherst, Massachusetts recently organized a march called *Make the Nights Safe for Women* in response to the fact that women's safety at night is negligible.

If rape by a single individual is an assault on a person's most precious possession, the body, then gang rape or group rape, the sexual attack by more than one man on a woman, is a multiple assault and thus the height of humiliation, degradation, and terror. Concern increases when we realize that although the *Uniform Crime Reports* do not itemize or differentiate group assaults from single-person assaults, studies have indicated that these multiple attacks comprise a large percentage of rapes. Amir (1971) points out that in his study in Philadelphia 43 percent of the rapes involved more than one attacker. Because there is more than one assailant, the victim finds it difficult to resist and little force is necessary to commit the crime. In multiple-rape situations, the victim is often further degraded by being forced to perform fellatio, be the object of cunnilingus, and the recipient of multiple men serially having intercourse with her.

We (John and myself) were walking along the highway trying to hitch a ride back to school. Three white males in their thirties stopped, asked us where we were going and then told us to hop in. Two of the men were sitting in the front and one sat in the back. I got in first. John followed. We sat in the back seat. The man in the back asked us if we were two women, and we said no. He talked a little about where we were going and it was just about then that the driver turned off the road and explained that he was taking us to school through another route. He asked us if there was a gas station on the road and we said we didn't know. Soon the man sitting next to the driver said to pull off the road so he could take a "piss." Shortly after that the driver pulled over and the man in the front seat said as he got out of the car, "Don't look." At that point the man sitting next to John pulled out a switch blade. He told John to get out of the car and pushed him out. At that point I began to cry. I could hear John say something about his glasses. I think he had a knife on John. At that point the man got back into the car, and the car sped away. The man in the back seat had a knife on me saying, "Don't do anything and you won't get hurt." At that point he began to touch me intimately and pull at my clothes, pushing me down, taking off his pants, etc. I don't know what happened to the knife. He asked me if I had any money and I told him I only had five dollars. He told me to give him the money while he tried to get me to touch him. I was crying. Just then a police car came by and the driver told the man in the back seat to cool it.

The man ordered me into the front seat and I went. He asked me my name and I told him. During all this time the man sitting next to me was touching me intimately. The car headed off the main road, and the man sitting on my right told me to be cool, and I wouldn't get hurt. He was holding the knife in his hand next to me. I turned to the man in the back seat, and asked him if he could possibly give me my money back. The driver in the front got angry and said it's one thing to do this but it is another to rob a woman—give her money back. Then after a heated discussion the driver showed me a small revolver. We turned off to a small dirt road and stopped. They told me to take off my clothes. They made obscene remarks about my body. The driver got into the back seat and began to play with me, made me touch him and pushed me on top of him. I was crying, and he told me to be quiet. When he was done he said "Who's next?"

The shorter one said "Me." I was crying so hard that he stopped and said, "Forget it." The other man got in back with me. After he finished, the second man got on me again for a long time and then he left me. They were asking me obscene questions and then told me to get dressed. It was getting light. They told me that they had really not raped me because I hadn't put up a physical fight. They didn't seem to think that the knife and gun were threatening devices.

Obviously, the three rapists had bought the legal definition of rape which implied that the woman had to demonstrate by physical means that she had tried to fight off her attacker for the incident to be defined as rape. However, in this case, the three men were caught, tried, and found guilty.

Women, the victims, can be the objects of rape at any age, in any place, at any time, and fear of rape is a universal concern for girls and women throughout their lives. At no age is safety assured. In no place, not even home, is a woman completely certain of protection from being violated. The violation of a woman's body is coupled with feelings of powerlessness, manipulation, loss of control, and inadequacy.

Victims are people who very often happened to be in the wrong place at the wrong time and who, therefore, were chosen by chance for their roles as victims.

The fifteen- to nineteen-year-old age group has a higher chance of getting raped than any other age group (Amir, 1971). The victim may be a child of five who is abducted and raped on the rooftop of an apartment complex while she screams in pain as her labia is torn and she hemorrhages from adult male genitalia being thrust into her small body. The victim may be a young woman walking home from work or an old woman as she lies sleeping at home.

Victims by definition are individuals who are subjected to deprivation, oppression, or suffering. They are people to whom something is done over which they have no control, yet in our society the concept of "Blaming the victim" is common, especially if the victim is a woman, and especially if sex is involved. Isn't the woman the seducer, the teaser, the sexual manipulator?

Marvin Wolfgang in his *Studies in Homicide* (1967) refers to victims as culpable. Amir (1971) states that ". . . the victim is always the cause of crime" (p. 254). Victims can be the causes of the crime committed against them according to Schafer. Precipitative victims are those whose behavior is such that it operates to entice the criminal to commit a crime against the instigating victim. "Walking alone in a dark, deserted place, for example, may tempt the criminal to rob, or an overly revealing dress of a female may allure to rape . . . In these cases the victim, since he ought to ponder the risk, cannot be seen as entirely blameless, and some responsibility should be carried by the victimized person" (Schafer, 1977, p. 46). Does this not relieve the criminal of responsibility for his behavior and does this not place the blame on the victim? The following is a rape account given to the police. Should the victim carry partial blame for her victimization because she used what would appear to be poor judgment?

Miss R, aged 20, was on her way back from town at 12 noon, on her bike heading for the home she was babysitting at. She was approaching Elm Street when she passed a stopped vehicle. As she passed it the driver said, "excuse me" at which point she stopped. Miss R is unsure of whether the driver was in the car or in the process of getting out of it, but by the end of the conversation he was standing outside his vehicle.

He asked for directions to Prospect Ave. Before she could finish giving him directions he interrupted her and asked if she knew of anyone who would want to do some modeling that afternoon. Miss R said yes, she had a friend that might be interested because she did some modeling for an art class at the University. He then said well, would you be interested? She told him she had never done any modeling before. He said there's nothing to it, it's really easy. He offered to pay her $6.00 an hour. She asked him if there would be any nude modeling and he said yes, some but there would also be some free sketching. Miss R agreed to do it, but she was assuming it was for a group such as a class. She told him she would have to ride her bike home at which point he said it would be at Park Street and did she know where that was? She told him yes and then decided to ride her bike there. He then left and she rode her bike to Park Street. She caught up with the car at the entrance of the complex where he had stopped to wait for her. She then followed him.

He got out of his car and she got off her bike and locked it to a pole. He entered the apartment while she was securing her bike. She entered his apartment and said she was thirsty and he asked her whether she wanted water or orange juice. He then gave her a drink of water and also asked her if she wanted a smoke and she said no I've quit.

He then said we can do it upstairs or downstairs, but there is better lighting upstairs for the pictures. This was the first time Miss R remembers him saying pictures and not modeling. She was also surprised upon entering the apartment to see no other people there. In referring to whether it was upstairs or down Miss R stated it didn't matter to her.

They then went upstairs to a bedroom which they entered and he opened the curtains. Miss R was unsure what to do so she asked him and he said he wanted to do the nude first. She began to get undressed while he was monkeying with his camera. While she was undressing, Miss R asked him if he was the same person who advertised in the College and he said he was. He said he was an art major at the University. She asked him if he was a photography major too and he said no, art.

After getting undressed, he motioned for her to get on to the waterbed, which she proceeded to do. At this point Miss R began to get nervous. He then asked her if she minded if he took his clothes off because he felt more comfortable. Miss R said alright. He then took his clothes off and approached her in bed. He laid down on the bed on his side and angled the camera and took a picture of her crotch. He then immediately set the camera on the floor and he said he had to let it set for four minutes. He then made a statement about the phone which was located on the other side of the bed and very quickly reached across her and then rolled on top of her. Miss R told him no as he began kissing her.

He began trying to insert his penis into her vagina and she began trying to push him off of her. When she wasn't able to move him, she began talking and kept saying no, I don't want this. She also said it's unfair for you to take advantage because you're stronger than I am. She asked him if he wouldn't rather be doing this with someone who wanted to. He didn't answer. At one point he said a couple of times he wouldn't hurt her. He also said if she put her legs around him it wouldn't hurt so much. She didn't. During the entire time she kept saying no.

He asked her if she realized she was beautiful? He then began to really "move" and he was by this time inside her. She said no, stop this, I've had enough, get off me and he stopped. He said don't you like people to make love to you? Miss R had gotten off the bed and was getting dressed when he asked her this. Her reply was "you weren't making love to me you were fucking me." She said it would take all day to explain the difference and she wasn't going to go into a discussion, but that she knew the difference. He then asked her to hit him with her shoe. She refused. He asked her if she wasn't going to stay and have the pictures taken and she said no. She told him he was crazy and an ass for attacking her. He said he didn't attack her. Then the phone rang and she left.

Is an intoxicated woman responsible for her rape?

Complainant stated she had had a fight with her boyfriend in his vehicle at approximately 5:30 P.M. January 15, 1975. He had then taken her home and left. At approximately 8:30 P.M. complainant decided to go to the hotel to try and locate him. She stated she had begun drinking about 6:00 P.M. and continued drinking before and after her arrival at the bar.

Complainant arrived at the bar and searched for her boyfriend, but failed to locate him. Since he likes to play pool she decided to wait outside the pool room to see if he would come out. At one point, a white male approached her and sat down with her. He asked complainant if she would like to go with him to which she replied no. Shortly thereafter a black male subject (hereafter referred to as subj. #1) joined them and bought everyone a beer. Complainant stated that at this point she was intoxicated to the point of feeling sick. The white male subject left and the black subject #1 asked her if she would like to go to a friend's house. She replied no because she wanted to stay near the pool room. Complainant then placed a telephone call home to see if her boyfriend had by chance returned home. Subject #1 followed her to the telephone and was joined there by another black male (hereafter referred to as subj. #2) who handed subject #1 a beer.

Complainant started to return to the table, but got sick and went into the ladies' room. Both subject #1 and #2 followed her and waited outside restroom door. A waitress entered and told complainant that her boyfriend was waiting outside door to take her home. Complainant then left rest room to check and found that it wasn't her boyfriend the waitress was referring to, but the two black subjects. She reentered rest room and was once again sick.

Complainant is unsure of what happened next except for being in a car which subject #1 was driving. Subject #2 was seated on passenger's side and she was in the middle. She thought they were taking her home. The next thing complainant remembers is a hallway, doesn't remember entering the apartment, but remembers sitting on a couch. At this point she noticed there was a female also present. She began to feel sick again and female subject told her where the bathroom was located.

Complainant stated she was in the bathroom vomiting for a while before subject #2 entered and slammed the door shut and may have locked it. Complainant was unable to say anything at this time due to the fact that she was sick. Subject #2 did not say anything to her just unzipped his pants. He approached her as she was kneeling in front of the toilet bowl and attempted to take her pants down. Complainant stated she told him no and began fighting him. He mumbled something like come on. He tried to spread her legs apart at which point she began to scream. When she began to scream subject #2 began hitting her on the back of the head with his fists.

Complainant tried to protect her head and gave a loud scream. Complainant is unsure if she blacked out. The next thing she remembered is a police officer standing over her, as she lay on her side on the floor asking her if she were alright. Subject #2 had pulled her pants down to her knees. Complainant was unsure if subject #1 and female subject had left the apartment after she entered the bathroom, but they did not come to her aid.

Blaming the victim is part of the process of making some sense out of tragedies which occur. Lerner (1970) presented the concept of a "just world." This theory suggests that a victim gets what he or she deserves because the victim is inherently bad or because the victim's behavior is responsible for the outcome. The rape of an innocent person or one who has a good reputation is unjustifiable. In order to prevent chaos in our thinking and to protect our view of the world as an orderly, equitable place, we tend to assign blame to the respectable person who is victimized. In other words, she must have done something wrong, or otherwise it would not have happened.

Not every victim reports the attack. In fact, it is estimated by the National Commission on the Causes of Violence (Mulvihill et al., 1969) that rape is three and one-half times greater than actually reported. The results of a National Institute of Law Enforcement study made in 1974 (Brodyaga et al., 1975) shed some light on the factors which influenced a victim's decision to press charges. In the majority of cases of physical abuse, evidence that penetration had occurred, degree of injury inflicted on the victim, whether or not a weapon was used, whether or not the suspect had previously been involved in a relationship with the offender, how quickly the crime was reported, and the victim's ability to identify the offender, are factors in the decision of whether or not to report the rape. The victim's decision to report the rape is also based on her concerns for being publicly identified, the degree of guilt she feels about her possible role in the rape situation ("My mother told me not to walk alone at night but I did anyway") and the support she receives from significant others.

One study which focused on rape victims who decided on their own to report the rape found that the degree of danger perceived by the victim, differences in social class, and the support they thought they would get from the important people in their lives, directly affected their decision to report the crime (Smith and Nelson, 1976).

Although prompt reporting is important in the prosecution of a rape charge, the victim sometimes delays in taking this action. In the following case a two-week delay occurred before the rape was reported.

Miss R. states that she had been raped by three to four men. She had been to a party to celebrate her return from Florida. When the party ended at midnight, she and her roommate left and they waited on the corner for some male friends they had arranged to meet. Before these friends arrived, another car came along with someone that her roommate knew. The roommate went off with this friend leaving Miss R. to wait. The car came along and the two men, one of whom Miss R. had seen on campus offered to drive her to her dormitory. She accepted the offer, and later when she was asked whether she would like to visit with them in their apartment she accepted their offer once again. She remembered nothing about the apartment complex she went into but she said that she went up a flight of stairs and then entered a dark room which contained only a mattress. There were three to five males in the room. Miss R. was unsure of the exact number, and could not remember whether or not they were fully clothed when she entered the apartment. At one point Miss R. noticed that the men who had brought her to the apartment had left.

The men who remained began to use obscenities with her and began to feel her body. They then removed her clothes and forced her onto the mattress. When she began to scream, someone put his hand over her mouth. While someone held her down and someone else kept her from screaming another raped her. She was raped by at least three men. When they finished with her they made no attempt to stop her from getting dressed and leaving.

Miss R. left the apartment and managed to get outside where she fell and knocked on another door. A man answered to whom she stated that she had been attacked and asked him if she could stay there until morning. She became sick and after this she lay down on the sofa. The man brought her back to her apartment the next morning. She did not know this man's name. She did not remember the car he was driving but did recall the fact that he had dark hair and wore glasses.

Upon returning to her apartment, she spent the day sleeping and being sick. She told her roommate that she had been raped. She also told her mother and another friend. When she was asked by the police why she had delayed in reporting this incident she stated that she felt there was nothing they could do since she had so little information to give them. When she was asked why she had waited to see a doctor, she stated that she had no other problems except nausea until recently when she began to bleed and had noticed a few sores in the vaginal area. The doctor had suggested that she notify the police. When asked why she could not give more specific details she stated that she had been very tired from her trip and had drunk some wine and was intoxicated.

Some women attempt to resist the rapist by screaming, fighting or running, while others passively succumb. At the Violence Research Unit at Denver General Hospital an attempt was made to objectively study the personality of the resistors and compare them with those who chose not to fight. Those women who resisted were women who in general had good verbal ability, were sociable, scored higher in dominance scale, and generally were accepting of themselves and felt that they were competent. The rape did not catapult them into severe depression, and they were able to understand the rapist's needs. Those victims who did not resist demonstrated fewer of these characteristics, they were less sociable, less dominant, less self-assured and self-accepting and less able to identify with the rapist (Selkin, 1975).

A woman who is raped feels outraged, violated, dirty, used, often guilty, and during the rape attack itself, she is fearful of her life. Rape is a traumatic situation which results in crisis because of the severely stressful characteristics associated with it. The act of being raped is often so anxiety-producing and overwhelming that the individual's normal coping mechanisms become inoperative. What has worked before no longer works. Crisis occurs because of the individual's unresolved increasing tension and anxiety related to the stressful situation.

The questioning which takes place in the police station, when the woman does report the incident, can be humiliating and degrading—a continuation of the rape. If there are no female investigators, the victim is further assaulted by men who find it difficult to identify with her, and who may have absorbed society's attitude toward the rape victim—she must have done something to deserve it.

Some communities, like New York City, have attempted to provide a supportive atmosphere for victims of rape by training female investigators in sex crimes and crisis intervention. It has also been suggested that when the police need to question a rape victim in a hospital, a female community volunteer should accompany the victim in order to provide reassurance.

In the District of Columbia, a rape victim is called by a visiting nurse who has obtained her number from the police department. The purpose of this contact is to offer and encourage the acceptance of assistance.

Hospitals are often ill-equipped to deal adequately with a woman who has been raped. Certain tests are necessary for evidentiary purposes, but the manner in which these tests are given is crucial to the emotional well-being of the woman on whom these tests are made. The Rape Crisis Intervention Center of Beth Israel Hospital in Boston is an example of an exemplary program. The personnel in the emergency room are given positive reinforcement in order to foster a sensitive approach to the rape victim. Immediately after the tests are made, the victim is offered counseling in order to help her deal with her emotional crisis.

Sutherland and Scherl (1970) identified three phases which rape victims go through. The first lasts from a few days to a few weeks and is a severe reaction which is characterized by shock, fear, and consternation. What appears to be an adjustment characterizes the second phase. It is during this period that the initial feelings of anger and bitterness are worked through. Resolving the conflict takes place in the third phase. The victim appears depressed and has an urgent need to share her feelings.

Guilt is prevalent initially after the rape. It is important, therefore, for counseling to provide the opportunity for this guilt to be expressed and for reassurance that the victim was not responsible for the rape. The anger, which is often expressed through nightmares also needs to be addressed. The act of rape seems unfair and without apparent reason.

Ines Garcia killed a man who was an accomplice to her rape. "I'm not sorry I did it," she said. "I am only sorry I missed Luis Castillo (the alleged rapist). I meant to kill him, too. That's the only thing I'm sorry about" (Ben-Horin, 1975, p. 114). The jury convicted her of second-degree murder.

Burgess and Holmstrom (1974) discussed the symptoms that rape victims display during the various post-rape phases they go through. Initially, the symptoms include nausea, inability to sleep or fitful sleep, an inability to keep food down. During the second phase, nightmares occur, particularly those in which the rape itself is relived. The victim is not able to continue functioning well, so that disruptions occur in her marital relationship, and sometimes these victims are unable to return to their normal routine. It is in the last phase that resolution begins to take place and the victim is on the road to being restored to her previous level of functioning. For those whose previous level of functioning has been problematic, referral for long-term therapy is made.

Continued support is necessary for those victims whose cases will be tried. Reliving the rape on the witness stand can be traumatic. Frustration and anger are very likely to re-occur in those situations where the rapist is not convicted of the crime. A "just world" is not necessarily a world in which a rape victim lives. Research at Boston College found that rape victims sometimes have not recovered from the rape trauma even as long as four to six years after the incidence.

The perpetrator of the crime is often not identified, not prosecuted, and when he is taken to court often not convicted. A study of the California Superior Court from 1966–1972 found that conviction for rape was lower than for assault, homicide, and other sex offenses (Burgess and Holmstrom, 1974).

The concept of compensation for victims of rape is gradually taking hold. New York State was the pioneer and since 1967 has awarded $12 million to victims. But women who are found to be responsible for the crime by provoking it, or the victims of rape by relatives are ineligible.

When compensation is not forthcoming from state government, victims are suing for damages. One such case resulted from a rape at the women's locker room at Catholic University, Washington, D.C. A young woman arriving early for intramural basketball practice was raped by a young, black male. She received $20,000 in compensatory damages as a result of a suit, claiming inefficient security measures. In 1975 in Maryland a victim's family was awarded $13 million which was later reduced to $1 million. The victim was raped and killed after forty-five minutes of fighting for her life in her own apartment. The rapist, under the influence of alcohol, had been part of a crew moving furniture to the apartment next door. His coworkers noticed that he was absent when they heard the woman scream but did not intervene. They finally called the employer. Both employer and landlord were found guilty of negligence. The employer because he had not carefully screened the man for the job and the landlord for not providing security measures which would be adequately protective.

The singer, Connie Francis, received $2.5 million in damages from Howard Johnson's Motor Lodges on the basis of the fact that adequate security had not been in effect to prevent her from being raped.

Rape is a heinous crime. Monetary compensation, although justified, does not remove the long-term effects of the terror, the humiliation, the pain, the physical injury, and the dysfunction that accompanies rape.

Myth: College campuses, long protected citadels, are virtually free of incidents of rape.

Fact: At one midwestern state university, seventeen instances of forcible rape were reported in 1976. Of the 168 campuses indexed in the 1976 FBI uniform crime reports, 157 rapes were reported.

Myth: Students bear full responsibility for their safety on campus.

Fact: Courts have recently determined that the total burden of prevention does not lie with either the actual or potential victim, and that a university's physical environment and lack of adequate security may contribute to rape victimization.

Myth: Any woman could prevent the rape if she really wanted to, since no woman can be raped against her will. "You can't hit a moving target." Rape victims are really asking for it.

Fact: In 87% of rape cases, the assailant either carried a weapon or threatened the victim with death if she resisted him. The primary reaction of most victims is fear for their lives.

Myth: The primary motive for rape is sexual.

Fact: Studies show the major motive for rape is aggression, anger and hostility, not sex.

Myth: Rape is an impulse act.

Fact: 90% of all rapes are planned, although the victim is not always known, according to a national survey of police reports on rape.

Myth: Only women with bad reputations are raped.

Fact: Reputation has nothing to do with it; the rapist's desire is chiefly control, not sex.

Myth: Black men usually rape white women.

Fact: In 93.2% of rape cases, both the man and the woman are of the same race (*The Problem of Rape on Campus,* p. 2).

References

Allison v. U.S. *Federal Reporter* 2d Series 409. St. Paul, Minnesota: West Publishing Co., 1969.

Arnold v. U.S. (358 A. 2d. D.C. Ct. App., 1976).

Anon. Girl Raped, Mutilated, Arrest Made. Associated Press. October 10, 1978.

_____. *The Problem of Rape on Campus Women.* Project on the Status and Education of Women. Washington, D.C.: Association of American Colleges, n.d.

_____. *Uniform Crime Reports for the United States.* Washington, D.C.: U.S. Government Printing Office, 1971.

_____. *Uniform Crime Reports for the United States.* Washington, D.C.: U.S. Government Printing Office, 1973.

_____. *Uniform Crime Reports for the United States.* Washington, D.C.: U.S. Government Printing Office, 1976.

_____. *Uniform Crime Reports for the United States.* Washington, D.C.: U.S. Government Printing Office, 1975.

_____. *Uniform Crime Reports for the United States.* Washington, D.C.: U.S. Government Printing Office, 1977.

_____. *Uniform Crime Reports for the United States.* Washington, D.C.: U.S. Government Printing Office, 1978.

Amir, Menachim. *Patterns in Forcible Rape.* Chicago: The University of Chicago Press, 1971.

Ben-Horin, David. Is rape a sex crime? *Nation* **221**:112–115 (August 16, 1975).

Brodyaga, Lisa, Gates, Margaret, Singer, Susan, Tucker, Marna, and White, Richardson. *Rape and Its Victims: A Report for Citizens, Health Facilities, and Criminal Justice Agencies.* National Institute of Law Enforcement Assistance Administration, U.S. Department of Justice, November, 1975.

Brownmiller, Susan. *Against Our Will.* New York: Simon & Schuster, 1975.

Bryant, Clifton D. (ed.). *Sexual Deviancy in Social Context.* New York: New Viewpoints. A Division of Franklin Watts, 1977.

Bullough, Vern L. *The Subordinate Sex.* Chicago: University of Illinois Press, 1974.

Burgess, Ann Wolbert and Holmstrom, Linda Lytle. *Rape: Victims of Crisis.* Bowie, Maryland: Robert J. Brady, 1974.

Cohen, Murray L., Garofalo, Ralph, Boucher, Richard and Seghorn, Theoharis. The Psychology of Rapists. *Seminars in Psychiatry* 3:318 (August 1971).

Coltrane v. U.S. (135 U.S. App. D.C., 1969).

Farrar v. *U.S.* (275 F2d, 1960).

Frank v. *State* (35 NW2d, 1949).

Furman v. *Georgia* (408 U.S. 238, 1972).

Gager, Nancy and Schurr, Cathleen. *Sexual Assault: Confronting Rape in America.* New York: Grosset & Dunlap, 1976.

Gebhard, Paul H., Gagnon, John H., Pomeroy, Wardell B. and Christienson, Cornelia V. *Sex Offenders: An Analysis of Types.* New York: Harper & Row, Publishers, and Paul B. Hoeber, Medical Books, 1965.

Groth, Nicholas A. and Burgess, Ann Wolbert. Rape, a sexual deviation. *American Journal of Orthopsychiatry* 47:400–406 (July 1977).

Hale, Matthew. *Pleas of the Crown* 635 (1680).

Harper, Timothy. Ousted Judge Says Feminists Stoop Low. Associated Press, January 1, 1978.

Hilberman, Elaine. *The Rape Victim.* New York: Basic Books, 1976.

Hill, Constance. *Arnold* v. *United States,* 358 A.22 (D.C. Ct. App., 1976) (en banc). *Duquesne University Law Review* 15:305–314 (1976)

Home, John. *Douglas,* 1756 in George H. Nettleton and Arthur E. Case (eds.). *British Dramatists From Dryden to Sheridan.* Boston: Houghton Mifflin, 1939.

Ireland, Marilyn J. Reform rape legislation: a new standard of sexual responsibility. *University of Colorado Law Review* 49:185–204 (Winter 1978).

Jackel v. *State.* (App. 506 SW2d, 1974).

Kattner, Steve. The general rule covering prior acts of misconduct. *The Baylor Law Review* 29:163–171 (1977).

LeGrand, Camille E. Rape and rape laws: sexism in society and law. *California Law Review* 61:919–941 (1973).

Lerner, M. J. The desire for justice and reactions to victims, in H. J. MaCaulay and L. Berkowitz (eds.). *Altruism and Helping Behavior.* New York: Academic Press, 1970.

Mulvihill, Donald and Tumin, Melvin (eds.). *Crimes of Violence.* Washington, D.C.: U.S. Government Printing Office, 1969.

Sagarian, Edward. Forcible rape and the problems and rights of the accused, in Deanna Nass. *The Rape Victim.* Iowa: Kendall/Hunt Publishing, 1977.

Schafer, Stephen. *Victimology: The Victim and His Criminal.* Virginia: Reston Publishing, 1977.

Selkin, James. Rape. *Psychology Today* **8**:70 (January 1975).

Smith, Daniel. *The Ladies' Book of Anecdotes.* New York: Carlton & Phillips, 1855.

Smith, Linda C. and Nelson, L. D. *Predictors of Rape Victimization Reportage.* Paper read at the American Sociological Association Annual Meeting, New York, August, 1976, pp. 15–16.

Sutherland, Sandra and Scherl, Donald. Patterns of response among victims of rape. *American Journal of Orthopsychiatry* **40**:503–511 (April 1970).

Wolfgang, Marvin E. and Riedel, Marc. Rape, race, and the death penalty in Georgia. *American Journal of Orthopsychiatry* **45**:658–668 (July 1975).

Wolfgang, Marvin (ed.). *Studies in Homicide.* New York: Harper & Row, 1967.

5. Home is Not a Haven

Incest is a word which creates feelings of repulsion in most people. What does it mean? *The Random House Dictionary* defines incest as "sexual intercourse between closely related persons" and also as "the crime of sexual intercourse, cohabitation, or marriage between persons within the degrees of consanguinity or affinity wherein marriage is legally forbidden" (p. 719). It is commonly used to describe sexual activity between a parent and an offspring. In this chapter incest will be defined as any overt sexual behavior between members of the same nuclear family, which ranges from genital fondling to oral or genital sex.

It is very difficult to find the true rate of incest in the United States, because it is one of the least reported crimes—loyalty to the family unit seems to discourage the filing of formal complaints. In addition, children tend to be fearful of sharing their experiences with others for fear of reprisal from the incest offender. Remember that the offender is a family member, usually of the immediate family, and, therefore, someone on whom the child relies emotionally as well as economically if it is the father. In father-daughter incest, the mother is often covertly in collusion, which makes reporting even less probable.

It is estimated that at least one in a million people have had an incestuous relationship, but the actual rate is thought to be much greater. Cases of incest have been reported with children as young as three years old.

Alfred C. Kinsey, in his classic study of the sexual behavior of females, published in 1953, found that 24 percent of the 4441 subjects from whom his information was elicited had been approached sexually by an adult male prior to their adolescence. In 23 percent of the cases the adult male was a relative (uncles 9 percent, brothers 3 percent, grandfathers 4 percent, other relatives 5 percent, and fathers in 4 percent of the cases). According to Kinsey, the sexual contact by the adult male ranged from an approach only, to actual coitus (3 percent). Kinsey did not make a systematic study of pre-adolescent boys who had sexual contact, but his 1948 study of the human male found few cases of incest.

Paul H. Gebhard, one of Kinsey's successors at the Institute for Sex Research, and his associates found that out of 3500 prisoners studied, 13.1 percent had been involved in incest compared with 3.9 percent of the average population (Gebhard et al. 1965).

The American Humane Society estimates that there are at least 200,-000 cases of incest each year and of that number approximately 5000 or more are father-daughter incest. The Child Sexual Abuse Project in San Jose, California estimates that there are about 36,000 cases nationwide of father-daughter incest each year based on their contact with 165 per million such cases in their area (Summit and Kryso, 1978).

Sexually delinquent girls and sex offenders report a higher incidence. Halleck (1962) found that 15 percent of the delinquent girls with whom he worked had experienced sexual activity with their fathers or stepfathers. Gebhard et al. (1965) noted that of the sex offenders they studied, 9 percent had been involved incestuously with a member of their family. Weber noted that the reported cases of incest favor girls ten to one. One hundred cases of sexual abuse by a parent or parent surrogate are reported to the Los Angeles Police Department each year, and a complaint is formally made in less than one-third of these. Cases at the Santa Clara Child Sexual Abuse Treatment Program increased from 31 in 1974 to 269 in 1976, indicating that the rate of incest may be underestimated (Weber, 1977).

According to Gebhard et al. (1965), the most common type of incestuous behavior of sex offenders studied is between first cousins, then a sibling of the opposite sex, aunt, then equally, niece and daughter, and least common of all, incestuous relations with mother.

Girls from three years of age and up have been victims of incest, and as would be expected, most of the incidents have occurred in the home. Freud found that many of his women patients reported incestuous incidents which he attributed to fantasy. However, with increasing research and objectivity, therapists are finding that many of these fantasies are facts. The oedipal situation is actualized behaviorally.

Some anthropologists have suggested that it is the prohibition of incest which dramatically differentiates man from the animal kingdom. It has also been suggested that incest taboos have a "biological imperative." In simple language this means that in some way humans are biologically programmed so that sexual activity within the immediate family is discouraged. The evidence for this theory is based upon the behaviors of animals who bond; that is, animals whose mates and offspring remain in close physical proximity as well as in interdependence with each other for a period of time. This closeness, then, increases the probability of incestuous behavior. As a result, the animals have over the course of evolution developed conduct which results in separation of the sexually mature offspring from the mother and from the family (Bischof, 1972).

Human families, as well as groups in the animal kingdom, are organized along sex and age lines. Sex, as well as generation, determines the role and degree of power of the individual and his/her position in the family group. When some animals, such as the red deer and the African elephant, are about to reach sexual maturity, males leave the nuclear family and form their own independent peer group. Other animals, such as the North American opossum, leave their family of origin and live in isolation, forming their own family group during mating and childrearing. These behaviors tend to reduce the possibility of incestuous acts (Bischof, 1972).

The male animal is thrust out of the cocoon to become an independent, fairly self-sufficient adult, but what of the female? She, as in human families, too, remains with the mother, who teaches her the female role of mothering. She continues to help with caring for the younger siblings. The fact that females are permitted to continue to live with the nuclear family while the male offspring are pushed out of the proverbial nest, increases the danger of father-daughter incest (Frances and Frances, 1976).

There are animals whose social structure is based on ranking. Battles between adult males decide who is dominant, and it is this dominance which determines who has sexual prerogatives. The baboons' social order is based on such ranking.

Human beings are animals who are also influenced by bonding. They form mating groups which have some degree of permanence and emotional attachment. The individuals within each group are differentiated according to sex and generation, and this differentiation results in different status within the family as well as concomitant differential role expectations. The male is expected to support the family and to relate to the outside world, while the female's responsibility is involved with the emotional aspects of the family as well as childrearing. The age status of individual members also determines the power and spoils that the person receives. Since the adult male and the adult female are powerful, because of their age, they determine the sexual prerogatives in the family and tend to keep the incestuous feelings of the offspring in check (Frances and Frances, 1976).

Some of the proponents of the biological imperative theory of incest believe that incest is prohibited because the results of inbreeding are negative. They cite recessive mutations such as color blindness, hemophilia, and albinism as examples of the possible genetic effects of incest (Harris, 1971).

Adams and Neel (1967) studied eighteen children of incestuous matings between brothers and sisters, as well as fathers and daughters. Using eighteen other children in their control group, they found that five of the children of incestuous union died within six months of birth, one had a cleft palate, two demonstrated symptoms of epilepsy, and three of the children had I.Q.s of 70 or below. Seven of the children of incestuous unions as compared with fifteen of the children in the control group were labeled as adoption-ready after six months of age. Of the children in the control group, three were being held for further observation but the other fifteen showed no signs of abnormality of any kind. This study suggests that there may be deleterious effects of inbreeding.

A larger study in Czechoslovakia of 161 cases of children of incest compared with 95 children who were offspring of matings between nonrelated individuals further supports the thesis that inbreeding can have negative results on offspring. In this study, 25 percent of the incest-born children showed some signs of mental retardation as compared to none in the control group. A larger percentage of the incest-born children had congenital defects as compared with the other group, and more than twice the number of control group children were considered normal as compared with the incest-born group (Seemanová, 1971).

Does the biological imperative mean that early people deliberately prohibited incest in order to prevent malformation of children? Does it mean that the aversion to incest is instinctual? There is no evidence to support the contention that early people in their wisdom could relate congenital defects to inbreeding. Many peoples even today do not make the connection between sexual mating, conception, and child-birth. We must then assume that eugenics was not the motivating force for the incest prohibition.

If there was a definite base for supporting the instinct theory, then how can we justify the large number of cases of incest which occur? Recently, it was estimated that between 1.5 and 5 percent of the population as well as perhaps as many as ten percent of the families in the United States are involved in incestuous relationships (Brody, June 13, 1979).

R. E. L. Masters in his book, *Patterns of Incest* (1963), relates details of incestuous conditions which were acceptable among the Hindus in India before British occupation. Life among them was filled with promiscuity, and so the little boys and girls emulated their parents' eroticism. Little girls lost their virginity to little boys sometimes at ten years old or less. If a girl was still "pure" by the age of ten, the saying goes, there are probably no close male relatives in her family. Incest among the Hindus, as described in Master's book by an observer, was not unusual, and in fact was the norm. Because boys and girls romped around partially clothed, there were many opportunities for them to play with each others' genitals. When aroused to penile erection, coitus would take place (Masters, 1963).

Incestuous relations were sometimes an integral part of the culture of some groups. In Ceylon, and among the Yakuts of Siberia, it was the brother's duty to deflower his sister before marriage. In Africa, in one of the hippo-hunting tribes, a man would have intercourse with his daughter the night before the hunt to enhance his ability as a hunter (Masters, 1963). The belief that venereal disease can be cured by having sexual relations with one's daughter if she has as yet not menstruated was noted to have existed and still might exist in the United States (Weinberg, 1958). Suffice it to say, some men have indeed indulged in this incestuous act for "medical reasons."

Marriage among brothers and sisters of royalty was common during the reigns of the Pharaohs in Egypt. These marriages ensured the continuance of the royal blood lines and also kept power and property within the family. Under the early Roman rule, marriages among siblings were not infrequent, also for the purpose of keeping property within the family (Middleton, 1962). Among the royal family of the Incas of Peru, as well as among the Hawaiian families of royalty, brother-sister marriages prevailed.

If repulsion to incest is instinctual, then how can we explain the fact that severe penalties have been established to discourage it? Among the Australian Aborigines incest was punishable by death. In New South Wales among the Ta-Ta-Thi the incestuous male was killed while the incestuous female was either flogged or pierced with a spearhead. In some groups sexual play between members of the same clan was also severely punished (Durkheim, 1963).

The Old Testament makes reference to incest and its consequences. Leviticus 20:20 states, "And if a man lies with his uncle's wife, he has uncovered his uncle's nakedness: they shall bear their sin; they shall die childless." Here we see that incestuous relations have been extended to include marriage partners of a relative; yet the same religious document makes reference to Sarah (who was his half-sister) marrying Abraham (Genesis 20:12).

And then there is the story of Lot and his incestuous relations with his daughters.

And Lot went up out of Zo-ar, and dwelt in the mountain, and his two daughters with him; for he feared to dwell in Zo-ar: and he dwelt in a cave, he and his two daughters.

And the firstborn said unto the younger, our father is old, and there is not a man in the earth to come in unto us after the manner of all the earth:

Come, let us make our father drink wine, and we will lie with him, that we may preserve seed of our father.

And they made their father drink wine that night: and the firstborn went in, and lay with her father and he perceived not when she lay down, nor when she arose.

And it came to pass on the morrow, that the firstborn said unto the younger, Behold, I lay yesternight with my father; let us make him drink wine this night also; and go thou in, and lie with him, that we may preserve seed of our father.

And they made their father drink wine that night also: and the younger arose, and lay with him; and he perceived not when she lay down, nor when she arose.

Thus were both the daughters of Lot with child by their father.

And the firstborn bare a son, and called his name Moab: the same is the father of the Moabites unto this day.

And the younger, she also bore a son, and called his name Ben-ammi: the same is the father of the children of Ammon unto this day (Genesis 19:30-38).

Frazer stated that if human beings had an instinctual aversion to incest, there would not be a need for legal prohibitions.

It is not easy to see why any deep human instinct should need to be reinforced by law. There is no law commanding men to eat and drink or forbidding them to put their hands in the fire. Men eat and drink and keep their hands out of the fire instinctively for fear of natural not legal penalties, which would be entailed by violence done to these instincts. The law only forbids men to do what their instincts incline them to do; what nature itself prohibits and punishes, it would be superfluous for the law to prohibit and punish. Accordingly we may always safely assume that crimes forbidden by law are crimes which many men have a natural propensity to commit. If there was no such propensity there would be no such crime, and if no such crimes were committed what need to forbid them? Instead of assuming, therefore, from the legal prohibition of incest that there is a natural aversion to incest, we ought rather to assume that there is a natural instinct in favour of it, and that if the law represses it, as it represses other natural instincts, it does so because civilized men have come to the conclusion that the satisfaction of these natural instincts is detrimental to the general interests of society (Frazer, 1910, 4, 97 F.).

Given all these examples of socially sanctioned incest as well as the penalties that some societies have established to deter incest, can we still support the thesis that aversion to incest is instinctual? I would think not.

Edward A. Westermarck, a noted sociologist, wrote in his book, *A Short History of Marriage*, which was first published in 1936, that people who are in close proximity to each other for an ongoing period of time as children become sexually tepid toward each other, and in fact may be repelled by the thought of sexual contact. Separating cultural conditioning from propinquity as a causal factor is difficult. It has been found that children born and raised on the Israeli kibbutz tend to avoid dating and thus marrying each other, even though their parents are not averse to it (Talmon, 1964).

Emile Durkheim (1963) states that "One cannot court a person to whom one owes and in turn owes you a respectful affection, without this latter feeling being corrupted or vanishing in one way or another.

In a word, given our present ideas a man cannot make a wife of his sister without her ceasing to be his sister. This is what makes us disapprove so strongly of incest" (p. 103). What is implied here is that if sexual access between father and daughter, mother and son, as well as brother and sister were permitted, there would be too much competition for sexual partners within the family which would then result in the destruction of the family unit (Harris, 1971).

Arthur Wolf (1968) in his study of the practice of adopting a daughter-in-law in China presented data which would tend to negate the theory of physical closeness during childhood resulting in sexual aversion. He found that in China there was a type of marriage in which mates were chosen by families soon after birth, and in which the prospective groom's family adopted the future bride. The girl then lived in the same household as her husband-to-be in a sister-brother relationship. Since custom dictated that the parents choose a child's marriage partner, there did not seem to be any feelings of aversion to marrying someone with whom you grew up.

Freud (1955), discussed incest in *Totem and Taboo*. He hypothesized that the early human group consisted of a horde dominated by an extremely jealous male who prohibited all other males from having sexual access to the females, although he himself had access to his own daughters. Eventually, the jealous patriarch banned the sons from the group as they grew up. One day, the angry sons returned and together killed their father. Because of the guilt they felt about the homicide, they did not allow themselves sexual access to their own mothers or sisters and so mated with people outside their group as did the other members of their immediate family. The practice of choosing mates outside one's group is called exogamy and Freud related exogamy to the incest taboo.

Freud did, however, support the concept that the sexual desire for parents is not decreased because of physical proximity but is very much a part of the child's development. These sexual feelings are viewed negatively by the parent and are therefore repressed by the child. Freud believed that the strict universal incest taboos are really a defense against the universally incestuous desires found in all humans.

Incest taboo has also been discussed as a vestige of marriage by capture; a situation in which warriors forcibly dragged young maidens back to their own territory, raping them to establish their "rights" and then making them their wives. This may very well have been established in order to avoid the possibility of marrying within one's group and thus avoiding the possibility of incest.

In 1949, Leslie White stated that people tend to select mates from those in close proximity and that the incest taboo really arose from the practice of exogamy (marrying outside the group) and was based on the concern for establishing alliances with several groups for shared assistance as a survival mechanism. Prohibiting the selection of a marriage partner from within the group, thus mandating that a mate be selected from an outside group, tended to ensure more binding ties between the two groups and to deter the natural selection of mates from within the family (White, 1949).

The noted anthropologist, Bronislaw Malinowski, theorized that the incest taboo was a universal phenomenon because if sexual access was permitted between members of the nuclear family, competition and hostility would destroy this basic unit (Malinowski, 1955).

Talcott Parsons (1954) analyzed the incest taboo in terms of its relationship to the structure of society and the process by which the child is socialized. He postulated that if erotic feelings were not contained in the family unit, socialization of the child; that is, molding the child to fit into the society, would not take place. The incest taboo, he said, therefore functions to support the roles within the family as well as supporting the integration of the total society.

Vera and Allen Frances (1976) propose that human destiny dictates that we live in a fairly small family unit, that there is a long period of dependency until maturity, and that natural dominance as well as the need of the human child to become a separate entity from his parents resulted in an elaborate system of incest taboos. Meiselman (1978) agrees that the tendency to avoid incestuous relationships exists and that the actual taboo against it has been culturally determined.

The mother begins to respond less often to the demands of the child and because of this, the very strong bond with the mother gradually lessens. Both mother and father, through the process of progressively blocking the child's needs, but still displaying affection towards the youngster, detach themselves from the child so that its correct place in the family can be established. "Since the mother is the original source of the child's erotic gratification . . . it follows that overt erotic interaction between the child and other family members also becomes tabooed" (Frances and Frances, 1976, p. 240).

Psychoanalytic theory further proposes that every child goes through a stage in development during which there are incestuous feelings towards the parent of the opposite sex, and that the resolution of conflict (love for parent of the opposite sex and fear of retaliation and punishment from the parent of the same sex) must take place so that the child can grow up to be a healthy, heterosexual human adult. This is the well-known oedipal conflict which is considered by psychoanalytic therapists to be the cause of neurosis.

We can see that many theories have been posited regarding the origin and function of the incest taboo and that there is no total acceptance of any one theory. Meiselman (1978) synthesized the major theories by stating that ". . . while the taboo on nuclear family incest probably had its origin in the advantages of avoidance of inbreeding, from the earliest times the incest taboo had been influenced by many other social conditions, taboos, and psychological factors that have nearly always been present in the nuclear family situation." She lists dominance relationships within the group, stress on corresponding generational age sets for mating and the nurturing relationship which is inherent in childrearing as factors having influenced the establishment of incest prohibitions.

As with men who commit rape, the fundamental motivating factors differ, there being parents who are sexually seductive with their children, and those who actually involve their children in sex play or sexual intercourse. Summit and Kryso (1978) attempted to examine these differences. They state that some parents encourage their children to play games which have sexual overtones and/or act out their own sexual curiosity by touching the child's genitals or sleeping with the child. This type of behavior is seen as an attempt by a parent to work out his/her own erotic feelings towards the child. An interesting case was brought to my attention by the head of an agency located in a rural area of Massachusetts. This case involved two married sisters who encouraged their own offspring, a son and a daughter to play sexually with each other. When the cousins visited, they were also given the same bed to sleep in. This began when they were nine years old and continued for three years, during which time they continued to have sexual relations with each other. The case came to the attention of the agency when the boy was twenty-one. He had become a drug abuser, who had been wandering around without a job and without a permanent home for several years.

Another type of parent-child sexuality includes the parent or parents who truly believe that encouraging open expression, viewing of the human body, and even sometimes viewing the sexual act itself will help the child feel more comfortable with its own sexuality. Summit and Kryso (1978) presented a case of a woman who bathed with her five-year-old son and then suddenly was shocked to find her little boy playing sexually with his sister. He had become aroused by his mother's nudity, even though that was not her intent.

Sexual seduction and incest also occur in families where this type of behavior is considered normal and natural. As one social worker said, "Incest has been going on in these families from one generation to another. It's their style of life. The family is usually satisfied with that way of life. They have sort of adapted to it. The communities in these rural areas have almost become used to the idea and seem to take for granted the fact that this kind of thing will happen."

The children themselves in these families are socialized to believe that incest is normal. The families are usually rural, the children socially isolated, and the incestuous relationships are often serial. It starts with the oldest daughter; then, when she becomes old enough to recognize the fact that the behavior is socially unacceptable, the next oldest daughter is chosen, and so on down the line. The families are generally patriarchal, with father supreme and his needs, especially sexual needs, of prime importance. Women, therefore, seem to be viewed as father's property. The father wants to meet his sexual needs within the family and does just that. Gebhard's (1965) study of sex offenders found that in most of the cases where incest was committed with an adult offspring, the families were of the "Tobacco Road type milieu." In this environment, although incest was not thought of as a particularly positive phenomenon, it was not looked at as an unusual occurrence.

It is in cases like this that the community outrage is not great, and therefore there is little intervention by social agencies because no one complains.

Sexuality between parent and child can also result from a parental psychotic episode where the parent's poor reality testing and inability of self control leads to sexual play or sexual intercourse. It is assumed that the incestuous act would not have occurred if the parent had not been psychotic. But it is interesting to note that just as with the rape offender, the male incest offender in the father-daughter relationship particularly is generally not diagnosed as being mentally ill (Meiselman, 1978). The mother, however, who has an incestuous relationship with her son, an infrequent occurrence, is generally psychotic (Frances and Frances, 1976). Does this mean that women have more self-control than men or is it considered more natural for the father to lust for his daughter? Is it also more natural for him to act on these feelings of lust so that he doesn't have to be mentally ill to do so?

There are those men who commit incest as an expression of their fear and hatred of women. This type of individual usually has had a history of great difficulty in his relationships with his own mother. He often beats his wife, as well as abusing his children, and may also rape. He sees his daughter as someone who belongs to him. By sexually abusing her, he is making a statement concerning his ownership and also punishing his wife, whom he hates as he hates all women. The following case history typifies this particular type of incest offender. This is the case of a man who treated his infant daughter abusively and then as she got older tried to shield her from hurt. When she was eight, he became overcome with anger and loss because she had been raped, and in order to correct the terrible harm he felt had been perpetrated, he and his wife allowed the little girl to watch them have sexual relations with each other. The father, also about this time, began to have sexual relations with his daughter. After two years of an ongoing sexual relationship between father and daughter, the mother, who had been the victim of incest in her own home, finally reached out for help, but only after she saw her daughter and husband performing fellatio (Summit and Kryso, 1978).

There are also a small number of incest offenders who are motivated by a desire to seek a sexual thrill with their own daughters because they are neurotically enthralled with the sexual arousal they feel by contact with children. This offender particularly enjoys the fondling and body contact with children as well as oral sex. Gebhard et al. (1965) describes this variety as being generally pedophilic and focusing their interest in sex with children on their own offspring. Most pedophiles are not usually sadistic people. There are a small number, however, who gain a sense of their own sexual adequacy by frightening and physically controlling a child. This kind of person, according to Summit and Kryso (1978) is usually impulsive, oriented towards violence, and all too often, is found in the position of a substitute parent.

One of these cases involved a mother and her 12-year-old daughter, both of whom were held prisoner by the stepfather. They were unable to leave the house for over a year, during which time they were both beaten and repeatedly raped. When the stepfather, who was an alcoholic, was finally apprehended, the mother and daughter were found to be covered with black and blue marks from the boards he had used to beat them with.

There are also occasional cases where a bloody rape of a young girl takes place. A violent assault took place on a nine-year-old child by her mother's boyfriend. The police, as well as the Hotline for Children, were called by neighbors, who heard bloodcurdling screams. This case was similar to the one discussed by Summit and Kryso. In this situation the mother's boyfriend originally raped the seven-year-old daughter and continued to have intercourse with her for a period of about a year-and-one-half, during which time he physically assaulted her in his attempt to have vaginal and oral intercourse. Although the child begged for her mother's intervention, her pleas were not heard by the unsympathetic mother, who later on allowed her subsequent two boyfriends to molest the child.

Cases of rape in incest seem to be rare, according to the small number of studies which have been made. Basically, particularly with younger children, the introduction into sexual relations is usually gradual so that pain does not occur. Maisch's study indicated that in only 6 percent of his cases the first incestuous act was a violent one (Maisch, 1972). However, those cases which do come to the attention of the courts tend to be associated with more violence (Meiselman, 1978).

There are also those parents who mix pornography with incest. These are people who emphasize ritual in their sexual act, and who attempt to take pictures of bizarre sexual activity.

A mother and father enlisted their children into shared sexual activity and then, having conditioned the children into orgiastic adventures, used them as bait to draw in neighborhood boys to provide the father with a continuing harem (Summit and Kryso (1978).

One social worker told about a case where the parents were taking pictures of their children naked, spread-eagled, playing sexually with one another. The family came to the attention of the police department when the clerk at the photography store looked at the pictures. The case was thrown out of court, however, since the family insisted that the pictures were taken only to be used by them and therefore did not violate any law, and the judge upheld their contention.

Who commits incest? What kind of man violates this taboo? What kind of life experiences did he have and what were the precipitating factors?

According to Summit and Kryso (1978) there are two general characteristics of those people who sexually abuse children and this includes the incest offender. One characteristic is the inability to control impulses and the other concerns role confusion, in which the adult uses the child to meet his own needs, rather than playing the parental role of meeting the needs of the child. Love becomes perverted into sexual abuse. "The objective distinction between loving support and lustful intrusion are disquietingly subtle" (Summit and Kryso, 1978, p. 237).

Fathers in incestuous relationships generally come from a background of emotional deprivation and/or physical desertion or abandonment (Lustig et al., 1966, and Weinberg, 1958). A Kinsey Institute study (Gebhard et al., 1965) of 1500 incarcerated sex offenders, compared with a control group of nonincarcerated men, divided the incest offenders into three categories: those whose offense involved a child under twelve, those whose offense involved a minor (a child between the ages of twelve and fifteen), and those who committed incest with an adult. This study corroborated findings in other research concerning the early turbulent family history of incest offenders. Most strikingly, a chaotic family was found in the background of those offenders who committed the incestuous act with children (59 percent) and adults (60 percent). For reasons which cannot be explained, fewer of the men who committed incest with minor children came from broken homes.

Meiselman (1978) points out that there is no direct correlation for all incest groups between family instability and incest. She based her position on the Kinsey Institute study, which found that those men who committed incest with children over the age of sixteen perceived their early relationships with their parents as happy. There seemed to be a striking correlation between a happy family life and the age at which a child is initiated into an incestuous relationship. She concludes that the better the early home life of the incest offender, the older the child will be when he/she is initiated into incest.

Research has found that in many cases of incest, the father's anxiety around separation and/or desertion is operative (Lustig et al., 1966). Lustig and his colleagues present a case of an incest offender, Mr. O., whose father sadistically beat his children even for minor transgressions. Mr. O.'s father would vacillate between rigid religiosity and alcoholism. The aloof mother gave the responsibility of nurturing and care to her daughters. When Mr. O. was six years old he began mutual masturbatory activities with his younger sister, and when the activity was reported to the parents by her, Mr. O.'s father beat him, and while doing so told him that he was too young to be indulging in these kinds of acts. Lustig feels that Mr. O. was given a mixed message by his father which implied that it's okay to have sex play with a member of your family but you have to be older. We can see how difficult it must have been for Mr. O. to identify with the inconsistent, repressive father.

Fears of desertion and separation anxiety run rampant. When his marriage is in difficulty, and there is a threat, real or imaginary, the father approaches the daughter in the hope of allaying his fears of being deserted, particularly by the wife who either threatens divorce, is away from the family a great deal, or who limits or actually withdraws from sex (Gutheil and Avery, 1977). Abandonment can be felt at the birth of a child and need not necessarily become an actual physical separation. Lustig et al. (1966), see incest as a method of dealing with tremendous anxiety around separation stemming from early abandonment or rejection or anxiety around the fear of abandonment or rejection. It is the father's method of keeping his wife from leaving him, or keeping sex within the family, and thus keeping the family intact. This dynamic was also noted in the incest offenders' children in the Gebhard study. Lustig relates the following case history in illustration of the dynamic. The mother became increasingly negative toward sex with the father and because of his persistent efforts to have intercourse with her, she threatened to leave him. Mother sent the daughter to give father his meals where he worked in a projection booth. It was at this time that the father seduced the teen-aged daughter into participating in sex with him. The daughter enjoyed the sexual experiences. Pressure was then off the mother sexually, thus neutralizing the mother's need to separate from father, and as a result the family remained intact.

Lustig and his colleagues also point out that in the six cases of father-daughter incest which they studied, there was a strong need on the part of the fathers to cover up their feelings of inadequacy as males by overcompensating in a patriarchal way. The father presents himself as a strong, authoritarian figure, which in reality is a facade. The father maintains his dominant position in the family by threats and physical abuse. Most often this physical abuse becomes apparent when the family resists the father's wishes or when he is under the influence of alcohol (Meiselman, 1978). Lustig and his colleagues noted that the incestuous father is often perceived by others to be a good father and husband, who fulfills the role expectations of fatherhood and spouse. Occasionally, an incestuous father has been labeled passive-dependent in some of the research, but generally there are few incestuous families in which the mother dominates. There have also been some cases noted of incestuous fathers who also beat their wives (Ralphing et al., 1967).

Alcohol plays a role in father-daughter incest because it acts as a destroyer of inhibition, thus neutralizing guilt, and as with the alcohol and the wife batterer, the alcohol perhaps provides an excuse or rationalization for the lack of restraint. The Kinsey Institute study of sex offenders paid particular attention to alcohol and its relationship to incest. In all three types of incest offenders, those who committed incest with children, those whose victims were twelve to fifteen, and those whose incestuous companions were adults, alcoholism was occasionally noted. Incidences of excessive alcoholism decrease as the age of the daughter who is involved increases (Meiselman, 1978).

The incestuous father is also usually a person who has not been involved in other criminal behavior (Gebhard et al., 1965). He therefore presents himself to the community as an average man. The study of men at Kansas State Reception and Diagnostic Center who were convicted of felonies developed a composite picture of those who had been involved in father-daughter incest. Compared to the rest of the prison population, the "average" incest offender was described as having an average I.Q. and a fairly stable work history as a semiskilled worker. Extramarital relationships were rarely indulged in, although their wives were characterized as nonsupportive and rejecting (Cavallin, 1966). In contrast the Kinsey Institute study of sex offenders found that extramarital relations were not unusual (Gebhard et al., 1965).

It is very difficult to make a true assessment of the socio-economic level of father-daughter incest offenders. Most of the objective research that was done concerned prison populations. As in child abuse, the middle- or upper-class family is able to hide the abuse and seldom comes to the attention of the authorities. They are therefore difficult to identify. Kaufman et al.'s (1954) study of eleven girls whose fathers had involved them in an incestuous relationship found that these fathers generally came from a poverty background themselves, had little education and did not have a steady work history.

Although there does exist a small group of incestuous fathers with exceptionally strong sex drives, the literature presents most of the incestuous fathers as having such difficulty with sex that they need to resort to the less common types of sexual behavior such as fellatio. Gebhard's (1965) study for the Kinsey Institute noted that sex offenders do not differ markedly in how frequently they had sexual relations; however, frequency does not necessarily reflect the degree of intensity of the sexual need. Gebhard did find that the fathers of incestuous relationships with daughters under twelve appeared to be obsessed with sex as could be seen by their need for extensive foreplay, their concern with sex involving the mouth and the genitals, and their emphasis on variety in the sexual postures they assumed.

This type of sexual behavior was deemed to be atypical for their socio-economic status (Gebhard et al., 1965). Hypersexuality often occurs just before the initiation of the incestuous act. Remember that the act of incest is usually preceded by the wife's withdrawal of sex to some extent, if not completely, from her husband. Is his desire for sex "normal" or is he oversexed? A case presented in the literature by Ralphing et al., (1967) describes a man who stated that he and his wife copulated three or four times daily over a ten-year period. Can we conclude from one case that hypersexuality is the norm for incestuous fathers? Even if a man's urge for sex is terribly strong and unmet, does this justify using his own daughter to meet his sexual need? It is fairly common for a young girl to become slightly seductive with her father at puberty. The mature father does not act on this seductive behavior, but the impulse-ridden incestuous father does.

Lustig and his colleagues (1966) describe the case of a man whose wife was consistently seductive with him but was reluctant to consummate the act. One night the mother behaved in a sexually teasing manner towards the father, and after giving him a drink refused to have sexual intercourse with him because he was drinking, a "Catch 22." Mother then dressed herself, put their ten-year-old daughter in bed with her husband and dispersed the other children to their rooms. By this time the father had an erection. Father had intercourse with the child. After all, the mother had told the two of them to take care of each other as she left the house, and so he did take care of his daughter.

An interesting case history is described by Gebhard and his colleagues (1965). This was the case history of a thirty-three-year-old man who was a bus driver, and who could not by himself earn sufficient wages to support his family. He became emotionally disaffected from his wife, resulting in a decrease in his desires for sexual intimacy from as frequently as several times each day to two times monthly. Instead of finding a sexual partner outside his family, he focused his sexual desires on his daughter, who was at that time eight years old. The liaison with his daughter took place over a four-year period. The father would concoct reasons for remaining home from work so that he could be with his daughter, lying with her under the covers or having her sit on his lap while they watched television and hugged and kissed each other. The daughter became fully entrenched as the wife in the family, both sexually as well as in terms of taking care of the household chores. His obsession with sex had pathological overtones. He watched in a mirror as he and his daughter practiced fellatio, and tried to involve his daughter in a sexual act with their family pet, a dog.

The background data in this case revealed that the man as an adolescent had been impacted by a report of an incestuous affair which had resulted in pregnancy, and had himself feared impregnating a woman before marriage. He petted mostly with women but used animals for sexual relations, possibly because he had difficulty in keeping an erection when trying to have intercourse with a woman. He met a fifteen-year-old physically handicapped girl with whom he succeeded in having sexual intercourse, and also made pregnant, and so they married. The psychologist felt that the man seemed to be able to maintain an erection with those whom he could feel superior to (Gebhard et al., 1965).

There are many examples in the literature of poor role modeling on the incestuous father's own father. In some cases there is generational incest. Stucker (1977) describes one such case of a patient called Mary. Mary's initiation into sex with her father began when she was eight or nine years old and occurred on the average of three or four times each week. Her father would come into her room while she was asleep and play with her breasts and genitals. When she awoke in terror, he identified her fear to her and her mother as a nightmare. Mary's mother drank excessively, and Mary did not tell her mother about the incestuous acts because she feared that her father would carry out his threats to kill her if she did. When she reached twelve her father consummated the relationship with actual intercourse. "It hurt. I remember crying; I didn't understand what he was doing" (Stucker, 1977, p. 66). Mary's father was physically abusive to her mother, as well as to her and the other children in the household. Mary's own mother had been the victim of sexual abuse by her stepfather when she was a child.

Ralphing et al. (1967) describe another case in which generational incest takes place. In this case the father, let's call him Tom, was a spectator to his own father and his eleven-year-old sister's sexual activities. He and his sister began to play with each other sexually shortly thereafter. The sister eloped when she was fourteen and when Tom reached the age of fourteen, his own mother seductively encouraged him to play with her genitals. This act was only committed once by him because he felt extremely guilty and aversive to it. He went away from his home when he reached sixteen. Meanwhile, his father continued to involve each succeeding daughter in incest. He tried to get the next oldest daughter to have intercourse with him, and since she adamantly refused, he resorted to crawling into her bed and playing with her sexually while she slept. He then attempted to do the same with his eight-year-old daughter, who also refused. In his own marital family, Tom had his sexual advances to his own two daughters spurned. His own wife had also experienced an attempted sexual seduction by her father when she was a teenager.

The incestuous father, in addition to the difficulties he might have had with his own father, seems to be bound to his mother in a dependent, fear-producing manner (Gutheil and Avery, 1977, and Gebhard et al., 1965). This dependence and preference for mother over father has an oedipal aura about it. As Ernest Jones said, "A man who displays an abnormal affection for his daughter also has a strong fixation on his mother" (Ernest Jones, in Cavallin, 1966, p. 1137). Is it possible that in the incestuous relationship the desire for mother is projected onto the daughter? The incestuous strivings are thereby consummated with a less-threatening object than one's own mother.

We tend to conclude that men who commit incest are mentally ill. But Cavallin et al. (1966), found in their study that none of the convicted felons who had been incestuous were considered psychotic at the time they were arrested. In two of their cases, psychosis was evident only after the incestuous act but not prior to it. Harbert et al. (1974), report the following case of a middle-aged man who was sexually involved for five years with his daughter. In this case, the affair with his oldest daughter involved mostly heavy petting and masturbating each other. This continued for five years until the daughter reached the age of seventeen. Even when sexually involved with his wife, the father had fantasies involving his daughter. His wife ended their marriage when she first became aware of the incestuous activity. At that time the daughter was sixteen years old.

This man had a psychotic episode which required admission to a hospital, and it was apparently precipitated by sexual involvement with his daughter after five years separation. This led to depression (Harbert et al., 1974).

According to the Kinsey Institute study, only one out of twenty men who committed a sex offense with children were psychotic at the time. Of those whose incest involved a minor (twelve to fifteen years old) only a small number were treated psychiatrically or institutionalized prior to sentencing. A history of mental illness was found in only 12 percent of the cases of the incest offenders vs. adults (Gebhard et al., 1965).

Although in most cases psychosis is not the precipitant in father-daughter incest, there seem to be a great many projective mechanisms operating as well as suspiciousness (Cavallin et al., 1966).

Basically, the incestuous father has homosexual needs. He projects his "feminine self" onto his daughter and his homosexual strivings are met through incest (Lustig, 1966). Paranoia and homosexual needs are evident in the incestuous father (Cavallin et al., 1966). Perhaps this accounts for the precariousness of the father's masculine identity as well as his rationalizations regarding the incestuous acts. "She enticed me;" "I wanted to instruct her in sex," etc. Gebhard et al. (1965), found, however, that the incest offenders had a minute number of homosexual contacts outside of prison, less than the "normal" control groups.

Oral sex is a frequent occurrence with incest offenders in incestuous acts involving young children. With older girls coital activity occurs in a large percentage of the cases, thus perhaps negating the need for oral sex (Gebhard et al., 1965).

Our all-American incestuous father is basically insecure, can come from any socio-economic group, has generally had a difficult early life experience because of separation from parent or parents or rejection by them. He is not mentally ill, is often viewed by the community as an "upstanding" man and has had no past criminal involvement. He is patriarchal, very often overprotective of his daughter and commits the incestuous act when there is perceived or real threat of abandonment. The act itself is often premeditated in the sense that the father is aware of what he is doing and the consequences of his behavior. In most cases, the incestuous act is committed in the girl's home.

Who is the mother in the father-daughter incestuous family and what role does she play? Most often, from the little we do know, the mother, like the father, comes from an early life experience which is peppered with deprivation. She often feels unloved by her own mother. She is unable to take on the responsibility of mothering, resents its imposition on her, and wants to be mothered herself (Gutheil and Avery, 1977). Mothers in father-daughter incest have generally been abandoned physically or emotionally in their early life experiences. They have tremendous feelings of hate and love toward their own mothers. This ambivalence is projected on to the daughter, who is then given the mothering role in an apparent role reversal. The daughter thereby is unable to separate from the mother, and the mother's and daughter's identities are meshed (Lustig et al., 1966). If, indeed, the mother came from a broken or rejecting home, the possibility of learning an adequate maternal role would have been diminished (Meiselman, 1978). There are also a number of cases in the rather sparse literature on incest of mothers who themselves were victims of incest.

Kaufman et al. (1954) in their study of eleven girls who were the victims of father-daughter incest, and their parents, provide us with additional information on mothers. The mothers in their study were abandoned by their own fathers. Their own mothers worked very hard to support the family but gave very little to them emotionally. The mothers, generally while young, escaped from the unhappy household either by finding a job elsewhere or by early marriage. They presented themselves as dependent, not very bright, disorganized homemakers and not personally well-kept. When they were studied in more depth, they were found to have an above-average intelligence and were not realizing their potential. They had tended to marry men like their own fathers. The mother's dependency needs and inability to play the mothering role lead her to become dependent on her daughter and to encourage the daughter to take her place. When she is confronted with the incestuous relationship between her daughter and her husband, she may deny its existence, blame the daughter for it, especially if she is an older child, or in very few instances leave the husband and seek a divorce.

Gutheil and Avery (1977) discuss the case of a woman who was involved in a sexual relationship with her father for nine years starting in her teens. Her mother was very much aware of what was going on since she accidentally walked into the room during one of the episodes, but said nothing and left.

In some instances the mother may not only have abdicated her role but may have physically deserted. A case that came to the attention of a social agency was that of a mother who periodically left home over a two-year period. The last time she had been gone for one year, during which time the sixteen-year-old daughter dropped out of school to take care of the family, which included a young brother who began to call her "mother." Daughter was involved in assuming the wife's role. When mother returned to the household, she and her daughter fought incessantly because her daughter refused to give up the role her mother wanted to resume. After the case came to the attention of the agency the daughter was enrolled in an alternative school to obtain her high school diploma, and she was helped to establish her own residence. When she was seventeen she visited home occasionally but moved back home when her apartment was involved in a fire, and the difficulty began all over again. Although there was no direct evidence that overt incest had occurred, the inferences were very apparent.

Gutheil and Avery (1977) discussed a case in which the parents were having constant difficulties, particularly because of the father's drinking. One night the mother awakened her daughter and encouraged her to talk to her father. In this case, one can see that the daughter was placed in the position of victimization since alcohol lowers the father's resistance to temptation. Gutheil and Avery point out that this was a perfect example of the re-enactment of the oedipal situation since the mother's own father also drank. The mother identified with her daughter and carried through psychologically with her own incestuous desires which had not been resolved during her own childhood and adolescence.

It is evident that in most cases of incest the mother's role, if she is present, is one of conscious or unconscious collusion. There have been few cases in the literature in which a mother has actively participated in the father-daughter incestuous relationship, although it is not outside the realm of possibility.

The woman whose husband is incestuous often demonstrates characteristics of passiveness, dependency, and what appears to be masochism (Meiselman, 1978). She allows herself to be dominated by her husband, who in many instances is authoritarian and dictatorial, and who rules the family with an iron fist. Even in the face of physical abuse, she remains in the household, unable to leave and make an independent life for herself and her children. Her apparent masochistic tendencies can be inferred from the fact that she often presents herself as a self-sacrificing, victimized woman who allows herself to be placed in this position in order to save the family (Meiselman, 1978). The mission to keep the family together may account for the fact that mothers usually do not report the incest, and even after it is reported by an outside agent or the child, the mothers are unable to believe it is so and in some cases give support to the husband and devise excuses for his behavior. However, the younger the child, the greater the chances are that the mother will report the crime to the authorities. In over half of the cases of incest with minors, the mother was the reporting agent (Gebhard et al., 1965).

In summary, the mother in the father-daughter affair is usually one whose own family life had been filled with deprivation. She has usually abdicated her role as mother and wife, either by being away from home a great deal of the time, by withdrawal and passivity, or by actual desertion. She encourages the daughter to take her place, and through the process of denial, is generally not consciously aware of the incestuous scenario.

We are now prepared to look at the victim of incest, the daughter. She is not always viewed as a victim in the literature on incest, nor is she viewed as a victim under the law. If she is seen as having been victimized, like the rape victim, there are occasional references to "her role." The view of the incestuous daughter as an easy mark is reported by Lustig and colleagues (1966), who state that they had found four cases in which after the incest was reported the girl had to repel male relatives who wanted to involve her in sexual relations.

The assignment of partial responsibility to the daughter in the incest drama generally increases with increasing age. Gebhard (1965) states that 58 percent of the daughters in his study of incest offenders involving girls over sixteen, participated voluntarily through encouragement or by not actively rebelling. It is assumed that non-resisting means voluntary, and by definition voluntary is defined as "by free choice." Does a daughter living in a home where she is financially as well as emotionally dependent really have freedom of choice to repel the demands of the most powerful figure in the household? If a young girl is unable to make decisions and therefore is not responsible for her behavior because of retardation, can the incestuous relationship be considered voluntarily participated in?

Gebhard et al. (1965), cite the following case as an example. A man with a borderline normal I.Q. was raised in Oklahoma, and when he reached the age of eighteen became a wanderer, supporting himself by doing skilled and semiskilled work. His first sexual experience was with a divorced woman who was twice as old as he was. The woman he married was pregnant at the time of their wedding, and it was her uncle who had impregnated her. After five years of marriage, they separated but did not divorce. Fifteen years later the man met his wife unintentionally, and shortly thereafter she and her daughter, then nineteen, and a divorced mother, came to live with him. He and his wife did not resume sexual activity because he was more attracted to her daughter, and because his wife was in the last stage of pregnancy by her common-law partner. A sexual relationship developed between the man and his stepdaughter, resulting in his impregnating her. One day, following an argument during which the police were called, the stepdaughter told the authortities about the incestuous activity. The man was arraigned and given a light sentence because of the fact that incest in the community in which he lived was not rare.

Active resistance to incest increased with the twelve- to fifteen-year-olds in the Kinsey Institute study and decreased in the over sixteen population (Gebhard et al., 1965). We can thus assume that an older child is more capable of fending off an incest approach, and that in most cases where incest is occurring in that age group, it is with the co-operation of the daughter.

The incestuous daughter is usually of average intelligence (Weinberg, 1958) unlike the image we have of a mentally retarded young girl. Although fathers and stepfathers often describe her as being sexually well-developed for her age as a way of explaining their sexual reaction to her, the literature on incest does not support this, nor does it support the concept of the daughter being especially physically attractive. Meiselman (1978) notes that onset of menarche was not obviously diverse in her psychotherapy sample from that of the general population. She does posit that perhaps the daughter's assumption of more adult roles encourages viewing her as an accessible sex object. "The general rule seems to be that in the eyes of these offenders puberty renders a female eligible for sexual exploitation" (Gebhard et al., 1965, p. 270).

The oldest daughter is most often chosen, probably because she is the most sexually mature, and because she is the one to whom the wifely role is transferred in cases where the mother is physically absent from the home or where she has abdicated her role. Gebhard et al., expressed the attitude towards women in the statement that "Bluntly speaking, society tells the father or stepfather of a female aged 16 or over, 'You must live on rather intimate terms with a female who is old enough for sex and who is sexually attractive, but you must not allow yourself to take advantage of the situation.' To the average person this dictate seems a reasonable law and one easy to obey. However, in certain circumstances even the most conservative person must admit that obedience to the law requires an iron will" (Gebhard et al., 1965, p. 249). Thus, we find that even the so-called objective researchers bring to their research their view of women as sex objects. If women are sexually exciting, then how can we fault the men for acting on their urges? Covertly, then, girls and women are viewed as sharing responsibility for their sexual abuse.

The daughter, who is often lacking in adequate mothering, looks to her father for emotional support and instead is sexually used by him. If she is a young child, she will often view this attention in a positive way since her father and mother do not give her positive feedback in other areas. She accepts her father's actions, since he is a very important adult in her life, and as an authority figure, he cannot err. In some cases she has positive feelings around being chosen by him, and therefore does not see his sexual actions toward her as assaultive in nature (Peters, 1976). If the daughter is angered by her father's actions, she very often displaces these feelings onto her mother because of her mother's inability or unwillingness to protect her.

Karl Menninger's contention that childhood sexual activity with an adult is not only uninjurious but may also be helpful to the child's mental health has been questioned by a number of researchers. Summit and Kryso (1978) state that in probing women who are in therapy who manifest symptoms of suicidal tendencies, depression, and whose self-esteem is very low, we often find early experiences of sexual abuse.

The findings of other research support depression as symptomatic of sexual abuse of girls and also add symptoms such as guilt feelings, difficulties in learning, difficulties with sexual adjustment as adults, as well as such somatic complaints as stomach difficulties and poor appetite (Kaufman et al., 1954). In some cases the girls react to the sexual activity by running away from home. They are unable to deal with the difficult home situation directly and use mechanisms of denial and repression in their attempt to cope with the overwhelming problem. In other cases, the daughter feels that it is her responsibility to keep the family intact by meeting her father's unmet needs. Judy's incestuous activity with her father began when she was nine years old, and by the time she reached eleven she and her father were involved in coitus. Her father had periods of depression, and Judy felt that it was her responsibility to help her father by giving him sexual relief. The incest continued until Judy reached the age of sixteen (Lustig et al., 1966). This case demonstrates the blatant example of the expression of women's role of nurturing *without* consideration of the needs of the nurturing person.

The amount of guilt felt by the daughter is directly correlated with her age (the younger she is the less guilty she will feel), and with the reaction to the incest that is expressed by her family upon discovery.

Negative effects of incest are not necessarily seen immediately. At Cedar House in Long Beach, California, the workers counseling abusing families found that there was evidence that 90 percent of the mothers who were reaching out for help had been sexually abused as children (Summit and Kryso, 1978). As mentioned earlier, there is a relationship between the mother's own experience with sexual abuse as a child and her role in fostering her husband-daughter incest involvement. It is also apparent that although children involved in incest may not demonstrate immediate psychiatric effects from the experience, the long-term influences are still operative, and may particularly come to the fore at the time of adulthood when normal sexual demands are made of the individual with which she is unable to cope.

Whether or not father-daughter incest is a precipatory cause of psychosis in the daughter has not been definitely resolved. In one particular case described by Peters (1976), the connection between incest and the development of schizophrenia was direct. This was the case of a father who involved his two daughters, age three and six, in sexual play, as well as attempts at coitus whenever he was drunk. Although there were no obvious effects on the children at the time, when the youngest daughter gave birth to a child, she had delusions around her father's having desire for the child. Her other sister also had a psychotic break during her first courtship. It is Meiselman's (1978) thesis that although incest is not the cause of psychosis, it is indicative of an already stressful situation, all of which can lay the groundwork for a mental break.

Mother-daughter incest seems to be extremely rare and is also rarely reported in the literature. This is an area which warrants further study.

There are several references, however, to father-son incest which came to the attention of therapists as a result of the son's fears around being forced into homosexuality.

Mother-son incest hardly exists, and when it does occur, is initiated by the mother who generally is psychotic at the time. This is quite different from the father in the father-daughter incest, who as we have mentioned, in most cases is not considered to be mentally disturbed. The infrequency of mother-son type incest is demonstrated by the fact that Weinberg in 1958 studied 203 cases of incest occurring within the nuclear family and found within that number only two cases of mother-son incest. Wahl (1960), in his description of two cases of maternal-son incest views this as one of the most shattering experiences, often resulting in a psychotic episode in the son.

Mother and child, be it daughter or son, have a strong interdependent relationship with each other, with the father on the outside (Schwartzman, 1974). In order to become a separate individual, the son identifies with the father, while the girl views her father as a love object. This, state Frances and Frances (1976), accounts for the fact that there is a greater repulsion to mother-son incest than to father-daughter incest. If the son becomes too attached to his mother, he will be unable to change his symbiotic relationship with his mother to become a separate individual whose sexual identity also differs from hers. "An ongoing erotic interest in his daughter does not so nearly threaten the individual identities of either partner as is true in the mother-son partnership. These issues are played out in early infantile development and then recur dramatically with adolescence" (Frances and Frances, 1976, p. 242).

I would like to propose that another reason for the almost nonexistence of mother-son incest is the fact that fathers have been imbued with power in the family. Power concomitant with the view of young women as "fair game" sexually, operates to lay the groundwork for possible father-daughter incest. Mothers do not have the power and do not generally feel that their husbands or children are "owned" by them, and because of their role training to be nurturing, giving, caring individuals, would find great difficulty in acting on any incestuous desires they might have.

As we have seen, although incest prohibitions are thought to be one of the strongest taboos, incest exists more frequently than we as a society would like to accept. Incest occurs most often with the girl as the victim and creates difficulties for her in the process of developing to a whole woman. Hopefully, as rape comes out of the closet, so, too, will incest so that those who have been victimized will be encouraged to confront their feelings, and those who are the victimizers will get help to prevent further victimization.

References

Adams, M. and Neel, J. V. Children of incest. *Pediatrics* **40**:55–62 (1967).

Bischof, N. The biological foundations of the incest taboo. *Social Science Information* **11**:7–36 (1972).

Brody, Jane. Personal Health. *New York Times.* Section III: 8 (June 13, 1979).

Cavallin, H. Incestuous fathers: a clinical report. *American Journal of Psychiatry* **122**:1132–1138 (1966).

Durkheim, Emile. *Incest: The Nature and Origin of the Taboo.* New York: Lyle Stuart, 1963.

Frances, Vera and Frances, Allen. The incest taboo and family structure. *Family Process* **15**:235–244 (1976).

Frazer, Sir James. *Totemism and Exogamy.* London: Macmillan, 1910 (4 vols.).

Freud, Sigmund. *Totem and Taboo,* in *The Complete Psychological Works of Sigmund Freud,* James Strachey (ed). London: The Hogarth Press and the Institute of Psycho-analysis, Vol XIII 1955, pp. 1–161.

Gebhard, Paul H., Gagnon, John H., Pomeroy, Wardell B. and Christenson, Cornelia J. *Sex Offenders.* New York: Harper & Row, Publishers and Paul B. Hoeber, Medical Books, 1965.

Gutheil, Thomas G. and Avery, Nicholas C. Multiple overt incest as family defense against loss. *Family Process* **16**:105–116 (1977).

Halleck, Seymour. The physician's role in management of victims of sex offenders. *Journal of the American Medical Association* **180**:273–278 (April 1962).

Harbert, Terry L., Herson, Michel, Barlow, David and Austin, James B. Measurement and modification of incestuous behavior: a case study. *Psychological Reports* **34**:79–86 (February 1974).

The Holy Bible. revised standard edition. Toronto: Thomas Nelson & Sons, 1952.

Kaufman, I., Peck, A. L. and Tagiuri, C. K. The family constellation and overt incestuous relations between father and daughter. *American Journal of Orthopsychiatry* **24**:266–277 (1954).

Kinsey, Alfred C., Pomeroy, Wardell B., and Martin, Clyde E. *Sexual Behavior in the Human Male.* Philadelphia and London: W. B. Saunders, 1948.

_____. *Sexual Behavior in the Human Female.* Philadelphia: W. B. Saunders, 1953.

Lustig, Noel, Dresser, John W., Spellman, Seth W. and Murray, Thomas B. Incest. *Archives of General Psychiatry* **14**:31–40 (1966).

Maisch, H. *Incest.* New York: Stein & Day, 1972.

Malinowski, Bronislaw. *Sex and Repression in Savage Society.* New York: Meridian Books, 1955.

Masters, R. E. L. *Patterns of Incest.* New York: Julian Press, 1963.

Meiselman, Karin C. *Incest.* San Francisco: Josey-Bass Publishers, 1978.

Middleton, Russell. Brother-sister and father-daughter marriage in ancient Egypt. *American Sociological Review* 27:603–611 (October 1962).

Parsons, Talcott. The incest taboo in relation to social structure and the socialization of the child. *British Journal of Sociology* 5:101–117 (1954).

Peters, Joseph J. Children who are victims of sexual assault and the psychology of offenders. *American Journal of Psychotherapy* 30:398–421 (1976).

Ralphing, David C., Carpenter, Bob L. and Davis, Allen. Incest: a geneological study. *Archives of General Psychiatry* 16:505–511 (1967).

Schwartzman, John. The individual, incest, and exogamy. *Psychiatry* 37:171–180 (May 1974).

Seemanová, Eva. A study of children of incestuous matings. *Human Heredity* 21:108–128 (1971).

Stucker, Jan. I tried to fantasize that all fathers had intercourse with their daughters—the story of Mary C. *Ms* 66–67 (April 1977).

Summit, Roland and Kryso, Joann. Sexual abuse of children. *American Journal of Orthopsychiatry* 48:237–251 (April 1978).

Talmon, Y. Mate selection in collective settlements. *American Sociological Review* 29:491–508 (1964).

The Random House Dictionary of The English Language. Jess Stein and Laurence Urdang (eds.). New York: Random House, 1967.

Wahl, Charles William. The psychodynamics of consummated maternal incest: a report of two cases. *Archives of General Psychiatry* 3:180–193 (1960).

Weber, Ellen. Incest—sexual abuse begins at home. *Ms* 64–66 (April 1977).

Weinberg, S. K. *Incest Behavior.* New York: Citadel Press, 1958.

Westermarck, Edward. *A Short History of Marriage.* New York: Humanities Press, 1936.

White, Leslie A. *Science of Our Culture: A Study of Man and Civilization.* New York: Farrar, Straus and Cudahy, 1949.

Wolf, Arthur P. Adopt a daughter-in-law, marry a sister: a Chinese solution to the problem of the incest taboo. *American Anthropologist* 70:864–874, 1968.

6. When She is Bad, She is Horrid: Women and Crime

There was a little girl
Who had a little curl,
Right in the middle of her forehead,
And when she was good,
She was very, very good,
But when she was bad, she was horrid.
          Henry Wadsworth Longfellow

This rhyme which is found in many children's books, and which is recited to little children, reflects the expected behavior of females in our society. Little girls and also women need to be sweet, cherubic, and good. When they deviate from these role expectations, they are considered to be very, very bad, even horrid. It is true that females are highly under-represented in crime in the United States. Perhaps as a result of the fact that female criminals are in the minority or perhaps because women are not considered the important people in our society, there has been very little written about the female offender. In 1968 it was suggested that one chapter would be all that was needed to present the available information on the nature and origins of female criminality (Simon, 1977).

    Cesare Lombroso, an early criminologist, attempted to explain why some people became involved in criminal activity. He was particularly enamored with the idea that there was a relationship between the structure of the skull, bodily characteristics, and criminality. He found, for instance, that receding foreheads were more prevalent in prostitutes (12 percent) than in other criminals (11 percent) or normal women (8 percent). In addition, he wrote

> Prostitutes are almost quite free from wrinkles . . . crooked noses and asymetrical faces; what they have more frequently are moles, hairiness,

prehensile feet, the virile larynx, large jaws and cheek bones, and above all anomolous teeth (Lombroso and Ferrero, 1899, p. 85).

Lombroso felt that women were less criminally oriented than men because they were born that way, but he also believed that although most women were enticed into crime by their husbands or lovers, there were a small number of what he termed "born criminals." It is this female-born criminal who manifests more intense negative characteristics than comparable men. Cruelty abounds in the female born criminal, who does not hesitate to kill her victim, and moreover enjoys watching her victim suffer in the process.

> . . . a woman of bad life, on finding herself at 42 abandoned by her lovers, took to persecuting her daughter . . . She hung her daughter from the ceiling by the armpits, knocked her on the head with a brick, and burnt her with a hot iron whenever she came near her (Lombroso and Ferrero, 1899, p. 150).

Lombroso also felt that women were naturally more impervious to pain than men and therefore less compassionate. He characterized women as being like children, morally lacking, greedy, wanting to retaliate and jealous. These weakenesses of character are usually overshadowed by "piety, maternity, want of passion, sexual coldness, by weakness and an undeveloped intelligence" (Lombroso and Ferrero, 1899, p. 151). When there is a lack of the aforementioned feminine characteristics, women can become more cruel than men. Lombroso, like Aristotle before him and Freud after him, believed that women were innately passive as a result of their stationary ovum, unlike men whose sperm were highly mobile. These phenomenon result, he felt, in a psychologically passive bent. Anatomy, therefore, really becomes destiny. In addition, he theorized that women were less varied than men.

> The woman, as distinguished from the man . . . stands at one or other extremity of the pole, being either perfectly normal or excessively anomalous. And when the anomaly is excessive, suicide and madness are one. Consequently women are very rarely criminal when compared with men, but when criminal they are infinitely worse (Lombroso and Ferrero, 1899, p. 288).

It is apparent that Lombroso did not think too kindly of the "weaker sex." Although few women became criminals, when they did transgress they were "horrid."

Although Lombroso's research methods were felt to be unsound, more recent criminologists such as W. I. Thomas (1907) and Otto Pollak (1950) presented theories based on similar hypotheses concerning the natural physiological and therefore psychological disposition of women (Klein, 1973). Thomas continued in the early 1920s to expound on Lombroso's basic premise of anatomical and physiological differences of men and women as they influence personality. In his book, *Sex and Society* (1907), he correlated being male with being vigorous and vital, as well as sexual, compared to femaleness, which he viewed as static, nonsexual, and cautious. The female is better able to survive, but she is also more concerned with the personal aspects of life than are men. She is less interested in sex than men and accepts a domestic life style so that she can express her maternal instincts (Thomas, 1907).

In *The Unadjusted Girl,* published in 1923, Thomas proposed that a poor girl who could not find a marriage partner might choose to express her feminine needs by becoming a prostitute (Crites, 1976).

Thomas perceived the female delinquent as a maladjusted person who has few morals and who attempts to meet her basic need for security by sexual acts (Vedder and Sommerville, 1970).

In 1934 Sheldon and Eleanor Glueck published a study of 500 delinquent women. They saw poverty and biological factors as strong influences on crime.

> ... a fundamental attack upon the problems of anti-sociality depends not only on the raising of the status of the economically underprivileged, but on the elimination or better control of the biologically handicapped (Glueck and Glueck, 1965, p. 309).

They attacked "irresponsible breeding among delinquents" and supported voluntary sterilization as a method of resolving the problem.

And then there was Freud, who viewed women as biologically inferior because they lacked a penis. The lack of a penis is interpreted to mean that they are being punished for something. The sex act itself, with the male penetrating the female, Freud felt, was an indication of innate male aggressiveness and superiority as opposed to the female, who is passive and inferior. Deviation from biologically determined female behavior was considered by Freud to be neurotic and to be an indication of penis envy.

> Of little girls we know that they feel themselves heavily handicapped by the absence of a large visible penis and envy the boy's possession of it;

from this source primarily springs the wish to be a man which is resumed again later in the neurosis, owing to some maladjustment to a female development (Freud, 1943, p. 278).

Thus, as Klein (1973) states, Freud believed that any woman who presented behavior which was considered masculine rather than feminine was deviant. A woman by nature has been destined to be charming, sweet, and beautiful, and a good wife. Any rebellious attempt to change that expectation would be viewed as "unhealthy."

Otto Pollak's book, *The Criminality of Women,* published in 1950, made a strong impact on the field of criminology. He questioned the extent of women's role in crime, stating that although it had been thought that the crime rate among women was very low, in reality women commit more crimes than they are given credit for. He presented the premise that women's crimes are hidden and that "women offenders are more deceitful than men." He proceeded to document this contention by citing a number of criminologists who supported that concept. Even Margaret Sanger, the crusader for birth control, is quoted as stating that women's ability and need to practice concealment is justifiable. Pollak alludes to the possible biological justification for this basic difference between males and females by discussing man's need to achieve an erect penis in order to copulate and the impossibility of hiding this erection. The construction of the woman's body allows her to practice deceit in sexual relations (feigning orgasm) unlike the man. Creating illusions also becomes part of the girl's adolescent development since she is required to refrain from demonstrating overt enthrallment with the members of the opposite sex.

> This interplay between physical and cultural factors seems, therefore, actually to result in a greater lack of sincerity in women than in men (Pollak, p. 11).

The role expectations of women in our society of mother, housekeeper, nurse, etc., place them in a relationship of passivity and thus provide them with circumstances favorable to committing crimes which are difficult to detect. Women, therefore, he argued, commit "hidden" crimes which are often not reported. These crimes include shoplifting, stealing by prostitutes, having abortions (at the time he wrote his book abortion was illegal in most states in the United States), and giving false testimony. When women do participate in visible crimes they tend to take a more inactive role than the male basically because they have been socialized to be the male's supporter behind the scenes. They therefore are often the accomplices; driving the get-away car, acting as lookouts, etc. (Pollak, 1950).

Otto Pollak made a third point about the low crime rate among women. He believed that chivalrous behavior on the part of men in the judicial system influenced the fact that few women were charged by the police, and if charged were often acquitted. The police are reluc-tant to charge young women because this would stigmatize them for the rest of their lives. Few juries, stated Pollak, are willing to convict women, and judges are definitely unwilling to do so.

In discussing the cause of female crime, Pollak accentuated the im-portance of menstruation, pregnancy, and menopause. These physical changes in women are associated with psychological difficulties which expose women to weakened inhibitions and a climate in which com-mission of a crime can take place. He does stress the fact that culture is a determining agent in the development of the psychological difficul-ties. Menstruation, with its flow of blood, is associated with injury, and as a result with feelings of guilt, particularly in the area of sex. As a connotation of adult womanhood, menstruation is often accompanied by hostility because of the role of inequality that the woman is ex-pected to play and the fact that she cannot achieve what men are al-lowed to achieve. The end result of all of this is an emotional setting which can foster criminal behavior. He cited early studies which found a high correlation between crimes of shoplifting, arson, stealing, and murders, and the menstrual cycle. He dismissed an American study which showed a significantly lower number of girls guilty of arson than boys by stating that although a person is predisposed to the commis-sion of a crime, he/she has to have favorable circumstances in order to actually commit it (Pollak, 1950). In other words, an individual has to find an opportunity for performing a criminal act. Girls are generally, according to Pollak, protected especially from being out at night. It is at night that arson often occurs.

The concept of premenstrual and menstrual tension and irritability has been associated with crime in recent studies. According to some research, the majority of crimes committed by women occur the week prior to or during the week of menstruation, particularly premeditated crimes. Two-thirds of the violent crimes, such as child abuse, assault or murder, were found to be committed during the ten days prior to menstruation. One study of college women noted that they had greater feelings of aggression premenstrually than in the other phases of the cycle. The French, as well as some of the legal authorities in the United States, believe that menstrual tension is an acceptable legal reason for the commission of a violent crime because it creates a situation in which the woman is incapable of making decisions and is temporarily insane (Marsh, 1978). A controversy exists as to whether or not hypoglycemia (low blood sugar) occurs premenstrually and whether or not it is actually the prime causal factor in the commission of a crime.

Some researchers have questioned the method used in the studies which associate the menstrual cycle with crime or behavior in general, and feel that even when a correlation does exist, the interpretation that menstrual tension has a direct influence on the commission of a crime is questionable (Parlee, 1973).

Pregnancy, too, states Pollak, is a time of great risk for expressing destructive behavior, particularly those crimes of abortion (a crime when he was writing) and infanticide.

> . . . the psychological characteristics of pregnancy, such as unmotivated changes of moods, abnormal cravings and impulses, and temporary impairment of consciousness, point also in the direction of criminal causation (Pollak, p. 130).

Vulnerability for commission of crime is also present during pregnancy because the woman is still influenced by the menstrual cycle for several months following conception. Pregnant women are therefore being affected by both negative factors which result from pregnancy itself as well as those factors which result from the menstrual cycle.

Menopause, states Pollak, is a difficult phase for women, especially those who are married. Inability to sleep, mood swings, low frustration tolerance, and depression characterize the woman in menopause. These are not solely biologically determined, but are the result of the social significance that is placed on this stage of development in women's lives. Menopausal women are viewed as decreasingly sexually appealing and very often view themseves in this manner, thereby finding it increasingly difficult to relate interpersonally. Comparing single and married women during the age of menopause, research has found that there is a higher crime rate for married women than single women. Otto Pollak therefore concludes that menopause creates more of a threat for the woman in a marital relationship than for one who is not, and therefore a greater vulnerability for committing certain crimes (Pollak, 1950).

Otto Pollak did, however, point out that women are not basically more immoral than men. Culturally, sexually promiscuous women and prostitutes, because they are free from the sexual restraints placed on women by our society are labeled as immoral. Prostitution until recently was defined as only a female crime. It is interesting to note that a crime by definition is "an act committed, or omitted, in violation of a public law either forbidding or commanding it" (Blackstone, 1916, p. 2151). Immoral behavior is not necessarily criminal behavior. It appears that more immoral behavior, particularly that of a sexual nature is defined as such when committed by girls or women. The double standard still exists.

Gisela Konopka (1966), a psychoanalytically oriented social worker, studied in depth a large number of girls who were serving time in Minnesota institutions for delinquency. She concluded that there were several basic factors which seemed to have contributed to their deviant behavior. One was the dramatic onset of puberty, which if accompanied by no or little preparation can create problems, since the beginning of the menses, said Konopka, is closely associated with bodily injury. The potential for becoming pregnant and its effect on sex, she states, is also related to the biological onset of puberty.

> Sex . . . has a more pervasive meaning to the girl. Intense romantic connotation—pervasive frigidity, sex as outlet for frustration, sex as a weapon—may be developed (p. 120).

The second factor which creates difficulty for girls and sets the groundwork for delinquency is the complicated process the girl must go through (the Oedipal stage) in which she must eventually identify with her mother. A nonsupportive, competitive mother or a rejecting, harsh father can make this identification difficult. The third important factor in female delinquency, according to Konopka, is the fast-changing position of women in our culture. Normative behavioral expectations are no longer stable. Anger about the "double standard" which still exists in our society, little opportunity and encouragement to express her hostility because she is supposed to be sweet, and the fact that even if she does work, her job will have low status and low pay,

add to a girl's difficulties and to her perception of marriage as a solution. In typical Freudian analysis, Konopka states that "thwarted am-
bition" has a strong impact on the way girls behave, but for the girl,
unlike the boy, it is not "related to economics. For girls it is directly
related to being a woman" (Konopka, p. 121).

All girls, according to Konopka, have to deal with the three preced-
ing situations. In some cases the behavioral reaction is delinquency.
Those girls who end up in institutions have additionally been influenced by loneliness and lack of confidence in adults because of past
experience. Adults in their lives have been brutal, unloving, and un-
trustable. All of these four influences tend to lead to a poor self-image
and antisocial behavior resulting in the reinforcement of a poor self-
image and so on ad infinitum.

Konopka proposed that girls, unlike boys who are in trouble, basically have strong dependency needs and no matter what crime a girl
has committed, she will demonstrate difficulty in the area of sex. Here
we see the view of women as basically sexual creatures.

Edwin H. Sutherland theorized that "differential association" influenced whether or not an individual became involved in criminal behavior. He proposed that one learns criminal behavior rather than in-
heriting a tendency toward it, that this behavior is acquired in the
process of interacting with other people; that peer groups and other
primary groups are influential in the learning process, and that personal needs and values alone cannot explain illegal behavior (Sutherland and Cressey, 1966). This differential association theory seems to
be more applicable to adolescent female delinquents than to adult
women. At least we really are not as yet certain as to how much differential association influences women to manifest criminal behavior.

Efforts to explain why a particular person commits a crime have
proposed that an individual who has a tendency for antisocial behavior
may be influenced by a criminal milieu. The individual may have per-
vasive guilt feelings which motivate him/her to act out in an antisocial
manner in order to assuage guilt through punishment. Criminal behavior may be present as an attempt to cope with feelings of inadequacy and insecurity (Abrahamsen, 1960). Psychoanalytic thinking
would also relate women's criminal behavior to the expression of penis
envy.

> The usual kleptomaniac is a woman who emotionally has never been
> able to obtain sexual gratification in a normal way because of her penis

envy and castration fear. To her the stolen object is symbolic of the penis and she takes it in revenge because she does not have the male organ (Abrahamsen, p. 129).

If we substitute the concept of penis as an actual sex organ and think about the power that the male genitalia gives the bearer in our society, then perhaps the kleptomaniac can be seen as a woman who feels frustrated and powerless because of the feminine role our society forces her to play. She steals in order to gain a feeling of power and control. Remember that being female is genetically determined, but the concept of femininity is culturally devised.

Actually, women criminals existed in our country almost from the beginning of its settlement. Great Britain peppered the new world with women prisoners from institutions such as Bridewell and Newgate. Sometimes these women volunteered to become wives of settlers in exchange for their freedom. Sometimes, however, they were brought here as slaves or wives without their informed consent. There are documented cases of at least 140 women from prisons and women who were seized while walking the streets at night who were sent to the colonies on slave ships and bought as wives in exchange for tobacco leafage in the early 1600s. Since the trip took two to three months, and since the conditions on the ships were deplorable, 15 percent to 30 percent of the women died in transport. It is estimated that approximately 9000 women prisoners had been sent to the colonies by the beginning of the revolution (Blumenthal, 1962).

Today interest in female crime and in the female offender has suddenly mushroomed, and so has female crime. Perhaps this awakened interest in criminality and women may be directly related to the apparent increase in violent crime committed by women within the past ten years.

Most of the available statistics on crime come from the FBI's yearly *Uniform Crime Reports,* which are actually only accurate in demonstrating the general direction of crime. The FBI receives its information from a national pool of law enforcement agencies in forty-three states. Numbers of arrests, as well as reasons for the arrests, are reported for specifically indexed crimes. Although these reports are what we have to work with, they have several limitations, and these should be kept in mind in analyzing the data. It is difficult to obtain a clear picture of trends because the reporting agencies and the population estimate change yearly. In addition, increase in the reporting of some crimes may really not reflect an increase in the actual commission of that crime. The crime statistics also may reflect the fact that there are more law enforcement people as well as more efficient methods used in discovering crime, and in identifying and capturing the criminal. Statistical methods have also improved, and in the past female crime was not always accurately reported or itemized (Rans, 1978).

Since the sources for crime information are limited, the *Uniform Crime Reports* will be used.

The *Uniform Crime Reports* state that the number of arrests is helpful in understanding the involvement in crime of people in terms of sex, race, and age, particularly for more specific crimes which are usually solved. There were 3 percent more females and 1 percent fewer males arrested in 1977 than in 1976. The ratio of males to females arrested was five to one. In spite of the decrease in male arrests, they comprised 84 percent of the arrests for all crimes indexed and 90 percent of the arrests for violent crimes (*Uniform Crime Reports in the United States,* 1978). It is apparent that although crime by females is increasing, they are committing far fewer crimes in proportion to their number. The number of people under eighteen who were arrested in 1977 increased by 3 percent from 1973. The increase was comprised of 11 percent for males and 19 percent for females. If one looks at the arrest rate over an eleven-year period, one sees a dramatic increase in crimes by women, if arrest rates are indicative of this. Since 1968 female crimes had increased by 57.6 percent, while male crimes had increased by 13.4 percent. We can conclude that the crime rate for women is increasing at a more rapid rate than that for men. The most dramatic increase actually occurred between 1960 and 1976 when female arrests increased by 101 percent, as compared to male arrests, for which there was a 22.8 percent increase (*Uniform Crime Reports in the United States,* 1978).

A large increase in the number of arrests for females seems to have occurred in the under-eighteen age bracket, up by 38.6 percent since 1968. Prostitution appears to be what the young female is most often arrested for, with an increase since 1968 of 245.4 percent, except for that vague category of offenses against family and children, which has shown an increase of 435.0 percent, and driving under the influence with an increase of 758.5 percent. There have also been appreciable increases in aggravated assault (158.7 percent), fraud (165.4 percent), embezzlement (233.5 percent), and stolen property offenses (229.8 percent) (*Uniform Crime Reports in the United States,* 1978).

Although female crime has increased over a ten-year period, proportionately the number of arrests still is below their representation in the total society. In 1970, for instance, although women comprised about 51 percent of the population, they made up only 14.4 percent of the total arrests. However, the arrests of female juvenile delinquents have almost tripled in number (Hoffman-Bustamante, 1973).

The total number of robberies in the United States in 1977 decreased by 4 percent from the previous year, 1976, according to the *Uniform Crime Reports.* But of every 100 persons arrested for robbery, one was a woman, and this figure indicates a decline in the number of women who are committing robberies if we can accept arrest figures as indicators of actual commission of crimes. Burglary, which is defined as unlawfully entering a "structure" in order to steal or commit a felony, has decreased since 1976 by 2 percent but since 1973 has increased by 14 percent. In 1977, of every 100 persons arrested for burglary, 6 were female. The person most frequently arrested for this type of crime was a male between the ages of fifteen and nineteen (*Uniform Crime Reports in the United States,* 1978).

Larceny-theft is defined by the FBI as "the unlawful taking, carrying, leading, or riding away of property from the possession or constructive possession of another." It includes crimes such as shoplifting, pocket-picking, purse-snatching, thefts from motor vehicles, thefts of motor vehicle parts and accessories, bicycle thefts, etc., in which no force, volence or fraud occurs (*Uniform Crime Reports in the United States,* 1978). This type of crime comprised 54 percent of the crimes indexed and showed a decline from 1976.

Let's take a look at shoplifting, which is considered predominantly a female crime. Eleven percent of the larceny cases are shoplifting cases, and shoplifting has increased 40 percent since 1973. Thirty-two percent of the arrests are of females, and this is the crime which they seem to be more often arrested for. The number of males arrested for this crime decreased by 3 percent since 1976, but the number of arrests for women increased by 1 percent, not a terribly startling increase by any stretch of the imagination (*Uniform Crime Reports in the United States,* 1978).

Aggravated assault, which involves attempting to severely injure another person, has risen by 6 percent since 1976 and by 24 percent since 1973. Arrests for this crime have also increased, but the number of males still exceeds the number of females by seven to one.

Although women tend to act alone when committing murder, they tend to be accessories to the crime in burglary and robbery (Ward et al. 1969, and Pollak, 1950). Pollak stated that women capitalized on their female roles and characteristics as part of their role as decoy or lookout.

Patterns of crime seem to be associated with access and opportunity. During World War II, when women were encouraged by an appeal to patriotism to leave home and assume what had previously been male jobs, crimes by women almost doubled, and the types of crimes committed were similar to those committed by males (Adler, 1975). A large number of women today are in the working world, and an increasing number of them are in positions in which they can commit fraud.

Therefore, female crime is increasing at a rapid pace and will probably continue as more women assume positions once reserved only for men.

> Lizzie Borden took an axe,
> And gave her mother forty whacks,
> And when she saw what she had done,
> She gave her father forty-one.

In the late 1800s Mr. Borden was found sadistically murdered, and his wife, too, was found in the same horrible condition upstairs in her bedroom. This case of double murder in Fall River, Massachusetts, created a stir throughout the country, especially when it was learned that both deaths were thought to be the responsibility of Mr. Borden's daughter, and the then Mrs. Borden's stepdaughter. After all, women were thought to be innately nonviolent and therefore Lizzie Borden's supposed act was considered unnatural and shocking. Although Lizzie Borden was acquitted people were horrified to think that there was even the slightest possibility that a woman could commit such a heinous crime. Fairly recently, a young woman was arrested in New York and accused of being a gun for hire. Women are able to commit violent crimes.

There is a concern today that women are committing violent crimes at an alarming rate. The fact is that since 1968 female arrests for murder went up 17.9 percent, for aggravated assault up 71 percent, while the figures for men are 30.8 percent and 52 percent respectively. The *Uniform Crime Report for the United States,* 1977 indicates an increase of 72 percent in arrests for violent crimes committed by women and

48.9 percent for men. The most dramatic increase is in the under-eighteen age group where female arrests for violent crimes increased by 138.8 percent. Ninety percent, however, of the violent crimes are committed by men. The largest increase in female arrests occurred for commission of crimes in the area of fraud (+206.3 percent), larceny-theft (+128.8 percent), buying or receiving stolen property (+234.2 percent) and driving under the influence (+186.0 percent).

It seems that because of our stereotyped expectation that women be nonviolent, we have become very concerned about the increase in violent behavior. Wolfgang points out that men are murdered and are victimized by being murdered almost five times as often as women. Women tend to kill members of the opposite sex, while more men kill members of their own sex.

Although there are racial differences in rates of homicide, within each racial group women commit significantly fewer murders than men (Wolfgang, 1967).

The fact that women tend to kill their husbands or lovers and members of their families (Ward et al., 1969) reflects their socialization pattern. Women are taught to focus on personal matters, and it is therefore relationship problems which precipitate murder. Difficulty with a lover or a battering husband can cause women to make them victims. Wolfgang's Philadelphia (1958) study found that almost 84 percent of the murders committed by women involved male victims with whom they had a close interpersonal relationship. The comparable figure for male murders was 59 percent.

Male victims killed by spouses comprise only 11 percent of the total number of men who are killed (Wolfgang, 1967). Women usually act alone without an accomplice when they do commit a murder (Ward et al., 1969). Wives generally meet their death in the bedroom by a beating, while they kill their husbands in the kitchen with a butcher knife (Wolfgang, 1967). It has been postulated that this may be due to the fact that women generally spend a great deal of time in the kitchen where controversies regarding finances are apt to be raised and where weapons are easily accessible. We can perhaps hypothesize that husbands kill their wives in the bedroom because it is there that sex most often takes place, and it is also, therefore, in that room that the male's sexual ability and masculine identity may come into question. Beating one's wife to death does demonstrate one's physical strength, and physical strength is still an indication of masculinity.

Actually, women, more often than men, commit murder with a minimum of violence, contrary to Lombroso's belief that they enjoy watching their victims suffer. Wolfgang (1958), found that about 67 percent of the women in his Philadelphia sample committed what he called "non-violent" homicide. The figure for men was 45.5 percent. A more recent study corroborates this with its finding that many of the victims (42 percent) of murder committed by women were defenseless. They were either sleeping, intoxicated, unwell, or old in 42 percent of the cases, and children in 19 percent (Ward et al., 1969).

Murder by females is usually unpremeditated (Ward et al., 1969). Wolfgang (1958), in his analysis of his Philadelphia study, discussed the concept of victim-precipitated murder, which he defined as murders in which the victim was the first one to display aggression, such as slapping or punching, towards the murderer. He found that women were twice as likely to be involved in victim-precipitated homicide as in murder in which the victim did not have a major contributory role. Wolfgang suggests several reasons for this. Perhaps husbands tend to exacerbate a hostile situation with their wives, so that they are attacked more often, than wives do with their husbands, or perhaps the behavior of the husbands is defined by their wives as assaultive, or perhaps husbands may retreat from the conflict, which results in their not acting out in a violent manner. No matter what the underlying reason behind the differences, it is unquestionably true that husbands play an important precipitory role in their own murder.

More men than women were found to commit suicide after killing their spouses (Wolfgang, 1967). It has been conjectured that perhaps when women kill their husbands they feel justified in doing so and therefore feel less guilty than their male counterparts (Goode, 1969). We do know that men commit suicide many times more often than women, although women make more attempts at it.

Women who murder generally come from intact homes in which there is no history of crime. They themselves had little experience with crime, were not involved with narcotics, but did drink excessively (Ward et al., 1969). Wolfgang (1967) found that there was a high correlation between alcohol and victim-precipitated murder. Since women tend to murder spouses and lovers, and since a high percentage of the murders they commit fall into the victim-precipitated category, the presence of alcohol, although not necessarily a causal factor, is not surprising.

Why is crime for women increasing? Otto Pollak (1950) did not be-lieve it really was increasing as rapidly as it appeared. He felt that crimes committed by women were hidden crimes, were under-reported and that women were also infrequently convicted because of the chiv-alrous attitudes of people in the law enforcement and judicial systems. Anderson (1976) presents the following thesis regarding the basic be-liefs concerning the dynamics of female crime which feed into the chiv-alry hypothesis. Women are thought to be naturally manipulative and thus they use their feminine wiles to encourage males to commit crimes. In their devious manner, therefore, they entice the male into risk-taking behavior while they themselves remain safe.

Anderson (1976) also discusses what she calls the concept of the "sexualized female;" that is, the perception that sexuality determines all behavior. In other words, regardless of what crime the woman commits, the basis for it is interpreted to be in nature because of the view of a woman as suffering from penis envy, having underlying pro-miscuous needs as well as being anatomically inferior, which all con-verge to impair the female's morality. The fact that men established the moral code, and that men are responsible for the laws of the land, results in women being viewed in a distorted manner, one which is highly influenced by sexism (Anderson, 1976). As we shall discuss later, women receive more punitive treament in many ways. They are sentenced to longer terms than men for the same crime and do not have the same educational and vocational opportunities in the institu-tions to which they are confined as are available for men.

And then there is the theory that women are committing more crimes, especially young women, because they are being influenced by the focus on feminism of the women's movement. The movement has questioned the traditional roles of woman as wife and mother, and has created dissatisfaction in young women with their lives. Cultural norms in flux, with their concomitant cultural lag, create disequilib-rium and an increase in social problems. The increase in crime is one of these social problems which may have been exacerbated by the women's movement. Dr. Donald Russell, director of the Judge Baker Guidance Center's Court clinic program in Boston, believes that be-cause girls are no longer accepting their mothering role they have more opportunity to become involved in more positive as well as more nega-tive types of activities (Katzeff, 1977).

There seems to be little support for the contention that the women's movement is a great contributor to the increase in female crime. One study by the National Study of Women's Correction Programs found that the majority of females in institutions are traditionally oriented. They have accepted the differential roles ascribed to males and females by society. They view the man's responsibility to the family as economic and the woman's as caretaker of the offspring (*The Women's Movement and Crime,* 1977). Another research project, supported by the California Youth Authority, did not find support for the contention that an increase in female crime is associated with the increasing desire of females to opt for nontraditional roles, and posited that the growth in drug use and drug addiction were causal factors (Katzeff, 1977).

When we consider the fact that the number of families headed by women has increased (Rans, 1978), that 70 percent of the women in prison are mothers (McGowan and Blumenthal, 1976), perhaps we can conjecture that women steal to meet their economic responsibilities to their dependents and to themselves.

It seems difficult for people to accept the fact that women may be committing more crimes basically for economic reasons, especially when one notes that the increase in crime is particularly evident in the area of fraud and larceny. Rans (1978) supports this contention with the following arguments. She states that it is a fact that the salary differential between men and women has increased almost to the point of doubling. In 1974 women's median income was 57 percent that of men's (Rans, 1978). When occupation was controlled, women's yearly earnings in 1974 ranged from 60 percent of the men's for service workers to 66 percent of the men's in professional and technical positions (Stromberg and Harkess, 1978). There has also been a tremendous increase in the number of working women, but many of them hold jobs which are low in status and low in pay, as clerks and service workers. In addition to a 73 percent increase of women in single-parent families, an increasing number of women are either single because they have not married or because they have been divorced (Rans, 1978). Rans points out that all these facts point to increasing economic pressure on women, especially when one reviews the characteristics of women in institutions. Many of them were unskilled, and if employed prior to incarceration, held low-paying jobs. In the California Youth Authority study, 60 percent of the 1600 incarcerated women studied had been married and only 10 percent were living with their spouse when institutionalized (*The Women's Movement and Crime,* 1977).

Most convicted women offenders are members of minority groups and poor. One researcher found that when women incarcerated in federal institutions had worked, about half of them had incomes of less than $280 monthly and one-third received a salary of less than $240 (Hovey, 1971). Minority women and poor women have not as yet become part of the women's movement in any great numbers.

Of course there are still those who, because of their belief in the biologically determined view of what little girls are made of, that is, sugar and spice and everything nice, find it difficult to accept the fact that females can be criminally oriented.

Until 1950 the doctrine of presumed coercion still existed in some manner. This rule under common law presumed that a married woman who committed a crime jointly with her husband, or where her husband was witness to her actions, was not acting as a free agent but was coerced by him to do so as an act of obedience (Kanowitz, 1969). The doctrine of coercion implied that a married woman was not a free agent, was incapable of committing a crime, and this doctrine reinforced the concept of husband and wife being one person under the law, usually the one being the husband. If we believe in the innate passivity and sweetness and light of females, it would be difficult to hold them responsible for criminal behavior, and I would not doubt that there are some law enforcement persons who hold that view today.

Throughout most of U.S. history women were barred by state statutes from serving on juries. All juries were, therefore, male except in situations in which a female defendant was pregnant and there was some question on the case, such as deciding whether or not to postpone her death sentence. Women would then serve on the jury, which had to determine whether or not the convicted woman really was pregnant. Women were first allowed to become jurors in 1898 in Utah, and Mississippi and South Carolina were the last two states to succumb. Although by 1957 women were allowed to participate on federal juries, in 1962, twenty-one states still had differential guidelines for jury duty for men and for women (Kanowitz, 1969). As late as 1961 the United States Supreme Court in *Hoyt* v. *Florida* (368 U.S. 57 1961) upheld the ruling of a lower court which agreed that although men as a class had to serve as jurors when called, women could be excluded from the list unless they registered their desire to be a juror. The Supreme Court ruling included the statement that a woman is still regarded as the center of home and family life (Kanowitz, 1969). Fair trial assumes a jury of one's peers and if women were not permitted to serve on juries or had to make an effort to be able to serve, one wonders whether women received and in some cases are receiving equal treatment before the law. The number of states that permit women on the basis of their sex alone to exempt themselves from jury duty has dwindled because of a number of court cases which have affirmed the right of a person convicted of a crime to be tried by a representative jury under the Equal Protection Clause of the U.S. Constitution. New York State now makes it mandatory for both males and females to serve on juries when called, unless the judge decides to approve a written or in-person request for exemption.

The National Commission on Causes and Prevention of Violence in 1969 found that in California, which seems to be representative of the whole country, 80 percent to 90 percent of the arrests were males. Seven times as many men as women are arrested for crimes which are considered to be serious, while twenty-two males to each female were incarcerated in a state or federal institution (Mulvihill and Tumin, 1969). In 1970 six males were arrested for every female, and yet that same year twenty-one males to every female comprised the population in state and federal institutions (Price, 1977). It is apparent that a higher ratio of males than females are sentenced to prison. It can be argued that the differential view of women, as well as the fact that female crime is not as serious as male crime, influences the disposition of cases (Crites, 1976).

State sentencing statutes for women have often been discriminatory. The Muncy Act in Pennsylvania (1913) provided that any woman over the age of sixteen whose crime by statute required incarceration for more than one year had to be given an indeterminate sentence to the Muncy State Industrial Home for Women. Although a judge was permitted to use his discretion in sentencing men, he was forbidden by law to do so with women. Pennsylvania by law decreed that the sentencing judge is responsible for determining parole if the sentence is under two years, and the responsibility of a parole board if longer. Women sentenced to Muncy automatically came under the jurisdiction of the parole board, which did not permit a legal advocate at its parole hearings. The Muncy Act resulted in women spending twice as long in prison for the same crimes that men committed (Armstrong, 1977).

What was the basis for the Muncy Act? Armstrong believes that it was based on the philosophy that girls who are delinquent have no sexual morality and produce mentally retarded children. If they are sentenced for a long period of time, their sexual delinquency will be curtailed (Armstrong, 1977).

The Gluecks in their book, *Five Hundred Delinquent Women* (1965) presented a case history of a young Irish immigrant called Annie, who at age nineteen married a man twenty-five years older than she was. After several years of marriage, Annie, with her husband's approval, left him and their daughter to live with her lover. Both were arrested on charges of adultery; both pleaded guilty. Annie's lover was given a one-year sentence to the House of Corrections in Massachusetts. Annie with her newborn child was given an indeterminate sentence of five years to the women's reformatory. It is apparent that Annie's transgressions were deemed more aberrant than her lover's.

The Muncy Act was challenged in 1967 by a woman named Daniels, who was originally sentenced to one to four years in a county prison for the commission of a robbery. The court, after one month, changed the sentence to an indeterminate one based on the Muncy Act. Daniels therefore might have had to serve all of the ten years maximally required for the crime instead of the four-year maximum given to her originally. Because of the manner in which the parole board had operated in the past, Daniels would probably not have been eligible for parole until she had served a minimum of three years as opposed to the original sentence. The Pennsylvania Superior Court ruled that there was no violation of the equal protection clause of the Constitution because there was a rationale for treating the two sexes differentially. Fortunately for Daniels and the other women in Pennsylvania, the Pennsylvania Supreme Court later reversed the decision of the Superior Court in ruling that discrimination did exist in sentencing, and that differential eligibility for parole for women and men committing the same crime under relatively similar circumstances was unjustifiable (Kanowitz, 1969).

In 1968 a thirty-eight-year-old woman was arrested and sentenced for breach of the peace and resisting arrest. Connecticut, where the sentencing took place, by law gave indeterminate sentences for these misdemeanors to women over eighteen for not more than three years or longer to coincide with the maximum provided for the particular offense. Misdemeanors committed by men generally incurred a sentence of one year and six months. The justification of the differential sentencing was that by keeping women and juveniles in institutions they could be provided with greater opportunities for rehabilitation

(Kanowitz, 1969). This Connecticut statute was struck down on the basis of the violation of the equal protection clause.

Rans (1978) states that although more females are arrested today than were in the past, and although the basic motivation for the commission of a crime by women is economic, women are not shown partiality during their trials. There is, however, still a reluctance on the part of judges to send women to prison because the crimes they commit are closely related to their sex roles and are nonviolent in nature, therefore, nonthreatening to society. In most cases where women do commit violence, it is related to family members or paramours (Crites, 1976), and when they commit violent acts other than murder they tend to play the role of accomplice or accessory to the fact (Ward et al., 1969). Crites does state, however, that it is in the area of sentencing where women are discriminated against.

Girls who misbehave in our society are still treated more harshly than boys by the judicial system. They are more often sent to institutions for status crimes, and their stay in the penal institution is longer than that of boys. A status crime is an act which would not be considered criminal if it were committed by an adult. These crimes include running away from home, "incorrigibility," violating curfew, truancy, and sexual transgressions. The President's Commission on Law Enforcement and Administration of Justice indicated that girls were sent to prison for antisocial acts which were less serious than those of boys in institutions, and that in 1965 over one-half of the girls who came before Juvenile Court were there because they had committed status offenses (Haft, 1974).

A survey in California of 238,376 persons under eighteen who were arrested found that of the 14 percent who were girls many were arrested for sexual misbehavior. In Detroit, police data indicated that the majority of girls came in contact with the juvenile system for status offenses, while boys were more often arrested for such crimes as burglary or assault (Gibbons, 1976). Girls are more often referred for ungovernability and running away than boys, 53 percent girls, 24 percent boys. They are in many cases products of broken homes and referred to the court by their parents (Datesman and Scarpitti, 1975).

Why is it that sexual transgressions by women are severely punished while similar behavior by men is considered more acceptable and generally not illegal? I would propose that this difference in attitude is the result of the view our society has of women as property, as well as the perpetuation of the myth that women by nature are sweet, passive, nonsexual, and nurturing. The girl who acts out sexually is behaving too much like a boy and must be punished.

Our society exerts greater control over and expects more controlled behavior from our girls than our boys. The sex role expectation for girls is narrower than that for boys, and when girls break through their limits, they are penalized for it. As Chesney-Lind (1977) points out:

> ... it is the symbolic threat by female delinquency to these values that best explains (1) why the juvenile court system selects out aspects of female defiance which violate sex role expectations rather than those that violate legal norms; and (2) why female delinquency, especially sexual delinquency, is viewed as more serious than male delinquency and is, therefore, more severely sanctioned (p. 54).

Sexual acting out behavior by girls was and in some cases still is seen as a terrible threat to society. In the early studies one researcher found that in an institution in Wisconsin housing 252 delinquent girls, case histories noted what was deemed unacceptable sexual behavior in 75 percent. Promiscuity was identified in 40 percent of the cases and about the same percentage of the total number were identified as having VD (Armstrong, 1977).

Looking at the rationale for the establishment of separate institutions for women gives us an understanding of the underlying attitudes toward deviant women. The first reformatory for women was established in 1873 in Indiana and then four years later in Massachusetts. The following report written by the superintendent of the women's reformatory in Massachusetts presents the basic reasons for this action.

> The reformatory was founded in order that women law breakers need not be sent to jails or houses of correction, but might be treated in an institution whose entire purpose should be their development. The problems were not complex as its founders saw it: sin was the cause of crime and conversion the cure ... (*Third Annual Report of the Bureau of Prisons of Massachusetts,* for the year 1918, p. 63).

The goal, then, in establishing reformatories for women was to rehabilitate sex deviants and alcoholics, whereas the Elmira, New York, reformatory was established for boys in 1876 with the prime focus to rehabilitate male felons.

Interest and sometimes obsession with the delinquent girl's sexuality is evident in some training schools. In one such school in Connecticut, the inmates were questioned in depth about their past sexual behavior, and their menstrual cycle. Pregnancy was viewed as punishment for the commission of an immoral act, sexual intercourse (Chesney-Lind, 1977). If a young woman is viewed as perilously close to becoming involved in vice, she can be committed for her own good under the acts which make status offenses crimes. The preoccupation with sex is also apparent in the fact that vaginal smears are automatically taken from girls who come to the attention of the Family Court of New York regardless of whether their transgression involved sex (Armstrong, 1977).

The view that sexually active women are dangerous and must therefore be punished is reflected in an Oklahoma statute which was declared unconstitutional in 1942. This statute made mandatory sterilization of what was termed habitual criminals, who were defined as those who had been committed three times for cases considered of "moral turpitude" other than acts of embezzlement (Gold, 1971).

The fact that almost half of the population in juvenile institutions consisted of minors whose crimes were status offenses rather than criminal offenses prompted states such as California and New York to rewrite their statutes in the early part of the 1960s with other states such as Connecticut following suit. The New York State statute is known as Persons in Need of Services (PINS).

Part of this statute dealt differentially with males and females. It reads:

> Person in need of supervision means a male less than sixteen years of age and a female less than eighteen years of age who does not attend school in accord with the provisions of part one of article sixty-five of the education law or who is incorrigible, ungovernable or habitually disobedient and beyond the lawful control of parent or other lawful authority (N.Y. Judiciary-Family Court Act 712(b) (McKinney Supp. 1971).

Is it not rather contradictory that a female in the State of New York can get married with her parent's consent at age sixteen, a male at age eighteen, but according to the PINS legislation, she is in need of supervision until she is eighteen? Does that mean that a female exchanges her parents for her husband as supervisor? Incorrigibility, ungovernability, and disobedience are such nebulous terms that they are often defined differently according to the sex of the person involved. Sexual promiscuity would be defined more negatively for girls than for boys because of the different cultural behavioral expectations of the two sexes. A large number of the 7000 cases of ungovernable youngsters in a large New York state institution are girls.

It is also interesting to note that although it is an accepted fact that female delinquents benefit by having both men and women in the treatment milieu, for many years the institutions for girls in New York were staffed only with females. This practice was based on the fear that female delinquents would attempt to seduce the male staff or accuse them of seduction (Gold, 1971). The myth of the female as seductress keeps rearing its ugly head.

In California, the statute pertaining to youngsters in need of supervision stated that:

> Any person under the age of 21 . . . who from any cause is in danger of leading an idle, dissolute, lewd or immoral life, is within the jurisdiction of the juvenile court which may adjudge such person to be a ward of the court (California Welfare and Inst. Code & 601 (West Supp. 1970).

A Connecticut statute states that:

> Any unmarried female between the ages of sixteen and twenty-one . . . who is in manifest danger of falling into habits of vice, or who is leading a vicious life, or who had committed any crime . . . may be committed . . . to an institution (Riback, 1971, p. 322).

Note that this statute referred to an unmarried female, whereas the statute appropriate to men had no reference to marital status. Riback states that the disparity in the two statutes in Connecticut serves to control a young female's sexual behavior until she marries, at which time her behavior becomes her husband's responsibility. The socialization process is geared to meeting the needs of males. Woman is seen as inferior, and all of this persuades the judicial approach to female behavior, which implies that females need to be protected more than males (Riback, 1971). Women tend, therefore, to be sentenced for behavior which is not considered serious if committed by a male, and to be given indeterminate sentences which in effect keep them in institutions.

Now that we have brought females through the courts, let us see what is in store for them in the institutions to which they are sent.

The rationale for sending people to prison is rehabilitation but, basically, what we in our society tend to do is to separate and isolate the deviant person from the community, which actually impedes the rehabilitative process. We do this with the mentally ill, the mentally retarded, the incompetent aged, and the criminal as well.

Deviant men and deviant women are, however, perceived differentially. Women, because the types of crimes they had committed were acts which negated their roles in society and were more often crimes against themselves (drunkenness and sex), rather than the more violent, antisocial crimes committed by men, were viewed as potentially rehabilitative. The institutions built to house them are comprised of individual buildings in what is euphemistically called a "cottage complex." The inmates often wear their own clothes. The physical settings of women's institutions are less forbidding than those for men. Barbed wire is nonexistent. Originally, most institutions for women also had farms on which the inmates worked (Gibson, 1976). The prisons were established in rural settings, and because there are so few of them, an offender would sometimes be shipped to an institution in another state, helping even more to isolate the female offender from her family.

Although the physical surroundings of most federal and state institutions for female offenders are palatable, women inmates do not have access to the many types of rehabilitative programs offered to men. They frequently do not have access to work programs, mainly because the institutions are located in rural areas, too far to transport them to urban centers where work would be available. Work programs, if they do exist, are geared to preparing or keeping the offender in her traditional female role. Female offenders are offered programs in sewing and other household skills, in spite of the fact that two out of three women inmates today are above average in intelligence (Price, 1977).

A national survey found that there were an average of about ten programs for job training available to men and only about two for each women's institution (Ramstad, 1975).

Women, like men who are imprisoned, are deprived of some basic needs such as need for control over their own lives as well as the need to feel safe in their environment. To be incarcerated with violent people threatens one's basic sense of security. Because there are few women's prisons, women sentenced for both violent and nonviolent crimes are often housed within the same institutions. There are no separate maximum and minimum security prisons for women. In fact, there are only two federal prisons for women, and generally each state has one institution for female offenders (Clinard, 1974). Women are usually herded into one cell in the county and municipal jails and are unable to participate in rehabilitative programs to which men have access (Price, 1977). In jails in rural areas, female offenders are not adequately separated from males, often do not have women caretakers and are the objects of sexual abuse (McGowan and Blumenthal, 1976). As a result of a suit brought by the women prisoners in a New York prison, restrictions were placed on the use of nonfemale guards. The federal judge ruled that inmates have the right to some minimal privacy. Male guards were assigned to the women's section and therefore gave women little privacy in their toilcting, showering, and undressing (Lubasch, November 26, 1978).

Another example of the disregard for the rights of women surfaced in March, 1979 with the filing of a class action suit by the American Civil Liberties Union against the city of Chicago because of that city's policy of strip-searching women accused of such a minor infraction of the law as a traffic violation. It is estimated that about 10,000 women were searched in this fashion, even though they had been accused of committing a nonserious misdemeanor. The discriminating treatment of women (men are not automatically strip-searched as women are), received wide publicity when a young college student in Chicago was apprehended after making an illegal left turn and not being able to produce her driver's license when stopped by a police officer. She was taken to the police station although the fact was she indeed had a license, and while her friend left to get it, she was stripped, had her anus searched, and then was forced to submit to a vaginal probe by the police matron, who did not bother to wash her hands or use gloves (*Time*, March 19, 1979, p. 36). Apparently indiscriminate strip-searching of women has been a practice in Houston, too.

Because there are so few separate institutions for women, there are more restrictions for them than for men, especially for those who have committed minor crimes. Ward and Kassebaum (1965) feel that isolation from families is a greater deprivation for women than for men because women are socialized to be family oriented and are prepared throughout their early lives to be wives and mothers. A large number of incarcerated women are indeed mothers. In the institution they studied, 68 percent of the inmates were mothers and 59 percent had children who were minors. A national survey of institutions housing a minimum of 25 female inmates found that about two-thirds of the inmates had children, many of whom the women had been responsible for prior to incarceration, and about two-thirds of the children were ten years old or younger (McGowan and Blumenthal, 1976).

If there are no relatives to care for the children left behind, the court places them in foster homes generally without any input or involvement of the incarcerated mother. Sometimes the court views the incarceration of the mother as abandonment of her child and therefore her child becomes legally eligible for adoption (Haley, 1977). In California a child under two is permitted to remain with his/her mother, while other states do not provide opportunities for frequent contacts between mother and minor child, and when women are permitted to have their children visit with them, they are separated from them by glass. Mothers have stated that the greatest difficulty in being in prison was their separation from their children (Haley, 1977).

Counseling programs in Hawaii do not have female personnel, and those women who have to serve more than a two-year sentence are sent to California so they can partake of rehabilitation services. Although there are eight half-way houses for male federal prisoners in the United States, there is not one such facility available for women (Ramstad, 1975).

Juvenile defenders fare even worse. Wooden (1976) found a tremendous disparity between the treatment of male delinquents in training schools and the treatment of girls. Females, he found, often did not have the use of toilets, but were issued containers such as coffee cans and chamber pots, and in one institution punishment for the girls consisted of issuing them soda bottles in which to urinate. In some facilities there was more food available for boys than for girls, and in addition to having access to less food, second helpings were forbidden to the girls. In another institution he found girls suffering from diseases of the skin attributable to poor nutrition. Pregnant girls are often particularly penalized, according to Wooden, by being placed in solitary confinement and by not being offered help in making a decision about the outcome of their pregnancy. Saline injected into the muscles was a form of punishment used in Massachusetts until the early 1970s (Wooden, 1976). He very aptly named the book he wrote describing these conditions as *Weeping in the Playtime of Others.*

An increasing number of women are turning to crime. An increasing number of them are apprehended, sentenced, and incarcerated. Facilities for women have not kept up with the numbers they are expected to house, nor have the rehabilitative programs within the institutions. The nature of crimes committed by women is also changing and is influenced by the change in the traditional roles that women were expected to play. To Henry Higgins, who asked, "Why can't a woman be more like a man?" the answer may very well be she is getting there but her treatment is still inequitable.

References

Anon. The women's movement and crime. International City Management Association, Washington, D.C. *Target* 6, No. 8 (September 1977).

_____. Outrage in the Station. *Time* 36 (March 19, 1979).

_____. Third Annual Report of the Bureau of Prisons of Massachusetts, for the year 1918.

_____. *Uniform Crime Statistics for the United States.* Washington, D.C.: U.S Government Printing Office, 1977.

_____. *Uniform Crime Reports for the United States.* Washington, D.C.: U.S. Government Printing Office, 1978.

Abrahamsen, David. *The Psychology of Crime.* New York: Columbia University Press, 1960.

Adler, Freda. *Sisters in Crime.* New York: McGraw-Hill Book Co., 1975.

Anderson, Etta A. The chivalrous treatment of the female offender in the arms of the criminal justice system: a review of the literature. *Social Problems* 23:350–357 (February 1976).

Armstrong, Gail. Females under the law—protected but unequal. *Crime and Delinquency* 23:109–120 (April 1977).

Blackstone, Sir William. *Commentaries on the Laws of England.* Vol. 11, William Craig Jones (ed.). San Francisco: Bancroft-Whiting Co., 1916.

Bloch, Herbert A. and Geis, Gilbert. *Man, Crime and Society.* New York: Random House, 1962.

Blumenthal, Walter Hart. *Brides from Bridewell.* Rutland, Vermont: Charles E. Tuttle, 1962.

Chesney-Lind, Meda. Judicial paternalism and the female status offender. *Crime and Delinquency* 23:121–130 (April 1977).

Clinard, Marshall B. *Sociology of Deviant Behavior.* New York: Holt, Rinehart & Winston, 1974.

Crites, Laura (ed.). *The Female Offender.* Lexington, Mass.: D. C. Heath & Company, 1976.

Datesman, Susan K. and Scarpitti, Frank R. Female delinquency and broken homes. *Criminology* 13:33–55 (May 1975).

Freud, Sigmund. *A General Introduction to Psychoanalysis.* Garden City, New York: Garden City Publishing Company, 1943.

Gibbons, Don C. *Delinquent Behavior.* Englewood Cliffs, N.J.: Prentice-Hall, 1976.

Gibson, Helen E. Women's prisons: laboratories for penal reform, in Laura Crites. *The Female Offender.* Lexington, Mass.: D. C. Heath & Co., 1976.

Glueck, Sheldon and Glueck, Eleanor T. *Five Hundred Delinquent Women.* New York: Kraus Reprint Corporation, 1965.

Gold, Sarah. Equal protection for juvenile girls in need of supervision in New York state. *New York Law Forum* **17**:570–598 (1971).

Goode, William J. Violence between intimates, in Donald J. Mulvihill and Melvin M. Tumin (eds.). *Crimes of Violence* 13. Washington, D.C.: U.S. Government Printing Office, 1969.

Haft, Marilyn. Women in prison: discriminatory practices and some legal solutions. *Clearinghouse Review* **8**:1–6 (May 1974).

Haley, Kathleen. Mothers behind bars: a look at the parental rights of incarcerated women. *New England Journal of Prison Law* **4**:141–155 (Fall 1977).

Hoffman-Bustamente, Dale. The nature of female criminality. *Issues in Criminology* **8**:117–136 (Fall 1973).

Hovey, Marcia. The forgotten offenders. *Manpower Magazine.* U.S. Department of Labor, January, 1971.

Kanowitz, Leo. *Women and the Law: The Unfinished Revolution.* Albuquerque, N.M.: University of New Mexico Press, 1969.

Katzeff, Paul. Equal crime. *Boston Magazine* 107–108, 206–210 (December 1977).

Klein, Doris. The etiology of female crime: a review of the literature. *Issues in Criminology* **8**:3–30 (Fall 1973).

Konopka, Gisela. *The Adolescent Girl in Conflict.* Englewood Cliffs, N.J.: Prentice-Hall, 1966.

Lombroso, Caesar and Ferrero, William. *The Female Offender.* New York: D. Appleton, 1899.

Longfellow, Henry Wadsworth. There Was a Little Girl, in Iona and Peter Opie (ed.). *The Oxford Book of Childrens' Verses.* New York and Oxford: Oxford University Press, 1973.

Lubasch, Arnold. Men Guards Limited at Women's Prison. *New York Times* 56 (November 26, 1978).

Marsh, Thomas O. Women and violent behavior: natural cycle suspected as link in crime. *Science Digest* 65–66 (September 1978).

McGowan, Brenda G. and Blumenthal, Karen L. Children of women prisoners: a forgotten minority, in Laura Crites (ed.). *The Female Offender.* Lexington, Mass.: ?. C. Heath, 1976.

Mulvihill, Donald J. and Tumin, Melvin M. (eds.). *Crimes of Violence.* Washington, D.C.: U.S. Government Printing Office, December, 1969.

Parlee, M. B. The premenstrual syndrome. *Psychological Bulletin* **80**:454–465 (1973).

Pollak, Otto. *The Criminality of Women.* Philadelphia: University of Pennsylvania Press, 1950.

Price, Ray R. The forgotten female offender. *Crime and Delinquency* **23**:101–108 (April 1977).

Ramstad, Sheryl A. Female offenders: a challenge to courts and the legislature. *North Dakota Law Review* **51**:827–853 (Summer 1975).

Rans, Laurel L. Women's crime: much ado about . . . ? *Federal Probation* **42**:45–49 (March 1978).

Riback, Linda. Juvenile delinquency laws: juvenile women and the double standard of morality. *U.C.L.A. Law Review* **19**:313–342 (December 1971).

Simon, Rita James. *Women and Crime*. Lexington, Mass.: D. C. Heath, 1977.

Stromberg, Ann H. and Harkess, Shirley. *Women Working*. Palo Alto, Calif.: Mayfield, 1978.

Sutherland, Edwin H. and Cressey, Donald R. *Principles of Criminology*, 7th edition. Philadelphia: J. P. Lippincott, 1966.

Thomas, W. I. *Sex and Society*. Boston: Little, Brown, 1907.

_____. *The Unadjusted Girl*. Boston: Little, Brown and Co., 1923.

Vedder, Clyde B., and Sommerville, Dora B. *The Delinquent Girl*. Springfield, Illinois: Charles C. Thomas, 1970.

Ward, David A. and Kassebaum, Gene G. *Women's Prison*. Chicago: Aldine Publishing, 1965.

Ward, David A., Jackson, Maurice and Ward, Reneé E. Crimes of violence by women, in Donald J. Mulvihill and Melvin M. Tumin. *Crimes of Violence*. National Commission on the Causes and Prevention of Violence. Washington, D.C.: U.S. Government Printing Office, 1969.

Wolfgang, Marvin E. A sociological analysis of criminal homicide, in Marvin Wolfgang (ed.). *Studies in Homicide*. New York: Harper & Row, Publishers, 1967.

_____. *Patterns in Criminal Homicide*. Philadelphia: University of Pennsylvania Press, 1958.

Wooden, Kenneth. *Weeping in the Playtime of Others*. New York: McGraw-Hill Book Company, 1976.

7. To Love, Cherish and Batter

Rap Brown once said that "Violence is as American as apple pie." Although he seemed to be referring to revolution, war, and racial violence, violence in America permeates personal relationships as well. The National Commission on the Causes and Prevention of Violence found that 13 percent of its representative American sample had experienced being slapped or kicked as adults, and 18 percent stated that they themselves had at some time in their adult lives slapped or kicked another person. Forty-one percent of the sample openly admitted ownership of a gun (Mulvihill and Tumin, 1969).

What do we know about violence in the family in the United States? The *New York Times* reported in 1972 that during a six-month period in New York City the number of people killed by relatives approximated the number of people killed in Ireland during three-and-one-half years of its civil disturbance (Steinmetz and Straus, 1973). In 1969 in the United States, one-quarter of the murders committed were committed within the family and more than one-half of these were interspousal. The FBI reported in 1963 that almost one-third of the intentional murders were intrafamilial, as well as two-thirds of the serious assault cases (Truninger, 1971). These statistics support Wolfgang's classic study of 5888 criminal homicides in Philadelphia between 1948 and 1952. He found that in one-half of the murders, the victim and offender were either friends or relatives. In 24.7 percent of the cases they were members of the same family. He also found that those murders involving spouses were more violent than others. Of 136 intrafamily homicides studied, 100 victims were spouses, 9 were sons and 8 were daughters (Wolfgang, 1958).

The FBI reports that in homicides which involve spouses the wife is the victim 54 percent of the time (Truninger, 1971). Other statistics which "boggle the mind" include the fact that 60 percent of all the calls in Atlanta received by the police during the night are calls involving domestic quarrels. Boston receives about forty-five daily calls of this kind. Domestic disturbances account for one-third of the homicides in Kansas City, and 31 percent of the aggravated assault cases treated in Boston City Hospital emergency room are women who have been assaulted in their homes, usually by their husbands or lovers (*Response,* October, 1976). Violence in the family is fact, not fiction. Half of the cases handled by Chicago's Court of Domestic Relations are assaults within the family (Parnas, 1967). O'Brien (1971) found that in his study of couples involved in divorce suits, 48 percent reported that incidences of violence were a regularly occurring phenomenon. Levinger's (1966) study revealed that 40 percent of the working-class women and 23 percent of the middle-class women gave physical abuse as a reason for divorce.

The false idea of the family as a sanctuary, as a haven, and as a positive support system is slowly fading. Abuse of children, like abuse of women, has occurred since time immemorial. It is interesting to note that the American Society for the Protection of Children was formed *after* the American Society for the Prevention of Cruelty to Animals. The story of its inception is as follows. In 1871 Mary Ellen was found by a group of church workers badly battered, tied to her bed, and undernourished. The perpetrators of this abuse had to be tried under the law which forbade cruelty to animals, because there was no comparable law for children at that time. Mary Ellen's case was responsible for the establishment of the American Society for the Protection of Children.

As one can see, children were considered to be the property of their caretakers to do with as they wished, and the privacy of the home was considered sacrosanct.

Although Mary Ellen's case occurred in the 1800s child abuse is still rampant today in spite of legal efforts to stop it. It is estimated that about 3 million children are abused each year (*Parade,* September 16, 1979, p. 8).

The family, as well as the society in general, supports physical punishment. In many states paddling a child in school for misbehavior is still legal, the death penalty has been reinstated in a number of states, and very few people would make the physical punishment of a child by parents an illegal act, although a law against slapping a child was recently passed in Sweden. Violence is therefore condoned and has become institutionalized by society.

Violence can be defined as

> . . . intentional use of force on another person. The physical force can be used for a variety of purposes: (1) to cause pain and injury as an end in itself (what might be called expressive violence); (2) the use of pain and injury or physical restraint as a punishment to induce the other person to carry out some act (which might be called instrumental violence). (Steinmetz and Straus, 1974, p. 4).

Simply, violence is ". . . any behavior which threatens or causes physical damage to an object or person" (O'Brien, 1971, p. 692). What is the difference between force and violence? Perhaps force is considered to be an acceptable norm while violence is an act which is considered to be socially non-normative. It is okay to punish a child by slapping him but not okay to slap him so hard that visible bruises result.

The mystique of the family as the peaceful cradle of safety and emotional support has influenced the lack of attention given to the family violence that does occur. Most recently, concern for the battered child has mushroomed so that legislation and services have grown to meet the needs of these objects of abuse. For battered women, however, consciousness has not been sufficiently raised, resulting in minimal public awareness and therefore limited community action.

Recent research supports the thesis that if violence in America is a common phenomenon, so is wife battering. Interestingly enough, although one can find voluminous material on violence in general, there has until recently been a sparcity of writing and research on physically abused wives. Wife battering, like rape, is beginning to come out of the closet, and as it does, we find that violence between spouses is a common occurrence.

Langley and Levy (1977) estimate that spouse abuse occurs in almost half of the marriages in this country, and FBI figures indicate that wife abuse is three times as common as rape (Kamisher, 1976).

Much of the tacit acceptance of wife abuse is culturally determined and grows out of a patriarchal system in which married women have had few, if any, rights. In many early societies, marriage by purchase existed, and it was the father who owned the daughter and who sold her to another man. Actually, according to anthropologists Hobhouse,

Wheeler and Ginsberg (1930), 303 out of the 434 tribes studied made use of what is called the progeny price in arranging marriages. This means that the woman's family is paid a price, ten cows, for example, in exchange for the loss of the young woman to her family and the loss of all future offspring she might produce. The woman's status is closely correlated with the amount of barter that is paid for her by the groom and his family. Apparently, this type of marital arrangement is commonly found in Africa (Hoebel, 1966). It is clear that one of the basic values of a woman lies in her ability to produce children and, until recently, our own society laid stress on the importance of women bearing children in marriage, because this was regarded as the fulfillment of their destiny and their reason for being.

Marriage by capture, although not necessarily the most often used technique in acquiring a wife, did exist. The Plains Indians practiced this type of bride selection. Sometimes captured women became slaves, not wives. In those cultures where bride capture no longer exists, mock capture is practiced as a remnant of the other more violent method of getting one's own woman. Among the Bushmen of southern Africa the groom grabs the bride at the wedding celebration and tries to abscond with her. He can keep his bride if he continues to hang onto her as her relatives beat him. The African Bahima bride becomes the target between her group and the bridegroom's people as each side tugs at her. The bridegroom's side finally wins and off they run, carrying the bride while her relatives merrily run after her (Hoebel, 1966).

Although bride price did not necessarily give a husband a right to do harm to his wife, payment for a woman, marriage by capture, and patriarchy in general, became fertile soil for the abuse of women, who were not, of course, given the same privileges.

Our Judeo-Christian tradition is basically patriarchal in nature and establishes the husband as superior and master to his wife. In ancient Assyria a woman was forbidden to strike her husband but her husband had the right to hit her. According to Cato, the Roman rule was that "If you find your wife in the act of adultery the law permits you to kill her without trial. If by chance she surprises you in the same condition, she must not touch you even with the tips of her fingers; the law forbids her" (Gellius, X:23 in Durant, 1953, p. 59). Under the Julian law a husband could kill his wife's lover but was forbidden to kill his wife unless he found her in an adulterous situation in his own home.

The patriarchal power is reinforced in the Old Testament. God becomes angry with both Adam and Eve for having eaten of the forbidden fruit but he says to Eve:

> I will greatly multiply thy pain in childbearing; in pain you shall bring forth children, yet your desire shall be for your husband, and he shall rule over you (Genesis 3:16).

The Christian church did not relieve wives of the iron fist of their husbands. "Wives," said St. Paul, "be subject to your husbands, as to the Lord. For the husband is the head of the wife" (Ephesians 5:22–23).

During the Renaissance, San Bernardin wrote about the guidelines for beating one's wife:

> And I say to you, men, never beat your wives while they are great with child, for therein would lie great peril. I say not that you should never beat them; but choose your time ... I know men who have more regard for a hen that lays a fresh egg daily than for their own wives. Sometimes a hen would break a pot or a cup, but the man will not beat her, for fear of losing the egg that is her fruit. How stark mad, then, as many that cannot suffer a word from their own lady who bears such fair fruit! For if she speak a word more than he thinks fit, forthwith he seizes a staff and begins to chastize her; and the hen, when she cackles all day without ceasing, you suffer patiently for her egg's sake (San Bernardin in Coulton, 1908, p. 14).

Unfortunately, even today many men beat their wives, especially during pregnancy.

Our common law and many of the attitudes we have toward women were brought over to the colonies from England. In the early 1600s women sold themselves to settlers in the colonies. "aggreeable persons, young and incorrupt ... sold them with their own consent to settlers as wives at the cost of their transportation" (Beard and Beard, 1930, p. 44). This practice was a remnant of marriage by purchase and placed women in the position of being the property of their husbands.

Under English common law, a husband and wife were considered to be legally one person. It was the husband, however, who had the power. At marriage women were relegated to civic death since they lost their individual legal and property rights. They could not sign contracts, could not sue, maintain title to their own earnings or property, even property they inherited, and in case of legal separation did not have title to their children (Kanowitz, 1969).

Man and wife are one person, but understand in what manner. When a small brooke or little river incorporateth with Rhodanus, Humber or the Thames, the poor riveulet looseth its name, it is carried and recarried with the new associate, it beareth no sway, it possesseth nothing during coverture. A woman as soon as she is married, is called covert in Latin, nupta, that is veiled, as it were, clouded, and overshadowed, she hath lost her streame ... To a married woman, her new self is her superior, her companion, her master (*The Lawes Resolution of Women's Rights* or *the Lawes Provision for Women*, 1632, pp. 124–125).

The commentaries of Sir William Blackstone, the well-known British jurist of the mid-1700s, were incorporated into the common law which was followed in the colonies. Blackstone gave full power to husbands over their wives and wrote "For, as (husband) is to answer for her misbehavior, the law thought it reasonable to intrust him with this power of chastisement, in the same moderation that a man is allowed to correct his apprentices or children ..." (Blackstone, *Commentaries*, 1765). Women continued to be viewed as and treated as children for many years. To some extent they are still viewed in this manner today.

As late as the early 1800s husbands in the United States were still permitted the right to chastise their wives.

In *Bradley* vs. *State*, Walker 158, Mississippi 1824, it was decided that:

Perhaps the husband should still be permitted to exercise the right to moderate chastisement, in cases of great emergency and use salutary restraints in every case of misbehavior, without subjecting himself to vexatious prosecutions resulting in the discredit and shame of all parties (Calvert, 1974, p. 88).

The ruling was overturned in *Harris* vs. *State* (14 S 266, 1894).

An 1874 North Carolina decision bluntly stated that the barbaric doctrine which permitted a husband to whip his wife as long as the switch he used was not larger than his thumb was no longer permitted.

Not until the Married Women's Act of 1839, first passed in Mississippi, did a married woman gain the right to own and control property, sue and be sued as an individual without her husband, work without his consent, and keep the money she earned. Single women over a certain age always had such civic rights.

Although there have been tremendous strides in viewing women as independent legal entities, vestiges of the woman as her husband's property still exist in America today.

Until recently most states had statutes prescribing formal procedures for changing names, but many of these same states exempted married women from the opportunity of taking advantage of these procedures (Kanowitz, 1969). When a husband legally changed his name, his wife's name automatically changed at the same time. However, there were no provisions for the reverse unless he consented.

Until recently, too, a married woman's legal residence was that of her husband's and in some states a married woman is entitled to possessions in the home after a divorce only if she can prove that she has paid for them.

A wife, then, is still not an independent entity and still the object of abuse.

It is estimated that today over 200,000 American husbands consistently batter their spouses (Zullo, 1976). The National Commission on the Causes and Prevention of Violence found that one out of four men and one out of six women approved of slapping a spouse under certain conditions. Many wives believe that given a certain circumstance, the husband should beat his wife (Parnas, 1967).

The family is a social unit which has become increasingly isolated. Since family members now work away from home, the family and the interactions within it have become less observable. Since social control and observability are positively correlated, what happens within the family unit is private and therefore less subject to accountability to others (Laslett, 1973). There is, therefore, no one to interfere with the violence, and so there is a greater tendency for violence to occur since the negative sanctions of others are unavailable. Battering is viewed as a private, family affair, and beating one's wife is considered to be a marital prerogative.

To some researchers power seems to be the overriding influence on battering one's wife. What better way is there to demonstrate who is in control than by the use of force? Very often the battering is triggered off by a minor event, such as the wife's refusal to get up out of bed at three in the morning in order to prepare food for a hungry, intoxicated husband, or for buttering the bread incorrectly. One woman I know was beaten by her husband if she served him soup which he considered too hot.

Whitehurst (1974) suggests that husbands who beat wives do so because of actual loss of or perceived loss of power. It is important to point out that the abusers who can be considered mentally ill are comparable in number to those of the total population who are defined as mentally ill (Straus, 1973). So men who batter are generally of normal mental health.

A study of twenty-three men in custody on charges of having assaulted their wives or cohabitors revealed the following: The husband was generally suspicious and jealous, had a tremendous need to assert himself and an inability to tolerate any threat by his wife to his superordinate position. The violent act is often precipitated by a minor event that is interpreted as a threat to the husband's superior position (Faulk, 1974). According to Gelles (1972) although wife battering crosses class lines ". . . violence is more prevalent in families where the husband fails to possess the achieved skills and status upon which his ascribed superior status as head of the household is based" (Gelles, 1972, pp. 137–138).

It has been suggested that there is a subculture of violence and that this subculture exists in those parts of American society which have little power to wield: the poor including blacks and other minorities (Wolfgang and Ferracuti, 1967).

Wolfgang's theory (Wolfgang and Ferracuti, 1967) of a subculture of violence was developed as a result of a study he made of crimes in the 1940s and 1950s. He found that most of the murders seemed to occur among a small portion of society. He concluded that this segment of society was separated from the dominant group and that within it existed norms and values containing expectations of violent behavior. For instance, he found that most of the murders he studied were committed by young males, usually black. It is people in the lower levels of the social structure whose resources are limited, who are unable to achieve goals, and who are therefore frustrated, who resort to violence. The more available resources an individual has, the less tendency there is to use overt force. Violence is used as a last resort when there are no other alternatives available (Goode, 1971). We can therefore conclude that the husband with low status, little income, and limited education would tend to use violence as a mechanism for coping more often than the individual with high status, good income, and education.

However, there are those who state that physical violence is characteristic of all socio-economic groups. "The middle class is not only as likely as others ever to have engaged in physical aggression, but has done so as often" (Stark and McEvoy, 1970, p. 53). These researchers posit that because of lack of privacy, acts of violence committed by the poor tend to come to the attention of the police and therefore become more public.

Job loss can precipitate violent behavior. In Birmingham, England, a six-month period when unemployment noticeably increased correlated with an increase in cases of wife battering (Steinmetz and Straus, 1973).

Alcohol is an important agent in violence. Lunde (1976) found that there is a close relationship between the amount of alcohol drunk and the commission of violent crime. Gelles (1972) noted that alcohol was positively related to incidences of wife abuse in about half the cases he studied. He raises the questions as to whether the alcohol intake impacts on the battering of one's wife or whether the individual drinks in order to disclaim responsibility for his violent behavior.

Jealousy is another personality characteristic of battering husbands. Spouses who batter feel insecure in their relationships and tend to abreact to perceived threats to their marriage. This may account for, or be the result of, the social isolation that families where wives are battered, as well as families where children are battered, find themselves in.

The existence of the double standard in our society relating to sexual behavior creates problems for the wife who violates the sexual norm of monogamy and for the wife who is defined by her husband as a transgressor. Our society builds in protection for the wife when her husband strays sexually. Although the wife is very hurt by her husband's infidelity, she may be able to forgive him because the myth in our culture is that man, by nature, is not monogamous. Whitehurst (1974) suggests that when we accept the idea that women are also interested in sex, perhaps when women do stray, husbands will not necessarily respond violently. We are not suggesting, and we do not think Whitehurst was suggesting that wife battering is usually caused by the woman's infidelity.

The mechanism of projection is one which is frequently used by the wife abuser. According to Elbow (1977), the abuser projects onto his wife the cause of the marital discord. His need for his wife's compliance is so strong that he does not allow her independence. His conflicting feelings of antagonism and need for dependence on his mother are transferred to his wife.

Why does a man need to resort to violence in order to maintain his homeostasis? Margaret Elbow (1977), the director of a family agency, discusses the common characteristics of wife abusers. As stated earlier, one of the basic mechanisms of defense of most abusers is that of projection. The batterer is unable to accept responsibility for his own behavior and projects the blame for his actions onto his wife. It is his wife's fault that he gets drunk or beats her, because she does not behave properly.

The abuser also has a strong need to have his wife adhere to his concept of a wife's role behavior. He becomes terribly upset if she does not. She is not permitted to be autonomous. He views her as an extension of himself.

Elbow (1977) also states that the abuser transfers onto his wife the feelings he has toward a significant person in his life such as his mother. He thus imbues his wife with traits that he feels the significant other possesses. Because the abuser has specific rather rigid expectations of what his marriage should be like, he expects his spouse to become like the person he thinks she should be.

Elbow (1977) points out that because the abuser often has some redeeming qualities, it is difficult for his wife to leave him. He does, however, find difficulty in being intimate; that is, giving and receiving affection and pleasure. Sexually, his behavior communicates to his partner that she is there to satisfy him, that her own satisfaction is immaterial, and that she is an object for release of his sexual needs.

In an attempt to understand why men abuse their spouses, Elbow divided the abuse syndrome into four categories. One such category is the controller. He is an individual who always gets what he wants, who uses people to achieve his desires, is often involved in illegal or semilegal activities, is not sensitive to his wife's needs, insists on controlling her activities, and becomes abusive when he feels that he is losing command.

The defender, on the other hand, like the controller, likes women whom he can dominate. Unlike the controller, this type of individual needs to have his spouse lean on him. He adheres to moral guidelines, and fears independence by his wife because he needs to feel he is protecting her, and because he also fears retaliation (actually unconsciously by his mother, whom the spouse represents) for his sexual and aggressive feelings, which were not allowed expression when he was a child.

The approval seeker, another type of abuser, is one whose need to achieve is never met because it is insatiable. He does not feel good about himself, he is self-rejecting. He seeks a wife who can nurture him and abuses her when he feels threatened, but stops quickly and feels guilty about what he has done. He encourages his wife to go for counseling but will not participate in the counseling sessions unless his wife threatens to leave him or actually leaves him.

The incorporator is the most dangerous type of abuser. He is desperate, generally abuses drugs or alcohol, cannot separate his identity from that of his wife, is extremely jealous, and is not dampened by the presence of family or friends in his need to attack or even kill his spouse.

Perhaps, instead of lumping all batterers into one category, viewing each situation individually may be helpful towards developing a treatment goal for each. This is also true, of course, for those who are being battered.

It is a fairly common myth in our society that women like to be treated roughly by men and that women enjoy being controlled by physical means (Whitehurst, 1974). Snell et al. (1964) studied twelve families out of thirty-seven where the husbands had been charged with assault and battery and referred to a psychiatric clinic. They labeled the wives they studied as masochistic and concluded that like the wife of the alcoholic, "a husband's behavior may serve to fill a wife's needs even though she protests it" (p. 110). This attitude affects the type of treatment abused wives receive and their self-image.

The tendency to discount complaints by women as being psychosomatic or exaggerated is demonstrated by the results of a study published in the *British Medical Journal.* In 1975 the Journal reported that seventy-one out of one hundred abused women who sought medical care for the effects of abuse were given antidepressants and tranquilizers. Forty who sought psychiatric help were given shock therapy (Edmiston, 1976). The victim herself is seen as the problem, rather than the problem being understood as one of victimization.

Gelles found that the battered wives in his study often felt that they deserved to be struck because they nagged (Gelles, 1972). One family service agency described to me how one woman, whose husband had difficulty with his impulse control, would argue with him while she was ironing. When he left the room in order to avoid striking her, she would follow him with her iron. Finally, when he lost control and burned her she would scream that he was trying to kill her. However, to assume the victim precipitated the violence is to deny the husband's responsibility for his behavior. No act of physical violence is justified by the fact that a person was verbally abused.

In many cases nagging is not necessarily the prelude to battering, often the victim simply happens to be accessible. One of the battered women I interviewed stated that no matter how hard she tried to be compliant, she ended up being beaten by her husband. "It was really a no-win situation." Another woman spoke about her battering being precipitated by her expression of anger with her husband's extramarital affairs. Scott states that research in the future will not support masochism as a prime factor in wife beating (Scott, 1974).

Hilberman and Munson's (1977) in-depth study of sixty battered women found that what appeared to be masochism was really intense passivity as a result of the "paralyzing terror," and fear of the inability to control the aggression they felt. The women felt worthless, incompetent, and powerless. They had been the objects of rejection by their own parents, rejection which had often been reinforced by the legal system as well as by social agencies. The women in the Hilberman and Munson study demonstrated chronic anxiety, inability to sleep, disturbed sleep patterns, and an abreaction to anger, thunder, lightning, and sirens. The passive reaction covers the extreme anger felt and is the women's method of protecting themselves from the effects of their own rage which is of homicidal intensity.

Many women who are battered loathe the battering but find it difficult to leave a terrifying situation. Shame is an important factor. The battered wife feels ashamed to let other people know about her situation. Like the rape victim, the battered wife often feels that there is something wrong with her, and that somehow she is responsible for or deserves the beatings. There is a sense of failure in the marriage and because wives in our society often feel that success or failure in marriage is their responsibility, women whose marriages are troubled feel guilt and a sense of failure (Owens, 1975). One young woman who married at seventeen against her parents' desires did not tell them of her abuse because "she made her bed and had to lie in it."

There is very often an emotional tie to the person who is the assaulter. The *New York Times* (October 10, 1976, p. 49) published a story entitled *Love Story* about a young woman who tried to break off a relationship with a Bronx lawyer when she found out that he was married. He, because of the rage around being rejected, hired some thugs to blind her with lye in 1959 so that she would not be attractive to any other man. After he had served fourteen years in jail, the woman married the lawyer who had blinded her. In 1976 the victim requested that her husband, who had been disbarred, should be permitted to practice law again. She stated that she loved him, that he was really a good man, and that she was really the one who suffered because of his inability to practice law.

A battered woman finds it difficult to take action against her husband. She often finds herself in a financial bind. The battered wife is generally not economically independent and has few, if any, marketable skills as well as no place to run to. Living with a battering husband is therefore seen as better than trying to make it alone (Owens, 1975).

Violence most often occurs in the home, specifically in the kitchen, generally with no nonfamily member present and usually at night (Gelles, 1972).

Wives are often beaten when they are pregnant. In ten out of forty-four families where violence occurred, the wives were pregnant at the time (Gelles, 1972). Could sexual frustration and/or jealousy be a factor? Or does the strain, financial or emotional, as well as the defenselessness of the wife at this time, play a role? Pregnant women are generally more vulnerable to attacks by their husbands. If people are perceived as nonretaliatory, then, as Howard Kaplan (1972) states, aggression is more likely to occur.

The victim of an aggressive attack is very often devalued. People need to feel that there is some order and justice in the world. Like the rape victim, the victim of wife abuse is considered to have somehow deserved her lot. An experiment with college students in which a rape victim was described supports this concept. The married woman or virgin was thought to be more at fault than the divorced woman in the rape attack. The greater responsibility was attributed to those people for whom it was difficult to explain rape. The need to support justice in the world results in attributing responsibility to the victim (Lerner, 1970). The battered wife is met with skepticism and sometimes hostility. "Any woman dumb enough to marry such a jerk deserves what she gets," said a family court judge (*Ladies Home Journal,* June, 1974, p. 66).

It is fairly universally accepted that behavioral norms are learned. Behavioral aggression can be learned by parental modeling. Bandura states that observation of parental behavior is as important a learning phenomenon as is the direct rewarding and punishing of behavior (Bandura, 1973).

It is in the family that norms and values are learned. Violence is behavior which is learned, and parents are the important role models for children. Women who observed violence between their parents are more likely to become battered wives than those women whose parents were nonviolent. In addition, Gelles (1972) found that a large number of the men in the families he studied came from homes where violence existed or themselves had been treated violently. A large number of battered wives have been found to have had fathers who were violent, and these wives had married early in order to escape a perilous home situation (Scott, 1974). There also appears to be a correlation between the frequency of being hit as a child and the likelihood of being hit by one's husband (Gelles, 1976). Gelles proposes that because a woman is hit in childhood, she views being struck as the norm and that her expectations of being the object of physical force motivate her husband to do so. Again we see an example of blaming the victim and allowing the victimizer to defer taking responsibility for his abusiveness. Perhaps, though, as Gelles points out, a woman raised in a violent home is more likely to marry a potentially violent person than a woman raised in a home where physical abuse was not used. The fact that women are viewed as legitimate objects of violence certainly has an effect.

Incest and wife abuse seem to have some relationship. One shelter for battered women in Arizona conducted a study of incest, using as its subjects 100 women whom it had served. Twenty-three percent of those studied had given a positive response and of these, 60.5 percent had had a sexual encounter with a family member before they reached the age of fifteen, and this encounter created severe psychic pain (*Response* 2, January, 1979). Fathers who committed incest were also known to be physically abusive to members of their family (Meiselman, 1978). One father not only involved his daughter in an incestuous relationship but also sadistically battered his wife while having sexual relations with her because it "turned him on."

Female incest victims seem to marry men who abuse them both physically and emotionally. Although they do not necessarily like being abused, they tolerate this treatment and allow themselves to be treated as punching bags. Meiselman points out that girls who are the objects of father-daughter incest feel that they have been used. Their relationship with men is therefore one of being victimized.

One study of battered women, consisting of those who were married or were living with a man, found that the women had normal I.Q.s, had difficulty in expressing emotion, tended to withdraw from interpersonal relationships, and had little self-esteem. They had to cope with a great deal of stress in their environment, had a less than supportive early life experience and demonstrated a great deal of anxiety and fear. A large number of these women escaped from an unhappy parental environment into marriage and a number of them were pregnant at the time. They held traditional concepts of the roles of husband and wife in the marital relationship. The husband did not help with the household chores even when he was unemployed, and the husbands dominated their lives, were not affectionate, and they were forced to submit to their husband's sexual advances at his desire. The women did not feel that they should have been beaten but did take responsibility for somehow causing the assault. They saw their man as having difficulties, felt sorry for him, and although they threatened to obtain a divorce after they were assaulted, they did not carry through on this threat. Instead, they resorted to periodic separations (Star et al., 1979).

Thus, we see battered women as basically insecure, dependent, nonassertive, self-deprecating individuals who are often immobilized and unable to take action to change their lot.

The battered wife is usually unable to share her difficulty with others. She is ashamed, feels that she has in some way been responsible for the difficulty and is also afraid that her husband will beat her more if she tells. She remains in the household, sometimes fearful of her life, often sporting a black eye and as I saw recently at a wedding, dancing cheek to cheek with her "loving" spouse.

What finally motivates her to leave or to reach out for some help? Reaching out usually occurs after repeated attempts at making up and hearing promises that the abuse will not happen again. When it is obvious to the wife (and this differs with each woman) that the husband's promises will not be kept, there is a greater chance that she will leave him (Truninger, 1971). The severity of the violent attacks is also correlated with the wish to seek outside aid (Gelles, 1976). Gelles found that the frequency with which a woman was struck affected what method of intervention she sought. Being hit monthly or weekly apparently resulted in taking immediate action like asking for police intervention, going to a social agency, separating or divorcing. Those hit on a daily basis are more likely to turn to the police, while those hit less frequently turn to the courts for separation or a dissolution of the marriage. Gelles also found that the woman with few resources, for example no job or little education, is less likely to seek help, and teenage children are instrumental in giving their mother support to take action. One mother I knew suffered a broken arm, numerous bruises and other injuries but remained with her assaultive husband until he began to batter their two-year-old daughter. At that point she left him, went home to her own mother, only to return to her beloved batterer several months later.

About as many women kill their husbands as men kill their wives. Wolfgang reported that a large number of homicides in which a female kills a male, especially if the woman is the man's wife, are what he called "victim precipitated" murders (Wolfgang and Ferracuti, 1967). One reason may be that wives are often provoked by their husbands. One woman who was seven months pregnant grabbed a broom stick, after having been beaten on several occasions, and as her husband lunged towards her, she stabbed him through the heart. Roxanne Gay stabbed her husband, Blenda Gay. He stood at 6 feet 5 inches, weighed 255 pounds and played for the Philadelphia Eagles. He met his death in December, 1976, after repeated beatings from him and no support from the police, whom she called on several occasions. Instead of protecting her from her husband, they suggested that he walk off his anger, and then discussed football with him.

A thirty-three-year-old woman used a kitchen knife to end the life of her lover, who had beaten her on at least twenty-five occasions. He had previously beaten her with a blackjack, hit and kicked her as well as ripped off her clothes. If she became unconscious, he would revive her with cold water and then resume his assaults. He also was 6 feet 5 inches tall and weighed in at about 260 pounds. After she had stabbed him, he still came towards her. She was convicted of manslaughter and sentenced to life in prison.

A study of assaults on women in the City of Springfield, Massachusetts, in which the victim named a "boyfriend" or "husband" as the assailant indicated that fists were most commonly used as the weapon and battering with feet was a close second (Hirsch, 1977). Boyfriends were more creative than husbands and used pipes, cars, clubs, and chains as their weapons.

When a woman does defend herself, she is apt to use a weapon thus equalizing her ability to cope with a usually physically stronger male.

Increasingly women are pleading justifiable homicide in the slayings of their wife-beating husbands and increasingly this defense has been successful. Six years after her marriage, one woman killed her husband with a kitchen knife. She had suffered constant beatings from him with a pistol, and then adding insult to injury he would literally pour salt into her wounds. Sometimes he would pull her out of bed by her hair to resume the battering. She finally left her husband. The killing took place when she returned to their home to discuss finances with him. There she was beaten again by him and his seventeen-year-old housekeeper. Mrs. Smith stabbed her husband because, according to her testimony, he lunged toward her threatening to kill her. Mrs. Smith was acquitted *(New York Times,* April 15, 1979, p. 28).

Refuges are one innovative approach to helping battered women. The Women's Aid movement began in London in 1971 by Erin Pizzey, who held meetings with women who wanted to talk and share their concerns. Many of these women were desperately trying to find a refuge from an intolerable home situation. The Chiswick refuge, one of the first in the world, was founded in response to this need. There are refuges for women scattered throughout the world in Canada, Ireland, Scotland, Germany, New Zealand, etc., which indicates that wife battering is a world-wide problem.

The first refuge in the United States was established in California, and California is one of the few states that has special legislation on wife battering. The California penal code states that "Any husband who willfully inflicts upon his wife corporal injury resulting in a traumatic condition, and any person who willfully inflicts upon a child any cruel or inhuman corporal punishment or injury resulting in a traumatic condition, is guilty of a felony, and upon conviction thereof shall be punished by imprisonment for not more than ten years or in the county jail for not more than one year" (Truninger, 1971, p. 263). In 1962 the California law was extended to give spouses the right to charge assault and battery in a civil action against spouses. Spousal immunity in many states prevents a wife from suing her husband. Even in California where wife beating is a felony instead of a misdemeanor, it is the district attorney's office which makes the decision regarding the disposition of the complaint. There is a tendency to avoid issuing a warrant for the husband's arrest. Visible evidence of beatings and the emotional condition of the complainant are factors in the decision making. Most district attorneys and assistant district attorneys are men and men are not socialized in our society to view women as independent adults (note the frequent use of the word "girl" in referring to an adult woman). Could there be a "Catch 22" situation for the woman who attempts to file a complaint? In New York City during the year 1966, 38 percent of the petitions of wife battering were withdrawn or dismissed. For the rest of the counties in New York state, the corresponding figure was 54 percent (Parnas, 1969–70).

A Washington, D.C. study indicated that of 7500 wives who tried to bring charges against their abusive husbands only 200 succeeded (Edmiston, 1976). It is true that battered wives tend to withdraw their complaints perhaps because there are few alternatives for them to start anew. There are few refuges for these women in the United States, although as women's groups become increasingly aware of the problem, more refuges are being founded. Other types of services for battered women are minimal, and with the standard police response of "adjust," the battered wife sees no alternative but to return to her husband if she has left, or to remain if she hasn't.

Refuges are important places where women can go for safety, for emotional support, and for time to think things over. Some refuges provide counseling services and access to job training. Legal services are also available as well as access to financial help. With support from the personnel of the refuge, a woman can file a complaint if she so desires and carry through with it.

What are some of the legal recourses a woman has? She can file for a restraining order against her husband but can expect little police protection unless she initiates divorce proceedings. Many states require that a lawyer be involved when a restraining order is applied for. Payment of legal fees, costs for filing papers, etc., are deterrents to taking this step (Truninger, 1971). If the majority of battered women come from the lower socio-economic group and are therefore poor, where are they going to find the funds to take this action? Police are also reluctant to enforce a restraining order, particularly because it is a civil matter.

A group of married women whose husbands had beaten them filed a suit on December 8, 1976 against the New York City Police Department and the Family Court because the police had, contrary to state law, rejected their requests to arrest their husbands, and the Family Court had denied them access to judges who would make a determination on their request for protection. One woman stated that in spite of the fact that her husband was choking and punching her in the presence of their children because she had started divorce proceedings, the police would not arrest him. The pleas by the neighbors to arrest her husband went unanswered because the police stated that it was a marital argument. One woman said that the Family Court would not issue an order of protection in spite of the fact that her husband had beaten her on a number of occasions and on one of them had broken her ribs. The court requested that she return with her husband to see the court's family counselor before a protection order would be issued.

The class action complaint read in part:

> Despite the widespread existence of this problem (wife assault), defendant police officers and court officials either deny the existence, prevalence, and seriousness of violence against married women, or they treat it as a private privilege of marital discipline, rooted in the view that women are the property of their husbands and that the state should not interfere. The police refuse to arrest violent husbands or give other needed aid and protection to plaintiff victims. While the Family Court was enacted to give practical advice to battered wives (who do not have lawyers to assist them), the Court personnel in fact deny women access to Court. Each agency sends women to the other. Neither agency enforces the law. Plaintiffs are left remediless. The result is increased fear, injury, or even death at the hands of their violent husbands (*Response,* Vol. 1, February, 1977, p. 6).

This case against the New York City Police Department and Family Court was settled out of court. The agreement involved a change in police behavior. Each reported or threatened wife beating would have to be investigated by at least one officer, and a husband must be arrested if justified on the basis that he has committed a crime even though the woman does not show marks of physical abuse. The New York City law in the past had stated that assault was an illegal act but apparently, as in other states, if a man was assaulting someone to whom he was married, the law became invalidated. Violations of restraining orders which result in beatings would also result in the arrest of the spouse, and wives must be told about their rights by the police (*New York Times,* June 27, 1978, p. 1).

Several other communities have taken similar action. In many states it is still difficult to obtain a temporary or permanent injunction, ordering the man to stay away from the home, unless the couple is legally separated or the woman has filed for divorce. Another problem that ensues when a battered wife leaves her household to protect herself is the possibility of being charged with desertion. There are efforts being made to remedy this situation.

The fact that only four states, Oregon, Delaware, New Jersey, and Iowa have laws which allow a woman to charge her husband with rape seems to support the concept in marriage of a woman's body being owned by her husband. Recently in Massachusetts a man was convicted of raping his wife, who was in the process of getting a divorce. Testimony by her eight-year-old son helped to convict the father. Whether the husband would have been guilty of rape if a divorce action was not in process is questionable. Marriage, by law, gives the husband access to his wife's body; therefore, in some states there cannot be a situation called rape in marriage.

Crisis intervention hotlines as well as on-going support groups have been established throughout the country in an attempt to provide services to women who are being battered. The support groups provide an opportunity to share feelings with others who have similar problems and thereby lessen the emotional isolation which is characteristic of battered women. Helping to improve the woman's self-esteem as well as working to eradicate her perception of violence as normative is crucial. Women must be helped to understand that their behavior will not avoid violence (Hilberman and Munson, 1977).

Removal from the home, especially in cases where the violence is severe is one of the first steps toward treatment. A residential, crisis-oriented shelter provides a place of safety for women and their children. It is important to note that there is always much movement from the shelter back to the home and then back to the shelter again.

Finding permanent housing for battered women and their children, and providing legal advocacy if they desire it are essential, as well as financial support when indicated.

Agency concern should also focus on the offspring in families where wife battering occurs. Support groups for these children would help them to work through their fears and guilt that somehow they have been the cause of the difficulty between their parents. Above all, the battered wife must not be pressured to take any steps (unless she is in physical jeopardy) but must be helped in a supportive manner to identify her options, many of which she may be unaware of, and look at where they will lead.

Peer-group counseling for batterers is also necessary to address the problem, although most men will not admit to being responsible for the difficulty and sometimes refuse to accept the fact that a problem does exist. One such group, *Emerge,* in Boston, offers specific advice as to how to defuse a potential battering. The man is told, as an emergency measure, to go for a walk, call a friend, or channel his extreme anger by screaming or punching a pillow instead of the woman he is living with. Group counseling focuses on the man himself and not the marital relationship. He is taught how to handle his angry feelings and is also taught conflict resolution.

Now that wife battering is no longer a taboo topic, perhaps women will increasingly feel less trapped and therefore less apt to take extreme steps in resolving their untenable situation. In November, 1977, for example, a thirty-year-old woman was charged with first-degree murder in the death of her husband. Although she had lit the gasoline she had poured under her wife-beating husband's bed, she was acquitted on the basis of temporary insanity. Mrs. Hughes had acted out the homicidal rage that Hilberman and Munson (1979) had noted in their victims.

References

Anon. *The Lawes Resolution of Women's Rights: or the Lawes Provision for Women.* London, 1632.

_____. Love Story. *New York Times.* 49 (October 10, 1976).

_____. *Parade Magazine. The Springfield Republican* (Sunday, September 16, 1979, p. 8).

_____. Police Will Arrest Wife Beaters in Reversal of New York Policy. *New York Times.* 1 (June 27, 1978).

_____. Response 1 (October 1976). Center For Women Policy Studies. Washington, D.C.

_____. *Response* 1. Center for Women Policy Studies, Washington, D. C. (January 1979).

_____. *Response* 2. Center for Women Policy Studies, Washington, D. C. (January 1979).

_____. *Response* 1. Center for Women Policy Studies, Washington, D. C. (February 1977).

_____. Wife Beating. *Ladies Home Journal* 66 (June 1974).

_____. Woman in Michigan Freed in Slaying. *New York Times* 20 (April 15, 1979).

Bandura, Albert. *Aggression: A Social Learning Analysis.* Englewood Cliffs, N. J.: Prentice-Hall, 1973.

Beard, Charles and Beard, Mary. *The Rise of American Civilization.* New York: Macmillan, 1927.

Blackstone, Sir William. *Commentaries on the Laws of England.* Vol I, William Craig Jones (ed). San Francisco: Bancroft-Whiting Co., 1916.

Calvert, Robert. Criminal and civil liability in husband-wife assaults, in Suzanne K. Steinmetz and Murray A. Straus (eds.). *Violence in the Family.* New York: Harper & Row, 1974.

Coulton, G. G. *From St. Francis to Dante,* a tr. of the Chronical of Salimbene, London. Philadelphia: Richard West, 1908.

Durant, Will. *The Renaissance.* New York: Simon & Schuster, 1953.

Edmiston, Susan. The wife beaters. *Woman's Day* 61, 110–111 (March 1976).

Elbow, Margaret. Theoretical considerations of violent marriages. *Social Casework* **58**:515–525 (November 1977).

Faulk, M. Men who assault their wives. *Medicine, Science and the Law* **14**:180–183 (July 1974).

Gelles, Richard J. Abused wives: why do they stay? *Journal of Marriage and the Family* **38**:659–668 (November 1976).

_____. *The Violent Home: A Study of Physical Aggression Between Husbands and Wives.* Beverly Hills, California: Sage Publications, 1972.

Goode, William. Force and violence in the family. *Journal of Marriage and the Family* **33**:624–636 (November 1971).

Hilberman, Elaine and Munson, Kit. *Sixty Battered Women: A Preliminary Report.* Paper read at American Psychiatric Association Meetings, Toronto, Canada, May 5, 1977.

Hirsch, Miriam F. *A Study of the Reported Assaults by Boyfriends and Husbands in the City of Springfield, Massachusetts,* 1977. Unpublished.

Hobhouse, L.T., Wheeler, G.C., and Ginsberg, M. *The Material Culture and Social Institutions of the Simpler Peoples,* London: Chapman and Hall, 1930.

Hoebel, Adamson E. *Anthropology: The Study of Man.* New York: McGraw-Hill Book Co., 1966.

The Holy Bible. Revised Standard Edition. Toronto: Thomas Nelson & Sons, 1952.

Kamisher, Michele. Behind closed doors: battered women. *The Real Paper* 13, 20–21 (February 11, 1976).

Kanowitz, Leo. *Women and the Law: The Unfinished Revolution.* Albuquerque, N.M.: University of New Mexico Press, 1969.

Kaplan, Howard B. Toward a general theory of psychosocial deviance: the case of aggressive behavior. *Social Science and Medicine* **6**:593–617 (1972).

Langley, Roger and Levy, Richard C. *Wife Beating: The Silent Crisis.* New York: E. P. Dutton, 1977.

Laslett, Barbara. The family as a public and private institution: a historical perspective. *Journal of Marriage and the Family* **35**:480–492 (August 1973).

Lerner, M. J. The desire for justice and reactions to victims, in J. Macaulay and L. Berkowitz (eds.). *Altruism and Helping Behavior.* New York: Academic Press, 1970.

Levinger, George. Source of marital satisfaction among applicants for divorce. *American Journal of Orthopsychiatry* **36**:804–806 (1966).

Lunde, Donald. *Murder and Madness.* San Francisco: San Francisco Book Co., 1976.

Meiselman, Karin C. *Incest.* San Francisco: Josey-Bass Publishers, 1978.

Mulvihill, Donald J. and Tumin, Melvin M. *Crimes of Violence.* Washington, D.C.: U.S. Government Printing Office, 1969.

O'Brien, John E. Violence in divorce prone families. *Journal of Marriage and the Family* **33**:692–698 (1971).

Owens, David. Battered wives: some social and legal problems. *British Journal of Law and Society* **2**:201–211 (1975).

Parnas, Raymond. Judicial response to intra-family violence. *Minnesota Law Review* **54**:585–644 (1969–70).

_____. The police response to domestic disturbance. *Wisconsin Law Review* 914–960 (Fall 1967).

Scott, P. D. Battered wives. *British Journal of Psychiatry* **125**:433–441 (November 1974).

Snell, J. E., Rosenwald, R. J. and Robey. A. The wifebeater's wife: a study of family interaction. *Archives of General Psychiatry* **11**:107–113 (August 1964).

Star, Barbara, Clark, Carol G., Goetz, Karen M. and O'Malia, Linda. Psychosocial aspects of wife battering. *Social Casework* **60**:479–487 (October 1979).

Stark, Rodney and McEvoy, James, III. Middle class violence. *Psychology Today* 52–65 (November 1970).

Steinmetz, Suzanne and Straus, Murray, The family as a cradle of violence. *Society* 50–56 (September/October 1973).

_____. (eds.). *Violence in the Family.* New York: Harper & Row. 1974.

Straus, Murray. A general systems theory approach to a theory of violence between family members. *Social Science Information* **12**:105–125 (1973).

Truninger, Elizabeth. Marital violence: the legal solutions. *Hastings Law Journal* **23**:259–276 (November 1971).

Whitehurst, Robert. Violence in husband-wife interaction, in Suzanne K. Steinmetz and Murray A. Straus (eds.). *Violence in the Family.* New York: Harper & Row, 1974.

Wolfgang, Marvin E. *Patterns in Criminal Homicide.* New York: John Wiley, 1958.

Wolfgang, M. and Ferracuti, F. *The Subculture of Violence: Toward an Integrated Theory of Criminology.* London: Tavistock, 1967.

Zullo, Allen A. and Fulman, Ricki. Wife beating in nice homes. *New Woman* 68–69 (March 1976).

8. Boggling the Mind: Women and Therapy

When I was growing up, our family would often respond to evidence of illogical behavior by saying "You're all right. The world is crazy." I have become aware in recent years of the deep meaning that this often-used statement expresses, particularly as it relates to mental illness. People who are out of step with expected behavior in a given society are labeled as being aberrant and treated accordingly. Thomas Szasz (1961, 1970), a psychiatrist, has written several books in which he postulates that mental illness is a myth and that the dynamics of mental illness and the treatment of those who are labeled mentally ill is analogous to the treatment of those described as being witches by the inquisitors of the Middle Ages (see *The Manufacture of Madness*, 1970, and *The Myth of Mental Illness*, 1961).

Basically, then, the definition of maladaptive behavior or "craziness" is dependent on the role expectations and behavior of a particular individual, and the degree to which these differ from the cultural norms (Horney, 1937). It is also dependent on the degree of tolerance the dominant group (the one which holds the power) in a particular culture has toward members of a minority group. In other words, degrees of tolerance of difference are closely related to the degree of acceptance by the dominant group of a minority. Out-group, in-group theory accepts the proposition that certain behaviors which are not accepted when manifested by persons of the out-group are tolerated when demonstrated by one of the members of the in-group. The dominant group in our society is the white male. Therefore, blacks, other racial minorities, and women are often viewed as "sick" if they do not conform to the norms established for them by the greater society. In addition, stereotyping of minorities has a detrimental effect on the mental health of all groups.

Women in the United States, although relatively equal in number to men, are by definition minorities. They do not have political, economic, and social power equal to that of men, and the manner in which the dominant group has defined the woman's role creates stress which may be the reason for the large number of women who seek therapy. Role definition also has a decided effect on their treatment by therapists of both sexes.

Myths surrounding women have ranged from viewing them as witches, innately evil and lustful (Alexander and Selesnick, 1966), to all "sugar and spice and everything nice," both extremes. The *Malleus Maleficarum* written in 1487 by a monk describes how witches can be identified. They were purported to be women who by devious means such as concocting a particular devil-like mixture were responsible for locusts and caterpillars over-running crops, were able to cause impotency in men and infertility in women. They were capable of causing a pregnant woman to abort and could sometimes do all this in addition to causing illness and death by just looking at a person in a certain way. Not only did they occasionally practice cannibalism with children but could also turn themselves into animals (Durant, 1957). Sprenger, the learned Dominican inquisitor who wrote the document concerning witchcraft, felt that women comprised most of the class of witches because more than men, they were sensuous, easily seduced by the devil and had an insatiable desire for sex. Their souls and bodies were basically tainted because woman was made by God from a less than perfect rib. Thousands of women and children were killed as a result of such beliefs, many of them being burned to death. It is fairly apparent that a large number of the people accused of being witches, and of being possessed by the devil, were actually people who were mentally ill. One theory proposes that the persecution of witches resulted from women being made scapegoats because of the eroding of celibacy among monks and nuns (Alexander and Selesnick, 1966). Women were thought to be particularly prone to witchcraft because of their basically evil character.

What else is woman but a foe to friendship, an unescapeable punishment, a necessary evil, a natural temptation, a desirable calamity, a domestic danger, a delectable detriment, an evil of nature, painted with fair colours! Therefore if it be a sin to divorce her when she ought to be kept, it is indeed a necessary torture; for either we commit adultery by divorcing her, or we must endure daily strife (*Malleus Maleficarum*, pp. 165–67, in Veith, p. 63, 1965).

According to the proponents of the scapegoat theory, it was becoming more and more difficult to impose sexual abstinence on the representatives of the Church. Some of the monasteries and nunneries were joined by underground tunnels, and in an effort by the surrounding townspeople to preserve the virginity of their young women, prostitutes were delivered to the monks in some areas. In an attempt to address this difficulty, the Church in the 13th century initiated a campaign against eroticism. Women were considered the cause of sexual stirrings in men and, therefore, were considered to be influenced by the devil. Men's sexual drive was unacceptable to them and so it was projected onto women. It was *women* whose lust was said to be insatiable. By punishing women who were identified as witches, men's guilt concerning their own sexual desires could be eased (Alexander and Selesnick, 1966). Actually, viewing woman as seductress and temptress is still evident, as can be seen by the fact that prostitutes, but seldom their customers, are arraigned, and the fact that the rape victim is often seen as having "asked for" her attack by dressing or behaving seductively.

In the mid-1800s even as women were beginning to wage an organized battle to achieve a more equal status, doctors who supervised asylums were expressing the view that not only the bodily mechanisms but also women's psyche and morality must be addressed in their treatment. These doctors believed that women's sexual development, as well as changes during pregnancy and childbirth, created a proneness to criminal desires. Mental illness was considered a female disorder. By their sexual nature women were thought to be prone to hysteria, which in turn was considered to be just a short step away from insanity (Dreifus, 1978).

Dr. Alfred Stille, who was the president of the American Medical Association in 1871, expressed concern about women who were attempting to compete with men and viewed their efforts as attempts at becoming male. He described women as unable to make decisions, unable to stick to decisions they do make, and unstable in the ability to rationally make decisions. Some of these same stereotypes about women still exist today. Women are called flighty; it is said to be a woman's prerogative to change her mind; and women are considered to be less serious minded than men.

Basically, throughout much of the 1800s, it was felt that illnesses of the mind which afflicted a woman were related to her sexuality, her masturbatory activities, her unacceptable and immoral sexual behavior; and most of all the base of woman's insanity was considered to be the womb. Surgical treatment, such as clitoridectomy (total or partial removal of the clitoris) as well as the removal of the ovaries was practiced. Clitoridectomy continued to be used as a form of treatment of masturbation as late as 1937 (Dreifus, 1978).

Titles such as "A case of insanity, caused by diseased ovaries, cured by their removal—a phenomenal triumph for operative treatment" (Meyer, 1894), and "Melancholia, masturbation: cured by removal of both ovaries" (Church, 1887), appeared in the medical journals in the 1800s, and one can conclude that clitoridectomies and female castration were not an uncommon treatment prescribed for women who were presenting unacceptable behaviors. At first castration of women was confined to those who were outpatients. In the latter part of the 1800s, institutionalized mental patients were the subjects of this mode of therapy. It was believed that women did not feel less female with the removal of the clitoris and/or the ovaries. Somehow or other the feelings and reactions that men would have to castration were not felt to operate with women (Dreifus, 1978). It is almost as if women psychologically were completely different "animals."

Hysteria, a word derived from the Greek *hysteron* meaning uterus, is an emotional disorder which has generally been assigned to women. The Egyptians, even before the word was coined by the Greeks, believed that the disease was caused by the uterus being in the wrong place and so they attempted to use a fumigation method in order to entice the uterus to return to its proper position. The wandering uterus concept as a cause of hysteria was also given credibility by Hippocrates and Plato in Greece (Alexander and Selesnick, 1966).

The symptoms of hysteria were very clearly identified by Thomas Sydenham, who lived from 1624 to 1689. He pointed out that symptoms of hysteria may appear to be that of organic disease, and he included among the symptomology heart palpitations, paralysis, and epileptic-like convulsions. He pointed out that hysteria was a common disease and that like other diseases it was caused by "animal spirits." Males, too, he stated, could manifest hysterical symptoms but he labeled these hypochondriasis (Alexander and Selesnick, 1966). In spite of Sydenham, hysteria continued to be associated mainly with women and a number of hysterical women continued to be burned as witches.

After the witchcraft era ended in the 18th century, hysteria continued to be mainly considered a disease of women, and hysterical women were often viewed contemptuously.

These patients are veritable actresses; they do not know of a greater pleasure than to deceive . . . all those with whom they come in touch. The hysterics who exaggerate their convulsive movement . . . make an equal travesty and exaggeration of the movements of their soul, their ideas and their acts . . . In one word, the life of the hysteric is nothing but one perpetual falsehood; they affect the airs of piety and devotion and let themselves be taken for saints while at the same time secretly abandoning themselves to the most shameful actions; and at home, before their husbands and children, making the most violent scenes in which they employ the coarsest and often most obscene language and give themselves up to the most disorderly actions (Carter, in Veith, p. 211, 1965).

In the early 1900s hysteria in women was still associated with their reproductive organs.

Even in the normal woman there is some derangement in the psychic life during the menstrual period; there are special sensibilities which are foreign to the mentality of the male, and which we have never been able to comprehend. I am led to believe that the various vague, conscious, or unconscious sensations which pertain to the sexual instinct play, even in the virgin of the most immaculate thoughts, a considerable role in the genesis of hysteria. But they produce unhealthy autosuggestions only in subjects so predisposed and those of weak mentality . . . Sadler, p. 226, 1914).

Freud (1953) also believed that women were more prone to develop neurosis and particularly hysteria because of the nature of their sexual development. He theorized that a woman must transfer her erotic zone from the clitoris to the vagina while a man's erotogenic zone remains the same from childhood until he becomes an adult. He felt that women were more susceptible to neurosis but particularly hysteria because of the necessity of changing erotic zones. One can almost deduce from Freud that to be female is to be neurotic.

The concept of the hysterical personality is used almost always for females. This includes behaviors which are sexually seductive, centered on self, containing underlying hostility and emotional instability (Jordan and Kempler, 1970). Psychoanalytically speaking, these symptoms are attributed to the fact that the woman has been unable to identify with her mother and therefore has not made an adult sexual adjustment. Women are the cause of all evil. Actually, when we view the symptoms attributed to hysteria, we find that many of them are exaggerations of the sex-stereotypes of women, such as deceitfulness, seductiveness, unpredictability, etc. The hysteric makes use of exaggerated female traits in order to cope. Halleck (1967) feels that every woman will manifest hysterical symptoms under extreme stress conditions.

Men are not considered hysterics but are labeled as sociopaths (Cloninger and Gutze, 1970). Studies have indicated that women comprise about 92 percent of those diagnosed as having hysterical personalities and men 85 percent of the patients who have been judged to have antisocial personalities (Warner, 1979). One researcher presented sufficient data to make a case for the concept that both disorders have common features, that the history of childhood experiences as well as experiences in adulthood is similar in both, and that there may be evidences of sex stereotyping in the dichotomous labeling. Males who are considered hysterical are those who tend to present behaviors which are considered feminine. In both antisocial and hysterical patients, there appear to be behavioral traits which are exaggerations of the sex-role stereotypes. Hysterics are considered to be more easily treated than sociopaths, which also fits into the commonly held belief by therapists that women make better patients.

Nymphomania is a disease label which is attached only to women. Although it is used colloquially to describe any female whose behavior does not follow the projected sexual norm, clinically it describes a female who has a compulsive, ongoing, uncontrollable need for sex which results in a self-image of worthlessness and personality characteristics of dependency and masochism (Ellis and Sagarin, 1964).

Historically, nymphomania was considered a genital neurosis disease, and Pinel, a well-known reformer of mental institutions, born in 1745, proposed that puberty was the time when the symptoms of nymphomania are first seen. He believed that "Nymphomania is most frequently caused by lascivious reading, by severe restraint and secluded life, by the habit of masturbation, an extreme sensitivity of the uterus, and a skin eruption on the genital organs" (Pinel, in Veith, 1965, p. 179). He listed the symptoms as those involving lewd thoughts, immodesty, inability to sleep or eat, depression, restlessness, and ambivalence around expressing desires. As the disease progresses, the woman forgets sexual reserve and abandons herself to her lascivious desires, attempting to seduce the first man she meets. If he repels her advances, she becomes enraged. In the last phase of this disease, Pinel states, her rage becomes extreme, expressing her desire to inflict injury and symptomatically she appears to be a violent maniac. Interestingly, one of the cases he described to illustrate his thesis was that of a young woman who was wed to an impotent man (Veith, 1965).

The hypersexual woman has often been viewed as maladjusted because her behavior does not conform to the accepted role of women. Women, by nature, were supposed to lack sexual desire, which was considered base. As late as 1908 immoderate masturbation was presented as the cause of nymphomania. The nymphomaniac is condemned by society much more than her psychiatric counterpart, the Don Juan, who has a compulsive need to bed one female after another. In fact, in many ways, the Don Juan is admired and most often never finds his way for psychiatric help. Because of the increase in the acceptance of female sexual activity, the term nymphomania is not as often used today as it once was.

Every society prescribes norms; that is, ways of behaving that are considered appropriate or inappropriate for a particular person occupying a given status in a society. These norms are influenced by what the culture values, and these values are supported by the moral yardsticks the society has adopted. Violation of the norms meets with sanctions which range in severity from death and expulsion to a mild reprimand. The norms of behavior for women have throughout the years differed from those of men and were developed through the ages from myths surrounding the female sex.

The myth of woman as a seducer is very evident in the description of the nymphomaniac who unabashedly goes to bed with one man after another. Even those women who were not so blatant in their sexually tainted behavior were, and to some extent still are, viewed as seductresses, including the child who "seduces" her father, uncle, brother, etc., into some form of a sexual relationship. If women were not seen as actively encouraging the passions of men to rise, then they were implicated in creating difficulty for them. "How often do we, from beholding a woman, suffer a thousand evils; returning home and entertaining an inordinate desire, and experiencing anguish for many days . . . The beauty of women is the greatest snare" (St. John Crysostom, Homily XV, 1886).

Cases of nymphomania are not very evident in psychiatric literature today.

Agoraphobia, literally meaning "fear of the market place," is another disorder more commonly found in women than in men. Actually, agoraphobia is defined as being an abnormal fear of open or public places. It is labeled "housewives' disease" because it is very often seen in and admitted to by women. It creates more constraints on a person than the other phobias and afflicts 2.5 million Americans; the majority of them (85–90 percent) are women (*Time,* November 7, 1977, p. 58). Freud felt that phobias were symptoms of extreme fear of one's sexual and aggressive drives. It has been proposed that men tend to confront their fears, a cultural phenomenon, while women withdraw from their fears. Women who are housewives, say some feminists, become phobic because they are confined to the house and have been socialized to believe in the dangers of the world outside.

One therapist, Alexandra Symonds (1973), noted that a number of self-sufficient, independent women suddenly develop phobias after getting married. She proposed that these women, instead of having fear of losing control, which Freud theorized was the basis for phobic reactions, actually were fearful of being in control. They were afraid of what would happen to them if they actively became involved, assertive, and aggressive. A significant number of women, said Symonds, are phobic because our culture traditionally sets up obstacles so that women have difficulty in self-actualizing and in actively participating in life.

The concept of agoraphobia with its symptoms of dependence, impotency, and powerlessness has been related to conflicts in sex roles (Fodor, 1974). A number of women are raised to become people who are not fully adult in terms of being independent, self-motivated, and having the other attributes of adulthood. When the demands of life become overwhelming, they retreat into the ultimate in female behaviors, thus handling the desires they view as masculine, those of assertiveness, activity, etc.; desires which conflict with their sex role and so create a great deal of anxiety. By being afraid to go out, one reinforces one's inability to leave or escape. Marriage, particularly, makes adult demands on women which they are often unprepared to meet both because of their upbringing, and as a result of the romanticized notions of marriage they learn from the mass media (Fodor, 1974). Phobias are closely associated with dependency. Perhaps if we desist from portraying girls in textbooks and in the media as timid, shy, nonassertive, and sweet, we would be encouraging more of them to develop into "real" people in adulthood. If we also encourage girls to become self-actualizing adults without boxing them into sex stereotypical roles, the incidences of agoraphobia will decline. Fodor presents evidence to support the thesis that phobic reactions in women are closely related to cultural conditioning.

In the past, women were viewed as being innately less intelligent than men, and therefore denied access to education. The belief prevailed that too much use of the brain by women could lead to emotional difficulties. In the 1600s the mental illness of the wife of the Governor of Connecticut was attributed to the fact that she had been an avid reader. "If she had attended her household affairs, and such things as belong to women, and not gone out of her way and calling to meddle in such things as are proper for men, whose minds are stronger, etc., she had kept her wits, and might have improved them usefully and honorably in the place God had set" (Winthrop, Vol. 2, 1826, p. 2116).

The belief that women were basically inferior to men was reinforced by the stress placed on their subordination to their husbands, which was legally supported. In addition, women were to be submissive, and those who were proponents of equality were considered to be more masculine than feminine or mentally aberrant (Haller, 1974).

Not only was woman thought to be innately of lower intelligence than man, but she was also naturally inferior in many other ways and biologically meant to be passive. Aristotle, himself, verbalized the superiority of the male and based his conclusions on the fact that men produced semen but females did not. Males, therefore, represent activity and females passivity, since their role is to furnish the substance which the sperm then molds. He argued that women were basically the weaker of the two sexes, less passionate in desires than men, more deceptive, and basically less moral. A woman's redeeming features were a body beautiful and a passion for labor.

> ... the temperance of a man and a woman is not the same nor their courage and justice, as Socrates supposed, but a man's courage is of a ruling and a woman's of a subordinate kind, and so with all the other virtues (Aristotle, 1905, p. 35).

One of our great founding fathers, Benjamin Franklin, believed that men were naturally superior to women and that women needed to be educated so that they could better obey their husbands.

Biological determinism was the base for Freud's theories, which were well accepted in the United States, and which comprise the building blocks of psychoanalytically oriented therapy.

Although Freud believed in the concept of bisexuality, he saw the differences in the anatomy of men and women as the cause of innate superiority and inferiority. Both girls and boys develop along similar lines until the age of five. At this stage in their development, they become increasingly focused on and interested in their genitals and those of others in the surrounding environment, particularly those of the other sex. The young girl suddenly discovers that she is missing a part of what she believes to be her genitals. She develops anger towards her mother, who is "mutilated" like her, and whom she blames for the loss of this envied endowment. The little boy, on the other hand, does not feel castrated because his organ is still intact, but fears that he, too, may some day be mutilated like the little girl, especially since he fears that his father will act in a punishing manner in response to his sexual desire for his mother. The boy's fear of castration is instrumental in beginning the dissolution of the oedipal complex in boys (Freud, 1971 b).

The little girl who sees the boy's penis and realizes she does not have one develops a desire to someday obtain this superior organ. She eventually exchanges her desire for a penis with a desire to give birth to a baby and achieves her wish for a penis by having a child, preferably a boy.

Freud places women in a "Catch 22." He states that the reaction of a little girl to what she perceives as a lack of an adequate sex organ is one of recognizing her inferiority, believing that it resulted from some punishable act; she recognizes that she is not the only one who is so deprived, and "she begins to share the contempt felt by men for a sex which is the lesser in so important a respect, and at least in holding that opinion, insists on being like a man" (Freud, 1971 b, p. 253). Therefore, states Freud, women are basically more jealous than men. Penis envy results in a negative reaction to masturbation because the girl discovers that her clitoris is inferior to the penis. "This impulse is clearly a forerunner of the wave of repression which at puberty will do away with a large amount of the girl's masculine sexuality in order to make room for the development of her femininity" (Freud b, 1971).

Freud also stated that in the cases where a girl refuses to accept castration and continues to believe that she indeed does have a genital organ like males, she "may subsequently be compelled to behave as though she were a man" (Freud, 1971 b, p. 253). One can see how behavior which was not considered feminine, such as aggression, could be easily labeled inappropriate behavior and the person demonstrating it "sick."

Freud equated femininity with passivity by virtue of the fact that in the reproductive system the male sex organ is more active while the vagina is a receptive organ.

Along with passivity, masochism psychoanalytically was viewed as being characteristically feminine. Freud (1971a) noted that there was a recurrent dream, particularly prevalent in women, in which a child and then the woman herself is being beaten. The first fantasy satisfies in a sadistic way the woman's jealousy; the second satisfies the woman's need for punishment because of her forbidden desires for her father (Freud, 1971a). Masochism means deriving pleasure from pain, and although, said Freud, it is also found in men, it is a feminine characteristic. Women feel pleasure in the pain of giving birth. Marie Bonaparte (1953), a disciple of Freud, believed that because of the basic functions of reproduction in women involving the menstrual cycle, the pain at first intercourse, as well as pregnancy and childbirth, endurance of pain is the destiny of women.

Helene Deutsch (1945), a classic Freudian analyst, continues to support and expand on Freud's theories of femininity. According to her, a girl becomes traumatized by her recognition of the loss of a penis and develops the masochistic desire to be overpowered. The mature woman is one who accepts the role of nurturing, who demonstrates passivity and is rewarded by sexual gratification. In other words, a woman's place is in the home, catering to her husband and the children she bears as her responsibility to the continuation of the human species.

Another characteristic which was particularly feminine according to Freud (1971 b) was a limited sense of justice. Whereas the boy is forced to abandon the oedipus complex shortly after he discovers the "castrated" genital organs of the little girl, she does not forsake the oedipus complex because she has already been castrated. The effects of this can continue late into a woman's life and the superego then does not become independent and objective. Freud very specifically points to the fact that change in the superego as it is forming probably is responsible for such character traits found in women as lack of a "sense of justice" and the strong influence feelings have in their lives (Freud, 1971 b). And so the stereotypes concerning women are perpetuated.

Karen Horney dissented from the traditional orthodox Freudian psychology and, in anger, walked out of the New York Psychoanalytic Society singing "Go down Moses." The year was 1941. Her stress was on the cultural influences on the development of personality.

When we realize the great import of cultural conditions on neuroses the biological and physiological conditions, which are considered by Freud to be their root, recede into the background (Horney, 1937, p. VII).

She goes on to state that what is considered maladaptive behavior has to be viewed within its cultural context. "The conception of what is normal varies not only with the culture but also within the same culture, in the course of time" (Horney, 1937, p. 15).

Horney proposed, much to the dismay of the traditionalists, that the psychology of women did not need to be related to that of men. She proposed that because men, in our society, control the work force, it has been difficult for women to sublimate by choosing a particular profession, and because women were unable to achieve in the basically male professions, their feelings of inferiority were reinforced. She also proposed that our culture influences women to develop masochistic tendencies. Psychoanalysis, states Horney, functions

... to reconcile women to their subordinate role by presenting it as an unalterable one, but also to plant the belief that it represents a fulfillment they crave, or an ideal for which it is commendable and desirable to strive (Horney, 1967, p. 231).

Erik H. Erikson, a neo-Freudian, does accept the cultural and social influences on personality but sees them as interacting with biological forces. Although he does not accept the castration complex for women, he does focus on the fact that because of the makeup of the female reproductive organs, the vagina and the uterus, which are essentially closed, the concept of "an inner bodily space" is operative (Erikson, 1967).

Although he views women as active rather than passive, nonmasochistic but having an ability to endure discomfort, he believes that their physiological makeup determines their psychological makeup and that their " ... somatic design harbors an 'inner space' destined to bear the offspring of chosen men and, with it, a biological, psychological, and ethical commitment to take care of human infancy" (Erikson, 1967, p. 5).

Erikson based his theory of the importance of inner space for women on one experiment involving 150 boys and 150 girls whom he saw three times during a two-year period. During each of his three contacts with each child he asked them to construct something with materials he had brought. He found that each sex appeared to employ the concept of space in a different manner. Boys built more towers, usually high, and if they built enclosures, these were related to the other buildings in some manner. Girls, on the other hand, built lower buildings, constructed a greater number of enclosures and more often than boys, placed things within these barriers (Erikson, 1967).

A more recent replication of Erikson's experiment using two groups of children of different ages found that none of the boys and girls in the five-and-a-half- to eleven-and-a-half-year-old group tended to build the same types of edifices. Only in the fifteen-and-a-half-year-olds, the older group, was there evidence of boys building towers and girls building more enclosures (Cramer and Hogan, 1975). The question can therefore be raised as to the influence of culture and role models on the behavior of the two sexes.

Thus, how women are viewed influences whether they are deemed to be behaving in a normal manner.

Commitment for insanity occurred when people did not behave role-appropriately. Chesler (1972) relates the story of Elizabeth Packard, who spent three years (1860–1863) in a mental institution because she did not change her behavior to suit her husband. She was a Bible school teacher, who taught that humans are basically good and not born evil. She was summarily whisked away to a mental institution in Jacksonville, Illinois and committed by her clergyman husband. At her husband's insistence, she was not allowed to see her children, and the monies that were rightfully hers by inheritance were confiscated by her spouse. Mrs. Packard, in subsequent published works, and in her publication of the fact that she felt she had not been insane when committed, was instrumental in the passage of a law in Illinois which made it mandatory to have a jury trial before committing a person to an asylum for the mentally ill.

The role expectation of each sex is predicated on the myths and beliefs surrounding their psychology and the kinds of contribution it is believed they can make to society. It has been postulated that women's role in our society creates a great deal of stress and results in the prevalence of mental disorders as well as increased visits to psychiatrists, and more frequent institutionalization.

Assumptions can be made that women's roles in our society make them candidates for emotional problems (Gove and Tudor, 1973). As Betty Friedan (1963) pointed out, the feminine mystique tells women that they should be happy in their housewife role, and that their identity comes from being someone's wife and mother, unlike men, whose identities are derived from their roles as father and husband, but more so from the work they do. If, for instance, a man is dissatisfied with the role he is playing at home, his occupation may offer him compensatory satisfaction. The woman does not have this choice. One can also assume that keeping house and mothering children is not the most satisfactory activity, and that these involvements can prove a source of frustration. Talking to "little people" all day and cleaning up the mess is not exactly the most rewarding experience. One study (Newberry et al., 1979) on the differences between working wives and housewives found that although the number of psychiatric symptoms did not differ between working and nonworking wives, there was a difference in the degree of satisfaction they culled from their activities. The bored housewife syndrome was evident. Housewives do not have high status, especially because they are unpaid, and in our society prestige and money are often correlated.

Even the working wife's prestige is not as high as that of her husband. Her income, no matter how high, is considered supplementary; to buy all the extras. She is also burdened by having to do most of the chores around the house despite popular belief to the contrary.

In addition, the rapidly changing expectations of women create difficulty because their roles are not clearly delineated, and women, therefore, do not know what is expected of them. Gove and Tudor (1973) worked under the assumption that inherent in women's roles is a greater degree of frustration and fewer rewards than in the roles of men. Citing studies which indicate that women's self-image is less positive than men's and that depression is more common among women than men, Gove and Tudor reviewed a large number of studies done after World War II in order to draw some conclusions regarding adult sex roles and their relationship to mental illness. In reviewing the sex of patients treated in outpatient psychiatric clinics, they found that proportionately a greater number of women were seen than men. This was also found to be true in terms of people treated by private physicians for emotional problems. Women were found more often than men to be treated in outpatient clinics, general, and psychiatric hospitals for short-term disorders precipitated by overwhelming stress. Generally speaking, women more often than men become mentally ill.

Sex stereotyping, like social class, plays an important part in labeling behaviors as maladaptive. Behaviors by themselves are not necessarily labeled deviant. Factors such as social class and sex also play an important part in the diagnosis of behavior as maladaptive. The type of role behavior of male and female is basically different (Parsons and Bales, 1955). Males are expected to act in a manner which is considered "instrumental;" that is, goal-oriented, and women in a more expressive way; that is, more sensitive and concerned with feelings.

Women are said to have a fear of succeeding (Horner, 1969). Originally, tests seemed to indicate that women were less motivated to achieve than men (Maccoby and Jacklin, 1974). Researchers soon realized that the apparent lack of an achievement motive had more complicated influences. Matina Horner's research on students at the University of Michigan found that women students presented a fear of success, particularly in competitive situations, especially when the competition was male. The women in the sample who demonstrated fear of success were also the same women who were intellectually well-endowed and who were academically successful. Horner concluded that motivation to achieve is affected by more factors for women than for men. If a woman does succeed, she has to face the signals she receives from society which tell her that she is less feminine. Achievement, motivation, and assertiveness are not acceptable female sex-stereotypical behaviors.

Women who succeed academically are viewed as more likely to encounter embarrassment and discomfort (Monahan et al., 1974). Woman's work is valued less than man's work by both women and men as well as by girls and boys (Mischel, 1974). These factors would have an influence on the development of the achievement motive in women.

Some later research on the fear of success motive has not supported Horner's thesis (Kimball, 1973), while others obtained results which correlated with her studies. The majority of the women in the later study did not manifest the fear of success (Breedlove and Cicerelli, 1974).

If role expectations differ for men and women, we could assume that deviating from these roles would lead to being labeled maladjusted and even mentally ill. Males are expected to behave in a more active manner and girls more passively even as they are growing up. Girls are given dolls to play with, while boys are given trucks. Males are encouraged to participate in more active sports than females, and females who become interested in what has traditionally been a male activity are suspect in terms of their femininity.

In one study of schizophrenics (Cheek, 1964), the male schizophrenic demonstrated a greater degree of withdrawal than normal males. The schizophrenic females, on the other hand, demonstrated characteristics of greater activity and dominance over those of the normal females. What this study appeared to support was the thesis that diverging from one's sex roles is associated with being labeled mentally ill. This result surprised the researcher who had expected to find all schizophrenics displaying similar behaviors of withdrawal, passiveness, and inability to express feeling. The male schizophrenics presented behaviors considered feminine and the female schizophrenics behaviors considered masculine. Alienation from sex roles appears to be evident in those diagnosed as schizophrenic.

When testing schizophrenics for sex-typed reactions, sex role alienation was found (Cheek, 1964). Female schizophrenics behaved more assertively than males, whereas male schizophrenics approximated normal females in demonstrating sensitivity. The authors speculate that because of harsh treatment during childhood, schizophrenics were unable to accept their "gender role identity," thereby developing a sense of alienation from their own sex, occasionally having the sense of being like the opposite sex. Hospitalized female schizophrenics were particularly openly hostile and lacking in sensitivity.

In looking at the characteristics of women who are rehospitalized for mental disorders, one finds that many of them displayed rejection of their traditional housewife roles (Angrist et al., 1961). The women who are returned to institutions were found to be more often those who were married, and those who had cursed and had resisted performing their household chores. Another example of being labeled mentally ill because one has not accepted the sex role assigned by society.

Phyllis Chesler in her book, *Women and Madness* (1972), proposes that mental illness results from behaving in a nonsex role stereotypical way. She argues that this holds true for men as well as for women, and that women who either behave in an ultrafeminine manner or who reject the feminine stereotypes are considered emotionally disturbed. The ultrafeminine behavior leads to hospitalization for what is considered the typical female diseases, such as severe depression, sexual acting out (for instance, nymphomania), paranoia, and suicidal symptoms. The nonacceptance of the feminine role creates fear in both the woman and her family and results in hospitalization for diseases which are considered more masculine in character such as "lesbianism," schizophrenia, and "promiscuity" which Chesler states is interpreted as "a flight into or flight from 'femininity' " (Chesler, 1972, p. 56).

An interesting example of difficulty in accepting the sex stereotyped role is what Rickles calls the Angry Woman Syndrome (Rickles, 1971). This syndrome is characterized by difficulties in the marital relationship, sudden bursts of anger without provocation, efforts to commit suicide, a negative orientation, fault-finding, tendency to drink excessively, as well as a tendency to abuse drugs. The angry woman, states Rickles, needs to be on time and to be neat, as well as to excel in whatever task she undertakes. Rickles further states that the woman with this syndrome appears to be seductive in dress but that in reality "softness" is not one of her strong points. She has difficulty in showing affection, and during sexual intercourse encourages her partner to call her derogatory names, such as "goddam bitch" and "whore."

> They seemingly adjust well, are successful in their careers, dress and comport themselves neatly, and give the appearance of outwardly attractive, well-organized personalities ... They strive to be successes in a socially accepted manner. They suffer from an identity crisis, not knowing where they belong (Rickles, 1971, p. 94).

Rickles discusses the relationship these women had with their parents. He does not, however, address himself to what appears to be an identity crisis; one in which the woman wants to be self-actualizing by succeeding in work, a standard set up by our culture as rewarding. It is difficult to juggle two roles, that of housewife, mother, and wife as well as that of professional. Could the anger be an expression of the frustration these women feel in response to the pressures with which they are finding difficulty in coping?

The role traditionally assigned to women in our society still does not lend itself to the development of positive self-esteem. A study of 153 women undergraduates at the University of Maryland concluded that the development of the ego and of self-esteem is best served by encouraging the development and expression of characteristics which are feminine as well as those which are masculine (androgeny). Women in whom both masculine and feminine traits were at a low level were found to have a low sense of personal worth. Interestingly, women with a preponderance of masculine characteristics had about the same rate of self-esteem as the androgenous women. The authors agree with previous studies that found that "stereotypic sex-role socialization for women, with its emphasis on a traditional feminine role, [is] related to negative self-evaluation" (Schiff and Koopman, 1978, p. 304). They also propose that "masculine characteristics, highly valued in our culture, may contribute significantly to self-esteem . . ." (p. 304).

College women, who appeared to be fairly well adjusted, were found to have had as a role model with whom they identified, mothers who were considered masculine because they were goal-oriented (Heilbrun, 1968).

One of these stereotypical roles associated with being female is that of wife and mother. In some ways, being married can be dangerous to a woman's health, particularly her mental health. Studies have found that married women have a higher rate of self-reported psychiatric symptoms than men (Langner and Michael, 1963, and Phillips, 1966). Some have argued that women feel freer to talk about their symptoms than men, while other research reported an actual difference in mental illness rates when response bias is taken into consideration (Clancy and Gove, 1974). Gove and Tudor (1973) noted that in reviewing scores of research studies, women in our industrial society show higher rates of mental illness than men. In one article Gove (1972) pointed out that because more of those (in the general population) who had never been married, and those who had at one time been married, had been found to have been mentally ill than those who were married, one would assume that single women stereotypically would comprise the greater number of the unmarrieds who were mentally ill, and thus account for the lower differential than in men of mental illness. Gove negates this contention and provides support for his proposal that it is the rate of mental illness in the married women that influences the fact that women have higher rates of mental illness than men. He attributes this to the role strain of being married regardless of whether one is or is not a working wife.

Gove also reports studies in which women more than men feel that they have marital difficulty and are less satisfied with the marital relationship as well as with their role as parent. Research "suggests that married women find their role limited and frustrating, and that their circumscribed range of activities and introspective tendencies (and/or opportunities for brooding) tend to magnify their problems" (Gove, 1972).

In 1914 a book entitled *Worry and Nervousness* (Sadler) stated that "The life of the average housewife and mother is too often made one of unnecessary drudgery and useless anxiety" (p. 512). The author, however, then discussed the fact that emphasis is placed on trifles rather than the important values like children. He in no way suggested that married women leave the house.

Gove (1972) states that single men and women are closely related to each other in terms of the role expectations, more so than married men and married women. More single people than married people become mentally ill, but more married women than married men develop emotional difficulty. Marriage, then, appears to create a strain on the woman in terms of her mental health.

We therefore see that role pressures, fear of success, lower self-esteem, as well as the institutionalized lower status of women (Knudsen, 1969) create the environment for the development of mental illness in women.

Women's physical complaints are often thought to be psychological rather than physical. Disorders such as pain during menstruation (dysmenorrhea), symptoms of nausea which often accompany pregnancy, discomfort during labor, as well as behavioral difficulties in babies, are often considered to be caused or exacerbated by psychological factors (Lennane and Lennane, 1973). In an article entitled "Alleged Psychogenic Disorders in Women—A Possible Manifestation of Sexual Prejudice," the authors present the aforementioned thesis that the organic difficulties are labeled psychogenic in origin because of the basic prejudicial attitude toward women. They point out that dysmenorrhea is associated with ovulation and generally abates by the time the female is either 25 or gives birth to a child. Dysmenorrhea is common, yet the medical profession persists in believing that it is caused by "nervousness" and that in the "high-strung" individual what is really a mild discomfort becomes exaggerated. The conclusion is that there is little one can do to relieve the pain. In 92 percent of the cases studied where medication was prescribed to stop ovulation, the pain ceased and yet dysmenorrhea is still persistently labeled psychogenic in origin.

Lennane and Lennane (1973) also point out that although physicians continue to view nausea during pregnancy as psychogenic; that is a reaction to the pressures and burdens of prospective motherhood, about 88 percent of women who are pregnant are affected in this way. The pains of labor are also real and not a figment of the patient's imagination as some people would like to think. Lennane and Lennane discuss one study which demonstrated that those women in labor who were thought to be neurotic and who were extraverted tended to be more fearful during labor but felt less pain than those who were considered relatively stable.

Last but not least, the authors of this thought-provoking article discuss the colicky baby and the assumptions that this disturbance relates to the mother's anxiety concerning motherhood and the feminine role. As with the previously mentioned disorders, colic is common in infants and responds to the treatment of the infant with drugs. Yet some doctors prescribe tranquilizers to the mother instead. The authors conclude that the consistent erroneous labeling of disorders as psychogenic is a function of prejudice. It lends itself to a denigration of women as well as to a poor treatment program.

What happens when a woman seeks help for what she perceives to be a mental disorder? If she goes to a psychiatric clinic, a physician, or is treated in a hospital setting, chances are her therapist will be a male.

If a woman finds her way to a Freudian oriented therapist, there is the danger that she may be viewed as a feminine woman if she strives for the traditional role of wife and mother, or a masculine woman if she chooses a career or both. Anatomy will be the determining factor in expected psychological characteristics of normality. The Jungian analyst also might subtly encourage the stereotypical sex roles (Friedman et al., 1979). But how about therapists with other orientations? What about the eclectic?

Sexism, the belief that men are better than women in a variety of ways and that therefore women should be subservient to them and should be viewed in terms of their alliances with men (Wolman, 1976), is as much a part of the fabric of our society as institutional racism. Because it is so much a part of our culture, it is often covert and subtle. Therapists are products of the culture in which they live and therefore reflect the attitudes, even the sexist attitudes of society.

The well-publicized Broverman and colleagues study (1970) entitled "Sex Role Stereotypes and Clinical Judgments of Mental Health" created a tremendous stir in the therapeutic community. Sex role stereotypes were defined as accepted beliefs that typify men and women.

Since certain behaviors in a culture are considered desirable, these desirable behaviors are considered the normal ones. The researchers hypothesized that clinicians will view characteristics of men and women differently in terms of whether they are considered healthy and normal. A questionnaire was distributed to forty-six male and thirty-three female clinicians who were divided into three groups. One group was asked to respond to the stereotype questionnaire in relation to their concept of an adult, healthy male, the second group in reference to an adult, healthy female, and a third group in relation to a healthy adult—no sex given. The results were decisive: "... clinicians tend to consider socially desirable masculine characteristics more often as healthy for men than for women. On the other hand, only about half of the socially desirable feminine characteristics are considered more often as healthy for women rather than for men" (Broverman et al., 1970, p. 4). The researchers point out that although this finding may not seem important, the consideration of healthy women as differing from men in that they are

> more submissive, less independent, less adventurous, more easily influenced, less aggressive, less competitive, more excitable in minor crises, having their feelings more easily hurt, being more emotional, more conceited about their appearance, less objective, and disliking math and science (Broverman et al., 1970, p. 5)

stereotypes them into behaviors which are not conducive to success, nor to mental health as the clinicians defined it for the healthy adult. The concept of a healthy, mature male is similar to that of a healthy, mature adult. The implication seems to be that a woman who manifests healthy, mature, adult behavior chances being labeled sick because she does not manifest the stereotyped characteristics of what is considered a healthy female. A woman, then, who is rebelling against the traditional feminine role may be viewed as neurotic.

By the way, it is important to mention that there was no significant difference in the responses of female and male clinicians. Minority group members often buy into the stereotypes preached by the dominant group. Other research has supported the Broverman findings in terms of the fact that sex bias affects clinical judgments (Abramowitz et al., 1976).

One doctoral study attempted to obtain attitudes of clinicians of both sexes toward patients of both sexes. As with the Broverman study, both male and female clinicians viewed the patients similarly. The conclusion of this particular researcher did not fully support the conclusions of the Broverman study that the characteristics of a mentally healthy adult were biased toward the traits considered masculine in our society (Stricker, 1977), but since this study was reported six years after the Broverman research, perhaps there has been an increase in awareness on the part of therapists concerning the possibility of sex bias in their practice.

Concern about the possibility.of sex bias in therapy triggered the establishment by the American Psychological Association in 1974 of a task force on sex bias and sex role stereotyping. The task force was concerned with such issues as:

1. Differential treatment associated with women of different classes. Low-income women were viewed by therapists as not as well liked, more dependent, more passive, and more authoritarian than middle-class women, and treatment reflected this view.

2. The fact that female patients tended to be kept in the therapeutic relationship for a longer period of time than males, actually on the average of twice as long. Female patients perceived that the therapist embraced the traditional stereotypes of marital relationships. The husband should dominate, and sexually acceptable behavior differs for men and women.

The results of the questionnaire which was sent to women members of the APA concluded that sex bias does exist. One form is the fact that therapists seem to encourage traditional roles for women and do not appear to be tuned into the career needs that women may express. The respondents also itemized ways in which sex stereotyping is reflected in expectations of women in therapy as well as the manner in which devaluation of women takes place: for example, labeling battered women as masochistic, which overlooks their victimization, as well as labeling assertive, motivated women as castrating bitches. The use of epitaphs, such as "seductive" and "manipulative" for female patients and the telling of sexist, off-color jokes were presented as additional examples.

Respondents also criticized the reliance on psychoanalytic theory, particularly Freud's theory of penis envy, in treatment of women, as well as treating women as sex objects by stressing their physical appearance and attempting to seduce them in therapy.

The Task Force recommended that the education of therapists be revised to address itself to sex bias, stricter ethical standards for therapists, raising consciousness of clinicians, as well as further investigation of sexual intimacy between female client and the therapist (*Report on the Task Force on Sex Bias and Sex-Role Stereotyping in Psychotherapeutic Practice,* 1975).

It is very difficult to assess how many therapists have actually involved their patients in sexual activity, but we do know that it does exist (Chesler, 1972) and that it has a detrimental effect on the client. In the Fall of 1971 sexual abuse in therapy was vividly brought before the public when (Raymont, September 7, 1971) published an article in the *New York Times* discussing the American Psychiatric Association's refusal to publish an ad in its official journal, *The Journal of American Psychiatry.* The ad was one that would have publicized Martin Shepard's book, *The Love Treatment.* The book is about sexual behavior between therapists and clients and included eleven discussions with women who allegedly had sexual relations with their therapist. A spokesperson for the American Psychiatric Association stated that the "subject was 'inappropriate' for the professional publication" (Raymont, September 7, 1971). Dr. Shepard, himself a psychiatrist, requested that an investigation be made to scientifically study sexual intimacy between therapists and clients. The secretary of the committee on ethics of the American Psychiatric Association responded, "It is my personal opinion that the association has many more compelling social issues to worry about than to concern itself with an issue on which there is so little data" (Raymont, September 7, 1971, p. 20). Sexual abuse of women apparently was not an important enough issue for him.

In 1973 *The American Psychiatric Journal* did publish a study of attitudes and practices of male doctors in terms of sexually toned and nonsexually toned touching (Kardener et al., 1973). Of the 460 physicians randomly sampled (these included psychiatrists, obstetricians, gynecologists, and surgeons), most voiced negative feelings regarding physical contact with patients that was nonerotic in character. However, it was the psychiatrists most often who were the ones who rationalized the possible need for this contact. Thirteen percent of the physicians stated that nonerotic contact helps in cases of sexual maladjustment "especially in the depressed, middle-aged female who feels undesirable" (p. 1079), for helping people learn about their anatomy and "in healthy patients by mutual consent making the therapy go fast, deeper, and increases dreams" (p. 1079).

Five to thirteen percent of the physicians sampled had been involved with their patients in an erotic manner and 5 to 7.2 percent had had actual sexual relations with their patients. In 80 percent of the cases more than one patient had been involved.

A replication of the Kardener et al. study was done in 1976, this time using female physicians as subjects (Perry, 1976). More of the women doctors favored and had participated in nonerotic contact than the male physicians previously questioned. Few of them, however, supported the concept of or had been involved in erotic touching, and not one had had sexual relations with a patient. The patient's sex did not influence the female physician's attitude towards touching. Half of the women were not averse to nonerotic touching, and in fact about 2 percent had engaged in that type of behavior. More of the women who touched their patients were younger than those who did not.

Again, in 1977, the Kardener et al. questionnaire was sent to psychologists only with some additional questions. In this study (Holroyd et al., 1977), the majority (70 percent of male and 88 percent of female) respondents could find no rationalization for erotically touching clients of the opposite sex. Nonerotic contact was reported by 27 percent of the therapists, and male therapists stated that it was usually the female patient who first touched. Five-and-a-half percent of the male and .6 percent of the women therapists stated that they had been involved in a sexual relationship with a client. In comparing the research on male psychologists with that reported by Kardener et al. on male physicians, Holroyd and colleagues found that the attitude towards an actual erotic and nonerotic contact was very similar. In discussing their findings, Holroyd and colleagues state:

> The consistency between male psychiatrists and male psychologists indicates that a steadfast, small minority of therapists believe in the therapeutic benefits of erotic contact and practice in selected situations. Erotic contact and intercourse are almost always between male therapists and female clients (p. 848).

It seems that sexual exploitation is more often a function of the male and the victim of this abuse, the female.

One wonders whose needs are being met when there is sexual involvement in a therapeutic relationship. Research seems to suggest that it is the therapist's needs most often which are paramount in this liaison. Loneliness, fear of being intimate, and feeling like a father to the client were voiced by the therapists as reasons for their behavior (Holroyd et al., 1977). For the patient, the sexual liaison often leads to extreme psychic pain.

Kardener (1974) writes about the physician-patient relationship as paralleling that of parent-child. An individual in need of professional counseling is feeling dependent and somewhat in the position of a child because she is vulnerable. He views the sexual relationship of therapist and client as incestuous in nature and therefore potentially highly destructive for the woman, the client. Even if the woman is being seductive, her seductiveness is really expressing a need to be loved and to belong and should not be taken advantage of. The therapist who is the initiator of sex must be aware of his needs which may very well include a need for power. If, indeed, it is the patient who is meeting the needs of the therapist, states Kardener, then the therapist should be prepared to pay the client what he himself charges others.

Chesler (1972) labels sex between a therapist and his client as "legal rape," and points out that this type of violence is not new and has been practiced by well-known psychiatrists for many years. It typically takes place between a man older than his patient by as much as ten to twenty-five years. William Masters of Masters and Johnson believes that regardless of whether the liaison was begun by the therapist or the client, the therapist should be charged with rape rather than malpractice basically because the client inevitably becomes emotionally dependent on the therapist during treatment and therefore is in no position to make an objective decision (Stone, 1976).

There have been several cases of convictions because of sexual involvement of the therapist with clients. One psychiatrist who was convicted and sent to prison drugged his victims before sexually assaulting them. He was convicted of statutory rape of one of his clients, a sixteen-year-old promiscuous girl (Stone, 1976). Stone points out that in those cases where adult females have consented to the sexual activity, there is no fraud or force involved and therefore in many states no rape. According to Michigan's law a doctor who involves himself in a nonethical manner while treating or examining a patient is legally liable, and in Ohio a psychotherapist can be convicted of sexual battery if he uses coercive measures which the client under normal circumstances would be able to resist to force his client to submit sexually, (Stone, 1976). Stone points out that husbands who sue their wives' therapists for malpractice because the therapists have had a sexual liaison with them do not succeed in the courts.

Unfortunately, it is very difficult for a sexually abused patient to gain redress from the professional associations. The burden of proof is solely on the client, and often she is accused of either "seducing" the physician or of fantasizing. One of my clients told me that when she complained to another therapist about her previous therapist's erotic contacts and attempts at involving her in a sexual relationship, she was told, "you provoke this with men because you are passive and manipulate men into this behavior." Again we see yet another example of the "blaming the victim" syndrome. The victim is responsible for the crime. My client, with great persistence and help from another therapist, did gather data and filed a formal complaint with the American Psychological Association. The therapist was reprimanded but is still practicing his form of therapy today.

In one state in the west, one physician who had acted in the most unacceptable manner sexually, retained his license because the board found that he had been "grossly negligent and immoral but not guilty of grossly negligent or ignorant malpractice" which were the only grounds for the revoking of a license (Seiden, 1976).

Psychiatric abuse of women has to cease and, hopefully, with the increased awareness and vocalization by women of their concerns in this area, some progress will be made along these lines. In 1975 a landmark case was instituted by Pamela Buckingham when she filed a malpractice suit against a psychiatrist, Dr. Robert Trahms of San Francisco. Ms. Buckingham, a secretary at the Golden Gate Disposal Company in the same city, asked for $1.6 million in damages. She testified that she had been in weekly therapy with the "good" doctor, and had not only paid him his $40 per session fee but had on many occasions been involved in sexual intercourse with him. She had also carried out his "therapeutic" suggestions to get involved sexually with as many men as possible. The end result was physical and mental chaos. Although Dr. Trahms refused to admit that these acts did indeed occur, he was found guilty. Pamela Buckingham was awarded $250,000 in damages, and the doctor's license was revoked by the California Medical Quality

Assurance Board. Pamela Buckingham was the first woman to have succeeded in a "love therapy" suit in California. The year was 1977.

References

Anon. Report of the task force on sex bias and sex-role stereotyping in psychotherapeutic practice. *American Psychologist* 1169–1175 (December 1975).
_____. The Panic of Open Spaces. *Time.* p. 58 (November 7, 1977).
Abramowitz, Stephen, Roback, Howard B., Schwartz, Joseph M., Yasuna, Amy, Abramowitz, Christine V. and Gomes, Beverly. Sex bias in psychotherapy: a failure to confirm. *American Journal of Psychiatry* 133:6:706–709 (1976).
Alexander, Franz G. and Selesnick, Sheldon. *The History of Psychiatry.* New York: Harper & Row, 1966.
Angrist, Shirley, Dinitz, Simon, Lifton, Mark and Pasamanick, Benjamin. Rehospitalization of female mental patients. *Archives of General Psychiatry* 4:363–370 (1961).
Aristotle. *The Politics of Aristotle.* J. E. C. Welldon trans. London: Macmillan and Co., 1905.
Bonaparte, Marie. *Female Sexuality.* New York: International Universities Press, 1953.
Breedlove, Carolyn J. and Cicirelli, Victor G. Women's fear of success in relation to personal characteristics and type of occupation. *The Journal of Psychology* 86:181–190 (1974).
Broverman, Inge K., Broverman, Donald M., Clarkson, Frank E. and Rosenkrantz, Paul S. Sex-role stereotyping and clinical judgments. *Journal of Consulting and Clinical Psychology* 34:287–295 (1970).
Carter, Robert Brudenell. On the pathology and treatment of hysteria. London: John Churchill, 1853, in Ilsa Veith. *Hysteria.* Chicago and London: The University of Chicago Press, 1965.
Chesler, Phyllis. *Women and Madness.* New York: Doubleday & Co., 1972.
Cheek, Frances E. A serendipitous finding: sex roles and schizophrenia. *Journal of Abnormal and Social Psychology* 69:392–400 (1964).
Church, A. Report of the annual meeting of the Gynecological Society of Boston. *Journal of the American Medical Association* 8:441–442 (1887).
Clancy, Kevin and Gove, Walter. Sex difference in mental illness: an analysis of response bias in self-reports. *American Journal of Sociology* 80:205–216 (1974).
Cloninger, C. R. and Gutze, Samuel B. Psychiatric illness and female criminality. *American Journal of Psychiatry* 127:303–311 (1970).
Cramer, P. and Hogan, K. Sex differences in verbal and play fantasy. *Developmental Psychology* 11:145–154 (1975).
Deutsch, Helene. *The Psychology of Women,* Vols. 1 and 2. New York: Grune & Stratton, 1945.
Dreifus, Claudia (ed.). *Seizing Our Bodies: The Politics of Women's Health.* New York: Vintage Books, 1978.

Durant, Will. *The Reformation.* New York: Simon & Schuster, 1957.

Ellis, Albert and Sagarin, Edward. *Nymphomania.* New York: Gilbert Press, 1964.

Erikson, Erik. Inner and outer space: reflections of womanhood, in Robert Lifton (ed.). *The Woman in America.* Boston: Beacon Press, 1967.

Fodor, Iris Goldstein. The phobic syndrome in women: implications for treatment, in Violet Franks and Vasanti Burtle (eds.). *Women in Therapy.* New York: Brunner/Mazel Publishers, 1974.

Freud, Sigmund A. Transformation of puberty, in *The Complete Works of Sigmund Freud,* James Strachey (ed.). London: The Hogarth Press and The Institute of Psycho-analysis, Vol. VII, 1953. pp. 207–230.

_____. A child is being beaten, in *The Complete Works of Sigmund Freud,* James Strachey (ed.). London: The Hogarth Press and The Institute of Psycho-analysis, Vol. XVII, 1971 a, pp. 179–204.

_____. Some psychical consequences of the anatomical distinction between the sexes, in *The Complete Psychological Works of Sigmund Freud,* James Strachey (ed.). London: The Hogarth Press and The Institute of Psycho-analysis, Vol. XVII, 1971 b, pp. 248–258.

Friedan, Betty. *The Feminine Mystique.* New York: W. W. Norton, 1963.

Friedman, Susan, Stanford, Gams, Linda, Gottlieb, Nancy and Nesselson, Cindy. *A Woman's Guide to Therapy.* Englewood Cliffs, N.J.: Prentice-Hall, 1979.

Gove, Walter R. The relationship between sex roles, marital status, and mental illness. *Social Forces* 51:34–44 (1972).

Gove, Walter R. and Tudor, Jeanette F. Adult sex roles and mental illness. *American Journal of Sociology* 78:812–835 (1973).

Halleck, Seymour L. Hysterical personality traits. *Archives of General Psychiatry* 16:750–77 (1967).

Haller, J. S. and Haller, R. M. *The Physician and Sexuality in Victorian America.* Urbana, Ill.: University of Illinois Press, 1974.

Heilbrun, A. B. Sex role, instrumental-expressive behavior and psychopathology in females. *Journal of Abnormal Psychology* 73:131–136 (1968).

Holroyd, Jean Corey and Brodsky, Annette M. Psychologists' attitudes and practices regarding erotic and nonerotic physical contact with patients. *American Psychologist* 32:843–849 (1977).

Horner, Matina S. Fail: bright women. *Psychology Today* 3:36–38, 62 (November 1969).

Horney, Karen. *Feminine Psychology.* New York: W. W. Norton & Co., 1967.

_____. *The Neurotic Personality of Our Time.* New York: W. W. Norton & Co., 1937.

Jordan, Brian T. and Kempler, Bernhard. Hysterical personality: an experimental investigation of sex-role conflict. *Journal of Abnormal Psychology* 75:172–176 (1970).

Kardener, S., Fuller, M. and Mensh, I. A survey of physicians' attitudes and practices regarding erotic and nonerotic contact with patients. *American Journal of Psychiatry* 130:1077–1081 (1973).

Kardener, Sheldon. Sex and the physician—patient relationship. *American Journal of Psychiatry* 131:1134–1136 (1974).

Kimball, M. Women and success—a basic conflict? in M. Stevenson (ed.). *Women in Canada.* Toronto: New Press, 1973.

Knudsen, Dean D. The declining status of women: popular myths and the failure of functionalist thought. *Social Forces* **48**:183–193 (December 1969).

Langner, Thomas and Michael, Stanley. *Life Stress and Mental Health.* New York: Free Press, 1963.

Lennane, Jean K. and Lennane, R. John. Alleged psychogenic disorders in women—a possible manifestation of sexual prejudice. *The New England Journal of Medicine* **288**:288–292 (1973).

Maccoby, Eleanor Emmons and Jacklin, Carol Nagy. *The Psychology of Sex Differences.* Stanford, California: Stanford University Press, 1974.

Masters, William and Johnson, Virginia. 29th Annual Meeting of the American Psychiatric Association, Miami Beach, Florida. May 10–14, 1976.

Meyer, J. A case of insanity, caused by diseased ovaries, cured by their removal— a phenomenal triumph for operative treatment. *Transactions of the American Association of Obstetricians and Gynecologists* **7**:503–504, 1894.

Mischel, H. Sex bias in the evaluation of professional achievements. *Journal of Educational Psychology* **66**:157–166 (1974).

Monahan, L., Kuhn, D. and Shaver, P. Intrapsychic versus cultural explanations of the "fear of success" motive. *Journal of Personality and Social Psychology* **29**:60–64 (1974).

Newberry, Phyllis, Weissman, Myrna M. and Meyers, Jerome K. Working wives and housewives: do they differ in mental status and social adjustment? *American Journal of Orthopsychiatry* **49**:282–291 (April 1979).

Parsons, Talcott and Bales, Robert. *Family Socialization and Interaction Process.* New York: Free Press, 1955.

Perry, Judith Adams. Physicians' erotic and nonerotic physical involvement with patients. *American Journal of Psychiatry* **133**:838–840 (1976).

Phillips, Derek. Rejection of the mentally ill: the influence of behavior and sex. *American Sociological Review* **29**:679–87 (1966).

Raymont, Henry. Psychiatry Journal Accused of Ban on Ad for Sex-Expose Book. *New York Times.* p. 20 (September 7, 1971).

Rickles, Nathan. The angry woman syndrome. *Archives of General Psychiatry* **24**:91–94 (1971).

Sadler, William S. *Worry and Nervousness.* Chicago: A. C. McClurg, 1914.

St. John Chrysostom. Homilies sur les statues in Vol. 3, Oeuvres, M. Jeannin Bar-le-Duc (trans). Nantes: L. Guérin, 1886.

Schiff, Ellen and Koopman, Elizabeth J. The relationship of women's sex-role identity to self-esteem and ego development. *The Journal of Psychology* **98**:299–305 (1978).

Seidan, Anne M. Overview: research on the psychology of women: II. women in families, work, and psychotherapy. *The American Journal of Psychiatry* **133**:1111–1123 (1976).

Stone, Alan A. The legal implications of sexual activity between psychiatrist and patient. *American Journal of Psychiatry* **133**:1138–1141 (1976).

Stricker, G. Implications of research for psychotherapeutic treatment of women. *American Psychologist* **32**:14–22 (1977).

Symonds, Alexandra. Phobias after marriage: women's declaration of dependence, in Jean Baker Miller (ed.). *Psychoanalysis and Women.* New York: Brunner/Mazel, 1973.

Szasz, Thomas S. *The Manufacture of Madness.* New York: Harper & Row, 1970.

_____. *The Myth of Mental Illness.* New York: Hoeber-Harper, 1961.

Veith, Ilsa. *Hysteria.* Chicago: The University of Chicago Press, 1965.

Warner, Richard. Racial and sexual bias in psychiatric diagnosis. *The Journal of Nervous and Mental Disease* **167**:303–309 (1979).

Winthrop, John. *The History of New England* 1630–1649 (2 vols.). Vol. 2, 2116. Boston: Thomas B. Wait, 1826.

Wolman, C. Therapy groups for women. *American Journal of Psychiatry* **133**:274–278 (1976).

9. Shaking Up Our Bodies: Medical Violence

Although there is a higher death rate for men, the rate of illness is higher for women. Adult women tend to be acutely ill more often than adult men. They visit their doctors more frequently than men do and they also are more frequent short-term patients in hospitals than their male counterparts (Nathanson, 1975). Although males do not become ill as frequently as women do, the illnesses they develop are usually of a more serious chronic nature and these illnesses tend to be more disabling (Verbrugge, 1977).

Americans are spending more and more on health care, and since women are recipients of health services 25 percent more often than men (*Health/Pac Bulletin*, March, 1970), they are also more often the objects of poor medical practice and possible abuse. Ninety-seven percent of the gynecologists in this country are men (Weideger, 1977). In her article, "A Funny Thing Happened on the Way to the Orifice: Women in Gynecology Textbooks" (January, 1973), Diana Scully reviews the negative attitudes towards women that are expressed in these books, and which it is safe to assume are adopted by the medical men in training who will be working exclusively with women. These negative attitudes as well as the view that women are basically reproductive agents may very well influence the medical violence that is perpetrated against "the weaker sex." We are referring to the unnecessary hysterectomies, the wholesale radical mastectomy approach, as well as the careless distribution of oral contraceptives in spite of their injurious effects.

The mass manufacture of the birth control pill is associated with the re-emergence of feminism in the United States. Did this long-awaited panacea really free women or is the result enslavement, or even worse, death?

Margaret Sanger, a name synonymous with contraception and birth control, was actually responsible for the financing of research in the early 1950s to find a contraceptive that could be easily used by most people. She raised funds for Gregory Pincus so that he could focus his work on reproduction and discover a "wonder" contraceptive. He, along with his associate, Dr. Min Cheuh Chang, was intrigued with the possibility of using progesterone as a deterrent to conception, particularly because progesterone had not been established as a carcinogen in past research. Estrogen had been found to have an exacerbating effect on cancer as early as the 1940s. Progestins, artificial progesterones, were used by Pincus and Chang in their experimental effort to block pregnancy. The use of progestins was facilitated by the production of oral doses. Meanwhile, Dr. John Rock, a gynecologist, was merrily working along on experiments with the hormones of the ovaries because of his interest in infertility. In 1955, after giving hormones to rabbits and rats, the three experimenters Chang, Pincus, and Rock, who had been sharing the results of their work, were ready to try their discovery, the pill, on people.

Inmates in mental institutions were the first human guinea pigs, and one wonders whether there was an effort made to obtain informed consent. These inmates and some medical students comprised the sixty people who volunteered to participate in the experiment.

At an International Planned Parenthood meeting Dr. Pincus reported on the pill and its ability to keep an ovary from producing egg cells. He also reported that the effect on eight male volunteers was infertility. They had been given ten milligrams daily of an early version of Enovid. One of the male patient's testicles shrank and a softening of the scrotum occurred after five-and-a-half months on the pill. Sex drive as determined by the rate of masturbation did not seem to be generally affected. Because of the influence of the Enovid on the testicles of this one inmate, the further exploration of Enovid as a male contraceptive was negatively affected. Steroids of any kind apparently affect the pituitary gland, which in turn decreases the secretion of the pituitary hormones, thus, within several months eliminating sperm production.

Later, 132 women in Puerto Rico were given the pill for a period of twelve months or more, and another group of 718 women took the pill for less than twelve months. The small number of women tested came as a surprise to the public and was not discovered until 1963, when Senator Hubert Humphrey, a Democrat from Wisconsin, and his Senate Committee on Government Operations were investigating the Food and Drug Administration.

Although there were five deaths among the women, there was no attempt made to examine in depth the possible effect of the pill on their illness. Following this obviously short and research-poor study, the FDA approved the pill for sale as a contraceptive in 1960, and the reemergence of the feminist movement took place. No longer would women have to fear the possibility of an unwanted pregnancy. No longer would women have to abstain from sexual intercourse for fear of pregnancy, or have sexual intercourse, always fearing the awesome possibility of unwanted motherhood. Women could now be sexually active before marriage and sexually active after marriage, knowing that the decision of whether or not and when to have children could be theirs. They could now space their children and plan their families. The sword of Damocles had been lifted from over the heads of the female sex.

In reality, psychologially this was true. What one forgets, however, is that the diaphragm had been available for use since the late 1800s, and that the diaphragm, if fitted correctly, and used in conjunction with foam, is about 99 percent safe, as safe as the pill, and as we will soon see, safer in terms of the possibilities of morbidity and mortality. We have never lost a woman yet as a result of the use of the diaphragm.

The original birth control pill marketed was purported to be pure progestin, thus avoiding the use of estrogen, which had been found to be associated with cancer, although not having a direct effect on its genesis. It was found, however, that when the pill began to be tested in Puerto Rico in 1956 somehow or other it contained some estrogen. An effort to purify the pill was successful, although the effects on women such as some bleeding, and the resultant concern that the suppression of ovulation had not taken place, resulted in reconstituting the pill to contain estrogen in spite of the knowledge of its deleterious effects. Pills containing progestin only are being used now, but are not as effective as the combined estrogen and progestin pill in preventing pregnancy.

Seaman and Seaman (1978) in their excellent book, *Women and the Crisis of Sex Hormones,* point out that up until the widespread acceptance of the use of the pill by physicians, most drugs were carefully used mainly on people with medical problems, people who were ill. The women who were and are being given the pill are generally healthy. Also, they state that estrogen was a known carcinogenic agent; yet it was added to the original pill, which contained only progestin, without much concern. The constant inhibition of the pituitary gland by the pill results in a drastic change in hormonal balance. Did anyone express concern as to what side effects would result? Very few did, and certainly not the manufacturer of the drug. Seaman and Seaman (1978) also point out that it was only after millions of women had become pill users that the necessary dosage was confirmed, and that was found to be one-tenth of the estrogen which the marketed pill contained.

Actually, Enovid had been used since 1958 as a method of relieving dysmenorrhea, particularly that called by doctors spasmodic dysmenorrhea, in which there is a hormonal imbalance involving an excess of progesterone in relation to estrogen (Weideger, 1977).

Not too long after its approval by the FDA and the beginning of its widespread use as a contraceptive, Enovid, manufactured by Searle and the most widely used pill, became suspect. The manufacturer had on file in 1962 about 132 reports that women taking Enovid had suffered an embolism (the blocking of a blood vessel), and thrombosis (intravascular coagulation of the blood, commonly known as a blood clot) (Seaman and Seaman, 1978). Apparently, there were also about eleven deaths associated with the use of the pill, and talk erupted concerning the possibility of rescinding its governmental approval. Alarmed at the possibility of losing a lucrative market, Searle created a large-scale conference in 1962 with a focus on increased research on the pill and its effects. From some of the jovial conversations at this conference, one could conclude that the side effects of the pill were not taken as seriously as they might have been. One wonders whether if there had been more women in the medical profession this might not have happened.

Although called for at this conference in Chicago, in-depth studies were not instituted. Finally, a British committee called the Dunlap Committee on the Safety of Drugs, with a small staff of twenty-five and a small endowment, was able to conclude that there certainly was a connection between use of the pills and blood clotting ailments. It was 1968, six years after the Chicago conference.

How does the birth control pill work? Each ovary contains thousands of follicles within which there is a cell with an undeveloped egg. These follicles are responsible for the monthly production of eggs triggered off by the secretion of Follicle Stimulating Hormones (FSH) secreted from the pituitary gland. The follicles in the process of developing, produce estrogen, which is one of the sex hormones. The estrogen travels through the blood stream to the pituitary gland, which in turn begins to decrease the manufacture of FSH when a certain level of estrogen is absorbed. The pituitary gland then switching rather than fighting, turns to producing LH (Luteinizing Hormone). When LH reaches the ovary, it joins with the estrogen to inhibit all but one of the follicles that had been stimulated. The chosen one develops until it matures, at which time its egg is expelled from the ovary. LH is responsible for the remaining follicle becoming the corpus luteum, and the corpus luteum is responsible for the manufacture of another ovarian hormone called progesterone. It also continues to produce estrogen. When a given amount of progesterone reaches the pituitary gland, it responds by ceasing secretion of LH, resulting in the breakdown of the corpus luteum since it is no longer being nourished. Progesterone and estrogen are therefore no longer manufactured and menstruation begins. If pregnancy had occurred the corpus luteum would have continued growing, the fetus would have been nurtured by the progesterone the corpus luteum manufactured until such time as the placenta was able to assume the function of providing nourishment. For an excellent summary of the menstrual cycle, see Paula Weideger's *Menstruation and Menopause* (1977) and the Boston Women's Health Book Collective's *Our Body Ourselves* (1973).

Estrogen and progesterone are synthetically produced and make up oral contraceptives. These hormones prevent pregnancy by preventing the egg from developing. Because synthetic estrogens are additions to what is manufactured by follicles when they are taken, the message to the pituitary gland is that it does not have to manufacture FSH and therefore an egg is not developed. If eggs are not developed, conception cannot take place since there is nothing for the sperm cell to fertilize.

There are two kinds of birth control pills, the combined and the sequential. According to Seaman and Seaman (1978) the combined pill, that which contains both progestin and estrogen, has a reliability rate of 99.5 percent. The pills which are not as effective and have caused more concern regarding their safety are the sequential pills, containing either progestin or estrogen, and which are taken in such a manner as to approximate the "normal menstrual cycle." Pills containing progestin only have been shown to be the least reliable of the three types. The reliability of oral contraceptives is unquestioned if women take the pills regularly. There are, however, incidences (an estimated 6 percent of pregnancies) resulting from lack of adherence to the prescribed daily dosage or what is called breakthrough pregnancy.

A *Newsweek* article of October 28, 1974 (p. 107) summarized a study by the New York State Department of Health which indicated that women who unknowingly continued to take the pill after pregnancy had occurred, gave birth to children who had birth defects related to the skeleton, including anything from a finger or toe that was missing to more severe skeletal abnormalities. In this study 108 women who had produced skeletally defective children were compared with a matched control group of 108 women whose babies had been born normal. Of the women who had defective offspring, 45 had taken synthetic hormones, as compared to four women in the control group. Five of the women who birthed deformed babies had been on the combined birth control pill, that which contains both progesterone and estrogen, while they were pregnant. Apparently they had used the pill as directed but became pregnant due to a quirk of some kind in their reproductive systems. Three of the women had taken a pregnancy test involving injections of progesterone. This test will cause the onset of menstruation in nonpregnant women. Six mothers had taken hormones to stop vaginal bleeding while pregnant. Although the researchers felt that the deformities might very well be related to endocrine hyperactivity of the mother, they did recommend that the withdrawal-type pregnancy tests not be used because other pregnancy tests are available, but postponed making a judgment on oral contraceptives until further study in spite of the fact that there are also other birth control methods available (*Newsweek,* October 28, 1974, p. 107).

Reading through the medical journals, one finds many references to myocardial reactions and myocardial infarctions as related to the use of the pill. In plain layperson's language, the articles refer to heart abnormalities. One such article in the May 19, 1977 issue of the *New England Medical Journal* (p. 1166–1167) cites several findings which indicate that women with myocardial infarction have been three to five times more likely to have taken oral contraceptives, and that those who are on the pill are almost two and one-half times as likely to develop myocardial infarction if thirty to thirty-nine years old and about four and one-half times if forty to forty-four. If they smoke or have high blood pressure, the risk increases (Hennekens and MacMahon, 1977).

Between 1970 and 1974 a study of a large number of women with myocardial infarction found that many of them were oral contraceptive users (Oliver, 1970). Another study reported in *The Lancet*, a prestigious British medical journal, indicated that the chance of heart disease increased four times for oral contraceptive users. If the pill user smoked twenty-five or more cigarettes daily the increased risk rose to twenty times. Length of time the oral contraceptive was used did not seem to affect the risk factor *per se* (Shapiro et al., 1979).

Reviewing a number of studies on the relationship between oral contraceptives and heart attacks, Dr. Howard Ory and his colleagues concluded that although pill takers increase their risk of getting a heart attack, unless there are other predisposing factors such as hypertension or smoking, there is only a slight increase in their risk of dying from it (Ory, 1976). I'm not too sure this is very comforting, since one's health can be very seriously affected and one's activities severely limited by heart disease.

Compared with men, women have had fewer incidences of cardiovascular diseases. Some people have proposed that as women gain entry into highly competitive tension-producing positions, they will become more apt to fall prey to the same diseases as men, especially that of heart disease. Valerie Beral, writing in *The Lancet* in November, 1976, refutes this contention. She states that although the influences of female employment on cardiovascular diseases have not been studied in depth, morbidity and mortality among women who work have not in any way been shown to be correlated with working. In fact, increase in education is associated with a decrease in death from heart disease, high blood pressure, brain disease associated with vascular difficulties, as well as cardiovascular difficulties in women. She also points out that evidence does not support the contention that the woman who is emancipated would be more prone to fall victim to cardiovascular disorders.

Beral also discounts increased change in diagnostic categories or the change in smoking habits as being responsible for the increase in mortality in cardiovascular diseases. She also contends that the increase in mortality rate is not the result of doctors' knowledge of the effect of oral contraceptives on the heart and blood vessels since the increase was noted before the association was made. In relation to cigarette smoking, she states "that changes in smoking habits which are probably contributing to the overall level of and the long-term trends in female cardiovascular-disease mortality, are unrelated to the distribution of oral contraceptive use and thus should not account for the associations described" (Beral, 1976, p. 1051). Noting that in 1973 alone, and in increasing numbers, about 50 million people throughout the world were on oral contraceptives, she further states that "findings support the previous studies in suggesting that there is a true increase in the risk of death from myocardial infarction, hypertension, cerebrovascular diseases, and possibly all cardiovascular diseases among women taking the pill" (Beral, 1976, p. 1051). She urges that the risks associated with taking the pill be cleared up once and for all.

British researchers found that those women who are oral contraceptive users are five times as likely to die from circulatory diseases, which include heart disease, high blood pressure and cerebrovascular disorders (*British Medical Journal,* October, 1977).

Another group of researchers working with the Family Planning Association in Oxford, England observed 17,032 women over a period of nine years. Although none of the women who were using diaphragms or IUDs died, there were forty-three pill-using women who succumbed. In both of these studies women who were thirty-five or older showed a higher rate of death from cardiovascular disease. Of the nine who died of cardiovascular disease, all used the pills for a period of from three to ninety-three months. Five were sudden and unanticipated deaths. One was a woman who died forty months after having a heart attack, and we wonder about the quality of her life during that period (Vessey *et al.,* 1977). Don't panic, suggests one review, because there has not been an increase in the risks themselves, rather a recalculation has occurred. After all, the number of people who died is not a large number, and people today aren't planning to use the pill during all of their reproductive years since there is a trend towards sterilization of the wife or husband (*British Medical Journal,* October, 1977). It is certainly easy to say don't worry as long as you are not the person who is taking the oral contraceptive and therefore not the person whose life may be in danger.

In addition to the danger of cardiovascular disease, there is a known danger of the possibility of blood clotting for those women who use oral contraceptives. Apparently the pill can cause the dilation of the veins, which results in the blocking of the blood flow and possible blood clot formation (Seaman and Seaman, 1978). The legs, feet, and pelvis are the areas in which blood clotting most often occurs. Blood clots don't always stay where they are formed, and if they are released can stop the supply of blood to a vital area, such as the brain, resulting in a stroke, or the heart, resulting in a heart attack, or the lung (pulmonary embolism). According to the FDA there are between 300 and 500 women each year who are killed by a pulmonary embolism associated with taking the pill (Seaman and Seaman, 1978). There are additional deaths from clots which have traveled to other vital organs of the body. Prior to the release of oral contraception on the market, there were very few young women who died of a stroke or what the physicians call a cardiovascular accident. Strokes for this population increased with the introduction of the pill, and the stroke victims did not have diseases such as diabetes or high blood pressure to cause them. In 1974 the *Canadian Medical Association Journal* (Gilder) described such a case in a twenty-two-year-old woman, and the author concluded that the pill was the culprit in her death.

The British were very concerned with the possible negative side effects of the pill. Two British doctors, W. H. Inman and M. P. Vessey (1968) of the British Committee on Safety of Drugs, established the fact through their research that blood clotting disease was related to estrogen and that the dosage and type of estrogen were important factors. They obtained data from 920 doctors in Great Britain and 305 doctors in Sweden and compared all the pills on the market between 1965 and 1969, looking at the relationship between the type of oral contraceptive and the incidence of thromboembolism (bloodclotting disease). They found that the most important factor in blood clotting difficulties was estrogen. The British issued a statement to their population urging women to keep their estrogen intake at not more than 50 micrograms for each pill. In the United States, however, the FDA refused to take action and waited for the publication of the full report of the study. Finally, the FDA issued a recommendation that physicians prescribe a low-dose pill. It was spring of 1970 and there were about 8.5 million women using oral contraceptives in the United States, with only one-half of them on low-dose pills (*Science News,* May 2, 1970, p. 430). The length of time on the pill is not a factor in thrombosis or the development of blood clots. The risk of developing a blood clot, however, is ten times greater for an oral contraceptive user than for those who are not on the pill (*The Lancet,* June 1973).

In the *Southern Medical Journal,* March, 1977, several doctors from Rochester, New York, described in detail a case of mesenteric venous thrombosis associated with oral contraceptives.

CASE REPORT

A 46-year-old white woman was admitted to another hospital on Oct. 17, 1972, with a three-day history of recurrent episodes of abdominal pain. She was awakened on the morning of admission by colicky, periumbilical pain which increased in severity and shifted to the right lower quadrant of the abdomen. This was accompanied by nausea without vomiting and several diarrheal stools. Her last menstrual period was normal, and occurred 3½ weeks before admission. She had been taking norethindrone with mestranol for six years. Her past history and family history were unremarkable. She gave no history of superficial or deep venous thrombosis.

Physical examination at admission revealed a well developed, well nourished, middle-aged woman in acute distress . . . (Nesbit and Deweese, 1977, p. 360–361).

After her operation she continued to run a fever rising to 102 degrees on about the fifth day after surgery. She complained of pains in the stomach and the back severe enough to cause great discomfort. Exploratory surgery revealed blood clotting in the veins. Twenty-five days after surgery, the patient was discharged from the hospital. She was taken off anticoagulants and did not again resume the use of oral contraceptives.

If this woman had not taken oral contraceptives (norethindrone and mestranol) she might not have become so acutely ill and have lost twenty-five days of her life in the hospital for the treatment of blood clotting.

Drs. Nesbit and Deweese (1977) conclude on the basis of their case, and the sixteen other cases they reviewed which were reported in medical journals, that there is a definitive suggestion that oral contraceptives are associated with mesenteric venous thrombosis.

The Royal College of General Practitioners in the United Kingdom has been conducting a long-term study beginning in 1968 of about 46,-000 women of child-bearing age and focusing on oral contraceptives and the difficulties they may create. Periodically, a paper is written regarding the Royal Academy's findings on the illness of users, nonusers and those who stopped taking the pill. They found that those who steadily took birth control pills had a mortality rate for circulatory disease that was over four times that of the controls, had four times the mortality rate for diseases of the heart and high blood pressure, as well as cerebrovascular disease. The increased rate of death of one death per 5000 for pill users is twice as much as the rate of accidental death in the study population. The study also pointed out that "the risk of circulatory disease increases with the duration of oral-contraceptive use and may persist after the pill is discontinued . . . This suggests that oral contraceptives induce changes in the circulatory system which are not immediately reversible" (*The Lancet,* October, 1977, p. 727).

The possibility of increased blood presure in users of oral contraceptives has been documented by the Walnut Creek Contraceptive Drug Study of 13,358 women between the ages of fifteen and twenty who were monitored from January, 1969 to December, 1972. Pill users had higher mean blood pressure than nonusers and the researchers wonder whether the effect of increased blood pressure relates to the increased rate of stroke and heart disease of those women on the pill (Fisch, 1977).

In a communication to the editor, published in the June 6, 1977 issue of the *Journal of the American Medical Association,* Dr. William B. Kannel of the National Heart Institute points out:

> While the changes in blood pressure, blood lipid values, and glucose tolerance noted may, on an individual basis, seem clinically trivial, it should be recognized that the impact on a whole population of women could be substantial. For example, a 10 mm Hg increase in blood pressure can increase the incidence of cardiovascular disease by 30%. The impact of a similar rise in the cholesterol level is roughly equivalent. In women, development of overt diabetes can erase their relative immunity to cardiovascular mortality. Add to this an independent effect of the oral contraceptives promoting myocardial infarction by an enhanced clotting tendency, and we have a potentially dangerous situation. It could eventually eradicate the female advantage in cardiovascular risk. (p. 2531).

He goes on to state that oral contraceptives have become a part of the fabric of our society, and he calls for taking positive steps toward understanding the effects of the pill as well as informed consent for women to whom oral contraceptives are prescribed.

It would seem that it is time to set some guidelines for monitoring women receiving oral contraceptives with respect to atherogenic traits and changes in blood coagulation. Indications and contraindications in the use of oral contraceptives and the time to consider alternative methods of contraception need to be more explicitly defined. Accepted contraindications now include thromboembolic disorders, cerebrovascular or coronary heart disease, known or suspected estrogen-dependent neoplasia, undiagnosed genital bleeding, or suspected pregnancy. More consideration should be given to adverse cardiovascular risk (Kannel, 1977, p. 2531).

And then there is the possibility of developing a primary liver tumor. The National Cancer Institute called on the American College of Surgeons Commission on Cancer to research the relationship between the pill and tumors of the liver. Seven hundred and forty-nine cancer research hospitals were contacted with 477 responding. Records were reviewed for the years 1970 to 1975 and 540 cases of primary liver tumors were identified in both sexes; 165 patients were men and 378 were women. Of the tumors in females, 166 or 43.9 percent were malignant and 212 or 56.1 percent were benign; 91.1 percent of the tumors in the males were carcinomas. Nearly half of all tumors were found in women who had taken oral contraceptives, and of those, 73.8 percent were not malignant (Vana et al., 1977).

A Central Registry had been set up in Great Britain to document the occurrence of benign hepatic tumors (tumors of the liver) in women since these tumors were rare before the introduction of oral contraception. Hepatic tumors seem to have a relationship to estrogen levels, and were most often seen in women who were in their later months of pregnancy or who had recently given birth. Length of time the pill was used was associated with the increased risk of developing a liver tumor. If a person takes oral contraceptives for five to seven years, the risk is five times the normal rate, and nine or more years of pill use increases the risk factor to twenty-five times normal. The documentation by the Registry suggests that benign tumors can become cancerous or may rupture or cause an ominous increase in liver size (*British Medical Journal,* April 1977).

Even the gall bladder is at risk for the woman on the pill. Apparently estrogen has an effect on the concentration of cholesterol, changing the bile composition and thus setting the stage for the formation of gallstones. Childbearing age is correlated with an increase in the development of gall bladder disease so again sex hormones may be the culprits (*The Lancet,* October 1976). If you are on the pill, you are twice as likely to develop gall bladder difficulties than if you are a nonuser (Seaman and Seaman, 1978).

Some research also suggests a change in glucose tolerance with the subsequent danger of diabetes attributed to oral contraceptives. One research project in Gainesville by Dr. William Spellacy at the University of Florida College of Medicine has been following the changes in metabolism that seem to be associated with oral contraceptive use. He has become particularly concerned with the fact that 5 to 15 percent of the women he has been studying who are on the pill have had major changes in their metabolism with long-term use of the pill, and that all pill users demonstrate some metabolic abnormality (Spellacy, 1969).

On November 12, 1978 the *New York Times* (p. 34) reported that oral contraceptives and cancer of the skin are linked together. A study in Walnut Creek of a large number of patients who belonged to a pre-paid health plan found that a woman who uses the pill for more than four years has ten times the risk of developing malignant melanoma (skin cancer). In another study in San Francisco it was found that there was an increase of 79 percent in skin cancers, from 1970 to 1975, half of the increase occurring in women who were potential child bearers. Use of oral contraceptives was suspect. Skin cancers in women comprise about 1 percent of all cancer. Five thousand cases of skin cancer, nearly half of them leading to death, occur yearly (*New York Times*, November 12, 1978, p. 34).

What relationship does the pill have to the skin? The pituitary gland is responsible for determining the rate of reproduction of skin pigment cells.

Skin pigment development is affected by estrogen and progesterone. Oral contraceptives contain sex hormones and many light-skinned oral contraceptive users develop dark skin patches. What has not been determined is whether the pill stimulates the pituitary gland, which in turn causes changes in the skin or whether the oral contraceptives have a direct influence on the skin cells themselves. Regardless of whether the pill directly or indirectly causes skin cancer, the *New York Times* (November 12, 1978, p. 34) reports that as far back as 1968 a psychiatrist at Metropolitan Hospital in Los Angeles suggested in the *Journal of the American Medical Association* that there might be a link between malignant melanoma and the use of the pill.

One study of a comparison of the rates of referral to the hospital of 1700 women who attended the Family Planning Association in British clinics and the method of contraception these women used, including the pill, the diaphragm, and the IUD, concluded that those women who used the pill tended to be referred to the hospital less often for difficulties in the menstrual cycle except amenorrhea (absence of menstruation), and less often for cancer and for nonmalignant breast lesions. They were referred more often than the users of the other methods of contraception for stroke, cervical erosion, and blood clotting (*The Lancet,* October, 1976). Diaphragm users were hospitalized less often for carcinoma of the cervix and dysplasia (abnormal tissue growth). However, referrals for hemorrhoids were more common. IUD users were seen in the hospital most often for varicose veins and for inflammation of a fallopian tube.

Although studies have found that the use of oral contraception hampers conception for several months after its use is discontinued, for those women who have borne children prior to using the pill, there is some question concerning permanent infertility in a number of women who have never been pregnant (*The Lancet,* October 1976). Although the combined oral contraceptives have less of a negative effect on future fertility, they have a wide effect on the biochemistry of the body which has not been determined as yet for those who are long-time users.

The so-called "oversuppression syndrome," meaning continuing infertility after cessation of use of the pill, was noted in 1968 and widely accepted as a consequence of oral contraceptives by the 1970s.

Often, pills to stimulate fertility are prescribed. These include Clomid and Gonodotropin, hormones derived from the pituitary glands of dead people or urine of women in menopause. Clomid stimulates the ovary and is prescribed in the hope that it will precipitate the menstrual cycle. Seaman and Seaman (1978) point out that although 70 percent of the people who take Clomid ovulate, less than half of them become pregnant. The side effects of this drug include stomachaches, tiredness, development of ovarian cysts, and symptoms similar to those that develop in menopause. Gonodotropin is expensive and can result in potentially dangerous conditions involving the buildup of fluid in the chest and the abdomen, decrease in blood pressure and even fatal coagulation of the blood in the arteries (Seaman and Seaman, 1978).

Oral contraceptives have been associated with eye disorders such as hemorrhages of the retina, double vision, short-term blindness, as well as infections of the bladder and kidney. Some women have been affected by a decrease in their sex drive, depression, and psychiatric difficulties (Seaman and Seaman, 1978).

The hormone estrogen has been found to be a carcinogen in a number of animal species, and it is logical to assume that it may also have a similar effect on humans.

Evidence has been accumulating over the years that there is an association between the pill and some types of cancer. As early as 1940 researchers had established the fact that estrogen has the potential of exacerbating a cancer that already exists (Seaman, 1969). Pill users are 300 percent more likely to have cervical "dysplasias," which are abnormal tissue changes in the cervix, than women who are nonpill users. These abnormal tissues detected by the Pap smear, often very closely resemble the tissues found in early cancer of the cervix (Seaman, 1969). What is indicting is the fact that for a number of patients who cease using oral contraceptives, the tissues revert to normal. Although this does not establish a direct relationship between the pill and cervical cancer, the researchers do caution that longer use of the pill may be more conclusive.

In 1970 research focused on the effect of the pill on both benign and malignant diseases of the breast. In 1975 the results of one study indicated that those women on the pill who had benign breast disease and had taken oral contraceptives for six years or longer were six to eleven times more likely to develop cancer than nonusers. The researchers did not conclude that there was a causal relationship between the pill and cancer but did indicate that if there is a cancer already in existence, pill use seems to encourage its growth (Fasal and Paffenberger, Jr., 1975).

Another research project in 1978 compared oral contraceptive users and nonpill users who developed cancer of the breast and found that contraceptive steroids have a detrimental effect on breast cancer (Spencer et al., 1978).

Concern for the association between oral contraception and uterine cancer resulted in having three major producers of the pill withdraw the oral sequential contraceptive from the market in 1976, although they did not recall those pills that had already been distributed.

Diethylstilbestrol, commonly known as DES, is a word that creates terror in 2.1 to 3.5 million daughters of women who had taken this synthetic estrogen in the 1940s, 1950s and 1960s in order to prevent miscarriage. It was in 1970 that the association of DES and cancer of the vagina (adenocarcinoma of the vagina) was made and reported in a medical journal. This type of carcinoma, which occurs in glandular tissue, is relatively rare in young women but more often is found in women over fifty. And yet, during the years 1966 and 1969 an alarming number of young girls with adenocarcinoma of the vagina came to the attention of the medical profession, especially Dr. Arthur Herbst and his colleagues at Vincent Memorial Hospital in New England. These researchers had noted that eight patients diagnosed as having this disease had been born between 1946 and 1951 and so a retrospective study for the years 1966 to 1969 was done to try to find those factors which the young women had in common, and which might be associated with the disease. Doctors at Vincent Memorial Hospital were surprised to find that between 1966 and 1970 seven young girls under the age of twenty-two were diagnosed as having adenocarcinoma of the vagina, whereas there was no evidence of such a case prior to 1966. None of the patients had been on oral contraceptives, only one had been sexually active, none had used douches which can cause irritation, and so a study was made using matched controls and involving an interview with the mothers of the subjects used in the study.

The study found that these mothers had presented a high risk of spontaneously aborting during the pregnancy with their daughters and that seven out of the eight mothers had taken diethylstilbestrol during the first three months of their pregnancy. The researchers concluded that use of DES by mothers during pregnancy "appears to have enhanced the risk of adenocarcinoma developing years later in the offspring exposed" (Herbst et al., 1971, p. 878). They hypothesized that stilbestrol changes the cells of the fetus and that this change resulted in malignancy years later. They recommended the disuse of stilbestrol for women who are pregnant, and a close examination of abnormal bleeding in adolescents, which is usually not considered a dangerous symptom for that population.

There is no accurate statistic for the numbers of women to whom stilbestrol was prescribed during pregnancy, and in reaction to the research done by Herbst and his colleagues, an editorial in the *New England Journal of Medicine*, April 22, 1971, urged that a central clearinghouse be set up to document the numbers of diagnoses of cancer of the vagina in young females for informational and evaluative purposes (Langmuir, 1971).

Interestingly enough the original Herbst article called for data which would confirm the conclusions of the effect of DES on the offspring, and on August 12, 1971, confirmatory data was given in the *New England Journal of Medicine* (Greenwald et al., 1971). The New York State Cancer Registry, which retrieves data on all cancers diagnosed in all of New York State, excluding New York City, noted that between 1950 and 1970 five women under the age of thirty had been reportedly diagnosed as having adenocarcinoma of the vagina, and that the data included a history itemizing the drugs used by the mother during pregnancy. Five of the mothers of the patients had taken a synthetic estrogen to prevent spontaneous miscarriage, and none of the patients were married at the time of diagnosis. Three patients in whom the diagnosis was made within a two-month period of onset died; the cause of death was advanced carcinoma. The mothers in the control group had not taken stilbestrol during pregnancy and none of their offspring suffered from the disease. In those DES offspring where treatment was given, some had to have a total removal of the vagina. Remember, this is in young women under the age of thirty. The researchers concluded that their findings raise "concern about the future. It is not known how many more vaginal carcinomas will be developing, whether other types of cancer will also develop in men or women, or whether a longer induction period may be present for those who received a smaller dose ... There can no longer be doubt that synthetic estrogens are absolutely contraindicated in pregnancy" (Greenwald et al., 1971, p. 392).

Although the Herbst et al. article raising concern with DES appeared in the *New England Journal of Medicine* on April 22, 1971, and copies of their findings were sent to the FDA, it was not until November of that same year that the FDA took some action to curb the use of DES. It is estimated that quicker action by the FDA would have prevented exposure to DES of about 20,000 women, 30 of whom will probably develop adenocarcinoma of the vagina or cancer of the cervix by the time they reach the age of thirty; a four in 1000 risk, which is forty-four times the risk of developing leukemia. For one-quarter of these young women, DES taken by their mothers during pregnancy means death (Seaman and Seaman, 1978).

As a result of an investigation by Congressman L. H. Fountain, Democrat, 2nd District of North Carolina, and his committee on DES in 1971 of the FDA's inaction, a mandate was issued and sent to doctors cautioning them about the effects of the drug on offspring if administered to pregnant women. The sale of DES continued to increase, however, because of its perceived validity as a pregnancy preventative if taken the morning after intercourse. The morning-after pill was widely used at health clinics of universities without informing the recipients of the possible danger to the fetus if pregnancy continued. DES's reliability as a contraceptive has been questioned (Jones, 1976).

DES is not only dangerous for female offspring but also for males, as well as dangerous for adult women who use the drug. Laboratory studies showed that male offspring of mice given DES during gestation had a high ratè of infertility (60 percent) and developed abnormalities of the reproductive system, including epididymal cysts. There are also reports of cancer of the testicles of offspring of mothers who took DES (Seaman and Seaman, 1978).

Suits are now being filed by DES offspring against major pharmaceutical companies in an effort to collect damages and special funds for detecting, preventing, and curing cancer of the cervix (*New York Times,* March 4, 1977, p. 16).

Several women who had taken DES for five years as treatment for being born with a lack of ovaries or congenitally defective ovaries developed cancer of the endometrium or changes which indicated the possibility of future cancer (Cutler et al., September 28, 1972).

If oral contraceptives have the potential of causing many side effects, what about the IUD? In 1975 it was estimated that about 4 million women in the U.S. used the IUD (Intrauterine Device) and that another 4 million had been users. The IUD is a copper or plastic device shaped in a loop or like a spring, a T, or a coil, which is placed by a physician into the uterus, and which, for reasons as yet unknown, prevents pregnancy. This foreign object may impede the development of the uterus lining, thus preventing the implantation of the egg, or it may cause changes which result in the egg being propelled at a fast rate through the Fallopian tube to the uterus so that when it does arrive the lining of the uterus has not as yet prepared itself for its implantation. Another theory suggests that it induces an increase in white blood cells which then inactivate the sperm. One of the positive reasons for using the IUD is that if desired, pregnancy can occur shortly after its removal, as well as the fact that once the device is inserted, the only involvement for the woman consists of occasional checking of the string to which the IUD is attached to ensure that the IUD is in its proper position.

In the 1800s a device similar to the IUD was invented. This was called a "pessary" and consisted of a device made of different types of materials including wood, metals such as gold and silver, as well as glass and ivory, which fitted over the cervix, but because this remodeled device caused so much difficulty and tended to induce infections, between 1930 and 1940 physicians considered its use unsafe (Corea, 1977). It wasn't until the late 1950s when there arose a concern with population growth that the IUD suddenly was presented as a good, safe birth control device. It has been suggested that there really was no new evidence of the increased safety of the device but that the pressure to widely distribute an easy, reliable contraceptive method was deemed to be crucial by population control advocates, and it was these advocates, particularly those represented by the Population Council (founded in 1959) who were instrumental in establishing the credibility of the IUD as well as being responsible for its expanded distribution (Corea, 1977).

The IUD appears to be safer than oral contraceptives. Between one and ten women out of 1 million, compared with twenty out of 1 million oral contraceptive users die as a result of use. It does not affect secretion of the hormones so that ovulation continues. Some women are unable to retain it, and if expulsion occurs without their knowledge, pregnancy can ensue. Pregnancy occurs in 2 to 4 percent of users, usually within a year of use, basically because expulsion of the device occurs in 2 to 20 percent of the women who use it, and it is during the first year that the user finds out whether or not she is able to retain the device (Katz, 1975). It is estimated that a large number of women (two out of three) are able to retain the IUD, and that a number of women who are able to keep the IUD request its removal because of various uncomfortable side effects, such as cramping or staining (Seaman and Seaman, 1978). Many doctors are not skilled in fitting the devices properly, which also adds to the numbers of unwanted pregnancies as well as discomfort for the user.

Side effects commonly noted with IUD users consist of staining between menstrual periods, pain during menstruation, as well as increase in menstrual flow (Martin, 1978). As with so many other prescriptions and devices prescribed for women, the consumer is not apprised of the potential dangers. In 1 in about 2500 cases, the IUD may perforate the wall of the uterus and in some instances find its way to the abdomen or to the bladder. One such case was reported in detail in the *Journal of Obstetrics and Gynecology* (September 1974).

A 40-year-old multipara (DK) with 9 living children had a Lippes Loop inserted 7 years previously, 2 weeks after the delivery of her last child. The insertion was done by a medical officer in a health center and was easy and painless, although a few days after insertion the patient experienced mild low backache lasting for 2 to 3 days.

She was admitted to our hospital April 17, 1972, with the chief complaints of pain in the lower abdomen, and burning and frequency of micturition for 8 months. The pain was mild to moderate in intensity, continuous, and situated over the pubic area, radiating toward the external genitalia during the act of micturition. She had nocturnal frequency accompanied by a burning feeling during every act of micturition. She had also been aware of a cloudy appearing urine. She had no menstrual complaints.

Six months previously the patient had been admitted to a gynecology unit with similar but milder complaints and with the history of non-expulsion of the loop. Curettage was performed but the loop could not be identified. On exploratory laparotomy at that time the uterus was found to be densely adherent anteriorly. Since no loop could be found, the abdomen was closed (Saronwala et al., 1974, p. 424).

The woman's abdomen was X-rayed during her most recent admission to the hospital, and it was found that the IUD, the Lippes Loop, commonly used, had perforated the uterus and the bladder and had caused the formation of a stone. The closed type of IUD has also been reported to cause obstruction of the bowel, and in 1968 the FDA received a recommendation from its Advisory Committee on Obstetrics and Gynecology that these devices be removed if perforation occurred. The Lippes Loop, which is an open type IUD, does not seem to perforate the bowel, so that the physicians' discretion determined whether or not one that was perforated be removed, basically because the surgical procedure for removal is accompanied by high risk (Whitson et al., 1974).

The Dalkon Shield, an open-type IUD, was released for use without extensive clinical studies in 1970. Because it was an open type device, a physician was not mandated to remove it in case of perforation and unfortunately perforation rates were fairly high (Whitson et al., 1974).

In 1973 the United States Public Health Services Center for Disease Control reported that it found women were hospitalized more often as a result of use of the IUD than they were if they were on oral contraceptives (Katz, 1975). With a sudden increase in the numbers of deaths and infections of the uterus reported as a result of Dalkon Shield use (11), as well as a fairly large number (209) of women whose IUD-related uteral infection resulted in miscarriage, the FDA became alarmed and proceeded to ban that particular device. Although the ban was eventually lifted after the Dalkon Shield was reconstructed, the negative publicity associated with it lingered on.

Pregnancies that occur while the IUD is intact are dangerous to both the mother and the fetus. IUDs are associated with pregnancy outside the uterus, pregnancy which is complicated by uteral infection, the threat of miscarriage, hemorrhaging after giving birth and even death. For the baby, the danger if pregnancy continues is premature birth as well as damage to the brain (Wilson, 1978). Physicians are advised to induce miscarriages in all pregnancies of this nature.

Menopause, commonly known as the change of life, actually is the period during which there is a cessation of menstruation usually taking place in women between the ages of forty-five and fifty. The fact that it is referred to as the "change of life" gives that natural physiological process an ominous tone. In our society the change is considered to be a negative one; a change from youth and sexuality associated with the ability to conceive and bear children, to old age and lack of sexuality associated with the fact that generally menopause and definitely post-menopause is a period of nonfertility.

It is during menopause that the secretions of progesterone and estrogen gradually decrease until the amount is stabilized, while the androgens decrease only slightly. The decrease of progesterone and estrogen means that egg cells (ova) are not produced and the menstrual flow ends. Because of the lessening in the secretion of estrogen, according to some researchers, a number of physiological symptoms occur such as hot flashes, cold sweats, and some discomfort in the breasts. After the menopause has ended there are also varying degrees of decrease in vaginal lubricating fluid which can have the effect of creating pain at intercourse. Dryness of the skin occurs and due to the shrinking of discs in the vertebrae, the length of the spine is reduced and consequently, height is also reduced.

It was estimated that in 1975 36 million American women were forty-five years or older and that by the time the year 2000 is reached, this figure will increase to 49 million (*A Statistical Portrait of Women in the United States,* 1976). The symptoms associated with menopause vary in intensity with each individual. However, it has been fairly well established that the woman's psychological reaction to the change within her body; that is the hormonal fluctuations, as well as the change from being a reproductive to a nonreproductive organism, has a profound effect on the degree of discomfort an individual woman will have.

For many years it had been assumed that treating menopausal women with estrogen therapy would prevent arterioschlerotic cardio-vascular disease (ASCVD). Concern mounted because there was an apparently steep increase in women having coronary heart disease (CHD) after menopause. The belief existed that possibly the decrease in the secretion of estrogen contributed to the high risk for these women, a conclusion reached because of the near equalization of heart attack risk between men and postmenopausal women. Some re-searchers refuted the association of postmenopausal heart attack risk by pointing out that actually what does happen is that the rate of death by heart attack in males decreases starting at the fourth decade of life and that there really is not a sudden increase in heart attack deaths of women during this same period (Shoemaker et al., 1977).

The death rates of men and women are also influenced by race, blood pressure, and socio-economic status (Shoemaker et al., 1977).

Shoemaker and his colleagues in an article in the *Journal of the American Medical Association* (October, 1977), discussed the benefits and the risks of estrogen replacement therapy (ERT). They concluded that as yet there is no hard evidence that estrogen is a factor in pre-venting cardiovascular disease in postmenopausal women.

Estrogen was also purported to prevent or at least decrease bone loss (osteoporosis) which results in bone breakage in postmenopausal women. Shoemaker et al. (October, 1977), cite the fact that one-quarter of women sixty or over develop fractures in the spine, and that in women who have reached or passed the age of forty-five, 75 percent of those with osteopenic bones will develop fractures and 80 percent will develop fractures of the hip, which result in death 16 percent of the time.

All individuals, male and female, experience bone loss as they age. Variables such as race, the amount of physical activity, diet, and skele-tal mass throughout the first three or four decades of life influence bone mass. In many studies which have concluded that there is a ben-eficial effect of estrogen in preventing or treating osteoporosis, the aforementioned variables have generally not been taken into account.

Shoemaker et al. (1977) do point out that there seems to be some benefit to treating young women who have hysterectomies with estrogen therapy since it appears to prevent osteoporosis until aging. The jury is still out on the effectiveness of estrogen therapy in the prevention of loss of bone mass.

Estrogen therapy was also advertised as the youth drug, a claim which has not been substantiated. It does not keep the skin soft or help to retain a woman's youthful feelings.

Estrogen is a widely used drug. Four times the amount of estrogen was sold in 1973 than in 1962 (Ziel and Finkle, 1975). This wonder drug was supposed to do many wonderful things such as relieving the symptoms of menopause, including hot flashes, inability to sleep, poor appetite, and depression. Some companies even marketed estrogen as the next best thing to the fountain of youth. The *Physicians' Desk Reference* in 1973 warned physicians that Milprem, a conjugated estrogen, could result in drug dependency and further stated that if the patient withdraws from the drug abruptly after having used it for a long period it may

> ... precipitate recurrence of pre-existing symptoms, such as anxiety, anorexia, or insomnia, or withdrawal reactions, such as vomiting, ataxia, tremors, muscle twitching, confusional states, hallucinosis, and rarely, convulsive seizures (*Physicians' Desk Reference,* 1973).

Premarin, a conjugated estrogen manufactured by Ayers was also listed in the 1973 PDR as effective in controlling the symptoms associated with menopause. What was not listed were the possible negative side effects that could occur as a result of using this drug. The supplement (B) to update the *Physicians' Desk Reference* in 1976 noted that there were indications of a link between estrogen therapy and endometrial cancer. Several studies were described: one by Smith et al., 1975 in which 317 women with endometrial cancer were retrospectively compared with patients with tumors (neoplasms) in the cervix, ovary or the vulva (the external portion of the female genitalia). Those women who had received estrogen therapy were over four times as likely to have developed cancer. No effort had been made in this study to identify the effects of the amount of estrogen taken and the length of time it was used.

The very significant Ziel and Finkle (1975) study was also cited. Ziel and Finkle noted that as early as 1933, estrogen had been identified as a carcinogen through studies on animals, and that in 1957 researchers were able to cause endometrial cancer with its use. Ziel and his colleagues compared those women identified as having cancer of the endometrium, whose cases were found in the reports of the Kaiser tumor registry in Los Angeles, with a control group who used the same health plan, the Kaiser Foundation Health Plan. The subjects in the two groups were the same age, lived in similar areas and had been members of this health plan for the same length of time. The authors reported that the risk of endometrial carcinoma was seven to one for estrogen users, and that the risk increased with the length of time the drug was used, with an increased risk of over thirteen to one for those on estrogens for seven years or longer.

Accusations of the exaggeration of the risk of estrogen were hurled at Ziel and Finkle. A response by the researchers and their colleagues to those questioning their original research took the form of having impartial experts review slides of the biopsy that was done on each of the patients diagnosed as having endometrial cancer reported in the study. In 74 percent of the cases there was unanimous agreement by all three experts that the diagnosis was correct, and in 99 percent of the cases at least one of the experts concurred with the original diagnosis (Gordon et al., 1977). The conclusion was again reached that conjugated estrogen has a role in the development of cancer of the endometrium.

The 1976 PDR also warned physicians about prescribing estrogen to patients with hyperglycemia (abnormal amounts of sugar in the blood), or to women with chronic mastitis (inflammation of the breasts). The PDR further cautioned that doctors "should be alert to the earliest manifestations of thrombotic disorders (thrombophlebitis, retinal thrombosis, cerebral embolism and pulmonary embolism)" (Supplement B-1976 PDR, p. 14). By 1979 the lists of contraindications and warnings for the use of premarin and other conjugated estrogens increased substantially.

On February 4, 1976, the *New York Times* reported that data issued by the National Center for Health Statistics indicated a tremendous increase in the death rate from cancer. The recorded rate of death from carcinoma increased more in 1975 than in any other year since World War II and increased more than any other death-causing agent.

To prescribe or not to prescribe estrogen therapy, that is the question. In an April, 1977, article in *Obstetrics and Gynecology,* Gray and colleagues reported on their study of 205 patients who had been diagnosed as having endometrial cancer, and a carefully matched control group which had no sign of this type of carcinoma when they underwent a hysterectomy. Risk of developing endometrial carcinoma increased with estrogen use to 11.5 times if used for ten years or longer. Relative risk had a relationship not only with the length of time used but the dosage. In spite of their findings, the researchers, all men, conclude

> The established or possible risks associated with the use of this medication must be balanced against its benefits . . . It has been estimated that in the near future 50% of women in the postmenopausal age range will have had a hysterectomy and therefore no longer be at risk for this disease. In addition the high cure rate of this cancer indicates that the impact of estrogens on the duration of life is certainly much less than its impact on the occurrence of endometrial cancer (Gray et al., 1977, p. 388).

It is frightening to think that physicians, generally without the knowledge of the patient, are prescribing without grave concern, a type of therapy which has a risk of provoking cancer on the grounds that the cancer, if it does develop, is curable.

It is particularly frightening since vasomotor changes (hot flashes, etc.) have not been definitively established as resulting from estrogen deficiency. Publications in the medical journals question this assumption (Aksel et al., 1976), and a letter to the editor in the April, 1977, issue of *The Lancet* urges the initiation of a large scale, carefully controlled study. In the same issue, in fact on the same page, a physician at the Department of Obstetrics and Gynecology of a hospital in Edinburgh, Scotland, denounced the advertising efforts of pharmaceutical companies which are focused on picturing women past menopause as suffering from a disease that can be treated with estrogen replacement. He also decried the fact that in their hard sell approach, these firms are claiming benefits which are not scientifically established, while these same advertisements to physicians question the validity of studies which have reported the link between endometrial cancer, carcinoma of the breast and estrogen. Why hasn't there been more of an effort made to find an alternative therapeutic program to relieve women of the discomfort of menopause? Hot flashes may be uncomfortable, but they are not dangerous and have been known to be controlled by Vitamin E (Seaman and Seaman, 1978). Vaginal atrophy, one of the results of the decrease of secretion of estrogen after menopause can be helped by the use of vaginal creams containing estrogen. Caution is suggested in using creams, however, because they are readily absorbed into the blood stream and can therefore have the same kinds of side effects as estrogen taken in pill form (Rigg et al., 1978).

Since 1977, the Food and Drug Administration required that estrogen be labeled as a possible carcinogen. In November of 1978 a Yale University study concluded that there was less of a risk from estrogen replacement therapy than had been previously reported (Horowitz and Feinstein, 1978). Shortly after the release of the Yale study researchers at Johns Hopkins University concluded that the risk of developing cancer of the uterus for estrogen replacement therapy users increases five times. Risk of cancer was confirmed by a group at Boston University, but their conclusion was that the risk increased ten times, and that those women between fifty-four and sixty years old who were on estrogen for more than eight years had an increased risk of twenty times of developing cancer of the uterus.

What effect, if any, does estrogen therapy have on the breast and the development of breast cancer? Estrogen stimulates the tissues of the breast readying it for cancer to develop or exacerbates the cancer that may already exist (Lipsett, 1977). Estrogen affects the development of breast tissue. Estrogen is also necessary for the secretion of prolactin, which influences the makeup of the cells in the breast (Lipsett, 1977). The occurrence simultaneously of endometrial carcinoma and cancer of the breast may therefore not be a coincidence, and the two diseases seem to occur together fairly frequently (McMahon and Austin, 1964).

1891 women who were given estrogen therapy were studied over a period of about twelve years to determine whether they developed carcinoma of the breast. To the surprise of the researchers, 30 percent had developed breast cancer. Although they did not conclude that there was a causal relationship between the use of estrogen and the development of cancer of the breast, they did conclude that estrogen was not a protective agent against the development of cancer of the breast as some researchers had implied, and that those women who had benign breast disease had a greater chance of developing cancer if on estrogen. The risk of breast cancer is twice as great for women on estrogen replacement therapy for five years or more than for nonusers (Hoover et al., 1976).

A report from the Boston Collaborative Drug Surveillance Program in Massachusetts (*Oral Contraceptives and Venous Thrombolic Disease Surgically Confirmed Gall Bladder Disease and Breast Tumours,* June, 1973), indicated that their research demonstrated an association between the use of estrogen in postmenopausal women and an increased risk of developing difficulties with the function of the gall bladder and the development of gall bladder disease for the same reasons discussed earlier in reference to oral contraceptives.

Estrogen replacement therapy can be responsible for uteral changes which might necessitate hysterectomy, and surgery is potentially dangerous in estrogen users because of the tendency for estrogen to affect clotting of the blood (Seaman and Seaman, 1978).

Responsible physicians are now calling for carefully selected use of estrogen therapy rather than prescribing it as standard procedure. Unfortunately, although there has been some decrease in the use of the drug, 8 million new prescriptions were written in 1975. Other approaches to relieving the symptoms of menopause should be attempted.

Carcinoma of the breast is a specter that most women feel hangs over their heads, especially because of the fact that there are 108,000 women yearly who are told by physicians that they are suffering from this disease and many of them are operated on because of it (Pines, 1980). Each year 35,000 women who have breast cancer die (Morris et al., 1978). After accidents and suicides, breast cancer among women in the twenty-five to fifty-four year-old age bracket takes the most lives (Rollin, 1976). The candidate for this type of carcinoma is a woman past menopause with a history of breast cancer in the family, usually one who never had children or who became a mother after the age of 20 (Rollin, 1976). The standard operating procedure for diagnosing and treating the discovery of a lump on the breast has been to hospitalize the woman for a biopsy, and if it shows a malignancy, while the patient is still under the anesthesia to do a radical mastectomy (removal of the breast as well as the muscles and lymph nodes), referred to medically as the Halsted method. The woman has to agree to "sign away" the breast should a malignancy be found, and she does not know whether or not she will be minus a breast when she awakens. The one-step procedure does not always lend itself to accurate diagnosis. Difficulty in determining malignancy is inherent in some of them (Pines, 1980). For some women, however, the one-step method is more comforting than the rather newly elected procedure whereby diagnosis and treatment is a two-step program. The biopsy can be done on an out-patient basis, and if proven malignant, treatment can begin. This later procedure allows time to discuss the possible options and to work through some of the anger and anxiety that is commonly evoked as a result of a cancer diagnosis.

Radical mastectomy as a method of treating breast cancer has been, until recently, an accepted, almost automatic surgical procedure since William Stewart Halsted invented it in 1882. But increasingly, in recent years, automatically performing a radical mastectomy, as opposed to other procedures, has been called into question. Why should women with cancers which have not spread undergo such drastic treatment? Is the survival rate higher than for partial mastectomy, radiation, or chemotherapy, or a combination of these treatments?

In 1976, a surgeon at the University of Pittsburgh, Bernard Fisher, released information on a continuing study of 1700 patients begun five years previously. Thirty-four medical centers contributed information on patients who had been diagnosed as having cancer of the breast. Those patients whose cancer had apparently not metastasized at the beginning of treatment were reviewed three years later. Rates of recurrence and death from cancer were similar in patient groups who had received a radical mastectomy, those who had been given a simple mastectomy, and those whose simple mastectomy had been followed with radiation therapy. In all three groups of patients, recurrence was linked to the fact that metastasis had already taken place before treatment was rendered (Brody, November 24, 1976).

A study by the National Institute in Milan, Italy, compared recurrence rates of carcinoma of the breast in those women who were treated by a partial mastectomy coupled with radiation therapy, compared with those whose therapy consisted of a radical mastectomy, and concluded that the recurrence rate was similar (Valagussa et al., 1978).

Another extensive survey involving 1686 women who underwent either a radical or modified radical mastectomy for breast carcinoma drew some interesting results. The study involved all the women in Rockford, Illinois surgically treated for breast carcinoma and medically followed from 1924 to 1972. The researchers conclude:

Radical mastectomy does not increase survival compared to more conservative operations and should therefore be abandoned except in special circumstances (Meyer et al., 1978).

Experiments are now being done with simple excision of the lump combined with chemotherapy.

It has been suggested that because most doctors are men, there is less concern for the psychological trauma of lopping off a woman's breast and that these same physicians would be very reticent to surgically remove a part of the male anatomy which is associated with maleness. Many surgeons perform a radical mastectomy without projecting the effect of the operation on the possible reconstruction of the breast, a technique increasing in frequency. Eighty percent of women who have mastectomies are potential candidates for reconstruction of the breast, particularly if there has not been extensive radiation damage (Wedemeyer, 1976).

The advocates of breast reconstruction do caution that the first aim of treatment should be the arresting of the cancer and that the operation itself should not be less extensive for the sole purpose of the possibility of reconstruction. Silicone gel implants, used for increasing breast size since 1962, is the technique employed. The breast reconstruction operation itself requires only a few days of hospitalization. The psychological benefits of approximating the normal breast are considerable.

Betty Rollin describes what she saw after her radical mastectomy.

On the left half of my chest, where a breast had been, was a flat, lumpy surface like the ground, covered with, instead of dirt, skin. Across the surface, a long, horizontal, red, puffy welt meandered crazily from the center of my chest, where a cleavage once was, to the other side, under the arm, and around toward the back (Rollin, 1976, p. 133).

An M.I.T. biologist noted in February, 1979, that physicians have adopted radical mastectomy, although there is not sufficient data to support its superiority over other less drastic techniques. He proposes that "there is abundant evidence supporting the proposal that more conservative procedures provide at least equal benefit with substantially less mutilation" (*New York Times,* February 4, 1979, p. 20E).

In addition to the physical pain following a mastectomy, simple, modified, or radical, there is the potential for a tremendous emotional upheaval. The breast is symbolic of a woman's femininity. Following the fad in the 1920s for flat chested women, emphasis has centered on the full-bosomed woman as epitomizing "sexiness" and beauty. Marilyn Monroe, as well as the "pin up girls" during World War II, such as Lana Turner, were hurtled to fame because of the manner in which they filled their sweaters. Padded bras are a big seller; silicone injections to increase the size of breasts are no longer a rare occurrence, and women on oral contraceptives delight in the fact that estrogen tends to increase breast size, and the sale of size C bras mushroomed with the rise in oral contraceptive use. Imagine, then, the psychological and emotional trauma of having a breast removed. One feels mutilated, defeminized, fearful of losing one's husband or the man with whom one lives or is involved. And there is also the fear of dying (Asken, 1975).

The British Journal of Medicine (April, 1978) reported a study of seventy-five patients and their psychiatric difficulties during the first year following mastectomy. Controls consisted of fifty patients whose breast disease had been diagnosed as benign. The women who had a breast removed had many more emotional difficulties than the women in the control group. More than twice the number (25 percent as compared with 10 percent) of the women needed to receive treatment because they manifested symptoms of anxiety and depression. Thirty-three percent of these same women were faced with difficulties relating to sex, as compared with 3 percent of the control group (Maguire et al., 1978).

Increasingly, concern is emerging for the psychological damage as well as the physical damage of breast removal. Increasingly, alternative options for the treatment of carcinoma of the breast are being explored as well as reconstruction of the breast for cosmetic reasons. Breast prostheses are now more easily accessible so that women need not stuff the empty cup of their bras with stockings or cotton, and bathing suits are now designed for the women with one breast, or no breasts. Reach for Recovery, an organization begun by a victim of carcinoma of the breast, helps patients who are referred by their physicians to discuss and work through their feelings as well as answering their many unanswered questions. It has been suggested that formal programs for information and discussion be set up within the hospital setting itself for these women (Swartz, 1977). A two-year follow-up study in London of patients who had undergone mastectomies found that psychological damage need not be extensive, and that much of the psychological healing occurs within the first year after surgery (Morris et al., 1977).

Even though the jury is still out on the benefits of radical mastectomy, along come a handful of physicians in the United States, Dr. Charles S. Rogers among them, who are performing "preventative mastectomies." The rationale for the "off with her breast" approach even before cancer is detected is that breast cancer is a deadly disease. Physicians cannot save about half of the women who develop it. Dr. Rogers uses mammograms to determine which women in the group who are considered high risks also have patterns indicating the likelihood of the development of cancer. He, as well as the other doctors using this approach, bases his treatment on the work of one man, Dr. John N. Wolfe, a radiologist in Detroit.

The death rate of patients with breast cancer has not changed over the past three decades (Campbell et al., 1976). Attempts were made to detect early cancers in order to increase the life expectancy of those with it. The mammogram was used in a wholesale fashion to do this. It was the American Cancer Institute which was instrumental in committing the government through the National Cancer Institute to involve hundreds of thousands of women in an X-ray program (mammograph) for early detection of breast cancer. Unfortunately, the implications of such a program had not been meticulously reviewed. Because mammography is sensitive to even the smallest change in tissue, tiny lesions of the breast were discovered, misdiagnosed by the pathologists as carcinoma and forty-eight mastectomies were performed which were later deemed unnecessary. Between 1972 and 1977 about 27,000 women were involved in the routine screening project and most of them were unaware of the risk involved. Many machines were not calibrated with precision so that women were exposed to more than necessary radiation. One woman reported to me that she had received two X-rays in the same breast at one session because the X-ray technician was experimenting with a newly developed cushion for the breast at the request of the manufacturer.

In March of 1977, almost five years after the beginning of the mass X-ray program, the Cancer Institute consulted with a panel of experts who voiced the belief that not only was the effectiveness of this screening method questionable but that it may also be the cause of cancer.

Because younger women's sensitivity to radiation is higher than that of older women, the Cancer Institute recommends yearly mammo-grams only for women over fifty. The debate still rages. The American Cancer Society disagrees with the conclusions made by the Cancer Institute. However, no longer are women being given regularly scheduled mammograms as part of a governmental project.

Off with the breast and out with the uterus. Hysterectomies, the surgical removal of the uterus, are the major operation performed most frequently, second only to tonsillectomy. The rate of hysterectomies increased from 6.8 per 1000 in 1968 to 8.6 per 1000 in 1973 in spite of the fact that there appeared to be no increase of "clinical indications" (*The Lancet,* January, 1977). In 1975 it was projected that about half the adult female population over forty will be told that their uterus must come out and about 378,000 will be relieved of their ovaries and Fallopian tubes while the gynecologists will reap the harvest of about $400 million. For 12,000 women, the reward will be death (Rodgers, 1975).

We have become a surgery happy society in general. A Cornell study found that about 11 percent to 13 percent of suggested surgery may in fact not be warranted. If these findings are projected to the total population in the United States, Dr. Eugene C. McCarthy of the Cornell University Medical College, and the person in charge of the study, states that over 2 million operations are performed unnecessarily. In the cases researched, individuals sought consultation after being told by the physician that elective surgery was indicated. Only one person in eight finally ended up on the operating table because his/her condition exacerbated, and one in eight underwent surgery in spite of the consultant's recommendation that it was not needed. In 70 percent of the cases in which the consultant contradicted the original opinion, the patients had not undergone surgery within two to three years and McCarthy concluded that the surgical procedure had been permanently postponed (Brody, May 3, 1976).

Not only are many operations unnecessary, but there are also an alarming number of physicians (about 5 percent of 320,000) of questionable competency who cause death because of bungled surgery and inaccurate prescriptions for drugs. A number of doctors, at least 16,000 of them, are considered to be less than competent because of lack of knowledge of the growing scientific research, lack of care in their practice or because of mental or drug problems, according to the Federation of State Medical Boards. This means that 7.5 million patients are being treated by doctors who are potentially hazardous to the patient's health (*New York Times*, February 1, 1976, IV, p. 11).

According to a Congressional subcommittee, about 11,900 deaths occurred in 1975 which were related to the performance of unnecessary surgery. Most surgical procedures are not life saving but are rather attempts to make the patient's life more comfortable. The American College of Surgeons under a mandate from Congress for peer review outlined surgical procedures for twenty operations but did not itemize the indications which necessitated doing the surgery (Brody, January 27, 1976, p. 71). Unnecessary surgery continues and incompetents continue to practice medicine. In thirteen years only about sixty-six doctors a year have been deprived of their license to practice medicine as a result of action taken by state regulating agencies (*New York Times*, February 1, 1976, IV, p. 11).

The problem in the United States seems to be the excess of surgeons. We have twice as many in relation to the population as Britain has, and U.S. surgeons operate twice as often as their British counterparts (Bunker, 1970). In an article in the *New England Journal of Medicine* (1970), John P. Bunker attempts to analyze the reason for the difference in the number of surgeons and the number of operations in the United States compared with that in England. He suggests that the difference is not only due to the attitudes of the United States surgeons, which support a more aggressive approach to practicing medicine, but may be a function of the insurance system. For instance, he pointed out that in a prepaid insurance program in New York, the physicians performed less surgery (50 percent) than under an insurance program operating on a "fee-for-service" basis such as Blue Cross.

Not only are there an excessive number of surgeons, but eight times as many surgeons as the projected need in the United States were being trained in 1976, according to a study made by the American College of Surgeons (Brody, January 27, 1976). The study also indicated that only 52,000 of the 94,000 doctors who operate have been educationally prepared for this specialty and certified by the American Medical Association to practice surgery. There aren't enough operations to go around since, according to the AMA, a surgeon needs to do about ten operations weekly to retain his/her skills.

The Federal Government became alarmed in 1975 at the large number of questionable operations being performed, particularly since an increasing amount of federal funds in the form of Medicare and Medicaid were being consumed. In 1977 HEW suggested that all surgical procedures should be done only after a second physician was consulted. The agency emphasized that second opinions were particularly necessary in tonsillectomies, gall bladder operations, and hysterectomies.

The first caesarean hysterectomy of a human being was performed on July 21, 1868. The patient died three days later, but the operation was considered successful. Until the 1940s a Caesarean hysterectomy was rarely used except in a life-saving situation. By 1951, with increased blood bank efficiency and advancement in the use of drugs to fight infections, the operation was deemed less hazardous and was recommended "for medically indicated sterilization, removal of a diseased uterus, or removal of a uterus no longer functionally useful in a woman near the climacteric" (Barclay, 1970). Although this type of operation is considered fairly safe, it can result in undue loss of blood, sometimes necessitating reoperation as well as possible trauma to the urinary tract (Barclay, 1970). It also takes some of the patients as much as eleven months to recuperate from the Caesarian hysterectomy procedure. The vaginal hysterectomy, in which entry is achieved through the vagina instead of the abdomen to remove the uterus, is also fraught with difficulties such as more fevers, more infected urinary tracts, as well as the possibility of reoperation because of difficulties ensuing postoperatively. Vaginal hysterectomies have also precipitated collapse of lungs, as well as formation of blood clots, obstruction of the intestines, formation of scar tissue, which in turn makes intercourse painful (Rodgers, 1975). Obviously, all operations have an element of risk associated with them. Yet hysterectomy is increasingly being recommended by doctors not only for medical reasons, but also for contraceptive reasons, as well as being chosen by women as a method of birth control. The questions to be asked are how much information is the patient given, and is there really informed consent? As we will discuss later in this chapter, the answer to the questions is related to the woman's socio-economic status.

There are some givens relating to rates of surgery. For instance, the numbers of operations are twice as frequent for the insured population than those uninsured (Bunker, 1970), and the rates of surgery are higher for those patients associated with a fee-for-service plan as opposed to a prepaid plan (Brody, 1976). If a second opinion is required, then the number of operations decline (Brody, 1977). Patients on Medicaid are twice as likely to be operated on as the general population (Lyons, 1977). These givens can also be applied to women and hysterectomies. The National Center for Health Statistics released data which indicated that there were twice as many hysterectomies performed in the southern states compared with the Western part of the country, and that 10 percent more uteri were removed in the south than the northeast, although there is no data to support the premise that southern women are prone to increased gynecological disorders (Rodgers, 1975).

A fairly recent approach to hysterectomies is the functional approach. In other words, a woman should have a hysterectomy even though there are no pathological indications. It has been suggested that the functional approach to hysterectomy takes into consideration the functions of the uterus, such as menstruation, reproduction, and a sexual function (the uterus does contract during orgasm). Each woman should review these three functions with her physician before opting for the operation. In other words, the thinking processes leading to a decision are deemed to be important (Burchell, 1977). A woman should define for herself whether or not a hysterectomy is necessary unless the pathology is such that there is no other alternative. Being part of the decision-making process may also positively affect the depression syndrome which commonly follows removal of the uterus. Emotional difficulty is particularly prevalent among women with a history of depression, those who have a malignancy, and those who are experiencing marital difficulty (Notman and Nadelson, 1978).

Although large numbers of psychologically healthy women experience increased sexual pleasure because of lack of fear of pregnancy, there is also the feeling among many that without the uterus the woman is no longer a woman and no longer sexually coveted.

It is estimated that since 1964 six million people in the United States have had themselves sterilized, men as well as women (Westoff, September 29, 1974). The increase in sterilization is attributed to the development of the vasectomy procedure for men as well as laparoscopy. Previous to the development of the laparoscopy technique of sterilization tubal ligation was used. This technique requires cutting open the abdomen in order to tie the Fallopian tubes. The laparoscopy consists of making small incisions in the abdomen through which the tubes are cauterized. The procedure is fairly inexpensive, less dangerous than tubal ligation, and does not involve a long period of convalescence. By 1973 the number of women sterilized had almost doubled since 1971, whereas the number of men sterilized decreased from 80 percent of the sterilizations to 57 percent (Westoff, September 29, 1974). For men sterilization is a completely voluntary act, but for women it may not be.

In 1974 the Office of Health, Education and Welfare determined that about 150,000 persons are being sterilized yearly with funds paid for by the federal government, and that in some cases, particularly among the poor and minorities, the sterilization took place without the person's informed consent. A highly publicized case was that of two black sisters, aged 14 and 12, one of whom was retarded, who were sterilized. The parents of the two Relf sisters sued the federal government, since the procedure had been done in a federally funded birth-control clinic and allegedly without their consent. The girls had been receiving Depo Provera, a contraceptive drug, and the parents assumed that the visit to the clinic was for the purpose of their routine injection. Non-English-speaking women have been known to sign papers in English giving consent for sterilization, and one doctor in South Carolina admitted to forcing women on Medicaid who were pregnant to consent to sterilization if they wanted him to deliver their baby. His rationale was that these women already had several children and were burdening the taxpayer. It is particularly distressing to find that in some areas of the country the sterilization rate for young black women is high. Between 1960 and 1968 the North Carolina State Eugenics Board released the figure that 1620 persons had undergone sterilization procedures. Of these, 1023 were black and more than half were under twenty years old (Coburn, 1974). Over a four-year period 3400 American Indians, the majority being women, were sterilized in the west (*New York Times.* November 24, 1976, p. 12).

Sterilization prevents one from becoming a mother in the future but is usually performed on those who already have children. Motherhood is holy or as Coleridge in his poem, *The Three Graves,* said,

> "A mother is a mother still,
> The holiest thing alive." (p.227)

Therefore, to want to do away with a potential child, the fetus, is considered by some to be sacrilegious. And yet, in all societies abortion does occur. In other words, at some time or other, a woman is unhappy with her potential motherhood and wishes to relieve herself of the burden of pregnancy. The law in many societies determines whether or not she can do this legally.

In 1873 Anthony Comstock was instrumental in attaching a rider to a postal service bill prohibiting sending what was labeled as obscene or lewd material through the mail, and this included everything related to contraception. Until that time the common law did not violently disapprove of abortion as long as it took place before quickening.

Margaret Sanger, the pioneer of the birth control movement, was impelled in the 1920s to crusade for contraception as a result of watching a young, poverty-stricken woman, Sadie Sachs, die of a self-induced abortion. Sanger, the attendant nurse, was deeply touched by the tragedy and wrote in her autobiography, "I was resolved to seek out the root of the evil, to do something to change the destiny of mothers whose miseries were as vast as the sky" (Sanger, 1938, p. 92). She focused on changing the laws prohibiting the sale and use of contraceptives and on attempts to educate women about birth control methods as a way of preventing pregnancy. Meanwhile, women were faced with unwanted pregnancies and were resorting to ingesting chemicals as well as the use of sharp instruments such as knitting needles, hatpins, and knives, or were seeking out an illegal abortionist, usually someone with little or no training to do the job. It was estimated that 8000 or more women died each year as a result of illegal abortions, and that in 1951 the death rate was still very high, estimated to be between 5000 to 6000 (Schur, 1965). The number of deaths decreased with the increased use of antibiotics to combat infection. The death rate dropped perceptively when abortion was legalized in 1973. However, as late as 1978, a twenty-two-year-old woman was tried and acquitted of abortion in Bowling Green, Kentucky under a state statute that made it illegal for anyone who was not a licensed physician to perform an abortion. Marla Pitchford had been impreganted by her college boyfriend, who strongly urged her to abort even though they had planned eventually to marry. Because she was beyond eighteen weeks pregnant, the clinics she contacted would not give her an abortion. Marla aborted herself with a six-inch knitting needle, was hospitalized for a high fever, given a drug to induce expulsion of the fetus and gave birth to a dead fetus and a knitting needle (*Time*, September 11, 1978, p. 22).

In writing about illegal abortions before the Supreme Court decision in 1973, Schur noted that there were about 330,000 illegal abortions performed yearly and an abortionist was instrumental in 300,000 of these (1968).

Women who had been raped were unable to get an abortion under the laws of most states, which allowed a nontherapeutic abortion only to save the life of the mother. Some states included the mental health of the mother as a legal ground for abortion.

Between 1967 and 1970 some states liberalized their laws to allow abortion if there was the possibility of a deformed child or where the female became pregnant because of rape or incest. It wasn't until 1973 that abortion was declared by the Supreme Court to be a woman's right in *Roe* v. *Wade* and *Doe* v. *Bolton.* The court ruled that the decision to abort is solely a matter between a woman and her doctor during the first three months of pregnancy. The state can establish guidelines for abortion during the second three months to ensure the safety of the woman and can, if it wishes, prevent abortions except for life-saving reasons during the last three months of pregnancy.

Even after Roe v. Wade and Doe v. Bolton a number of hospitals, particularly municipal hospitals, were either refusing outright, or were setting up barriers to granting abortions.

In 1977 Congress passed the Hyde Amendment which meant that states did not have to pay for abortions under their Medicaid program. Later, in the spring of 1980 the Supreme Court of the United States upheld the constitutionality of this amendment. This meant that again, as before 1973, women with money could obtain abortions while poor women could not. Thirty-three states decided to limit their funding. In Connecticut Medicaid will only pay for an abortion in order to save the mother's life. This means that a poor, pregnant victim of rape or incest might have to carry her baby to term because of lack of funds. Because pregnancy and childbirth carry higher risks than abortion, one study reported in the *American Journal of Public Health* (September, 1977) projected that there could be a significant increase in the number of deaths of women of childbearing age as a result of the federal guidelines (Petitti and Cates, Jr., 1977).

Since the Hyde Amendment, which restricts Medicaid-funded abortions to cases where the mother's life is in danger, and to pregnancies resulting from rape or incest, and only if the rape or incest is promptly reported, there have been three abortion-related deaths of women according to the National Center for Disease Control in Atlanta. One attempt at abortion consisted of douching for several days with Drano. Instead of aborting, the consequence was surgical removal of the uterus and treatment for kidney disorder.

In the Fall of 1978 two newswomen, Pamela Zekman and Pamela Warrick of the Chicago *Sun-Times* began their exposé of the violence committed by the abortion clinics on Michigan Avenue in Chicago. They presented documented data supporting the contention that women were being used and abused for profit. They noted that non-pregnant women were given abortions, and that some women who were more than twelve weeks pregnant had been aborted illegally. They also established the fact that because of poor conditions and lack of sterile environment, women who had abortions had serious side effects such as cramping, infections, and damage to their internal organs, sometimes resulting in later removal of the ovaries and/or uterus.

Zekman and Warrick noted that unqualified personnel, including a doctor whose license was withdrawn, were doing the abortions and doing them very quickly, even before the painkillers administered had time to become effective. The two newswomen decried the fact that referral services were charging for their service and that one of the referral sources was a doctor who allowed his dog into the operating room and permitted the animal to drink the blood found on the floor. They stated that pathology reports when indicated were very often not ordered, that records were kept poorly and that instead of counseling, the so-called counselors were really salespeople pushing abortions (Chicago *Sun-Times,* November 12, 1978, p. 1).

All four abortion clinics located on Michigan Avenue are directed by men who seem to be impervious to the fact that they enrich themselves by causing difficulties and sometimes even death to women. The Illinois Department of Public Health is held responsible for its laxity in enforcing the guidelines for the licensing of health clinics. People, especially women, put their faith in doctors. This blind faith was obviously unwarranted and dangerous, particularly in the abortion mills in Illinois, where about twelve women lost their lives allegedly from poor abortion procedures. One wonders why it took an exposé by two women to develop concern and action to stop the abuses.

As has been established in this chapter, women's reproductive system is constantly being barraged by drugs, devices, and surgical procedures to prevent pregnancy, to increase fertility and maintain youth. Many of these therapies and procedures along with the "off with the breast" and "out with the uterus" psychology of physicians, most of whom are males, are often implemented without the informed consent of the patient, a woman. As the feminist movement gains momentum, so does the self-help health movement for women. Women are learning about their own bodies, especially the reproductive system, which was at one time the prerogative of the medical profession. They are establishing health centers for themselves whose purpose is to deal with health issues such as abortion and to help women become better informed of medical procedures and effects so that they become more actively involved participants as patients. As early as March, 1971, the first Women's Health Conference was held and today centers have sprung up throughout the country. Perhaps if women had been well informed health consumers a large number of deaths, disfigurements, and suffering might have been prevented.

References

Anon. Alleged Sterilization of Indians Denied. *New York Times* 12 (November 24, 1976).
The Boston Women's Health Collective. *Our Body Ourselves.* New York: Simon & Schuster, 1973.
_____. Contraception and health. *The Lancet* 2:942–943 (October 1979).
_____. Enough to Move FDA. *Science News* 97: 430–431 (May 2, 1970).
_____. Hazards of The Pill. *Newsweek* 107 (October 28, 1974).
_____. Letter to the Editor. *The Lancet* 746 (April 1976).
_____. *Health/Pac Bulletin* (March 1970, p. 1).
_____. Liver tumours and the pill. *British Medical Journal* 2:345–6 (April 1977).
_____. Mastectomy Debate. *New York Times* 20E (February 4, 1979).
_____. Mortality among oral-contraceptive users. *The Lancet* 2:727–731 (October 1977).
_____. Mortality and oral contraceptives. *British Medical Journal* 2:918 (October, 1977).
_____. *New York Times* 34 (November 12, 1978).
_____. Oral contraceptives and venous thromboembolic disease, surgically confirmed gall bladder disease and breast tumours. *The Lancet* 1:1399–1404 (June 1973). Report from the Boston Collaborative Drug Surveillance Program.
_____. *Physicians' Desk Reference.* Oradell, N.J. : Medical Economics Company, 1973.

_____. Physicians' Desk Reference, 1976 Supplement B. Oradell, N.J. : Medical Economics Company, 1976.

_____. *Physicians' Desk Reference,* 1973, Supplement B. Oradell, N.J.: Medical Economics Company, 1976.

_____. *A Statistical Portrait of Women in the United States,* Publication 58. Current Population Reports Special Studies Series, U. S. Department of Commerce, Bureau of the Census, 1976, p. 28.

_____. The Scarlet Letter. *Time* 22 (September 11, 1978).

_____. Skin Cancer Link Found in Birth Control Pill. *New York Times.* 23 (November 12, 1978).

_____. 3 in Suit Say Drug Produced Cancer. *New York Times* 16 (March 4, 1976).

_____. What every woman needs to know. *The Lancet* 1:232 (January 1977).

_____. U.S. Doctors: About 5 Percent are Unfit. *New York Times* 11 (February 1, 1976).

Aksel, S., Schomberg, D. W., Tyrey, L. and Hammond, C. B. Vasomotor symptoms, estrogens, serum estrogens, and gonadotrophin levels in surgical menopause. *American Journal of Obstetrics and Gynecology* **126**:165–169 (1976).

Asken, Michael. Psychoemotional aspects of mastectomy: a review of recent literature. *American Journal of Psychiatry* **132**:1:56–59 (1975).

Barclay, David L. Caesarean hysterectomy. *Obstetrics and Gynecology* **35**:120–130 (1970).

Beral, Valerie, Cardio-vascular-disease mortality trends and oral contraceptive use in young women. *The Lancet* **2**:1047–1051 (1976).

Brody, Jane E. Hysteretomies Reduced Sharply Under Monitoring Plan in Canada. *New York Times* B4 (June 9, 1977).

_____. Cornell study finds 11% of surgery is unnecessary. *New York Times,* p. 62, May 3, 1976.

_____. Incompetent Surgery is Found Not Isolated. *New York Times* 24 (January 27, 1976).

_____. Belief in limited breast surgery is supported by cancer research. *New York Times* 9:3, November 24, 1976.

_____. Incompetent surgery is found not isolated. *New York Times,* p. 1, January 27, 1976.

Bunker, John P. Surgical manpower. *New England Journal of Medicine* **282**:135–144 (1970).

Burchell, Clay R. Decision regarding hysterectomy. *American Journal of Obstetrics and Gynecology* **127**:113–117 (1977).

Campbell, D. J., Banks, A. J. and Oates, G. D. The value of preliminary bone scanning in staging and assessing the prognosis of breast cancer. *British Journal of Surgery* **63**:811–816 (1976).

Coleridge, Samuel Taylor. The Three Graves, in Ernest Hartley Coleridge (ed.). *Coleridge Poetical Works.* London : Oxford University Press, 1917.

Corea, Gena. *The Hidden Malpractice.* New York: First Jove/HBJ Book, Harcourt, Brace & Jovanovich, 1977.

Cutler, Bruce S., Forbes, Anne P., Ingersoll, Francis M. and Scully, Robert E. Endometrial carcinoma after stilbestrol therapy in gonadal dysgenesis. *New England Journal of Medicine* **287**:628–631 (1972).

Fasal, Elfriede and Paffenbarger, Ralph S., Jr. Oral contraceptives as related to cancer and benign lesions of the breast. *Journal of the National Cancer Institute* **55**:767–773 (1975).

Fisch, Irwin P. and Frank, Jess. Oral contraceptives and blood pressure. *Journal of the American Medical Association* **237**:2499–2503 (1977).

Gilder, S. S. B. Overseas report. *Canadian Medical Association Journal* **3**:1058–1066 (1974).

Gordon, Jack, Reagon, James W., Finkie, William D. and Ziel, Harry K. Estrogen and endometrial carcinoma. *New England Journal of Medicine* **297**:570–571 (1977).

Gray, Laman A., Christopherson, William M. and Hoover, Robert N. Estrogens and endometrial carcinoma. *Obstetrics and Gynecology* **49**:385–389 (1977).

Greenwald, Peter, Barlow, Joseph J., Nasca, C. and Burnett, William S. Vaginal cancer after maternal treatment with synthetic estrogens. *New England Journal of Medicine* **285**:390–393 (1971).

Hennekens, Charles H. and MacMahon, Brian. Oral contraceptives and myocardial infarction. *The New England Medical Journal* **296**:1166–1167 (1977).

Herbst, Arthur I., Ulfelder, Howard and Poskanzer, David C. Adenocarcinoma of the vagina. *The New England Journal of Medicine* **284**:878–881 (1971).

Hoover, Robert, Grady, Laman A., Cole, Philip and MacMahon, Brian. Menopausal estrogens and breast cancer. *New England Journal of Medicine* **295**:401–405 (1976).

Horowitz, Ralph I. and Feinstein, Alvin R. Alternative analytic methods for case-control studies of estrogens and endometrial cancer. *New England Journal of Medicine* **299**:1089–1094 (1978).

Inman, W.H.W. and Vessey, M.P. Investigation of deaths from pulmonary, coronary, and cerebral thrombosis and embolism of women of child-bearing age. *British Medical Journal* **2**:193–199 (1968).

Jones, V. *Effectiveness of Diethystilbestrol as a Contraceptive in Rape Victims.* Paper presented at the American Public Health Association, October 17, 1976.

Katz, Barbara. The IUD: out of sight, out of mind. *Ms.* **IV**:108–115 (July 1975).

Kannel, William B. Communication to the editor. *Journal of the American Medical Association* **237**:2530–2531 (1977).

Langmuir, Alexander. Editorial. *New England Journal of Medicine* **284**:912–913 (1971).

Lipsett, Mortimer. Estrogen use and cancer risk. *Journal of the American Medical Association* **237**:1112–1115 (1977).

Lyons, Richard D. Medicaid Surgery Reports to be Twice U.S. Rate. *New York Times* A17 (September 1, 1977).

Maguire, G. P., Lee, E. G., Bevington, D. J., Küchemann, C. S., Crabtree, R. J. and Cornell, C. E. Psychiatric problems in the first year after mastectomy. *British Medical Journal* **1**:963–965 (1978).

Martin, Leonide L. *Health Care of Women.* Philadelphia: J. B. Lippincott, 1978.

McMahon, B. and Austin, J. H. Association of carcinoma of the breast and corpus oteri. *Cancer* **28**:275–280 (1964).

Meyer, Alfred C., Smith, Simmons S. and Potter, Meredith. Carcinoma of the breast. *Archives of Surgery* **113**:364–366 (1978).

Morris, Tina, Green, Steven and White, Patricia. Psychological and social adjustment to mastectomy. *Cancer* **40**:2381–2387 (1977).

Nathanson, Constance. Illness and the feminine role: a theoretcial review. *Social Science and Medicine* **9**:57–62 (1975).

Nesbit, Robert R. and Deweese, James A. Mesenteric venous thrombosis and oral contraceptives. *Southern Medical Journal* **70**:360–362 (1977).

Notman, Malkah T. and Nadelson, Carol C. *The Woman Patient.* New York: Plenum Press, 1978.

Oliver, M. F. Oral contraceptives and myocardial infarction. *British Medical Journal* **2**:210–213 (1970).

Ory, Howard, Cole, Philip, MacMahon, Brian and Hoover, Robert. Oral contraceptives and reduced risk of benign breast disease. *New England Journal of Medicine* **294**:419–422 (1976).

Petitti, Diana B. and Cates, Willard, Jr. Restricting Medicaid funds for abortions: projections of excess mortality for women of childbearing age. *American Journal of Public Health* **67**:860–861 (1977).

Pines, Maya. Reducing the Trauma of Breast Cancer, *New York Times* 35–37 (April 6, 1980).

Rigg, Lee A., Hermann, Harold and Yen, Samuel S. C. Absorption of estrogen from vaginal creams. *New England Journal of Medicine* **298**:195–197 (1978).

Rodgers, Joann. Rush to surgery. *New York Times* 34 September 321, 1975.

Rollin, Betty. *First, You Cry.* Philadelphia: J. B. Lippincott, 1976.

Sanger, Margaret. *Margaret Sanger: An Autobiography.* New York: Norton, 1938.

Saronwala, K. C. Singh, Ravinder and Dass, Hacharan. Lippes loop perforation of the uterus and urinary bladder with stone formation. *Obstetrics and Gynecology* **44**:424–427 (1974).

Schur, Edwin. *Crimes Without Victims.* Englewood Cliffs, N. J.: Prentice-Hall, 1965.

Scully, Diana. A funny thing happened on the way to the orifice: women in gynecology textbooks. *American Journal of Sociology* **78**:1045–1049 (1973).

Seaman, Barbara. *The Doctors' Case Against the Pill.* New York: Peter H. Wyden, 1969.

Seaman, Barbara and Seaman, Gideon. *Women and the Crisis in Sex Hormones.* New York: Bantam Books/Rawson Associates, Publishers, 1978.

Shapiro, Samuel, Rosenberg, Lynn, Sloane, Dennis, Kaufman, David, Stolley, Paul D. and Miettinen, Olli S. Oral contraceptive use in relation to myocardial reaction. *The Lancet* **1**:743–746 (1979).

Shoemaker, E., Stanton, E., Furney, J. Pete, and MacDonald, Paul C. Estrogen treatment of postmenopausal women. *Journal of the American Medical Association* **238**:1524–1530 (1977).

Smith, D. C., Prentice, R., Thompson, D. J., and Herrmann, W. L. Association of Exogenous estrogen and endometrial carcinoma. *New England Journal of Medicine* **293**:1164–1167 (1975).

Spellacy, W. W. A review of carbohydrate metabolism and the oral contraceptive. *American Journal of Obstetrics and Gynecology* **104**:448–460 (1969).

Spencer, J. D., Mills, Rosemary R. and Hayward, J. L. Contraceptive steroids and breast cancer. *British Medical Journal* **1**:1024–26 (1978).

Swartz, Marc D. An information and discussion program for women after a mastectomy. *Archives of Surgery* **112**:276–281 (1977).

Valagussa, Pinuccia, Bunadonna, Gianni and Veronesi, Umberto. Patterns of relapse and survival following radical mastectomy. *Cancer* **41**:1170–1178 (1978).

Vana, Joseph, Murphy, Gerald P., Aronoff, Bille L. and Baker, Harvey W. Primary liver tumors and oral contraceptives. *Journal of the American Medical Association* **238**:2154–2158 (1977).

Verbrugge, Lois. Sex differences in morbidity and mortality in the United States. *Social Biology* **23**:275–296 (1977).

Vessey, M. P., McPherson, K. and Johnson, Bridget. Mortality among women participating in the Oxford/Family Planning Association Contraceptive Study. *The Lancet* **2**:731–733 (1977).

Wedemeyer, Dee. After mastectomy: the options for breast reconstruction. *New York Times* **56**:1, December 9, 1976.

Weideger, Paula. *Menstruation and Menopause*. New York: Alfred A. Knopf, 1976.

Westoff, Leslie Aldridge. Sterilization. *New York Times* 30 (September 29, 1974).

Whitson, Leland, Israel, Robert and Bernstein, Gerald S. The extrauterine Dalkon shield. *Obstetrics and Gynecology* **44**:418–423 (1974).

Wilson, E. S. B. Septic abortion and I.U.D.'s. Letter to the Editor. *British Medical Journal* **1**:719 (1978).

Zekman, Pamela and Warrick, Pamela. The Abortion Profiteers. *Chicago Sun Times* 1 (November 12, 1978).

Ziel, Harry K. and Finke, Wm. D. Increased risk of endometrial carcinoma among users of conjugated estrogens. *New England Medical Journal* **293**:1167–1170 (1975).

10. To Self-Destruct: Alcoholism, Drug Addiction, and Suicide

Karl Menninger (1966) proposed that there is a large amount of destructiveness in the world; that fate and nature are not solely responsible for this destruction, and that large numbers of people are self-destructive.

People attempt in many ways to escape from situations which they feel are intolerable. Drinking, drug abuse, and the ultimate in escape, suicide, are universal coping mechanisms which are also universally highly destructive.

Even as violence is as American as apple pie, so is drinking alcohol. Unfortunately, drinking excessively has become a problem for about 10 million Americans, although it is estimated that about 100 million are regular alcohol users (Stockton, 1978). Alcoholism can be defined as "a chronic behavior disorder which is manifested by undue preoccupation with alcohol to the detriment of physical and mental health, by a loss of control when drinking has begun (although it may not be carried to the point of intoxication), and by a self-destructive attitude in dealing with personal relationships and life situations" (Chafetz and Demone, Jr., 1962).

The World Health Organization apparently considered alcoholism enough of a world-wide problem to adopt a working definition which states that

> Alcoholism is a chronic behavioral disorder manifested by repeated drinking of alcoholic beverages in excess of the dietary and social uses of the community and to an extent that interferes with the drinker's health or his social or economic functioning (Blane, 1968, p. 9).

What do these definitions have in common? Firstly, to be labeled an alcoholic, the individual's life must focus on the consumption of alcohol, which in turn affects the individual's relationships to people, especially those which are close personal relationships, and results in the inability to function in a constructive manner, not only socially but economically. Health problems accompany what the American Medical Association has labeled a disease, the disease of alcoholism. These health problems are mental as well as physical. In other words, an alcoholic, by definition, is a person who drinks too much and who, because of this excessive consumption, functions inadequately on most levels.

In most societies, as well as in the United States, drinking is more of an activity associated with males than with females. Wakes, rites of passage, and social events are often occasions for drinking alcohol in many cultures. Generally, although heavy drinking by men is acceptable, women are permitted to drink only lightly, and drunkenness by women is frowned upon (Child et al., 1965).

Many people think of the alcoholic as the skid-row person and therefore do not recognize alcoholism in others. The skid-row alcoholic comprises a very small percentage of the total and the majority of them are men. Women, perhaps because they tend to be protected by their families or perhaps because of their role in society, tend not to gravitate to a skid-row life. The skid-row alcoholic is one who cannot stop drinking once started, and continues until he cannot drink any more. He tends to find others who have similar lifestyles and spends the days with his companions consuming alcohol. If he does have a sex life, it is with women who are his drinking companions or female friends, usually single, middle-aged working women, who have the need to nurture, and express this need by taking care of him, as well as taking him into their homes for periods of time ranging from one night to several months (Wiseman, 1970). Homeless men drink more than homeless women, according to a study done in 1973 (Garrett and Bahr). A comparison of women in a shelter with men clients known to an institution for homeless men, found that not only did women drink less, but that they tended to drink alone while the men gravitated to drinking in groups. The women felt that their excessive drinking was deviant, while the men did not perceive their drinking behavior as too aberrant (Garrett and Bahr, 1973).

Most alcoholics are not skid-row "bums" and many alcoholics are women. But there is still no definitive idea of the number of women alcoholics. Estimates indicated that almost 5 million of the 10 million persons suffering from alcoholism are women (*Good Housekeeping,* September 1977). Some researchers have proposed that 70 percent of the alcoholics are men (Albrecht, 1973), while others suggest that if women's drinking was not hidden, there would be as many known women alcoholics as there are men who are alcoholics.

From our present knowledge we find that although women become alcoholics, they seem to do so less often than men. This phenomenon has been related to the pressures placed on women of all ages to refrain from drinking, and the association of the consumption of alcoholic beverages with masculinity. Although women in our society do drink, they drink less than men. One theory suggests that those groups in our society who are not active participants, and who are considered underprivileged, tend to drink lightly if at all basically because they embody the traditionalism of the society. Those people who are not economically independent, women, children, welfare recipients, individuals serving prison terms or in mental institutions, are pressured to refrain from consuming alcohol basically because their behavior is a reflection on those on whom they are dependent (Knupfer, 1964). Knupfer also suggests that female virginity is more highly prized than male purity, and that the fear that excessive drinking will lead to loss of sexual control, and therefore loss of virginity, is the basis for the social sanctions against alcoholism in women.

Today alcoholism for women is increasing at a faster rate than it is for men. Cirrhosis of the liver, a disease related to chronic alcoholism, has climbed for women, and one-third of the membership of Alcoholics Anonymous is comprised of women as opposed to one-fourth prior to 1971 (Anderson, 1977). The consumption of alcohol by women in the United States began increasing during World War II and continued to rise twice as rapidly as that of men by 1969 (Gomberg, 1974). We can conjecture that because the traditional housewife role for women was discouraged during the war years as women were wooed to the defense industries, women also abandoned the feminine nondrinking patterns, and they began to adopt more masculine behaviors. For instance, whereas wearing dungarees was frowned on for the "gentler sex" prior to World War II, Rosie the Riveter was so attired as she was pictured holding a riveting machine with her hair in a kerchief. Rosie the Riveter, of course, was the role model established in order to attract more women to work in factories manufacturing war materials.

Age and social class appear to be variables in determining social drinking among women as well as among men. There is a direct relationship between level of social class and drinking. The higher the social class, the greater the frequency of consumption of alcohol (Cahalan et al., 1969). Women are two years older than men when their drinking problem begins (Mulford, 1977).

Until fairly recently, most of the literature on alcoholism, and much of the research, has been directed toward male alcoholics. The study of alcoholism in women has been woefully sparse. The reason for the paucity of literature is difficult to explain. It may very well be because women are generally closet drinkers (Fraser, 1974) and have not in the past drunk so much that their jobs were jeopardized (many drinkers are housewives in the home) and have not frequented bars as often as men. In fact, some bars prohibited women from buying drinks unless accompanied by a male companion. Women's drinking, therefore, did not gain public attention. The lack of previous attention to alcoholism in women may also be a result of the fact that since men are the dominant group, it was assumed that what held true for the males also could categorize females. Today women are indeed drinking more; alcoholism, indeed, is a female problem as well as a male problem, and there are indeed some definite differences between alcoholism in women and the same disease in men.

As pointed out earlier, men drink more often than women and tend to have more drinks at any one time (Cahalan et al., 1969). Among high school students, males are twice as likely to report drinking than females, and in all social classes, more girls than boys are abstainers (Wechsler and McFadden, 1976). Not only do boys drink more than girls, but they become drunk more often. The number of girls who drink, particularly in secondary school, has increased and continues to become more like that of boys, although boys still continue to consume more alcohol on each drinking occasion (Wechsler and McFadden, 1976).

Women alcoholics tend to begin their drinking at a later age than male alcoholics (Lisansky, 1957). Alcoholism in women, when it begins develops more rapidly over a shorter period of time than alcoholism in men and without progressing through well-defined stages (Fort and Porterfield, 1961). Women also tend to point to specific life events as precipitating their alcoholism (Lisansky, 1957; Curlee, 1970; Hoffman and Noem, 1975). Those under the age of twenty point to menstrual difficulties, broken love affairs and unwanted pregnancies which led to abortions, as events in their life triggering their excessive drinking. Middle-aged women viewed difficult marriage, feelings of guilt, jealousy, birth of a child, as well as ill relatives or a death in the family, as the cause of their alcoholism, while women over forty blamed menopause (Wall, 1937). The conclusion drawn is that alcoholism in women is closely related to a specific stressful life situation or crisis. Men, apparently, do not often cite a precipitant, which leads researchers to the conclusion that excessive drinking by men is not generally precipitated by a life event. Men seem to slowly increase their drinking patterns as a response to the pressures of daily living (Mulford, 1977).

Below thirty and over sixty appear to be the "safe" years in terms of alcoholism. There are fewer alcoholics among both men and women in these age groups. Alcoholism in women seems to peak during middle age, between thirty-two and forty-nine. Mulford (1977) found in his study of 3132 problem-drinking men and 395 problem-drinking women that half the women were in their middle years, as compared to 42 percent of the men. Middle age, one could conclude, places a great stress on women. The "empty nest syndrome" rears its ugly head with concomitant strains on the marital relationship because of the decrease in the wife's responsibilities as well as the fact that she is no longer needed to play the mothering role. Concern for the change in beauty, or fear of loss of it as she ages, can create stress and lowering of self-esteem, especially if the main identity the woman has is as a pretty possession to be displayed by her husband. It is an interesting fact that housewives comprise the larger group of women alcoholics (*Good Housekeeping,* September, 1977).

What significance does marriage have to alcoholism? Both men and women who were married were older when they had their first drunk experience than those who had never married. The married alcoholics were not arrested as often as nonmarried alcoholics and also apparently had fewer previous hospitalizations (Bromet and Moos, 1976). The Bromet and Moos study also found that those who were married were less apt to do their drinking at bars or with their friends than those who were not married.

Alcoholics marry ratio-wise as often as the general population (Rosenbaum, 1958). However, alcoholic men and alcoholic women were frequently found to have multiple marriages; women alcoholics three times the rate of the general population and men twice the rate (Mulford, 1977). It has been suggested that there is a one-in-ten chance that a woman will marry someone who is suffering from alcoholism. The odds for a man marrying an alcoholic woman are one in fifty. Alcoholics, both male and female, tend to marry others who also drink (Lisansky, 1957).

Marriages for alcoholic women are usually unsatisfying and are often characterized by extreme jealousy and brutality, chronic conflict, unfaithfulness; disillusionment, and loneliness (Kinsey, 1966). Marriage does not offer the emotional rewards needed by the woman who drinks excessively. Alcoholic women often marry men who dominate them by aggressive or passive means, who are unkind and insensitive (Wood and Duffy, 1966). Both the husbands and the wives are unable to give of themselves in the relationship, relate poorly on the sexual level, and are unable to communicate with each other (Wood and Duffy, 1966, Kinsey, 1968).

Women alcoholics, more so than men, feel that there is no one that they can talk with and share their problems. Men who have spouses are more likely to feel that they have someone with whom to communicate than women (Mulford, 1977). It appears that the woman alcoholic seeks out for marriage someone who she thinks will give her some security, but who will not make demands of personal intimacy which she is not able herself to respond to (Wood and Duffy, 1966). The husband of the female alcoholic exacerbates his wife's difficulties by his own excessive drinking and his destructive attitude towards his wife's imbibing (Rosenbaum, 1958).

Although the alcoholic husband often introduces his wife to alcoholism, few husbands drink excessively because of their wife's drinking habits (Lisansky, 1957; Wanberg and Knapp, 1970). However, spouses who drink a great deal are more common among alcoholic women than alcoholic men (Mulford, 1977). Nine out of ten spouses of alcoholic women will abandon their drinking wives, but only one out of ten wives abandon their alcoholic spouse (*Good Housekeeping*, September, 1977). Emotional problems are also characteristic of many spouses of women alcoholics. Two-thirds of the women treated for alcoholism in one psychiatric hospital were married to men who had a psychiatric illness, and one-third of the husbands drank heavily (Rimmer, 1974).

Marital status, apparently, is an influential factor in alcoholism. One study states that:

Compared with the unmarried, married women alcoholics have different family and background characteristics (i.e., they were older when they first drank to get drunk and when they first recognized their drinking as a problem, their fathers were less likely to be heavy drinkers, and they less often had prior alcohol treatment), have more positive self-concepts, less anxiety and less physical impairment, and more often engaged in solitary drinking (Bromet and Moos, 1976, p. 311).

The researchers conclude that the causes and accompanying dynamics may differ for the single and the married woman who becomes alcoholic.

Before we look at a more in-depth analysis of why women drink, let us review some of the theories as to why people in general drink. According to Chafetz and Demone (1962), alcohol is viewed as an antidote for depression. It is also used to blot out uncomfortable feelings, especially those with which the individual is unable to cope. If one drinks, then one becomes less than responsible for the behavior which may be expressed. The alcoholic who acts out the repressed feelings is usually unaware of the very conflicts she/he is expressing, so alcoholism can act as a support of one's defense mechanisms. Alcohol is also used to help a person face a situation which is too anxiety-producing to face without the alcohol as a crutch. For instance, drinking before going on a job interview, etc. Chafetz and Demone also state that alcohol can deaden one's feeling just like a narcotic and can also be used in order to gain acceptance where everyone else is drinking heavily. A sober mate meets with less acceptance by an alcoholic spouse than one who also drinks.

As early as 1919 the psychological concept of alcoholism as an escape from the difficulties of life was voiced (Chafetz and Demone, Jr., 1962). The theory was that the alcoholic has difficulties in coping with the demands in life and drowns difficulties in alcohol. In other words, the alcohol anesthetizes the drinker so that there is no pain (anxiety, depression) felt at least while drinking is going on.

Freud postulated that there was a homosexual component to alcoholism. Alcoholics, said Freud, are latent homosexuals, orally dependent. Men who drink too much seek out the company of other men in bars, etc., thus fulfilling their homosexual feelings (Chafetz and Demone, Jr., 1962).

Karl Menninger (1966) proposed that alcoholics have a desire to destroy themselves based on extreme anger towards their parents, anger which creates guilt. By drinking, the alcoholic expresses this rage simultaneously as she/he gratifies oral needs. Alcoholism, suggested Menninger, is a slow way of committing suicide.

Learning theorists propose that people learn to drink and that some learn to be problem drinkers (Albrecht, 1973).

Unmet dependency needs and fear of one's desire to be dependent are often cited as a basic conflict of the alcoholic. Since women, culturally, are permitted more often to express dependency, they can attempt to cope with this need by direct means rather than the indirect means employed by men (Blane, 1968). Those societies in which infants are discouraged from being dependent, where there are many people caring for the child, where the child is expected to achieve, and in which dependency in adults is curtailed, have problems with excessive drinking among their people (Bacon, 1974). Societies differ in their expectations of behavior from children and adults and in their stress on independence and dependence. Those societies which stress individuality and which highly stress independence for adults lay the groundwork for dependency-independence conflict, and in those societies there seems to be a high rate of alcoholism.

As stated earlier, it is more acceptable for women to openly be dependent, since culturally, femininity is associated with the acceptance of reliance on others. The woman suffering from alcoholism insists on having her needs met, while the man, because of the social sanctions against dependency as being nonmasculine, recognizes these needs as unacceptable and in an apologetic, sometimes meek manner, strives to have them achieved (Blane, 1968). It has been suggested that the fact that women can be more openly dependent influences their ability to seek out and accept treatment for alcoholism, while the male alcoholic must continue to resist seeking help. More women than men studied were found to have attempted to obtain help for their alcoholism more than once (Mulford, 1977). Men more readily express their perceptions that their drinking habits are worsening (Wanberg and Horn, 1970) and women, it has been suggested, are less inclined to admit the severity of their problem but less inhibited in seeking help for it.

Although all women alcoholics, like male alcoholics, cannot be pigeon-holed into one type of personality or having the same kind of background, there are some characteristics which they appear to have in common. Mulford (1977) found that the women alcoholics he studied were better educated than the men, and they did not have as many of the problems with which excessive drinking is often associated, such as involvement in accidents, conflicts with the law, and physcial harm. If women are generally secret drinkers, and if much of their drinking is done in the home, then they would not have the opportunity to openly defy conventions and are protected from the public display of behavior which might result in legal sanctions.

Drinking to relieve feelings of being alone, to help fall asleep, to relieve anxiety, and to block out anxieties, were found to be cited by more women than men. Interestingly enough, the majority of married men (52 percent) and an even larger number of married women (68 percent) said they drank because they felt very much alone (Mulford, 1977). This supports the concept that the marriages of alcoholics are not satisfactory, and that although marriage for the male alcoholic is nonfulfilling psychologically, it is even less so for the women. Both men and women seem to learn to use alcohol in order to relieve psychological pressures and because drinking is less acceptable for females than for males, women learn to rely on "spirits" as a panacea later in life (Mulford, 1977).

Heavy drinking has been associated with the drive for power, and it has also been posited that alcoholism as well as heavy drinking, is associated with the desire to feel powerful. While the drive for and the desire to feel powerful may very well be a dynamic behind drinking by men, research so far has not supported this thesis for women (Wilsnack, 1973 a).

Women alcoholics, it has been proposed, are "sicker" than male alcoholics (Rathod and Thomson, 1971; Winokur and Clayton, 1968) and most alcoholic women suffer from emotional difficulties in addition to their drinking problem (Fort and Porterfield, 1961). Why are alcoholic women psychiatrically in worse condition than alcoholic men? Karpman (1948) believed that women are forced to repress their feelings more than men and attempt to find ways of expressing themselves that are more conventional. If the repressed needs build up to the point of near-explosion, and are unable to be handled by previously employed methods, alcoholism may result as an expression of the difficulty. Since the tension fighting for expression is so intense, the expression of it in the form of alcoholism is more vehement. Kinsey (1966) points out that treating women alcoholics in a hospital is more difficult than the treatment of men, and women alcoholics try to commit suicide and succeed in doing so at a higher rate than men. Thoughts of suicide and delusions are often found in females hospitalized for alcoholism and more women than men are diagnosed as suffering from a depressive reaction in addition to alcoholism (Winokur and Clayton, 1968; Curlee, 1970).

Researchers like Kinsey (1966) question the conclusions drawn that women alcoholics demonstrate more pathology than their male counterparts. He points out that what is considered to be pathological is often influenced by the double standard of behavior, that as many women as men are successfully treated for alcoholism in the hospital, and that women in general have a higher rate of attempted suicide. He also stresses the fact that alcoholic women coming for treatment may be demonstrating greater pathology because they are treated after a number of years of inebriation and may be demonstrating in their behavior the results of "greater disapproval, rejection and alienation rather than a pre-alcoholic condition" (p. 7).

It is true that most women alcoholics appear to have psychiatric hospital admissions at a high rate and are also institutionalized for a longer time than men (Curlee, 1970). Curlee proposes that because women alcoholics are more prone to seek out treatment, and because it is easier to accept a diagnosis of mental illness for women rather than inebriation, women are seen as having greater pathology. The prognosis of alcoholic women and that of men seems to be similar (Beckman, 1975). If this is so, is the alcoholic woman really sicker?

Women, in general, are more often diagnosed as being emotionally disturbed, while men tend to be identified as sociopathic (Gove and Tudor, 1973). This pattern is also demonstrated in diagnosing alcoholic women. Most alcoholics suffer from depression (Weingold et al., 1968), and women in general are diagnosed as depressed more often than men. It is no wonder, then, that the woman alcoholic demonstrates a greater frequency of depressive disorder than the male inebriate.

How does the alcoholic woman feel about herself? Most alcoholics generally have poor perceptions of themselves and are very angry individuals who lack a sense of trust (Kinsey, 1966). The poor self-concept of the alcoholic has been well-documented (Charalampous et al., 1976). The alcoholic drinks to feel good about herself but is only drawn into a cycle of guilt, more drinking, and more guilt. Although women inebriates see themselves as lacking in attractiveness physically as well as in personality characteristics, and unable to meet the expectations of adulthood (Kinsey, 1968), male alcoholics as well as their female counterparts lack self-esteem (Clarke, 1974).

Women alcoholics come from a family in which their mothers were unable to demonstrate warmth. Mothers were characterized as insisting on perfection, inflexible, and emotionally contained (Wood and Duffy, 1966). Mother was the dominant one in the family, and father, if he was available (in most cases he is alcoholic, psychotic, or has left the family through death or desertion) was ineffective (Wood and Duffy, 1966; Kinsey, 1968). Most of the women felt deserted emotionally in childhood, although they may have been living with their family. About half of the alcoholic women have fathers who were also alcoholic and almost one-third have close relatives with psychiatric illnesses (Wood and Duffy, 1966; Schuckit, 1969). Many of their brothers also drink heavily, and depression is evidenced in a large number of the female relatives (Schuckit, 1969; Winokur and Clayton, 1968). Parental drinking among male alcoholics shows no appreciable difference from that of the female alcoholic's parents (Hoffman and Noem, 1975). Often the alcoholic was not the preferred child in the eyes of the dominant parent, and she found it difficult to do anything right for the dominant one. Characterizing the patients in their study, Wood and Duffy (1966) state

> Our patients grew up submissive and passively resentful, always lacking self-confidence. Every one developed feelings of worthlessness and inadequacy which utterly negated her generally superior beauty, talent, and intelligence. Frequently she expressed the feeling that she was basically like the father, who obviously failed to please the perfectionistic mother (p. 342).

The parent's marital relationship was less than good, and sex, a prohibited subject, was imbued with dirtiness. Wood and Duffy (1966) point out that as she becomes an adult, the alcoholic woman looks for a relationship with someone who will give her security and on whom she can lean. She marries someone who controls her and cannot meet her emotional needs of acceptance. Her husband, in order to make his wife be more sexually accepting, teaches her to drink, and so they live, but not happily and not forever after.

Adolescence presents a severe crisis for the female alcoholic to which she responds by submissiveness, lack of trust of others, and often an identification with a judgmental type of religion (Jones, 1971).

Problem reactions by women are often attributed to their physiological changes as a result of the menstrual cycle, childbearing, and menopause. These changes are also used to rationalize unacceptable feelings and behaviors. So why not identify premenstrual difficulties, pregnancy, and menopause with the onset of alcoholism? It has been done. The argument goes that women are closely tied to their physiological functions, especially those which are particularly female. These functions affect their feelings and consequently the manner in which they behave. The beginning of the menses, therefore, can trigger off excessive drinking. Menopause, if it does result in depression, lays the groundwork for alcoholism, as also do gynecological problems such as uteral or ovarian surgery (Lolli, 1953).

Although there appears to be a relationship between alcoholism and female physiological functions, it is the way the woman feels about these functions that is important (Lisansky, 1957). Kinsey (1966) found that there were a surprisingly large number of alcoholic women in his study who were homosexual, infertile, or nonorgasmic, and this would lead one to believe the thesis that there is a direct relationship between female physiology and the onset of alcoholism. But, says Kinsey, when one analyzes the data in more detail, one finds that the individual had begun drinking heavily before the physiological difficulty began.

Women who attribute their drinking habits to premenstrual tension have been reported to use alcohol to relieve this tension. "Acceptance or nonacceptance of feminine role behavior, heightened by the perception of premenstrual physiological changes, may serve as a significant stress for alcoholic women" (Belfer and Shader, 1971). Since drinking is culturally basically a masculine behavior, the question can be raised whether alcoholism is associated with a conflict around femininity.

Alcoholic wives who are infertile, it has been proposed, perceive their inability to bear children as a question of their supposed lack of femininity, and suffer a concomitant loss of self-esteem. The woman who drinks excessively often drinks in reaction to her inability to perform as a woman. The more she drinks to feel more feminine, the more her femininity is questioned, and the cycle continues. This pattern has been labeled "femininity by the bottle" (Wilsnack, 1973 a). If, as has been found to be true in many cases, the mother of the alcoholic woman was the domineering parent and the father a passive personality, role confusion can take place. The female alcoholic may sometimes develop what are perceived as masculine traits, which in turn creates conflict around her concept of herself as a woman.

Basically, sex role preference, sex role behavior, and sex role identification differ. Preference implies viewing the behavior associated with a specific sex as desirable and a wish to appropriate those behaviors. Sex role behaviors are those identified with a particular sex, and sex role identification means taking on as one's own those behaviors (Lynn, 1959). If at any point one of these processes of adopting a sex role fails, or does not develop concurrently, the resultant tension may lead to excessive drinking (Parker, 1972).

Alcoholic women have been found to demonstrate conscious feminine preferences but have expressed more masculine preferences on the unconscious level and in their choice of masculine behaviors. They seem to identify and take as their own their mother's masculine manner but do not identify with their passive fathers (Wilsnack, 1973, b). Although they appear to feel consciously feminine, their assertiveness may have raised concerns and anxieties regarding their ability to be a "real" woman. Perhaps, the alcoholic is truly attempting to establish herself as a woman (Wilsnack, 1973, b).

In one comparison of women alcoholics with women who drank moderately, it was found that for alcoholic females, the sex role preference is lessened in spite of the fact that the way they react emotionally (how they express fear and pity) becomes more feminine in character. This creates a conflict situation. The decrease in sex role preference and the increase in feminine emotional responses may symbolize an effort to compensate for masculine behaviors (Parker, 1972).

Is it true in Shakespeare's words, that "The lady doth protest too much" (Shakespeare: *Hamlet,* III, ii)? Some researchers do not think so (Kinsey, 1966, Beckman, 1978).

Alcoholic women have difficulty in adjusting to the role expectations of adulthood, do not negate but do find satisfaction with feminine roles. It may very well be that they accept the feminine role but have not been able to meet these role expectations. Their style appears to be more masculine, and they have difficulty and concern about being a mother and wife (Kinsey, 1966).

More recent research (Beckman, 1978) found a very small number of their alcoholic women subjects demonstrating sex-role conflicts. Nonalcoholic women in treatment demonstrated similar femininity, masculinity, and androgeny patterns. The researcher concluded that:

> ... all women who show pathology are likely to evidence similar types of sex-role identification. It indicates that (although sex-role identity problems may not be of major significance in alcoholic women) whatever problems alcoholic women have in the area of sex-role identification seem characteristic of female psychopathology or emotional disorder in general rather than alcoholism per se. Thus, sex-role identity conflicts may characterize women with all types of disturbed or pathological behaviors. Perhaps all types of internal conflicts are more typical among women evidencing psychopathology or emotional disorders (Beckman, 1978).

As the differences in role behavior of males and females become more blurred, we will find an increase in alcoholism among women. This increase may result from an increase in identification of women as alcoholics, which is already influencing our statistics. It may also result from the fact that women will be taking on more masculine roles, particularly at work, and with the assumption of masculine behaviors, will also come an increase in drinking. We know that alcoholism is associated with exposure to alcoholic beverages so that we can assume that with an increase in exposure at an early age, the groundwork will be laid for more females developing an alcohol problem.

On the other hand, as more women enter the work force, housewives' disease of boredom will decrease, and boredom has been proposed as a factor in the development of excessive drinking (Fraser, 1974).

When the average person thinks about a drunk woman, the individual thinks of promiscuity. Basically, however, alcoholic women tend more often to be sexually witholding. As one researcher pointed out:

> They find sexual relations frightening, uncomfortable, and painful; sexual activity is minimal, sometimes nonexistent. Frigidity and unresponsiveness replace warmth and participation (Blane, 1968, p. 116).

How does our society view the woman inebriate? She is perceived as more deviant than the man, since drinking is unladylike behavior. Alcoholics in general are perceived to have low morals, to have characteristics of irresponsibility, unreliability, selfishness, and to be unredeemable. The alcoholic woman is viewed as being less feminine but the male is seen as lacking in masculinity. Stafford and Petway (1977) therefore conclude that the double standard for women alcoholics no longer exists. On the other hand, other researchers support the contention that women alcoholics are viewed especially harshly (Kinsey, 1966). Kinsey suggests that this may account for the reluctance to face the fact that alcoholism is a problem facing women, resulting in little research in that area.

The alcoholic woman is often also a pill popper. Drug abuse is not a new phenomenon for women. In the 1800s opiates were very inexpensive and easily accessible. Physicians readily prescribed them to relieve menstrual distress and the difficulties of menopause. The majority of opiate users during the 19th century were women (about 61 percent), and it is estimated that women users of opiates outnumbered men about three to one (Brecher, 1972). Their age ranged from twenty-five to fifty-five, and since menopause occurred earlier in women than it does today, one can assume that a significant number of these women were menopausal. It has been postulated that women used opiates more extensively than men not only because doctors prescribed them for the distress associated with menstruation and menopause, but also because alcohol consumption by women was not considered ladylike and was therefore tabooed. As Brecher says, men went to the bars to drink while women stayed home to get their high. After the Harrison Act was passed in 1914, equalization of addiction between the sexes took place. The Harrison Act placed restrictions on the sale of opiates as well as the manner in which the physician prescribed them.

Opium is a drug which relieves pain and induces sleep. Like alcohol, it is a depressant which helps ease anxiety and creates a sensation of "all is well" with the world. Morphine and codeine are nonsynthetic derivatives of opium, while heroin is synthesized from morphine. All are potentially addictive.

Although the addiction dangers of opium were well known, medication containing large doses of this drug was still being prescribed for "female discomfort" in the 1940s. I know because it was prescribed for me.

During the 19th century much of the dispensing of opiates was geared to the relief of pain, but it was also recommended to replace alcohol, which was perceived as a more dangerous drug (Brecher, 1972). Brecher points out that even as late as the early 1940s alcoholics were being persuaded by their physicians to substitute morphine for drink. I became aware very recently of the case of a young woman, addicted to Percadan, a synthetic narcotic, as a result of a painful injury of the arm. She was told by several physicians to use alcohol as a substitute. Today, I suppose, alcohol is viewed as the lesser of the two evils.

Opiates were used as tranquilizers and women became addicted to them. Today women are still addicted to tranquilizers, although these are not necessarily narcotics. In fact, more women are addicted to prescription drugs other than narcotics than men. These include the drugs prescribed for depression; tranquilizers, barbiturates, as well as sedatives. In 1971 women made up 53 percent of the population, yet used these drugs six times as often as men (Chambers, November 1971).

One in-depth study by the Alcoholism and Drug Addiction Research Foundation in Toronto compared the use of mood-altering (psychotropic drugs) prescription drugs of women in an urban area in Canada with that in the United States (Cooperstock, 1971). The drugs studied were those that were prescribed by a physician, in other words, drugs legally issued. Almost one-quarter of the prescriptions were written for drugs which have a mood-altering effect. Forty-four percent of the mood-altering drugs prescribed were sedatives and hypnotics and comprised the largest group. The next most frequent prescription (40 percent) was for the so-called "psychotherapeutic" drugs which consist of drugs to combat depression, and tranquilizers. Only 16 percent of the prescriptions of mind-altering drugs issued were for stimulants.

The "mind boggling" result of this study was the fact that 69 percent of the prescriptions for all drugs were dispensed for women. This, according to Cooperstock (1971), the author of the article, is not surprising since studies in the United States have found that women are issued about 67 percent of the mood-modifying prescriptions. In fact, the majority of all prescriptions (60 percent) are written for the female population.

Tranquilizers are the most popular of the prescription mood-altering drugs and so are the sedatives. In 1961 research was done on patients who were part of a prepaid medical plan (Shapiro and Baron, 1961). In any one week, the physicians who were visited by patients in their office, or who visited patients in their home, prescribed mood-altering drugs 12 percent of the time, and tranquilizers comprised half of them. More than twice the number of the psychotropic drugs were prescribed for females. There was also a marked difference in age range between female and male patients and the type of drug prescribed. A large number of antidepressants was prescribed for women fifteen to forty-four, a larger number than in any other group. The author notes that this is considered the childbearing age. Frequency of visitations to physicians by women did not, according to the researchers, adequately explain the differential in drug prescriptions.

In 1967, the percentage of women using prescription psychotropic drugs was still proportionately large according to Brecher (1972). At that time 66 percent of the people using those drugs were female, about the same percentage that existed in the 1800s for female opiate users. Although in 1967 women comprised a little more than half the population, they made up 56 percent of the people visiting the doctor's office and used 60 percent of the prescribed drugs.

Of the following, women comprised most of the users; 60 percent of all prescriptions for barbiturates, 66 percent of nonbarbiturate sedative and hypnotic agents, 68 percent of the drugs prescribed as tranquilizers, 71 percent of those issued to combat depression and 80 percent of amphetamines. The majority (68 percent) of psychoactive drugs were medically advised to be used by women (Brecher, 1972, p. 484). Women are the recipients in greater numbers of drugs geared toward helping psychological difficulties. Women appear to have been and still are the legal pill poppers.

Why are women destroying themselves with the abuse of drugs and why are physicians prescribing more of the mood-altering drugs to the female segment of the population? There are those who believe that drug advertising, especially the advertising in the psychiatric and medical journals, plays an important role. One of the proponents of this thesis is a physician, Robert Seidenberg (1971). He proposes that the drug industry is strongly influencing doctors but particularly psychiatrists. *Psychiatry Digest,* says Seidenberg, is received at no charge by almost 20,000 psychiatrists and is supported by payments from advertisers. Psychiatrists are bombarded with pictures of distressed and depressed women and are told what to prescribe for what ails them. Since there are so many drugs on the market, psychiatrists are unable timewise to make an in-depth evaluation of each drug and therefore tend to be influenced by what appears in the psychiatric journals. The American Medical Association does not evaluate or censor material it accepts for its journals. There is, however, even if it is not meant to be, an implicit approval of the drug as well as implicit approval of the advertising gimmick. Seidenberg points out that at least $200 million is spent each year on psychotropic drug advertisement, and that advertising has been established as an important influencer in all areas. Seidenberg harshly criticizes the type of advertising which presents women who are reluctant to wash dishes, do housework, or give their children baths, as "sick" and the suggestions that they be given drugs so that they can better adjust to their tedious situation.

Seidenberg also attacks those ads which encourage doctors to prescribe drugs to women who bother the doctor because they do not follow through on suggestions, although they request help; those women who have symptoms such as insomnia, headaches, and stomach upsets, and who call the physician often; those women who have emotional problems but who want to be told that their difficulties are physical in origin; and those who are very demanding and want the physician to give them more attention. Seidenberg takes issue with this type of ad because it encourages doctors to tranquilize their women patients because they are bothersome. Then, points out Seidenberg, there are ads encouraging physicians to prescribe tranquilizers because a woman's family complains about her behavior. One ad shows a raging man. The caption reads, "Women are impossible!" The ad is not suggesting tranquilizers for him but for his wife, whose premenstrual tension is causing her a great deal of anxiety as well as irritableness.

The basic attitudes toward women, the basic prejudices and stereotypes of women, are reflected in the drug ads. Women are portrayed in negative ways. One ad reads in part, "She has insomnia ... so he's awake. Restless and irritable, she growls at her husband. How can this shrew be tamed? ..." Seidenberg strongly believes that advertisers mold the opinions of doctors.

> ... the concept of mental illness for which drugs might be prescribed can be expanded to include otherwise (formerly) acceptable idiosyncratic behavior or capriciousness, the burden of giving a child a bath at night, or a distaste for washing dishes might be converted into medically treated syndromes. Similarly, displays of anger, irritability, or possessiveness become indications for tranquilization. And, addiction to food, alcohol or self-administered drugs are to be replaced by addiction to those medically prescribed. Similarly, attitudes toward groups of people—women for instance—can be influenced by an inordinate use (quantitatively) of pictures of them as "sick" or disturbed. One can create the image of women as not only the weaker sex but the sicker sex (p. 22).

I have noticed in thumbing through the medical journals, that the drug advertisements are now beginning to include increased numbers of men as patients needing chemical help.

Another explanation for the proportionately large number of women using psychotropic drugs is the thesis that these drugs are substitutes for alcohol. Men escape by drinking and women by popping pills. Alcohol consumption, as was noted earlier, is associated more with masculine behavior, and is therefore less acceptable as an outlet for women. Alcoholic women in the United States have been found to become users of other drugs more frequently than alcoholic men (Curlee, 1970). Alcoholics in general easily become addicted to other drugs, particularly tranquilizers and sedatives (Fox, 1973) so that doctors are cautioned not to prescribe those drugs without strict controls. Sedatives and tranquilizers are prescribed to relieve the distressing symptoms associated with alcohol withdrawal.

Ruth Cooperstock (1971) attempts to explain why more women than men use psychotropic drugs and why more men use illegal drugs.

She proposes that Western society permits women, more so than men, to verbalize how they feel, whether or not it is positive or negative, and allows them to identify these feelings as problematic when so indicated. Because women can express emotion, are encouraged to identify certain emotions or degrees of emotion as maladaptive, they are better able than men to seek out help from the medical profession and to share with their physicians the difficulties they perceive they are having. Because the doctor is molded by and reflects attitudes, values, and expectations of behavior of the female sex, he, and it usually is a he, anticipates that the woman will voice her feelings and therefore assumes that more women than men will need to have psychotropic drugs prescribed to them. And so he meets this expectation. Cooperstock supports her arguments by citing a study which demonstrated that men tend to see their problems as physiological in origin, while women view their difficulties as having an emotional origin (Phillips and Segal, 1969). Cooperstock points out that the findings in her study demonstrate that men, when they are prescribed tranquilizers, are given specific muscle relaxants as opposed to a general tranquilizer. General tranquilizers would most often be prescribed to those people who have what are perceived as emotional problems.

Men are not as apt to use prescription drugs as often as women. If they do use these drugs, they are apt to get them from nonmedical sources. Cooperstock points out that the self-medication behavior of men may result from the fact that they may not feel they need to go to a physician, or because going to a physician would be a sign of weakness which is not masculine. Men then point to specific symptoms when they do complain and women to more general difficulties. The doctor, on the one hand, expects women to complain more and to have diffuse complaints and so issues prescriptions of mood-modifying drugs to them. Cooperstock points out that the large number of psychotropic drug prescriptions written for women is not due solely to the types of diagnoses made. In Cooperstock's words, "Much evidence exists to demonstrate that holding diagnosis constant, women patients receive more mood-modifying drugs than men" (p. 243).

Tranquilizers are usually prescribed for people who have reached "mid-life." The use of minor tranquilizers has been found to rise for women in the thirty to forty-four age group and to reach its peak between sixty and seventy years old (Parry et al., 1973). One study of women over thirty years old, most of whom were well-educated and from the middle class (Linn and Davis, 1971) gives us some understanding of the middle-class woman who uses mood-modifying drugs. The authors do tell us that, because random sampling was not used, generalization to other populations should be done with caution.

What did the research find out about these middle-aged women who were taking psychotherapeutic drugs? Firstly, they used nonprescription drugs to ease the pain of headache,but tended not to use them for other symptoms. Of the 46 percent of the sample who were using prescription drugs, 84 percent said they were prescribed by a physician. There was a relationship between ongoing health difficulties and the use of these drugs. The more often an individual visited a physician, the greater the chance that she would be prescribed a psychotherapeutic drug. Those women using psychotherapeutic drugs were also found more likely to be on additional medication. The women having family or friends who were receptive to their sharing of health problems and to their talk about medication were more apt to be users. It appears, then, that one's reference group is also a significant factor in determining psychotherapeutic drug use. Broken marriages were associated with drug users. The authors conclude that religion was also an important variable which affects drug behavior. For instance, medical information, emotional and/or social problems appeared in this study to be highly significant to Protestant women and the rate of drug use but not to the other religious groups.

Blaming the drug industry and physicians is really not sufficient by itself as an explanation of the abuse of prescription drugs by women (Borgman, 1973). What did a three-year, in-depth study of the psychosocial history of twenty-three women in their middle years of life who were perceived by their families as abusing medication find? The medication these women took included barbiturates, tranquilizers, stimulants, as well as codeine. Sometimes an overdose, either accidental or purposeful, would occur. Medication was simultaneously taken with alcohol consumption. Social relationships suffered when periodically they would try to abstain from using drugs.

Most of these women had remained married, were never accused of violent behavior or promiscuity during their marriage, and almost half of them had been employed but had made frequent job changes. Their children generally were not labeled as problem children, and their adult offspring had either married and left home or broken the parental silver cord by establishing a career and living away from the family. The women were manipulative in obtaining the medication they wanted and were resourceful in the manner in which they asked their physician for the prescription. Outwardly, they appeared fairly mature. However, there were evidences of actual immaturity. They expressed feelings of being alone, not being happy, of leading a boring life, of not having the support they felt they needed from friends and relatives and basically of being unable to fend for themselves. All this with an overriding expression of hopelessness. They were extremely demanding, but unable to accept efforts to meet their expressed needs without criticism. Physical ailments were verbalized which, after extensive medical tests, were deemed to be psychosomatic. They were dependent on their families but resented it. The husband was the authoritarian figure in the family and controlled his wife in finances, regulation of his wife's time, and deciding when and if she could use the car.

Borgman (1973) proposes that in order to survive, these women relied on drugs. The time and energy spent in getting and using the drugs helped make their lives feel less empty. They viewed the medical prescriptions by the physician as an indication of care and acceptance. The use of medication was viewed as a statement of their independence, and the volatile responses to their medicaton abuse from their family added spice to their lives. What is extremely interesting is that the onset of the use of medication was not in most cases associated with any specific life crisis. Borgman states that:

> The more usual pattern was a gradual increase in medicine-taking until it resulted in obvious mental confusion, lethal danger, and public intervention by the family. Diminution of responsibility for care of children probably increased feelings of boredom, uselessness, and loneliness while reducing the incentive for self-control. In some instances, the husbands became less tolerant and more rejecting of their wife's demands and hypochondria as the couple entered middle age (p. 531).

The personality needs of women, then, are a factor in their abuse of drugs. We have all heard about the "bored housewife syndrome" and its cousin, "housewife's fatigue" accompanied by many other somatic complaints. Is the working woman less apt to be a pill popper? In an extensive study over a six-year period, Parry and colleagues (1973) found that both those women who were employed and those whose profession was "housewife" had about the same amount of "high level" use of minor tranquilizers. The women who use prescription drugs, such as tranquilizers and sedatives with duration are usually those who have poor educational background and who are in the low socio-economic class. Parry and his colleagues thus negated the stereotype that it is the bored middle-class housewife who does most of the pill popping. They suggest that the noticeable fact that there is a higher rate of prescription drug use among women than men may be due to the fact that there is

> among women, a greater likelihood of visiting the physician, biological differences associated with the reproductive cycle, demands and allowances characterizing female social roles, and less use of alternate substances for coping with emotional distress, e.g., alcohol (p. 782).

Some attention has been given to the women who become addicted to drugs as a result of medication sanctioned by their physician for the relief of pain. Even as early as 1944 (Pescor), it was noted that female narcotic addicts reported a painful physical condition as the reason for being introduced to narcotics. The pain, however, may not be physical but psychological in origin. Dr. Glaser (1968) has labeled such a woman "pain-prone." These women are able to obtain their drugs legally from their doctors, and Glaser noted that most of the women he studied had a large number of major surgical procedures for nonorganically based pain, followed by prescriptions of narcotics, basically because, posits Glaser, the physician feels more comfortable treating a condition that can be labeled organic. Women who are pain-prone, suggests Glaser, should be treated for their psychological distress. But unfortunately, the psychiatrists to whom many of the women he studied were referred, were apparently unable to be of very much help. Glaser stresses the prevention of addiction in pain-prone women, and places the responsibility for this prevention on physicians, who should be more selective in prescribing narcotics. Some of these women became addicted after being given drugs for menstrual cramps.

There were differences noted between the pain-prone women and others addicted to narcotics. The pain-prone women were older when they first began to use drugs, generally in their mid-twenties, began to use them for the relief of pain, were more apt to be divorced, were better educated, and a sizable number of them were in the nursing profession. The pain-prone person is usually not involved with the use of heroin, prefers not to take the drugs intravenously, and generally belongs to a higher socio-economic group than those who do. One of the striking similarities between the pain-prone group and other narcotic users was the fact that a large number of both groups also consumed barbiturates and alcohol.

When most people think of drug abuse, they think of narcotics and illegal drugs. Women are also involved in this type of self-destruction, but not to the extent that males are.

The National Institute of Drug Abuse reported (Annual Summary Report, 1977) that almost 75 percent of the patients admitted to drug programs which received funds from the federal government were men. Of the heroin addicts, 27 percent were women as opposed to 73 percent men, and 31 percent compared with 69 percent males addicted to other opiates were women. As has been found in other surveys, although 84 percent of the alcohol abusers were men, only 16 percent were women. Abuse of barbiturates was also more of a masculine venture; 33 percent of the barbiturate abusers were female, while 67 percent were male. Females, as usual, were found to abuse tranquilizers more than any other drug.

There apparently is a pattern of high use of drugs and an association with a particular stage in one's development. A national survey of over 4500 respondents who were twelve years or over concluded that family life was an important influencer, especially the drug habits of the mother. If a mother had taken psychotherapeutic drugs prescribed by a physician and smoked or drank moderately, her teenage children would be higher alcohol and illegal drug users. Father's drinking or drug habits did not appear to be a significant influence (Cisin et al., 1977).

Addicted females were found to be bereft of friends twice as often as male addicts and tended to state that they did not have a good friend half the time. Women who were addicted demonstrated questionable self-esteem and more depression than nonaddicted women. Both male and female addicts concurred that both men and women view the addicted women more negatively than they do the addicted men. They also agreed that if one compares a female addict with a male addict, the female is viewed as "worse" than the male. Addicts, themselves, seem to have a double standard as it applies to men and women with the same drug problem.

How else do male and female addicts differ? A study of 100 patients who had been admitted to the United States Public Health Narcotics Hospital in Lexington, Kentucky (Ellinwood, Jr. et al., 1966) found the following. Both men and women gave the same reasons for beginning to use drugs, among them to be part of a group because they were curious, and for enjoyment. Medical necessity was reported as an introduction to drugs by one-fifth of the sample. The age at which both men and women began to use drugs did not differ, both in the Ellinwood (1966) as well as the Pescor (1944) studies. The addiction process was faster for women, but it was the male who got into trouble with the law because of crimes against property, while women prostituted themselves to support their drug habit and abstained from drugs less often than men. The researchers posit that this may be due to the fact that women could support their habit by prostitution, which is *not* a crime against property, and law enforcement is primarily involved in preventing or punishing crimes against property as opposed to crimes against the person. Thus women did not come to the attention of law enforcement officials, perhaps also because of the tendency for our society to view deviance of women in a medical manner rather than legally.

The female addict's mother often suffered from alcoholism, as well as being involved in a criminal career. Although about 40 percent of both male and female addicts came from broken homes, the women experienced earlier removal from parental environs. A high incidence of incest was found to have occurred in the history of the addicted women studied. The perpetrators of the incestual relationships were family members who were older, such as their mother's lover or their own stepfather. As adults, many of the women were unable to achieve orgasm and many of them became homosexual. Uncles and cousins were more often the perpetrators of incestuous relationships in the history of 188 female addicts who were receiving treatment at Odyssey House (Benward and Densen-Gerber, 1975). That study found that the rate of incest was higher in white, poor families where there were a large number of siblings, and a number of the women also said that the incest had occurred before they were nine years old.

Ellinwood, Jr., and colleagues (1966) found that female addicts tended to rebel by acting out sexually. As expected, the women addicts were diagnosed as being neurotic or psychotic, while the men were labeled as sociopaths or suffering from personality disorders. The researchers conclude that since females are usually not as deviant in their behavior as males, and since drug addiction is deviant behavior, there often is someone in their lives with whom they have identified in this deviant manner, generally a mother who is an alcoholic.

Where does the female addict begin to use drugs? Would you believe she is usually initiated by a male no matter what kind of drug it is? For example, in the case of prescription drugs, the physician is usually a man. Women who marry a husband who is an addict frequently become addicts themselves, but this is not the case for the man who marries a drug-addicted female. The same pattern holds with the alcoholic. In nonmarital relationships, too, it is the male in whose company the female first uses drugs (Suffet and Brotman, 1976).

Broken marriages are frequently noted in the lives of the narcotic users as well as with the alcoholics. A study of addicts at the United States Public Health Hospital in Lexington drew some interesting conclusions concerning spouses of narcotic users (O'Donnell et al., 1967). Husbands who are alcoholic or narcotic addicted tend to influence their wives so that they, too, "catch" their addiction, but the reverse does not generally happen. Although some of the women in the study had been involved in a deviant culture early in their youth and had therefore tended to choose a deviant man as their spouse, most of the women had not been introduced to drugs until a number of years after their marriage.

More female addicts than male addicts report having children, and more women continue to retain responsibility for their offspring in spite of their addiction (Eldred and Washington, 1975). The effects on their children are obvious. Addicts who become pregnant place the fetus they are carrying in grave jeopardy. The pregnancy is usually unplanned, which lends itself to possible child abuse. Complications include breech delivery, premature birth, and toxemia. Babies born of addicted women weigh less and are usually born addicted (Stone et al., 1971). The numbers of pregnant addicts appear to be on the increase (Finnegan, 1975).

Whether it is a young woman addicted to narcotics, or a middle-aged mother abusing prescription drugs, the act itself is an act of self-destruction. It can lead to accidental or deliberate overdosing or the deadly effects of mixing drugs and drink. The National Institute of Drugs found that in one year ending in April, 1977, emergency-room treatment was given to about 47,000 people who had combined alcohol and drugs. Death resulted for 2500 of them (Stockton, 1978).

Suicide is a taboo word. Often when someone dies by his or her own hands, it is referred to as an accidental death and is not in any way identified as a purposeful act by an individual resulting in his or her own destruction. Although many people at one time or another have thoughts, either fleetingly or consistently, of doing away with their own lives, sharing these thoughts is not encouraged by others, and the topic of death itself, and especially suicidal death, is rarely discussed. Yet, one percent of all deaths are a result of suicide (Lester et al., 1979). People in the United States kill themselves each year, and a large number of them are women. In fact, women attempt suicide more often than men, while men accomplish their demise twice as often as women (Weissman and Klerman, 1977). The ratio of male-completed suicides to female-completed suicides has decreased in the past several years from three to one to its present two to one, and some people believe females will soon reach equal status in at least one area, that of killing themselves.

Suicide can be attempted or completed, it can be passive or active. A person can try to kill herself, but either not succeed in doing so intentionally, or be interrupted and saved in the nick of time. An individual can be passively suicidal, for instance, by not taking the prescribed medication for a serious illness, or an individual can take action to destroy herself by jumping out of the window (which was a more common method in the thirties than today), gassing herself, or any one of the many other available techniques. The method by which one chooses to die is also significant in helping to understand the dynamic behind the action. All suicides are not the same, and the motives for killing oneself may differ from one person to another, although there are some basic commonalities.

A simple definition presented by Ruth Cavan (1965) states that "suicide is the intentional taking of one's own life or the failure to save one's life when death threatens" (p. 3).

Other suicidologists have not only differentiated between attempted and completed suicide, but have also added a third category, that of suicide ideas (Beck et al., 1973). Completed suicide is defined as "a willful, self-inflicted, life-threatening act which has resulted in death." Attempted suicide means "a willful, self-inflicted, life-threatening act resulting in physical injury but not in death," and ideas of suicide, "suicidal ideation and acts that indicate a loss of desire to live, but which have not yet resulted in physical injury" (Beck et al., 1973).

Reasons for suicide have been offered by psychologists as well as by sociologists. Emile Durkheim (1951) divided suicide into anomic, egoistic, and altruistic, which are all a product of the individual's relationship to society. The altruistic suicide is one which society expects to occur because the mores dictate self-destruction in a given situation. An example of this type of suicide was the suttee custom formerly found among women of the Hindu religion, who flung themselves on their husbands' funeral pyres, and thus died with their mates. The individual desires of the widow were not taken into account. She had no choice but to follow the accepted custom or be ostracized by others, apparently a fate worse than death.

Anomic suicide, said Durkheim, is that which results when the individual's characteristic position in relation to society suddenly changes, leaving her with coping skills that are no longer relevant. Examples of this would include a sudden death in the family, a separation from a loved one, being fired from a job, or, as was true in the 1930s, the crash of the stockmarket, which left men, ordinarily the sole bread winners at that time, not only unemployed, but with no savings.

An interesting study in this area was reported in 1954 by Henry and Short, Jr. They reasoned that although economic growth and cultural change had resulted in opening doors for women in the work market, the opportunities for them were still minimal, and their husband's occupation was still indicative of family status. The man was the important figure in striving for upward mobility. Henry and Short, Jr., posited, therefore, that the business cycle would have a relationship to the suicide rates of males. Their study concluded that there was a marked difference among women and men in their response to fluctuations in the business cycle as determined by the number of suicides. Males responded more to the business cycle, and a decline of the business index was accompanied by a decided increase in suicides by men.

Durkheim believed that the more individuals were integrated into society, the less suicide would occur. Role conflict or a sudden change in roles would therefore affect the suicide rate. One recent study (Stack, 1978) attempted to discover whether the increase in women entering the labor force had any effect on the rates of suicide on men. The researcher hypothesized that increased entry into the work world by women would create a role conflict for men. If role conflict is related to integration into society and to anomic suicide, the results should show a positive correlation—and so they did. Whereas women who work have two basic roles, that of mother and worker, if a man's primary role, that of wage earner, is threatened, role conflict will occur. Interestingly enough, Stack also concluded that the suicide rate for females was less affected by their working.

Durkheim's last but not least classification of suicide was that which he called "egoistic" suicide. This is the direct opposite of altruistic suicide. Whereas in altruistic suicide the person kills herself because it is expected by society, in egoistic suicide the person kills herself because she feels that no one cares, and she does not feel that she is a significant part of the society in which she lives. There is a relationship between significant others and lethality. One measure of the strength of the person's intent to commit suicide is whether or not there are significant others in the person's life. People who are "alone" are more apt to accomplish their desire to die.

Freud (1955) believed that humans were imbued with an aggressive and destructive drive, both instinctual, both related (and both part of the death instinct). He stressed the concept that suicide involves a death wish against others, which results in guilt and the direction of the destructive impulses toward oneself. Menninger (1964) accepted

Freud's thesis but expanded it by classifying suicide according to motives.

> There are accidental suicides, there are suicides which are substitutes for murder, there are suicides which are a cry for help and suicides which are miscarriages of an attempt to get oneself rescued (p. 268).

Since females attempt suicide more often than they complete the action, it would be helpful to review some of the material on the differences among attempters and achievers.

White males comprise the largest number of completed suicides. This group (the completed suicides) has also been found to have people who are considered normal mentally and fewer who are in good health (Lester and Beck, 1975). High rates of completed suicides were also found in the inner city where there are ways of dramatically accomplishing the act, such as tall buildings and high bridges (Schmid and Van Arsdol, 1955). People with broken marriages, especially those who are divorced tend to be completers. Completed suicides for males increase as they get older. The age of thirty-five appears to be the time when female completed suicides peak (Schmid and Von Arsdol, 1955).

Widows are more likely to commit suicide than widowers. One study found that the ratio of completed suicides to attempted suicides among widows was five to one, whereas among widowers it was two to one (Shneidman and Farberow, 1961). One can infer that the loss of a husband is more traumatic than the loss of a wife.

Single people are more often suicide attempters than completers (Shneidman, 1970). It has been suggested that one reason females become attempters rather than completers of the suicide act is that they tend to choose methods which are generally less lethal than those chosen by men. Guns are more lethal than drugs because they can kill instantly, yet more women use drugs as a means of attempting self-destruction. Maris (1969) suggests that the method chosen by women may reflect the fact that guns are generally not part of their environment and shooting oneself is messy. Realistically, says Maris, the differential method is a reflection of differences in motivation. Women attempt suicide in response to domestic rather than occupational difficulties. Maris also posits that women who attempt suicide are not genuinely seeking death but expressing anger and a cry for help. The attempter is usually a married woman who is also a mother. It appears that difficulty in marriage is very often viewed by women as well as the society as a whole as the wife's responsibility. If a marriage fails, then the wife must have done something wrong. Jobs are still perceived as secondary in importance to the marital relationship, and so even if she does work, the woman's marriage is perceived to be the important job.

Phyllis Chesler (1972) views the many suicide attempts made by women as being a result of their performing the feminine role, which is to nurture, to care for, and to depend on a male. Studies on attempted suicides have shown that women more often than men respond to a relationship crisis with suicide attempts. Male attempters and completers of suicide focus on occupational difficulties, as compared with marital problems, which precipitate the suicidal actions of females (Breed, 1967; Maris, 1979). This is a reflection of sex role socialization patterns in our society in which men are socialized to be instrumental; that is to do and to change, and women are socialized to be expressive; that is to be concerned with emotions and relationships.

The presence of a "significant other" is an important factor influencing suicide intent. Married people have someone else who will be strongly affected by their actions. Marriage and children decrease social isolation and therefore the more children there are in the family, the less chance there is that the individual will commit suicide (Maris, 1969). Durkheim believed that marriage helped to immunize people against suicide. Apparently, women are less immunized by having children. Female suicides sharply increase between the ages of fifteen and thirty-five. Maris (1969) states, "One of the most significant events in this time period is marriage and the raising of children" (p. 162).

Discussions on suicide often point to the dependency factor. In an effort to obtain information on the sociological and psychological influences on the decision to commit suicide, a retrospective study was made of over 200 people who had been patients at a neuropsychiatric hospital and who had committed suicide, comparing them with patients who had not (Shneidman, 1970). One of the factors of prime importance that emerged was the conflict between dependency needs and the desire to be independent. The person who was dependent and also dissatisfied with life, the "dependent-dissatisfied" person, has increased lethality. This individual was a complainer, a controller, and a demander wanting support from the people around her/him, but ending up creating a situation in which they became alienated from her/him. The danger of this situation is that the staff at the hospital or other people around often begin to take the threats of suicide less seriously and are surprised when the person carries out the threats (Shneidman, 1970).

The suicide rate for males increases ratio-wise to females with age. Female rates hit a high at about thirty-five years of age and do not change appreciably thereafter. Maris (1969) concludes that:

> the older males are, the more illness, the fewer significant others, the more occupational problems, anomic and social isolation, the greater the wish to die, and the higher the suicide rate. Young females have more marital problems, more familial constraints, a greater wish to kill, use less lethal methods, and have a lower suicide rate than males (p. 114).

In an effort to evaluate intent, a study was made of the admissions to a hospital over a two-year period during the month of August, of people who attempted suicide (Dorpat and Boswell, 1963). Judges were asked to rate the behavior on a five-point scale, ranging from "gesture," "ambivalent suicide attempt," to "serious suicide attempt." They found that those who completed suicide used more lethal methods, such as hanging and guns, and that those who attempted, but didn't succeed, used drugs. Suicide lethality in terms of intent increased with age, and a large number of the people in both groups, attempters and completers, had shared their suicidal thoughts with others and had attempted suicide in the past. Women, therefore, who attempt suicide are making a statement and their attempts can become accomplished facts if they do not receive help.

Sometimes the attempted suicide accidentally dies. Those who are ambivalent tend to arrange it so that their suicide attempt will coincide with a rescue (Dorpat and Boswell, 1963). One case in point is the woman who swallows a large number of pills at 5:30, expecting that her husband, who is usually prompt, will be returning home from work at six o'clock. He is delayed and she is dead. Dorpat and Boswell (1963) believe that the person who makes a suicide gesture really does not want to die but wants to make a change in a relationship, such as having a love affair renewed. The ambivalent suicide attempter, like the alcoholic, tries to blot out the world in order to achieve peace. Both also want to see how much the significant others in their lives care, and can determine that by the amount of concern displayed when they are rescued. Dorpat and Boswell also state that those who are serious in their efforts to kill themselves, and those who succeed have commonalities of suffering from depression, feeling that there can be no change, and that no one really cares, and there are few, if any, close people in their lives.

Several researchers have noted that there is an element of risk-taking in suicide attempters (Lester and Lester, 1971; Weiss, 1957; Adams et al., 1973). The attempters feel that there is nothing to lose, so they might as well take a chance, for instance, to see whether their husbands really do love them. It is interesting that at least one researcher, E. Stengel, believes that manipulation of a relationship is the basic motive behind the suicide attempts of women. He believes that women manipulate because other means of control, such as economic or physical power are not available to them. He therefore concludes that women are not actually flirting with death in their suicide attempts (Lester and Lester, 1971). The myth of the woman manipulator again rears its ugly head.

There is a relationship between depression and suicide (Silver et al., 1971). People who are depressed often commit suicide and those who are suicidal are often depressed (Weissman and Klerman, 1977). Based on the diagnosis of women who seek psychiatric help, more women than men suffer from depression. Chesler (1972) believes that depression is learned behavior for women in response to their female role. Men learn to be drug addicts and alcoholics and are called social deviants. Women learn to be dependent, to be depressed, and to attempt suicide, and are called mentally disturbed. She points out that depression has been considered a response to a loss; a loss of a loved one whom one may have felt ambivalent about, a loss of the self we would like to be, and a sense of loss of significance in life. Whereas men traditionally respond to frustration with aggression, women, says Chesler, are taught to respond by turning hostility inwards with depression resulting. She points out that women who are depressed do not overtly act out their anger in a physical manner, and that any expression of hostility is usually verbal rather than physical in nature. Women, states Chesler, do not tend to channel their hostility into physical activity as men do. Physical strength is unfeminine and expressions of it go unrewarded and are even occasionally punished. She cites a study that indicated verbal hostility was less often expressed by depressed women than by nondepressed women, and that improvement in their depressive symptoms resulted in even fewer expressions of hostility. Depressed men, on the other hand, expressed greater hostility, verbally, than depressed women. She concluded that "it is safer for women to become 'depressed' than physically violent" (p. 45).

In an effort to understand the differences in depression among men and women in the United States, Weissman and Klerman (1977) reviewed and analyzed evidence culled from reported studies. They concluded that, indeed, women have a higher rate of depression than men, and that this phenomenon exists in most countries. Both men and women react to death with similar expressions of grief in terms of duration of symptoms and type of depression. Stress is assumed to be positively related to depression, and stressful situations are believed to be precipitating factors in depression. Weissman and Klerman point out that women presented more symptoms in response to the same stressful situation than men. They do suggest that these findings may be skewed by the fact that concrete precipitating life events are usually emphasized on stress scales, and that women might be reacting to socio-economic status, health difficulties, or the stress of large families, which might affect them more than men, and which the stress scales are not geared to measure. Although men resort to alcohol more than women to resolve their depression, or become involved in criminal behavior, Weissman and Klerman state that more women than men are depressed, that this is not solely a result of the fact that women more often come to the attention of medical personnel; or because they are permitted to express feelings more than men, and are not discouraged from seeking medical help as men might be in terms of concepts of masculinity and feminity. Women are in reality more often depressed than men, and this difference may be genetic and/or due to female physiology and endocrine functions (Weissman and Klerman, 1977).

They cite evidence in various studies which have shown that those people who are clinically diagnosed as depressed have a greater frequency of depression in members of the immediate family than those in the greater population. Studies of both fraternal and identical twins indicate the tendency of one twin to develop the same type of illness as the other. They do point out, however, that there is not enough support for a genetic sex difference in depression, but suggest that this avenue be further studied.

As would be expected, researchers have attempted to link premenstrual tension and/or the menstrual cycle with depression and attempted as well as completed suicides. MacKinnon et al., (1959) found a correlation between suicide and the period of activity of the corpus luteum. We know that the week before menstruation many women (70 percent) retain fluids resulting in weight gain and bloating. It also is an accepted fact that fluids which are retained in the area of the brain can cause depression and irritability (Weideger, 1977). Some studies have shown that a significant number of women who commit suicide are menstruating at the time (Wetzel and McClure, Jr., 1972). There have been conflicting conclusions from different studies relating the premenstrual symptoms to suicide thoughts and attempts. However, Wetzel and McClure, Jr. (1972) refuse to accept the possibility that no relationship exists between periods of the menstrual cycle and suicide. They express the hope that future research, more carefully designed, would correlate some part of the menstrual cycle with a greater potential for suicidal behavior, and thus help physicians predict and prevent suicidal attempts as well as completions. What they do not address themselves to is an encouragement of further research to explore how much, if any, premenstrual tension and suicidal behavior may be influenced by the way women and their physiology are perceived, as well as their own perceptions of their bodies and their function.

The myth of a physiological basis for depression as an inevitability during menopause has existed since time immemorial. Weissman and Klerman (1977) note that this is indeed a myth. Research has established the fact that depression which occurs during menopause is not separate from personality characteristics which prevail before the "change of life," and the menopausal woman is not a higher depression risk than women of other ages. Pauline Bart (1971) studied the history of over 500 hospitalized women aged forty to fifty-nine. This was their first hospitalization for psychiatric reasons, and half of them had suffered from depression. The inference from this study is that women who were most likely to become depressed during the menopausal period are those who were excessively involved with their children, or who were unable to allow the children to separate from them. This phenomenon is more common in housewives, and it is the housewife who more often becomes depressed than the woman who is employed. The "empty nest" syndrome includes depression, especially for the woman whose main focus is the household and the children in it.

Depression is more common among the housewives in the middle-income bracket than in those who are working-class (Bart, 1971).

The relationship between marriage and depression, and marriage and suicide is interesting. The rates of mental illness are higher among married women than among those who are single, divorced or widowed, whereas marriage appears to be an insulator for men (Gove and Tudor, 1973). Married women are generally restricted in their roles; the role of housewife does not provide structure as does a work role; there is little prestige associated with it and no pay, and the married working woman has extra pressures to cope with, hypothesized Gove and his colleagues.

Statistics in the past generally supported Durkheim's thesis that marriage insulates against suicide. Many past studies have found that the suicide rate among both married women and men was lower than among those who were single (Cavan, 1965; Dublin, 1963). The explanation was that married people were less likely to be socially isolated and therefore were more affected by outside controls. Today, though, the relationship between marital status and suicide appears to be changing. A study of the death certificates of almost 900 reported suicides in Ohio between 1960 and 1970 found that, although more men than women commit suicide, both men and women who are married have a higher rate than their single counterparts. The rate of suicide among married women is two times that of single women. Divorcees commit suicide more often than those women who are widowed, and both widows and divorcees have a lower suicide rate than widowers and divorced men (Rico-Velasco and Mynko, 1973). Marriage, then, is losing its effect as a deterrent to suicide (Shneidman and Farberow, 1970), and for women, depression and mental illness are a risk in marriage. Perhaps Chesler is correct. Women do the feminine thing and flagellate themselves, while men act out.

Powerlessness is another factor which is thought to influence suicidal behavior. The person who is suicidal has a feeling of impotency.

Males who threaten suicide have a lower level of feelings of powerlessness than those who attempt to kill themselves. For female attempters and threateners, the degree of difference of powerlessness is negligible. Lack of power for males appears to be related to suicidal behavior (Wenz, 1977). Why, may we ask, is powerlessness less disturbing for females? We might propose, as have other feminists, that women do not have and never had power. Women also are not expected to be dominant. In fact, Phyllis Chesler (1972) states that "women are in a continual state of mourning for what they never had—or had too briefly, and for what they can't have in the present, be it Prince Charming or direct world power" (p. 44).

Completed suicides among drug addicts, as well as alcoholics are frequently high (Frederick et al., 1973; Pitman and Snyder, 1962). Menninger (1966) spoke of the alcoholic as self-destructive, and many alcoholics have had a long history of depression before manifesting overt suicidal behavior. In alcoholics suicide has been found to be precipitated by a loss of a relationship through death or separation, of work, or because of deteriorating health (Pitman and Snyder, 1962).

Drugs are often used in suicide attempts, especially barbiturates. In 1968, 1602 people committed suicide, using these drugs, and a number of deaths which were considered accidental were the result of the lethal mixture of barbiturates and alcohol (*Drug Use in America,* 1973).

Before 1950 most of the suicides resulted from shooting, hanging oneself, or from gas. In the ten-year period between 1953 and 1963, three times as many people used drugs to self-destruct as in the years previously. Suicide with a barbiturate overdose was the second favorite method used in 1972. It is women who tend to overdose by using psychotropic drugs more often than men (McGuire et al., 1976).

As we have seen, there is a relationship between alcoholism, drug abuse, and suicidal behavior. Women who have presented these symptoms have low self-esteem, use drugs, alcohol, or suicidal attempts to blot out anxiety and are attempting to work through their dependency-independence conflict. Popping prescription pills and attempted suicide are more acceptable feminine behaviors than excessive drinking, which is considered masculine. More women, then, pop prescription pills and attempt suicide than men. It has been proposed that as the roles of men and women become less differentiated, so will the self-destructive behavior. More women, therefore, will become alcoholic, perhaps increase their use of illegal drugs, and succeed in killing themselves as often as men.

References

Anon. *Annual Summary Report, 1977.* Data from the Client Oriented Data Acquisition Process. National Institute on Drug Abuse, Statistical Series, Series E, No. 6. U.S. Department of Health, Education and Welfare, 1978.

_____. *Drug Use in America: Problem in Perspective.* U.S. National Commission on Marihuana and Drug Abuse, Washington, D.C.: U.S. Government Printing Office, March, 1973.

_____. The shocking facts about women and alcohol. *Good Housekeeping* 185:207–208 (September, 1977).

Adams, Russel L., Giffen, Martin B. and Garfield, Frances. Risk taking among suicide attempters. *Journal of Abnormal Psychology* 82:262–267 (1973).

Albrecht, Gary L. The alcoholism process: a social learning viewpoint, in Peter C. Bourne and Ruth Fox (eds.). *Alcoholism.* New York and London: Academic Press, 1973.

Anderson, George M. Women drinking: stigma and sickness. *America* 137:434–437 (December 17, 1977).

Bacon, Margaret K. The dependency-conflict hypothesis and the frequency of drunkenness. *Quarterly Journal of Studies on Alcohol* 35:863–876 (1974).

Bart, Pauline. Depression in middle-aged women, in Vivian Gornick and Barbara K. Moran (eds.). *Women in Sexist Society: Studies in Power and Powerlessness.* New York: Basic Books, 1971.

Beck, Aaron, et al. Classification and nomenclature, in H. L. P. Resnick and Berkley C. Hathorne. *Suicide Prevention in the Seventies.* Washington, D.C.: U.S. Government Printing Office, 1973.

Beckman, Linda J. Sex-role conflict in alcoholic women. *Journal of Abnormal Psychology* 87:408–417 (1978).

_____. Women alcoholics. *Journal of Studies on Alcohol* 36:797–824 (1975).

Belfer, Myron L. and Shader, Richard I. Alcoholism in women. *Archives of General Psychiatry* 25:540–544 (1971).

Benward, Jean and Densen-Gerber, Julianne. Incest as a causative factor in antisocial behavior: an exploratory study. *Contemporary Drug Problems* 4:323–340 (Fall 1975).

Blane, Howard T. *The Personality of the Alcoholic.* New York: Harper & Row, Publishers, 1968.

Borgman, Robert D. Medication abuse by middle-aged women. *Social Casework* 54:526–532 (November 1973).

Brecher, Edward M. *Licit and Illicit Drugs.* Boston: Little Brown, 1972.

Breed, Warren. Suicide and loss in social interaction, in Edwin S. Shneidman (ed.). *Essays in Self-Destruction.* New York: Science House, 1967.

Bromet, Evelyn and Moos, Rudolf. Sex and marital status in relation to the characteristics of alcoholics. *Journal of Studies on Alcohol* 37:1302–1312 (1976).

Cahalan, D., Cisin, I. H. and Crossley, H. M. *American Drinking Practices: A National Study of Drinking Behavior and Attitude.* New Haven: College & University Press, 1969.

Cavan, Ruth. *Suicide.* New York: Russell & Russell, 1965.

Chafetz, Morris E. and Demone, Harold W., Jr. *Alcoholism and Society.* New York: Oxford University Press, 1962.

Chambers, Carl D. and Schultz, Dodi. Women and drugs. *Ladies Home Journal* **88**:130 (November, 1971).

Charalampous, M. D., Ford, B. Kathryn and Skinner, Thelma J. Self-esteem in alcoholics and nonalcoholics. *Journal of Studies on Alcohol* **37**:990–994 (1976).

Chesler, Phyllis. *Women and Madness.* New York: Avon Books, 1972.

Child, I. L., Barry, H., III and Bacon, M. K. Sex differences: a cross-cultural study of drinking. *Quarterly Journal of Studies on Alcohol* Supplement No. 3:69–71 (1965).

Cisin, Ira, Miller, Judith D. and Harrell, Adele V. *Highlights from the National Survey on Drug Abuse: 1977.* Washington, D.C.: U.S. Government Printing Office, 1977.

Clarke, Sandra K. Self-esteem in men and women alcoholics. *Quarterly Journal of Studies on Alcohol* **35**:1380–1381 (1974).

Cooperstock, Ruth. Sex differences in the use of mood-modifying drugs: an explanatory model. *Journal of Health and Social Behavior* **12**:238–244 (1971).

Curlee, Joan. A comparison of male and female patients at an alcoholism treatment center. *The Journal of Psychology* **74**:239–247 (1970).

Dorpat, Theodore L. and Boswell, John D. An evaluation of suicidal intent in suicide attempts. *Comprehensive Psychiatry* **4**:117–125 (1963).

Dublin, Louis I. *Suicide: A Sociological and Statistical Study.* New York: The Ronald Press Co., 1963.

Durkheim, Emile. *Suicide.* Translated by John A. Spaulding and George Simpson. Glencoe, Illinois: The Free Press, 1951.

Eldred, Carolyn A. and Washington, Mabel N. Female heroin addicts in a city treatment program: the forgotten minority. *Psychiatry* **38**:75–85 (1975).

Ellinwood, E. H., Jr., Smith, W. G. and Vallant, G. E. Narcotic addiction in males and females: a comparison. *The International Journal of the Addictions* **1**:33–45 (1966).

Finnegan, Loretta P. Narcotics dependence in pregnancy. *Journal of Psychedelic Drugs* **7**:299–231 (1975).

Fort, Twila and Porterfield, Austin L. Some backgrounds and types of alcoholism among women. *Journal of Health and Human Behavior* **2**:283–292 (1961).

Fox, Ruth. Private Treatment of the Problem Drinker, in Peter G. Bourne and Ruth Fox (eds.). *Alcoholism.* New York: Academic Press, 1973.

Fraser, Judy. The female alcoholic. *Grassroots* 9–15 (August 1974 Supplement).

Frederick, Calvin, Resnik, Harvey L. P. and Wittlin, Byron J. Self-destructive aspects of hard core addiction. *Archives of General Psychiatry* **28**:579–585 (1973).

Freud, Sigmund. Beyond the pleasure principle, in *The Complete Psychological Works of Sigmund Freud,* Vol. 18, James Strachey (ed.). London: The Hogarth Press, 1955. pp. 7–64.

Garrett, Gerald R. and Bahr, Howard M. Skid row women. *Quarterly Journal of Studies on Alcohol* **34**:1228–1243 (1973).

Glaser, Frederick B. Narcotic addiction in the pain-prone patient. *The International Journal of the Addictions* **3**:149–161 (Spring 1968).

Gomberg, Edith S. Women and Alcoholism, in Violet Franks and Vasanti Burtle (eds.). *Women in Therapy*. New York: Brunnel/Mazel Publishers, 1974, pp. 169–190.

Gove, Walter R. and Tudor, Jeanette F. Adult sex roles and mental illness. *American Journal of Sociology* **78**:812–835 (1973).

Henry, Andrew F. and Short, James F., Jr. *Suicide and Homicide*. London: Free Press of Glencoe, Collier-MacMillan Limited, 1954.

Hoffmann, Helmut and Noem, Avis A. Alcoholism among parents of male and female alcoholics. *Psychological Reports* **36**:322 (1975).

Jones, M. C. Personality antecedents and correlates of drinking patterns in women. *Journal of Consulting and Clinical Psychology* **36**:61–69 (1971).

Karpman, B. *The Alcoholic Woman*. Washington, D.C.: Linacre Press, 1948.

Kinsey, Barry A. *The Female Alcoholic*. Springfield, Illinois: Charles C. Thomas, 1966.

_____. Psychological factors in alcoholic women from a state hospital sample. *American Journal of Psychiatry* **124**:1463–1466 (1968).

Knupfer, Genevieve and Room, Robin. Age, sex, and social class as factors in amount of drinking in a metropolitan community. *Social Problems* **12**:224–240 (1964).

Lester, David and Beck, Aaron T. Extrapolation from attempted suicides to completed suicides. *Journal of Abnormal Psychology* **84**:563–566 (1975).

Lester, David, Beck, Aaron T. and Mitchell, Betsy. Extrapolation from attempted suicides to completed suicides: a test. *Journal of Abnormal Psychology* **88**:78–80 (1979).

Lester, Gene and Lester, David. *Suicide: The Gamble with Death*. Englewood Cliffs, N.J.: Prentice-Hall, 1971.

Linn, Lawrence W. and Davis, Milton S. The use of psychotherapeutic drugs by middle-aged women. *Journal of Health and Social Behavior* **12**:321–340 (1971).

Lisansky, Edith S. Alcoholism in women: social and psychological concomitants. *Quarterly Journal of Studies on Alcohol* **18**:588–623 (1957).

Lolli, Georgie, Alcoholism in women. *Connecticut Review on Alcoholism* **5**:9–11 (1953).

Lynn, D. A. A note on sex differences in the development of masculine and feminine identification. *Psychological Review* **66**:126–135 (1959).

MacKinnon, I. L., Mackinnon, P. C. B. and Thomson, A. D. Lethal hazards of the luteal phase of the menstrual cycle. *British Medical Journal* **1**:1015 (1959).

Maris, Ronald W. *Social Forces in Urban Suicide*. Homewood, Illinois: The Dorsey Press, 1969.

McGuire, Frederick, Birch, Herman, Gottschalk, Louis A., Heiser, Jon F. and Dinovo, Eugene C. A comparison of suicide and non-suicide deaths involving psychotropic drugs in four major U.S. cities. *American Journal of Public Health* **66**:1058–1061 (1966).

Menninger, Karl A. *Man Against Himself.* New York: Harcourt, Brace & Norel, 1966.

_____. *The Vital Balance*. New York: Viking Press, 1964.

Mulford, Harold. Women and men problem drinkers. *Journal of Studies on Alcohol* **38**:1624–1639 (1977).

O'Donnell, John A., Besteman, Karst J. and Jones, Judith P. Marital history of narcotics addicts. *The International Journal of the Addictions* **2**:21–38·(1967).

Parker, Frederick B. Sex-role adjustment in women alcoholics. *Quarterly Journal of Studies on Alcohol* **33**:647–657 (1972).

Parry, H. J., Mitchell, B., Mellinger, G. D., Cisin, I. H. and Manheimer, D. National patterns of psychotherapeutic drug use. *Archives of General Psychiatry* **28**:769–783 (1973).

Pescor, M. J. Comparative statistical study of male and female drug addicts. *American Journal of Psychiatry* **100**:771–774 (1944).

Phillips, D. and Segal, B. Sexual status and psychiatric symptoms. *American Sociological Review* **34**:58–72 (1969).

Pitman, David and Snyder, Charles R. (eds.). *Society, Culture and Drinking Patterns.* New York: John Wiley, 1962.

Rathod, N. H. and Thomson, I. G. Women alcoholics. *Quarterly Journal of Studies on Alcohol* **32**:45–52 (1971).

Rico-Velasco, Jesus and Mynko, Lizbeth. Suicide and marital status: a changing relationship. *Journal of Marriage and the Family* **35**:2939–2944 (1973).

Rimmer, John. Psychiatric illness in husbands of alcoholics. *Quarterly Journal of Studies on Alcohol* **35**:281–283 (1974).

Rosenbaum, Bernice. Married women alcoholics at the Washingtonian Hospital. *Quarterly Journal of Studies on Alcohol* **19**:79–89 (1958).

Schmid, Calvin and Van Arsdol, Maurice D., Jr. Completed and attempted suicides: a comparative analysis. *American Sociological Review* **20**:273–283 (1955).

Schuckit, Marc, Pitts, Ferris N., Jr., Reich, Theodore, King, Lucy J. and Winokur, George. Alcoholism. *Archives of General Psychiatry* **20**:301–306 (1969).

Seidenberg, Robert. Drug advertising and perception of mental illness. *Mental Hygiene* **55**:21–30 (1971).

Shapiro, Sam and Baron, Seymour. Prescriptions for psychotropic drugs in a non-institutional population. *Public Health Reports* **76**:481–488 (1961).

Shneidman, Edwin. Preventing suicide, in Edwin S. Shneidman, Norman L. Farberow and Robert E. Litman. *The Psychology of Suicide.* New York: Science House, 1970.

Shneidman, Edwin S., and Farberow, Norman L. Statistical comparisons between attempted and committed suicides, in Norman L. Farberow and Edwin S. Shneidman. *The Cry for Help.* New York: McGraw-Hill Book Co., 1961.

Silver, Michael A., Bohnert, Michael, Beck, Aaron T. and Marcus, Donald. Relation of depression of attempted suicide and seriousness of intent. *Archives of General Psychiatry* **25**:573–576 (1971).

Stack, Steven. Suicide: a comparative analysis. *Social Forces.* **57**:644–653 (1978).

Stafford, Ruth A. and Petway, Judy M. Stigmatization of men and women problem drinkers and their spouses. *Journal of Studies on Alcohol* **38**:2109–2121 (1977).

Stockton, William. Dual addiction. *The New York Times Magazine* p. 10 (August 6, 1978).

Stone, Martin L., Salerno, Louis J., Green, Marvin and Zelson, Carl. Narcotic addiction in pregnancy. *American Journal of Obstetrics and Gynecology* **109**:716–723 (1971).

Suffet, Frederic and Brotman, Richard. Female drug use: some observations. *The International Journal of the Addictions* **11**:19–33 (1976).

Wall, J. H. A study of alcoholism in women. *American Journal of Psychiatry* **93**:943–952 (1937).

Wanberg, Kenneth W. and Horn, John L. Alcoholism symptom patterns of men and women. *Quarterly Journal of Studies on Alcohol* **31**:40–61 (1970).

Wanberg, Kenneth W. and Knapp, John. Differences in drinking symptoms and behavior of men and women alcoholics. *British Journal of Addiction* **64**:347–355 (1970).

Wechsler, Henry and McFadden, Mary. Sex differences in adolescent alcohol and drug use. *Journal of Studies on Alcohol* **37**:1291–1301 (1976).

Weideger, Paula. *Menstruation and Menopause.* New York: Alfred A. Knopf, 1976.

Weingold, Harold P., Lachin, John M., Bell, A. Howard and Core, Raymond C. Depression as a symptom of alcoholism: search for a phenomenon. *Journal of Abnormal Psychology* **73**:195–197 (1968).

Weissman, Myrna M. and Klerman, Gerald L. Sex differences and the epidemiology of depression. *Archives of General Psychiatry* **34**:98–111 (1977).

Wenz, Friedrich J. Subjective powerlessness, sex, and suicide potential. *Psychological Reports* **40**:927–928 (1977).

Wetzel, Richard D. and McClure, James N., Jr. Suicide and the menstrual cycle: a review. *Comprehensive Psychiatry* **13**:369–374 (1972).

Wilsnack, Sharon C. Femininity by the bottle. *Psychology Today* **6**:39–43, 96 (April 1973 a).

_____. Sex role identity in female alcoholism. *Journal of Abnormal Psychology* **82**:253–261 (1973b).

Winokur, George and Clayton, Paula J. Family history studies: comparison of male and female alcoholics. *Quarterly Journal of Studies on Alcohol* **29**:885–891 (1968).

Wiseman, Jacqueline P. *Stations of the Lost.* Englewood Cliffs, N.J.: Prentice-Hall, 1970.

Wood, Howard P. and Duffy, Edward L. Psychological factors in alcoholic women. *American Journal of Psychiatry* **123**:341–345 (1966).

11. In the Name of Beauty

To be born a woman is to know—
Although they do not talk of it at school—
That we must labor to be beautiful
(William Butler Yeats: Adam's Curse).

Actually, laboring to be beautiful is a task that women throughout history have had to undertake. There have been periods, from time to time, during which men worked hard to present themselves as elegant and desirable, but for women beauty was most often associated with popularity and preferability, and for women being wanted by a man, especially for marriage, was commonly associated with survival. Women depended on men to support them and to legitimize their existence. Marriage was the expected goal for all women, and those who did not achieve this status were often thought to have failed because of their lack of appeal to the other sex.

Although we all have heard the old English proverb that "Beauty is but skin deep," physical attractiveness is an important factor in the development of relationships, particularly heterosexual ones. Experimenters have demonstrated that when people are shown photographs, they tend to imbue good-looking people with favorable personality characteristics (Byrne et al., 1964; Miller, 1970, and Barocas and Karoly, 1972). Plato said that all that is beautiful is good, so it is evident that the equation of beauty and goodness has existed for over two thousand years. Shakespeare himself said, "She never yet was foolish that was fair" (The Rape of Lucrece). And Keats pointed out that

Beauty is truth, truth beauty—that is all
Ye know on earth, and all ye need to know (Ode
on a Grecian Urn, p. 234).

It was Robert Browning's belief that

If you get simple beauty and naught else,
You get about the best thing God invents
(Fra Lippo Lippi, p. 430).

People who are considered to be attractive are also assumed to be popular and coveted for friendship (Barocas and Karoly, 1972). Actually, in many instances this is a fact.

In 1966, an interesting study was made on whether or not people placed a high priority on the attractiveness of potential dates (Walster et al., 1966). College students were invited to a dance and randomly paired by a computer. Four college students rated the ticket purchasers according to their perceived level of attractiveness. The participants in this research filled out a questionnaire which elicited information on their popularity and self-esteem. The results indicated that there is a relationship between perceived attractiveness and self-reported popularity. In addition, those who see themselves as being attractive and having a pleasing personality expect their date to have the same attributes. Whether or not a woman was asked for a date after being matched for the dance, depended on her degree of physical attractiveness. The man's physical attributes, whether favorable or unfavorable, did not affect this variable. The women who were considered pretty were those who were more frequently dated. What surprised the researchers was the finding that women were also concerned with physical attributes, and whether or not a man was physically good-looking influenced whether or not he was liked, and whether or not he was desirable as a date. The experimenters suggest that perhaps the importance of physical attractiveness may only be operative for first encounters. It appears to be true that the first characteristic one notices in social interactions is physical appearance, and it is this first characteristic which seemingly determines whether or not an individual wishes to further encourage a relationship (Brislin and Lewis, 1968).

A later study over a period of five encounters (Mathes, 1975) supports the fact that physical attractiveness is influential on whether or not a person is liked, and points to evidence which suggests that this influencer does not decrease or increase with increased contacts. Researchers have found that physical attractiveness has an important influence on attraction felt toward a stranger regardless of sex (Byrne, et al., 1964). In our society a pleasing physical appearance is valued. The way one looks, as well as whether one is male or female is the first and most obvious noticeable characteristic. Physical appearance is also an important determinant in the degree of attraction one feels towards an individual. Whether or not we are consciously aware of this phenomenon, people who are physically attractive are not only thought to have desirable personality characteristics and desirability as dating partners, but are also viewed as being happier in their marriage, skilled as parents and in general successful in life (Dion, et al., 1972). Goodness and beauty are intertwined.

Not only is social life determined by our physical attributes but also our mental health, especially if we are female. Concern with the effect of physical unattractiveness on mental illness led to research in this area, using as subjects a group of patients hospitalized for mental illness who were not physically ill nor mentally retarded. The control group consisted of employees at a university, as well as a group of shoppers (Farina et al., 1977). Efforts were made to rule out the possibility of the influence of mental illness or of hospitalization on attractiveness. The findings in this study supported the thesis that women who were mentally ill were seen as unattractive. Both with the patients and the subjects used as controls, attractiveness was related to adjustment. Those who were poorly adjusted were also rated as physically less pleasing, although there was no cause and effect relationship between the two. The researchers did conclude that there was a relationship between a patient's degree of attractiveness and her in-hospital treatment. Those who were considered to be less physically attractive had fewer visitors, were not thought of as being pleasant to the same extent as those who were better looking, remained in the hospital for longer periods of time, and had a lower degree of interpersonal interactions. The authors postulate that these phenomena are also operative with unattractive people outside of a hospital environment, and that being physically unattractive may have a negative effect on adjustment.

Studies have also demonstrated that physical attractiveness is an important influencer. If one is attractive, one is able to have more influence on how hard another will work (Kahn et al., 1971), on how much sympathy one receives (Shaw, 1972), and on how seriously one's errors are perceived (Dion, 1972). Even whether or not a person will have his or her request met is influenced by the degree of physical allure (Chaikin et al., 1974). Perception of positive prognosis by counselors is associated with physical attractiveness of the client, particularly as it relates to women (Barcos and Vance, 1972).

Children, as well as adults, are influenced by a person's physical demeanor. Nursery school children seek out as companions for play those who have an attractive physical appearance (Jackson and Huston, 1975). Because people are physically pleasing, it is believed that they are socially reinforced in a positive way, which leads to increased desire for relationships with others as well as assertiveness.

Women who are pleasing in appearance were found to be more assertive than those women who were considered physically unattractive (Jackson and Huston, 1975). Because people who are attractive are often thought as having other positive traits, the attractive individual receives positive social messages, which in turn increases her self-esteem and consequently her assertiveness.

Women soon learn to use their bodies in order to obtain their desires. Unlike the male, who uses such manipulative techniques as deluding, women manipulate with their looks. Success in college is positively correlated with the physical attractiveness of the female (Singer, 1964). Beauty is power. Said Aristotle,

> Beauty he declared to be a greater recommendation than any letter of reference (Aristotle: quoted by Diogenes Laertius, p. 461)

The way we picture our bodies (body image) is basic to the way we feel about ourselves (self-esteem) (Gutze, 1969). For the women in our society, developing a realistic self-concept is difficult. The feminine ideal is one which is free from facial hair, smells sweetly, and bulges, but only in the right places. If a young woman cannot achieve these unrealistic standards, she may see womanhood as unobtainable. "Conflict and self-denial" may occur (Gutze, 1969). A person's image about herself is closely enmeshed in the way others see her. Charles Horton Cooley (1922), a well-known sociologist of his time, pointed out that an individual develops a self-image based on how she or he is viewed by others, accepted or rejected, approved of or disapproved of. The judgments that are made by others toward a person are incorporated into the view the individual develops of himself or herself. This, Cooley called the "looking-glass self." Our society gives messages to women, that they must not get old, and that they must continue to be sexually appealing.

Gutze (1969) posits that in order for a female to develop a body image that is associated with femaleness, there has to be a divergent sex in the society from which she can see herself as being sharply different.

It is necessary that a woman perceive that she is different from men. The differences must be in terms of (a) appearance, (b), function, (c) feeling, and (d) external identification (1969, p. 115).

The body image should include cultural aspects, such as "fad and fashion" as well as physical attributes. Because, states Gutze, women are becoming more assertive, and because the basic roles of women are in flux, there is confusion around what are masculine and what are feminine behaviors. In order to address itself to this, states Gutze, fashion dictated toplessness and mini-skirts in the 1960s in order to sharpen the body-image of the female.

The physiological function of women, basically that of menstruation, has social significance which determines for the woman how she feels about her body and about herself. Weideger (1977) speaks about "the menstrual uglies." Just prior to menstruation a woman may look peaked, feel tired, and break out with eruptions of the skin. She also may feel bloated. Although the change in appearance may be minor, women often feel intensely unattractive, and therefore anxious because they feel that they have lost their good looks. As Gutze (1969) points out, being svelte is viewed as important for women in our society. Feeling bloated, then, makes a woman feel fat, and therefore unattractive. Beauty may be only skin deep, but unfortunately, for women, surface beauty is essential.

The concept of beauty is the concept held by men. Arlene Dahl (1965) demonstrates, perhaps in an exaggerated way, the fact that men are the reference point in our culture, and Dahl in no uncertain terms states that this is how it should be. Who is Arlene Dahl? She was a famous movie star who wrote a column on beauty and was, herself, beautiful. As the book jacket adorning her book, *Always Ask a Man* (1965) states:

> Miss Dahl's flawless outward appearance is indicative of the beauty and serenity of her inner substance—living proof that the lady follows her own advice.

Dahl always asked her father to approve whatever it was that she was wearing and following her father, it was "the man" in her life to whom she referred, including her son. After all, said Dahl, one man usually represents the thinking of most men.

The Geisha Girl is supposedly modern man's ideal of womanhood. She is taught to do the things that please him. She is beautiful, serene, intelligent (she generally speaks several languages) and skilled (she sings, dances or plays a musical instrument). It's not difficult to understand why men find her irresistible (p. 20).

What a tremendous burden is placed on women to attempt to achieve femininity. To be feminine is to do for others, then, and not to be self-actualizing, and few women can hope to achieve the standard of beauty that is established as the model. Many women try, though. One company in the cosmetic business manufactures 2500 shades of nail polishes and there is also lipstick to match for most of them. The Revlon Company alone earned about $125 million profit on sales in 1979. The cosmetic industry plugs into a woman's need to feel attractive, which in turn will make her feel good.

Beauty is relative. Standards of beauty differ with each generation and in different parts of the world.

Beauty, like supreme dominion,
Is but supported by opinion
(Benjamin Franklin: *Poor Richard's Almanac,* 1741).

Tattooing and scarification as a method of beautification of the body was found among primitive groups and is still somewhat in existence today. Although tattooing is associated with lower-class people in America, such as lower-ranked sailors and unskilled laborers, in Polynesia it was associated with upper-class status. Not only were the face, the body, the legs, and arms tattooed but occasionally the tongue was also so treated (Hoebel, 1966).

Girls in one Guadalcanal society were reported to still be subjected to face marking as a rite of passage from childhood to adulthood, even though boys in that same society do not have to participate in any special rite as in the past (Hogbin, 1964). The decision as to when this rite is performed is determined by the girl's father in consultation with his wife's brothers, and usually occurs when breast development becomes evident. The girl is kept awake all night to become fatigued so that the excruciating pain can be diminished. When the rite is performed, the family stays far from the hut in order to be shielded from her cries of pain. A pointed bone is used to etch the designs since tattooing would not be effective on her brown skin. The last act of the "operator" is to pierce her nasal septum so that she can wear a shell or ivory ornament. After six hours of etching, the girl is conveyed to the village, where she is bedded down for several days. After that time her scabs are rubbed off her face at the beach. Although this rite was performed as a rite of passage, it would not be wrong to assume that the resultant effect made the girl more attractive and also more marriageable. In the United States tattooing is associated with masculinity. Although in Polynesia, as well as among the Ainu of Japan, a tattooed body was considered beautiful, an Englishman may view the results in a different manner.

> Ainu women appear at first sight astonishly ugly, dirty, and thoroughly spiritless. Pitiably miserable and unattractive do they look. They have dark, sooty-coloured tattoo marks upon the upper and lower lips, and sometimes a line of the same disfiguring ornamentation across the foreheads. Various patterns are engrained upon the backs of their grimy hands. Their feet are unshod; their hair, matted and unkempt, reaches down to the shoulders in front, and is cut in a kind of crescent shape behind. In addition to all this, their garments are slovenly, untidy, and their countenances sullen and dejected (Batchelor, n.d., p. 34).

Another nonobjective writer of the 1800s in his book, *Romantic Love and Personal Beauty* (Finck, 1887) states:

> The standard of primitive taste is not harmonious proportion and capacity for expression, but exaggeration. The negro woman has naturally thicker lips, more prominent cheek-bones, and a flatter nose than a white woman; and in selecting a mate, preference is commonly given to the one whose lips are thickest, nose most flattened, and cheek-bones most prominent; thus producing gradually that monster of ugliness—the average negro woman (p. 61).

Not only is Finck's description of the Negro woman filled with contempt for a group of people who look different and have different concepts from his own of what is beautiful, but his attitude points out the degree of difficulty black women in our society had and may still have in their attempts to be accepted as attractive in a society where dark skin and certain facial features are devalued.

The concept of beauty is also culture-bound. Women in our society (and some men now) perforate their ears to adorn them with metal, while some tribes pierce the nose so that a ring can adorn it.

Among the Fulanis of West Africa, women wear heavy earrings made of gold. The jewelry is so weighty that it needs to be supported by a strap wound around the head. Because the amount of gold worn by the women indicates the socio-economic status of the family, as the wealth of the family increases, more gold is often attached (Gerster, 1975).

In some cultures women with flat heads were thought to be beautiful, so from early infancy on, the forehead was pressed with a board bound to the head in order to achieve the desired shape. The Incas and other people of the Andes, as well as the Flatheads of Idaho, viewed this type of deformation of the cranium as beautiful. Flatheads were not beautiful to all groups. With some, elongating the cranium was preferred, and this was accomplished by using cloth to bind the head. The mother binds the skull of the infant with bark cloth almost immediately after she gives birth. Each day the cloth is unwrapped and then rewrapped in order to keep the cloth tight until the infant's head is properly shaped; that is, elongated.

There were also those people who saw beauty in long necks. Women, from early childhood on would have their necks stretched by wearing metal rings. Elongated necks were esthetically pleasing. Husbands would remove the rings in order to punish their wives since without the rings, the women could not hold their heads erect (Daly, 1978).

And then there were the Chinese, who saw beauty in small feet, but only in women. Apparently, the custom, which lasted for at least one thousand years, was adopted by the Koreans and was considered the utmost in fashionability by the 12th century A.D. It was a sign of upper-class status, since those whose feet were bound were unable to take anything but small steps, and because of the pain of standing on their feet, were unable to do any meaningful work. Footbinding did not have any religious overtones, but was purely a social custom. The woman whose feet were large was dishonored and was unable to obtain a good husband. This barbaric custom is thought to have been started in A.D. 934 during the Tang Dynasty by a prince's concubine (Bashford, 1916). The fact that it was rapidly adopted and lasted for such a long time would appear to indicate that it served a purpose.

Mary Daly (1978) believes that there was method to the madness of Chinese footbinding. Instead of isolating their wives and daughters as the Indians did, Daly believes that the Chinese bound their women's feet so that they would not be able to stray and would remain pure. In addition, the result insured women's dependency on men. She believes that by having a woman, the mother, perform the painful, sadistic act, women learned that it was not men but other women who were the source of their distress. She also sees the act of footbinding as ritualistically sadistic, since details, including how large the bandages should be, as well as the preferred size of the feet, were standardized.

Binding the feet would begin anywhere between the ages of three and seven. James W. Bashford (1916), Bishop of the Methodist Episcopal Church, who lived in China, describes the process as follows:

> It consists in binding the smaller toes under the foot and of bending the large toe upward and backward in such a way as to make a bow of the foot to a considerable extent the extension of the limb in a straight line. The effect is always to deform the foot, sometimes the bones are crushed in the process, and usually the woman is crippled for life (p. 130).

Footbinding was an agonizing process, sometimes causing infection and gangrene and sometimes resulting in death. Although after the bandages were removed there was no continuing pain, the young girl had difficulty in walking (Latourette, 1934).

Small feet were supposed to be signs of beauty. Women, however, were not given a choice, and when one reviews the general status of women during that era in China, it is not surprising that this sadistic practice could be imposed on them.

> ... when one remembers that under this teaching and under almost universal practice, the Chinese woman was treated as inferior to man, and that this inferiority is considered to inhere in her very nature and to continue throughout eternity; when one remembers how the daughters have been liable to infanticide and slavery, how wives have been from the earliest times under the power of their husbands; how in addition to the grosser tyranny of a bad man every Chinese wife becomes practically the slave of her parents-in-law, and may be subject to refined cruelty upon the part of a mother-in-law, which even a coarse husband would not think of practicing; when one remembers that the physical torture of bound feet is only a symbol of the mental cramping and spiritual torture which marks the entire life, then the grim decision sometimes reached by mothers to drown their baby girls, partly out of poverty and to avoid the alternative of selling them as slaves, and partly out of discouragement over woman's

lot in general, and the more desperate decision to commit suicide themselves, are sad comments on the lot of women in the most populous nation on earth (Bashford, 1916, pp. 131–132).

Feet became a symbol of civilization among the men of classical China. They proudly wore shoes to differentiate themselves from the noncivilized people who went barefoot. Peasants, of course, wore shoes made of straw, while the upper class had shoes made of fine cloth (Schafer, 1967).

In 1904 a public school system was proposed in China, but this system only offered education to girls at the lowest grade. The Dowager Empress and several other princesses also established schools for the daughters of high-ranking officials. Since they ruled that girls with bound feet would not be accepted, the custom of footbinding began to be abandoned (Williams, 1923).

During the early fifties high spiked heels were fashionable in the United States. Even if one learned to balance on these spikes, one could not move fast. The high-heel craze appeared just about the time that the back-to-the-home movement was advancing. Could it be that women were being encouraged to be more "feminine" so that they would accept the feminine role of marriage and motherhood?

The back-to-the-high-heel craze as we approach the 1980s is creating a big flap among doctors. There are those like Dr. W. Norman Scott, who is one of the orthopedic surgeons associated with the Knickerbockers, who says that if fashion is important, then it's okay to wear the high heels as long as you take the shoes off when your feet begin to hurt (*New York Times Magazine,* August 12, 1979, p. 52). A podiatrist, Dr. Richard Lotwin, believes that there should be a law against producing high-heeled shoes. In order to balance on them, a woman must "arch her back, throw her rear end out, lock knees, put her weight on the ball of her foot and jam her toes in the front of the shoe" (*Douglas,* August 22, 1979). Dr. Lotwin avers that extensive damage is done by wearing these shoes since there is pressure on the lower part of the body. Diabetic women may develop gangrene, and normal women callouses, bunions and corns. Lotwin posits that high-heeled shoes originate with men to prevent women from being free. With high heels, how fast can a woman run?

High heels are not a 20th century phenomenon. In the 15th and 16th century, courtesans in Italy were enamored with shoes which increased the height of the wearer as much as twenty inches. Rosencranz (1972) points out that sometimes women could not walk unless aided, and that although there was an attempt to ban this fashion, it lasted for centuries. Rosencranz believes that men are intrigued with watching women walk in a short, birdlike manner, and that because of this, high heels will consistently reappear as fashionable.

There is still a tremendous pressure on women to be fashionable, and so American women spend much time in selecting and buying clothes and deciding what to wear. Whereas a man can wear a basic suit for many occasions, a woman "needs" a variety of clothes to retain her chicness and femininity. Clothes for women come in many styles, in many lengths and in a myriad of colors. Some colors are more "in" one year than another, and the length of skirts and dresses varies from year to year. Sudden changes in skirt lengths used to send women scurrying to the stores for new clothes. Fortunately women today are not as much pulled up and down by the strings of the skirt-length yo-yo.

Clothes in all societies serve various functions (Barber and Lobel, 1952). Apparel can be utilitarian, can be esthetically pleasing and in many societies also serves the function of denoting social status. Barber and Lobel give as an example the fact that prior to the French Revolution dress and social rank were prescribed by law. Princesses and duchesses were the only ones who were allowed to wear silks, and fur muffs could only be worn by women of the upper echelon. So, too, the mandarin's very long fingernails and gowns identified him as a member of the nonworking class in ancient China.

A recent study using the Clothing TAT was done to find out the differences in clothing awareness between the various social classes and between men and women. This instrument is a modification of the classic TAT, which presents pictures of ambiguous situations in the belief that where there is ambiguity an individual will reveal his or her own personality needs and traits by what he or she projects on to the picture. As might be expected, women had more clothing awareness than men, and middle- and upper-class women rated higher in clothing awareness than those of the lower socio-economic group (Rosencranz, 1972).

In many societies different styles of clothes are appropriate for different age statuses, often associated with the style of living (Rosencranz, 1972). Young people wear clothes that generally do not impede their movement, whereas older people in our society tend to dress in a more conservative fashion. Among the Bushmen of Africa, babies wore no clothes until they reached one year. The younger women wore a small apron in front, while the older women wore one in the back, also. Younger women and men often paint their body and face (Schapera, 1963).

Clothes, states Rosencranz, in her book, *Clothing Concepts* (1972), are symbols not only of economic status, age and role, but also symbols of femininity and masculinity.

The majority of societies prescribe different clothes for males and females. If the clothes are basically the same, then, for instance, the length may differ or the ornaments each sex wears are dissimilar. Sometimes color is rigidly prescribed for each sex. Pink was for many years a female color in the United States. Today, in the United States, there is a trend toward unisex clothes, mainly adopted by youth.

What is fashion? It has been defined as "styles of cut, color, silhouette, stuffs, etc., that are socially prescribed and socially accepted as appropriate for certain social roles, and especially with the recurring changes in these styles" (Barber and Lobel, 1952, p. 126). Note that the Puritan women were forbidden to adorn their clothes with embellishments such as lace, etc., mainly because frivolous clothes might impede their ability to work in the home. "For a woman to put herself into a Fashion that shall prejudice wither her Health or her Work is to break all the commandments," said Cotton Mather (1710, p. 7).

The intertwining of women's clothes and role can be seen by looking at history. The English were blessed with the corset through the Normans, who shared it with them in the 12th century. Clothes became a symbol of status concurrently with the development of the idea of "lady" (Bullough, 1974). A lady was one who was sweet, good, untouchable, and pure. In fact, during the Middle Ages, there seemed to be among the upper classes a separation of eroticism and marriage. In the 1300s women plucked out their forehead hairs, used wine to wash their tresses and wanted to be slim and shapely (Ecob, 1892). It was at the end of the15th century that the "busk" and the "farthingale" became a part of women's costume. By the 16th century the busk, which was the early form of corset, was like an iron cage. Later the iron cage became a bone apparatus but the purpose remained the same—to keep the waist tightly constricted and coupled with voluminous petticoats, sometimes weighing as much as 15 pounds, the result was partial immobility.

A number of books were written both by men and women during the later 1800s decrying the corsets. One must remember that tightly laced corsets were generally worn by the upper-class women, who did not have to work. Working women needed to retain their physical mobility, and as a result of not adhering to this convention sported larger waistlines. J. H. Kellogg (1891) suggested that dress was resulting in what he called the "physical decadence" of the American woman, and that the small waist was actually unnatural and a physical deformity. In fact, said Kellogg, who incidentally was also the inventor of Kellogg's Cornflakes, the American woman, by wearing these waist-cinching contraptions, was causing more damage to herself than the Chinese women whose feet were bound. He listed the injury that corsets create as including

1. Downward displacement of all the abdominal and pelvic organs, and numerous functional and organic diseases growing out of this disturbance for the static relations of these organs.

2. Lack of development of the muscles of the trunk, which by long compression and disuse, to a very large degree lose their functional activity, resulting in relaxation of the abdominal walls, weakness of the muscles of the back, general physical feebleness, and destruction of the natural curves of the body, which are not only necessary for health, but also essential to physical grace and beauty, as the development of many bodily deformities, such as drooping shoulders, flat or hollow chest . . .

3. An ungraceful and unnatural carriage of the body, in sitting, standing, and walking.

4. An abnormal mode of respiration. (Kellogg, 1891, p. 13).

Kellogg compared women with men and found prolapse of the stomach and bowel to be more common in women than in men, over six times so.

Kellogg's sentiments were echoed by a woman before her time, Helen Gilbert Ecob. In 1892 she wrote a book called *The Well-Dressed Woman,* in which she also decried the constricting clothes that women wore and called it one of women's follies. She pointed out that women were becoming increasingly invalided, and that in her belief this deterioration was not preordained but was a result of the way women lived. To support her argument, she pointed to accounts of primitive tribes where women were described as being more robust and better developed than the men, and in some cases able to carry larger loads than the men, who were used as porters. She lamented the physical deterioration of the American woman.

> Women are designated as the weaker sex. They are compared to the tender, clinging vine, depending for their strength on the masculine oak. The elements in nature which suggest strength—the sea, the sun, the wind—are poetically expressed in the masculine gender. The chivalry of the feudal ages and the gallant deference of the present day are humiliating tributes of society to the weakness of women. They are the mock homage of power to helplessness. Woman is regarded, and regards herself, as a being of feeble physical power, preordained to hysterics, tears, and nervous prostration. She rarely attempts any work which involves endurance or an outlay of muscle. She has accepted with patient resignation the enervated life to which she believes herself called . . . and at length woman has learned to glory in the shame of her physical degeneracy. Tears, which are a disgrace on the cheek of man, are her refuge and weapon. The slim, tapering finger which tells of polished idleness, flabby muscles, the dainty form and delicate complexion, are objects of admiration. Why should a powerful physique in man be universally admired, and the small, insignificant physique of a woman be dubbed by the words piquant, petite, dainty, and the like? (pp. 18–19).

Ecob also proposed that the differences in the way women and men breathe, which had been thought to be genetically determined, were really a result of environmental influence, particularly the differences in dress. She made a plea to men to help change women's costume and stated that many husbands, brothers, and sons encourage their women to be corseted because they look more like ladies in that attire.

Kellogg (1884), although concerned with the effects on the health of the wearer of corsets and voluminous petticoats, also expressed concern about the effects of this fashion on vice. The way clothes are worn creates difficulties in the ovaries and uterus, particularly those associated with congestion and "derangements" and

> . . . have long been recognized as the chief pathological condition in hysteria, and especially in that peculiar form of disease known as *nymphomania,* under the excitement of which a young woman, naturally chaste and modest, may be impelled to the commission of the most wanton acts. The pernicious influence of fashionable dress in occasioning this disorder cannot be doubted (p. 193).

In the latter half of the 19th century, women activists were also concerned with dress reform. One of them, Amelia Bloomer, was an advocate of a new costume consisting of shorter dresses and trousers. She and others like her who wore this apparel were ridiculed. Clergy were particularly adamant in their attack on the morality of the trousers, since donning them would put the woman in the position of being able to spread her legs (Bullough, 1974). The Bloomer costume became associated with women's rights and because both were subjected to enormous ridicule, the Bloomer attire soon lost its appeal.

Women during the 1800s obtained their identity from their roles as wives and mothers and as clothing was constricted, their expression of sexual feelings was also restricted. Women, that is, normal women, were thought to be devoid of sexual desires, to have the moral responsibility for uplifting the baser sex, the male, and were taught that their body was repugnant (Hymowitz and Weissman, 1978). Aversive feelings towards one's body still exist today among a number of females. Many women avoid touching their genitals and are reticent about monthly breast self-examination. The beautiful woman in the 1800s was one who was weak, pale, and fragile. Her dress helped her to achieve and retain this state.

In the 1920s the beautiful woman was the sexy woman, which meant that her body could be revealed. The flapper made the scene. She was a woman who wore short skirts, bared arms, loose dresses, and red, red lipstick (Hymowitz and Weissman, 1978). Although flat breasts were the vogue, and flappers achieved this style by binding them, the deadly corset was out and freedom of movement emerged. Hymowitz and Weissman state that whereas purity was the virtue of the 1800s, the sexy look was in during the 1920s. Although the thrust had been to allow women to be sexual human beings, the result was to make women feel and be viewed as sex objects. Purpose—ensnare a man into marriage and keep him there. Sex before marriage was taboo, but one was expected to be fully sexual after the ceremony.

Sociologists have proposed that in the United States, particularly between 1930 and the 1950s, a woman's status was determined by that of her husband, particularly his occupation. Because there is an open class structure, a man can establish his status through the conspicuous consumption of his wife, particularly her clothes (Barber and Lobel, 1952). Conspicuous consumption still exists. The display of diamonds and other expensive gems, as well as ownership of mink coats, is still a characteristic norm of the upper middle and upper classes. Today, however, it is fashionable to wear one's mink coat with a pair of terribly expensive designer jeans. In fact, that outfit has become a uniform in some parts of the fashionable sections of Manhattan.

Before World War II, it was unfeminine in the United States for women to wear slacks. There was also concern with maintaining divergent roles of men and women. During the war, with the increased shortage of "manpower," women were encouraged to come out of the home and enter the defense factories, doing work such as riveting which had previously been a male domain. Women were also encouraged to wear dungarees, and tie their long tresses back with a kerchief in order to work more efficiently and to lower the danger of industrial accidents. After World War II women in the 1950s were encouraged back into the homes, into marriage and motherhood, and the stereotypical view of women "exiled her not only to the bedroom and the maternity ward, but to the kitchen, nursery, and dressing table" (Ryan, 1975, p. 285).

Clothes have been symbols of role expectation for women. The awareness of this was dramatically demonstrated in September of 1968. At that time a group of women activists, protesting the Miss America contest, which they contended kept women oppressed by the message it shared about the image of women, urged women to throw into what they called the Freedom Trash Can "girdles, curlers, false eyelashes, wigs . . ." (Morgan, 1970). This was known as the bra burning ceremony but in actuality no bras were burned.

Not only is there fashion in clothes but also in body weight. Many women today wish they lived during the time when fat was beautiful. Four hundred years ago beautiful women were round and fleshy, as was graphically depicted by Peter Paul Rubens in his paintings. Corpulence was associated with wealth as well as with health, and this remained more or less true until the last half of the 19th century. At that time the top and bottom of a woman's body were supposed to be plump but the waist had to be narrow. Whereas in the past exercise and diet were associated with the laboring class, today they are touted as important for the maintenance of good health. Today jogging is in vogue not only because it is supposed to strengthen the heart muscles but also because it reduces most of your body fat. Some joggers have gone so far as to reduce themselves to looking like concentration camp victims. People who are fat are viewed so negatively that an association of fat people emerged to combat prejudice. Only recently have fashions concerned themselves with the heavier woman, and finally at least one house of fashion is designing clothes for just that group, as well as using large sized women as its models.

Because of the association of slimness with sexiness, women have tried most anything to reduce their weight, sometimes even killing themselves in the process. Before amphetamines became rigidly controlled, women were popping pills to lose weight, often having these pills prescribed by their physicians. We are an "instant" society, so why not instant weight reduction?

In 1970 Hot Pants were marketed as the panacea for weight reduction. A bargain at $14.95, Hot Pants were a pair of shorts made of plastic that could be inflated and were "guaranteed to reduce your waist, abdomen, hips and thighs a total of 6 to 10 inches in just one day or your money refunded" (Klemesrud, 1971, p. 58). How do these Hot Pants work? After the pants are inflated with a pump, the wearer is instructed to perform a series of exercises during which the heat generated by these exercises causes a reduction in size of the body areas. The Food and Drug Administration pointed out that the manufacturer's claim is more hot air than truth and that exercising without the use of these pants would also take inches off in desired areas of the body. Their conclusions were based on studies performed on a prison population, half of which wore the pants and exercised, while the other half of the subjects did the exercise alone. Some of the physicians interviewed expressed concern regarding the deleterious effects on veins as a result of the use of this reducing device. The reason reducing gadgets were allowed to flood the market devoid of regulation by the government was the fact that the laws place responsibility on governmental agencies to prove that the advertisement is false, while with prescription drugs the responsibility to prove accuracy is placed on the shoulders of the manufacturer.

If Hot Pants are ineffective, how about joining a Health Spa? In 1972 the then $220 million industry was being investigated because of fraudulent claims (Lichtenstein, 1972). Apparently the type of advertising used, the type of contracts one must sign, as well as the exercise regime were questioned. When a spa advertises that by exercising alone without a concomitant diet one will lose weight, fraud is being perpetrated on the gullible consumer. Some spas have advertised that a person could lose ten pounds and at least eight inches after exercising for eight weeks, but do not say that people have to deprive themselves of food to do this. As with reducing gadgets, spas are not government-ally regulated.

Well, then, if Hot Pants do not work and the exercises alone are not sufficient to drastically reduce weight, how about pills? In 1970 two women in Rochester, New York died within two weeks after taking a particular type of diet pill which contained thyroid hormones, digitalis, amphetamines, and vitamins (*New York Times*, February 8, 1970, p. 66). Both women had been in good health. One was twenty-four and the other twenty-seven years old, and both were only slightly over-weight. The diagnostic assessment of the immediate cause of death was complications of the heart which resulted in edema of the lungs. A number of deaths from diet pills had resulted over the years and mal-practice suits were filed against physicians who had prescribed them. In September of 1968 one firm manufacturing diet pills in Texas was enjoined by a federal judge to rid itself of all the pills that contained digitalis and thyroid hormones, and yet pills containing these sub-stances were still on the market in 1970 and resulted in the deaths of two young women who wanted to be beautifully thin.

In 1972 one woman, weighing 215 pounds, under the supervision of a weight-loss clinic in New Jersey which put her on a daily intake of 500 calories and daily vitamin injections, died. She decided to hurry the weight loss process by starving herself for four days. Her blood salts changed, which resulted in a change in heart rhythm. Death was due to a heart attack (*New York Times*, October 11, 1972, p. 22).

It was also in 1972 that the Bureau of Narcotics and Dangerous Drugs reduced by 80 percent the amount of amphetamines that could be produced and placed amphetamines in the same category as co-caine. The Bureau also suggested that pills used for reducing should be strictly controlled (*New York Times*, October 11, 1972, p. 22).

At least ten women are known to have died from using liquid pro-tein diets which caused irregularities in the heart (*New York Times*, November 25, 1977, p. 21)

These diets have been advertised as the last chance to lose weight. What does this liquid protein consist of? Would you believe "low quality, partly digested protein derived from cattle hides and tendons. Artificial flavors and saccharin are added to disguise the otherwise horrid taste" (*New York Times*, November 25, 1977, p. 21). Since liq-uid protein has been advertised as a food instead of a drug, the government can only make sure it is pure but does not have any control over its regulation.

Diets are the topic of conversation at many a cocktail party, and businesses such as Weight Watchers and Diet Workshop have made millions of dollars. They have also been instrumental in helping people lose weight sensibly.

The desire to be thin is a compulsion with some people. One model weighing 97 pounds states that she forces herself to regurgitate after each meal so that she will stay slim.

The female breasts have been imbued with many symbols and have been the focus of attention for many years. Statues even during the Neolithic era were breast-focused. Breasts are symbolic of sexuality, of fertility, and of motherhood, and last but not least a sign of beauty. Miss America has usually been a well-endowed, young, voluptuous woman, and not flat-chested. The breasts are symbols of femininity with whatever that implies. In different cultures, throughout different periods, the veneration of the female mammaries has taken different forms. Bernice Cohen Sachs (1978), a physician, traces the breasts as "sex symbols" and as "releasers." Man, states Dr. Sachs, has imbued the breasts with mystical powers. In some cultures such as that of the Djuras and certain tribes living in Peru, large-breasted women were seen as being potentially dangerous since they could beguile men to destruction. Although there are a few examples of breasts being viewed as dangerous attributes, Dr. Sachs points out that most often they are seen in a positive manner. Fertility goddesses had well-developed breasts because fertility was viewed as originating in that part of the woman's anatomy. Sometimes there was also the belief that it was through the nipples that the seed which was to grow into a child penetrated the body of the mother. In Sparta, therefore, diamonds adorned women's breasts to indicate that they had strength, and circles of metal were placed over the nipples in order to ward off evil.

Dr. Sachs points out that during the Christian era, breasts were presented mainly as functional in nurturing and some of the artists portrayed lewd women having their breasts (perhaps the symbol of purity) attacked by serpents. Although, states Sachs, race and climate influence the size and shape of the breasts, their utilitarian function occasionally results in mutilation. The Basuto women deliberately force their breasts to become long so that their babies can be fed while the mother continues her work. All a woman has to do is to fling her elongated breast over her shoulder. In some areas of the South Pacific elongated breasts were thought to demonstrate beauty. Large breasts keep women and those physically close to them warm and so Eskimos like their women fat. In our society large bosoms are coveted. Most of our women sex symbols have had ample breast development. For example, Lana Turner, who made the sweater a sexy garment during the 1940s, Marilyn Monroe, and most recently, the country singer, Dolly Parton. Woe, then, to the female with less than adequate breasts.

Thousands of women in the United States, evidently feeling inadequate because of their small breasts, are seeking surgery to increase their size. This surgery, known as mammary augmentation, is the most common cosmetic surgery requested. About 250,000 are done each year (McCormack, August 21, 1979). Kinsey's study (1948) found that men were more sexually stimulated by a woman's breasts than by her genitals, and this subtle or not so subtle message is being received by inadequately developed women who feel less feminine because they do not conform to the sexy woman stereotype.

Are women who seek breast augmentation unstable? One study at Johns Hopkins (Edgerton et al., 1960) found that those women who sought cosmetic breast surgery to increase the size of their breasts had been diagnosed as having some psychiatric problem. Another study at the same hospital noted that more than half of the eighty-five women who had been admitted for mammaplasty demonstrated symptoms of hysteria, depression and a poor self-image (Edgerton et al., 1961). The average patient was found to be a woman between the ages of twenty-seven and thirty-three of middle income family. She was married, a mother, usually white and Protestant. Sixty-six percent of the women had felt self-conscious about the small size of their breasts since they reached the adolescent years, while about thirty-three percent became concerned after giving birth. Perhaps they had hoped that pregnancy and motherhood would result in a permanent increase in breast size. Before breast augmentation, several of the women reacted strongly to having their breasts touched, almost as if it were a phobia. Most of the women seeking mammaplasty had been depressed sporadically since adolescence, and depression had also been evident following the birth of a child. They came predominately from nonintact homes, felt rejected, and had experienced a large number of operations during their adolescent period. Needless to say, they felt fairly poor about themselves as women. The breast augmentation helped increase self-esteem, and a number of the eighty-five women said that they would have the operation again under the same circumstances.

A more recent study (Shipley et al., 1977) found that women seeking breast augmentation were not any more unstable than the control groups of small-busted and average-busted women with which they were compared. The average woman seeking breast surgery in this study was a thirty-one-year-old married woman who did not have any children. She was also not just a housewife but worked outside the home. The researchers concluded that women who desire to have the size of their breasts increased through surgery are not psychiatrically unsound. In contrast to the small-breasted and average-breasted woman, this woman, however, was found to be more concerned with being physically appealing and being stylishly dressed, and she viewed her small breasts as a negative trait. One must view this study with some caution since there were only twenty-eight subjects in each group. The generalizability of the results to a wider population is questionable.

Silicone was first developed for medical use in the 1950s. Injected into the body, however, it tended to result in negative reactions, including infections. In 1960, Japanese plastic surgeons began to use silicone injections to eliminate wrinkles in the face, and in lieu of a surgical face lift (Reinhart, 1975).

Silicone injections were popularized in the United States when a go-go dancer suddenly made headlines. Her 36" breasts had within several weeks been increased to a 42" for all to see, as she performed her topless dance. Thousands of women sought to increase their breast size, resulting in a shortage of pure silicone. Some companies began to use paraffin or olive oil to dilute the medical silicone, and silicone for commercial use was also sold for the purpose of increasing breast size. After four deaths and complications such as gangrene, resulting in the necessity of amputating the breast, lung infections and the migration of the injected silicone to the vital organs, as well as blindness, the American Medical Association became alarmed, warned doctors of the perils and the Food and Drug Administration made its use illegal in the United States (Reinhart, 1975).

Breast augmentation by injection continued to be sought by women who traveled to Mexico to have it done. Surgeons in the San Diego area were seeing an increasing number of women presenting complications from silicone injections received in Tijuana. Sometimes it took anywhere from two to six years for the symptoms to appear. The Dow Corning Corporation was licensed to make the medical silicone serum, Medical Fluid 360, to be distributed only to those physicians doing governmentally sanctioned research, and not in augmentation of the breast, but in reconstruction of the face as a result of cancer surgery, accident, etc. (Holles, 1974).

Women seeking silicone injections are usually afraid of the surgery necessary for a gel implant. In addition, silicone injections are cheaper.

Breasts, no matter how large or small, or how they are shaped, influence one's self-image and self-concept. Understanding the dynamics behind a woman's desire for breast augmentation is important for the surgeon who has to make a decision, not based on the physical attributes of the patient alone, on whether or not to perform such surgery. A two-part study (Baker et al., 1974) attempted to understand the psychodynamics of those who had undergone the operation. One part of the study consisted of an in-depth psychiatric analysis of 10 patients before and after their operation, and the second part, an analysis of a mailed questionnaire to 132 patients who had been operated on to increase the size of their breasts. As in past studies, the 10 women chosen for an in-depth analysis were white and middle-class. Only half of them were married at the time and although none of the patients wanted breasts that were significantly large, they did not want to have to wear padded bras, and requested the surgery after learning that someone they knew had their breasts augmented. The husbands of those who were married were not supportive of the operation. It was usually the patient herself, who wanted it. These women, as in other studies, felt inadequate during adolescence because of their small breasts to the point of, in some cases, a fear of being seen naked by men. Some had gynecological surgery and felt that in the cases where the surgery was a hysterectomy, they had lost some of their womanhood. Following the breast augmentation, the 10 women, who were studied in depth, felt that their sexual pleasure had increased and were happy about having chosen to submit to the surgery.

In reviewing the answers to the questionnaires filled out by the larger sample of 132 patients, the majority of them reported having the surgery because of their own needs. Breast augmentation, for a large number of these patients resulted in increased self-esteem, increased self-confidence, increased feelings of happiness, as well as increased sexual pleasure. It is fair to conclude, then, that breast augmentation serves a vital personality need for many small-busted women. It is sad, though, that women feel the need to subject themselves to elective surgery in order to feel better about their bodies. Surgery, no matter how minor, is fraught with possible complications and dangers. As long as women continue to be viewed as sex objects, and as long as breasts continue to remain the symbol of sensuality for women, breast surgery for purely cosmetic purposes will continue.

It has been estimated that breast augmentations are increasing at a rate of about 25 percent each year (Frank and Frank, 1975). If, as some of the studies have reported, women who seek out this type of surgery are as psychologically sound as most women, then we wonder whether we can conclude that mutilating one's body to conform to a concept of beauty has not become an integral part of our culture, particularly as it relates to women.

Not only are there surgical procedures for increasing the size of the breasts (usually done with silicone implants), but there are also operations, indeed more complicated and therefore more risky, for decreasing the size of the breasts. Too large a bosom is as unattractive in our culture as too small a bosom. Perhaps an overabundance of mammary tissue is associated with aging and being excessively matronly. One's breast development, like the chairs, which Goldilocks tested out in the three bears' house, should not be too small or too large, but just right, whatever that may mean.

If a woman's bosom is adequate, what about her face and nose? If the nose is inadequate, rhinoplasty, a nose job, is in order, especially if she is interested in becoming an actress. Candidates for nose jobs are usually sensitive about what they consider to be a nose that is too long and one that they feel might have been more acceptable on a man. In one study (Meyer et al., 1960) many of the patients who had requested rhinoplasty stated that their noses looked like those of their fathers. Most of the patients were not fat but would be considered unattractive. Some of the patients demonstrated psychiatric disturbances following the operation. Remember that having a nose fixed changes one's physical appearance, which has a significant effect on one's self-image and sense of self. Consciously, the majority of the women studied, thirty in all, wanted to have their nose changed in order to increase their social relations and to become better prospects for courtship. The researchers also found that the patients had felt discomfort about the size of their noses since adolescence. They stated, too, that

The operative procedure functions symbolically as a disavowal of the restrictive aspects of paternal identifications and an active striving towards greater comfort in the feminine role (p. 201).

Conflict in sexual identity, then, is a motivating factor in having one's nose changed with cosmetic surgery. One surgeon, it was reported in the *New York Times* (September 27, 1971, p. 30), had a patient who could not accept looking "prettier." He accommodated her and shaped her nose back to the one she had originally thought of as being ugly.

Although men are increasingly having their faces lifted, women still outnumber them. In 1971 twenty times the number of face lifts were performed on women than on men (*New York Times,* September 27, 1971, p. 30). A woman reaching the age of forty suddenly finds that she is beginning to show such signs of aging as wrinkles, bags under the eyes and generally, a sagging face, which is the result of skin loosening itself somewhat from the tissue underneath. Gravity tends to pull the skin down as it becomes less elastic with aging. States an article in *Vogue Magazine:*

> Your skin loses its elasticity, its ability to spring back and it sags, giving you that ugly "old-bag" look. A meloplasty reverses this aging process. Your surgeon tightens, re-drapes, and cuts off the excess bagging skin and by this simple but major process pulls up the corners of your mouth, your jowls, your fleshy chin, your flabby neck. There you are rejuvenated, lifted up. What more could you want? (Morant, 1975, p. 84).

After all, who wants to be an "old-bag?" That expression, however, seems to be used most often for aging women and not for aging men. It has been said that aging men are mature and desirable. Women, because they are identified so closely with being sex symbols, lose their sexiness with age. Even the married woman, who already has achieved her goal of having a man of her own, still often feels impelled to stop the aging process by any means necessary, even though her husband continues to show signs of getting older. Susan Sontag (1975) says that the concept of beauty is allied with females and femininity. Women are socialized to view themselves in body parts, hair, breasts, etc., while men view themselves as a total aggregate. Women are socialized to be overly concerned with how they look instead of who they are. They are, therefore, socialized to be narcissistic, dependent and nonadult.

Aging is highly traumatic for the American woman, and has been for years. She is pressured to retain her "beauty" but old is not beautiful as clearly stated by Finck in the late 1800s in *Romantic Love and Personal Beauty.*

> Wrinkles in the face are signs of advanced age, or disease, or habits of profound meditation, or frequent indulgence in frowning and grief. The wrinkles on a thinker's forehead do not arouse our disapproval, because they are often eloquent of genius, which excuses a slight sacrifice of the smoothness of skin that belongs to perfect Beauty. In women, however, we apply a pure and strict aesthetic standard, wherefore all wrinkles are regarded as regrettable inroads on Personal Beauty. Old women, of course, form an exception, because in them we no longer look for youthful Beauty, and are therefore gratified at the sight of wrinkles and folds as stereotyped forms of expression bespeaking a life rich in experiences, and associated with the veneration due to old age, are characteristic but not beautiful. (Finck, 1887, p. 451).

Even the stomach is not immune from reconstruction to make one appear more youthful. One woman recently sued her surgeon for putting her navel off center. She had undergone surgery for tightening of her stomach and one year later had surgery again to have her belly button put back in its proper place. The woman won her case and was awarded $854,000 (*Time,* May 14, 1979, p. 106). In March of 1979 the United States Government banned free cosmetic surgery for its military service personnel and their dependents. About 500 nontherapeutic cosmetic operations were being performed free of charge each year.

In Russia, too, the desire for cosmetic surgery has prompted women to travel thousands of miles to the Institute of Cosmetology in Moscow for face lifts, rhinoplasty, and other surgical procedures to improve their looks. After all, say the women, one must suffer in order to be beautiful. The kinds of letters received in Moscow are similar to the ones which deluge the plastic surgeons on Fifth Avenue in New York City. One woman wrote that she had led a life full of stress and difficulty, and that although she was presently happy, her face was mapped with wrinkles, and she wanted to look more appealing. She had become emotionally involved with a man four years her junior but she looked ten years older than he, and she wanted to do something about the lines in her face (Shipler, 1979).

The cosmetic industry is booming in the United States, with billions of dollars being spent on beauty services as well as products. Although men are increasingly becoming consumers in this area, most of the beauty salons and cosmetics are female oriented. Some cosmetics have recently become suspect as carcinogenic but their sale has not decreased.

In 1975 the possibility of a relationship between hair dyes and cancer and birth defects was found. At that time 20 million Americans were dying their hair in an effort to be glamourous in appearance, or to retain their youthful looks. One researcher found that 169 of the hair dyes he tested changed the genetic makeup of bacteria. The University of California biochemist stated that those known carcinogenic chemicals he used in his tests also caused mutations, and many of the chemicals in hair dye are closely related to these carcinogenic substances. He concluded that there is a good possibility that hair dyes, since they are like their mutogenic cousins, may be responsible for birth defects and may also cause cancer.

Hair dyes do not have to be approved by the FDA, nor are they regulated in the same manner as dyes used in other cosmetics and in food. Apparently, the cosmetic industry was instrumental in having hair dyes exempted from the Food, Drug and Cosmetic Act in 1938 (Brody, 1975).

Hair dyes were known to be absorbed by the skin, as evidenced by urine samples taken from users. After one of the chemicals in hair dye was found by Japanese scientists to cause liver tumors when orally injested by rats, and if injected into the skin, tumors of the muscles, it was withdrawn from use. The FDA had, for a number of years pressured Congress to allow it to more tightly control hair dyes and cosmetics but has not been successful in its efforts.

Since the hairless look is the feminine look, women spend time and money to remove such unwanted signs of masculinity, and shaving or chemicals are often used. Electrolysis, a time-consuming, sometimes painful process, but apparently satisfactory for many women, particularly those with unwanted facial hair, is another method employed to remove this symbol of masculinity.

One would think that when beauty is finally achieved all would be well, but not so. There are "hazards to being beautiful" suggests an article in the *New York Times* (Barden, 1974). Dr. Ella Lasky, a psychotherapist, states that self-esteem for women is heavily dependent on attractiveness. Some of what she called "the beautiful people" flirt their way through life trading on their physical attractiveness. The problem becomes magnified when the woman's looks begin to slowly disappear as the aging process takes place, or when she is confronted with a situation that cannot be addressed through flirtatiousness. Beautiful women feel good about themselves because they look good, and men because they are doing well either in their careers or in whatever sport they play.

B. Scott Teunis, a plastic surgeon, states that men want to look good "but they are definitely afraid of looking beautiful" (O'Brien, 1979). So when he does a blepharoplasty (surgery of the eyelids), he makes a concerted effort not to give the man a wide-eyed look commonly associated with femininity. As one author put it,

> . . . some men, because of their looks, need more stroking, more reassurance. Yet because of the prejudices against them, they can't complain about the perils of being beautiful—that would be unforgivably narcissistic. If beautiful men reach for power, they must defuse the impact of their looks. If they already have it, they must use it to make other men feel better looking, acting as if they never stare in a mirror and admire themselves (O'Brien, 1979, p. 23).

A woman, on the other hand, is very often valued for her beauty which enhances the status of the man to whom she is attached.

References

Anon. A Big Mistuck. *Time* 106 (May 14, 1979).
_____. Deaths of 2 Women in Rochester Tied to Use Of Diet Pills. *New York Times.* 66 (February 8, 1970).
_____. Legal Barriers Seen to Government Plan to Curb Diet Liquid. *New York Times.* 21 (November 25, 1977).
_____. Plastic Surgery: It's No Longer Reserved for the Vain and the Rich. *New York Times.* 30 (September 27, 1971).
_____. Study Doubts Value of Diet Pills and Calls for Strict U.S. Curbs. *New York Times.* 22 (October 11, 1972).
Baker, James L., Kolin, Irving S. and Bartlett, Edmund S. Psychosexual dynamics of patients undergoing mammary augmentation. *Plastic and Reconstructive Surgery* 53:652–659 (1974).
Barber, Bernard and Lobel, Lyle S. "Fashion" in women's clothes and the American social system. *Social Forces* 31:124–131 (1952).
Barden, J. C. The hazards of being beautiful. *New York Times* 62:3 (May 2, 1974).

Barocas, Ralph and Karoly, Paul. Effects of physical appearance on social responsiveness. *Psychological Reports* **31**:495–500 (1972).

Barocas, Ralph and Vance, Forrest L. Physical appearance and personal adjustment counseling. *Journal of Counseling Psychology* **21**:96–100 (1974).

Bashford, James W. *China: An Interpretation*. New York: The Abingdon Press, 1916.

Batchelor, Rev. John. *The Ainu of Japan*. New York: Fleming H. Revell Company, n.d.

Brislin, Richard and Lewis, Steven A. Dating and physical attractiveness: replication. *Psychological Reports* **22**:977–981 (1968).

Brody, Gary S. Fact and fiction about breast implant "bleed." *Plastic and Reconstructive Surgery* **60**:615–616 (1977).

Browning, Robert. Fra Lippo Lippi, in *The Poetical Works of Robert Browning*. London: Oxford University Press, 1962.

Bullough, Vern L. *The Subordinate Sex*. Chicago: University of Illinois Press, 1974.

Byrne, Donn, London, Oliver and Reeves, Keith. The effects of physical attractiveness, sex, and attitude similarity on interpersonal attraction. *Journal of Personality* **36**:259–271 (1964).

Chaikin, Alan, Derlega, Valerian, Yoder, John and Phillips, David. The effects of appearance on compliance. *Journal of Social Psychology* **92**:199–200 (1974).

Cooley, Charles Horton. *Human Nature and the Social Order*. New York: Scribners, 1922.

Dahl, Arlene. *Always Ask a Man: Arlene Dahl's Key to Femininity*. Englewood Cliffs, N.J.: Prentice-Hall, 1965.

Daly, Mary. *Gyn/ecology*. Boston: Beacon Press, 1978.

Diogenes Laertius. *Lives of Eminent Philosophers* Vol. 1. R. D. Hicks trans. Cambridge: Harvard University Press, 1925.

Dion, Karen, Berscheid, Ellen and Walster, Elaine. What is beautiful is good. *Journal of Personality and Social Psychology* **24**:285–290 (1972).

Douglas, Bruce. High Heels Should be Banned. United Press International. August 22, 1979.

Ecob, Helen Gilbert. *The Well Dressed Woman*. New York: Fowler & Wells, 1892.

Edgerton, M. T., Meyer, E. and Jacobson, W. E. Augmentation mammaplasty: II further surgical and psychiatric evaluation. *Plastic and Reconstructive Surgery* **27**:279–302 (1961).

Edgerton, M. T., Jacobson, W. E. and Meyer, E. Surgical-Psychiatric study of patients seeking plastic (cosmetic) surgery: ninety-eight consecutive patients with minimal deformity. *British Journal of Plastic Surgery* **13**:136–145 (1960).

Farina, Amerigo, Fischer, Edward H., Sherman, Scott, Smith, Wayne T., Groh, Thomas and Mermin, Paul. Physical attractiveness and mental illness. *Journal of Abnormal Psychology* **86**:510–517 (1977).

Finck, Henry T. *Romantic Love and Personal Beauty*. New York: Press of J. J. Little Co., 1887.

Frank, Arthur and Frank, Stuart. Cosmetic breast surgery. *Mademoiselle* **81**:74 (November 1975).

Franklin, Benjamin. The Complete Poor Richard's Almanac. Barre, Massachusetts: Imprint Society, facsimile edition Vol 1. 1733–1747, 1970.

Gerster, George. River of sorrow, river of hope. *National Geographic* 148 (August 1975).

Gutze, Henry. Female body-image in personality and culture, in George D. Goldman and Donald S. Milman. *Modern Woman.* Springfield, Illinois: Charles S. Thomas, 1969.

Hoebel, Adamson E. *Anthropology: The Study of Man.* New York McGraw-Hill Book Co., 1966.

Hogbin, Ian. *A Guadalcanal Society.* New York: Holt, Rinehart and Winston, 1964.

Holles, Everett R. Silicone injections traced to Tijuana. *New York Times* 30:6 (July 19, 1974).

Hymowitz, Carol and Weissman, Michaele. *A History of Women in America.* New York: Bantam Books, 1978.

Jackson, David and Huston, Ted L. Physical attractiveness and assertiveness. *Journal of Social Psychology* **96**:79–84 (1975).

Kahn, A., Hottes, J. and Davis, W. Prisoners dilemma game: effects of sex and physical attractiveness. *Journal of Personality and Social Psychology* **17**:267–279 (1971).

Keats, John. Ode On a Grecian Urn, in Norman H. Buxton (ed.). *The Complete Poetical Works of John Keats.* New York: Oxford University Press, 1934.

Kellogg, J. H. *The Influence of Dress.* Battle Creek, Michigan: Modern Medicine Publishing Co., 1891.

_____. *Plain Facts for Old and Young.* Burlington, Iowa: I. F. Segner, 1884.

Kinsey, Alfred C., Pomeroy, Wardell B. and Martin, Clyde E. *Sexual Behavior in the Human Male.* Philadelphia: W. B. Saunders Co., 1948.

Klemestrud, Judy. Reducing devices called ineffective. *New York Times* 58:5 (September 28, 1971).

Latourette, Kenneth Scott. *The Chinese: Their History and Culture.* New York: The Macmillan Company, 1934.

Lichtenstein, Grace. Fraud complaints on health-spas rise. *New York Times* 1:1 (December 26, 1972).

Mather, Cotton. *Bonifacius (Essays to Do Good).* Reprinted in Gainesville, Fla.: 1967 (Original, Boston, 1710).

Mathes, Eugene. The effects of physical attractiveness and anxiety on heterosexual attraction over a series of five encounters. *Journal of Marriage and the Family* **37**:769–773 (November 1975).

McCormack, Patricia. More Faces are Being Fixed These Days. United Press International. August 21, 1979.

Meyer, Eugene, Jacobson, Wayne, Edgerton, Milton T. and Canter, Arthur. Motivational patterns in patients seeking elective plastic surgery. *Psychosomatic Medicine* **22**:193–203 (1960).

Miller, A. G. Role of physical attractiveness in impression formation. *Psychonomic Science* **19**:241–243 (1970).

Morant, Jay. Diary of a face-lift. *Vogue* p. 84 (May 1975).

Morgan, Robin (ed.). *Sisterhood is Powerful.* New York: Random House, 1970.

O'Brien, Patricia. The dangers of being too good-looking. *Esquire* **92**:19–23 (September 1979).

Reinhart, Al. Doctor Jack makes his rounds. *Esquire* **82**:114–16 (May 1975).

Rosencranz, Mary Lou. *Clothing Concepts.* New York: The Macmillan Company, 1972.

Ryan, Mary. *Womanhood in America.* New York: New Viewpoints, A Division of Franklin Watts, 1975.

Sachs, Bernice Cohen. Breasts: sex symbols and releasers. *Breast, Diseases of the Breast* **4**:26–30 (1978).

Schafer, Edward H. and the Editors of Time-Life Books. *Ancient China.* New York: Time-Life Books, 1967.

Schapera, I. *The Khoisan Peoples of South Africa.* London: Routledge and Kegan Paul, 1963.

Shaw, J. Reactions to victims and defendants of varying degrees of attractiveness. *Psychonomic Science* **27**:329–330 (1972).

Shipler, David K. In Soviet, too, Quest for Beauty Leads to the Plastic Surgeon. *New York Times.* January 8, 1979 p. 18.

Shipley, Robert H., O'Donnell, John M. and Bader, Karl. Personality characteristics of women seeking breast augmentation. *Plastic and Reconstructive Surgery* **60**:369–376 (1977).

Singer, Jerome. The use of manipulative strategies: Machiavellianism and attractiveness. *Sociometry* **27**:128–150 (1964).

Sontag, Susan. A woman's beauty: put-down or power source? *Vogue* 118–119 (April 1975).

Walster, Elaine, Aronson, Vera, Abraham, Darcy and Rottmann, Leon. Importance of physical attractiveness in dating behavior. *Journal of Personality and Social Psychology* **4**:508–516 (1966).

Weideger, Paula. *Menstruation and Menopause.* New York: Alfred A. Knopf Publishing, 1976.

Williams, Edward Thomas. *China Yesterday and Today.* New York: Thomas Y. Crowell Company, 1923.

Yeats, W. B. Adams Curse, in Peter Allt and Russell K. Alspach (eds.). *The Variorium Edition of the Poems of W. B. Yeats.* New York: Macmillan Co., 1968.

Appendix A
A CASE OF INCEST*

She was eleven, she was beginning to—she hadn't started menstruating. I think she had had one period, but then she didn't have another one for almost a year later. Her breasts had begun to develop a little bit. She was beginning to develop. There were never any attempts before that. It was over a period of months. It started out, apparently, over the summer. It was very, very hot. She and her father and her brother were painting his apartment, her father's apartment. And because it was so hot, she was painting the wall and they had their shirts off. They were painting in the briefest possible clothes. It was up near the ceiling and it was hot. I know her brother wasn't around when this happened. He never had any indication of this for months.

But the first thing that her father did was play with her breasts, and it started out, as I say, because she had her shirt off. I know that one of the things that her father said for a long time was that she knows she acted sort of seductively towards him. She knows she did. I've done a lot of reading and I think that girls at that age do act seductively towards their fathers. My own feeling on this thing is that fathers don't take—you know—they think their daughters are cute, or they're embarrassed, or they tell them to knock it off, but they don't feed into it, and that's what he did. Maybe she tried to pretend, to practice learning with Daddy. And then it began developing. Like I said, it started in the summer, and very slowly over the next few months, more and more things.

He got her to masturbate herself in front of him, and then masturbate him, until finally they were having intercourse. This happened almost every weekend that she went to visit him. Late at night, after my son was asleep, he would come and take her from her bed and take her into his bed. He was very gentle about it, very kind, and it was almost the only time that he was ever nice to her. The rest of the time he was yelling at her. He didn't beat her, but he certainly came close. He got angry at her and threw her away from him, that kind of thing.

She liked it because he was very gentle with her. It felt good. She knew on at least one level that it was wrong. Partly, I think because he kept telling her that she shouldn't tell anybody about this, because if she did, she and he would be in a lot of trouble. But, he made it very clear that she would be in trouble, too. It was very gentle; it almost made it harder for her to hate him. And then, of course, she came to him willingly. She sort of initiated some of these which meant she went through a lot of guilt over that. In fact, when we were interviewed by the police, I told her

* The following is a verbatim statement by the mother of a case of incest involving her eleven-year-old daughter and her husband.

337

to be honest with the police, totally honest, and she said to the policewoman, "It was my idea some of the time." And the policewoman said, "That's okay. We understand. At your age you're too young to make these decisions. It's not your fault." But in a way, he turned her, or was trying to turn her, into the wife I never was. Because in reading her statement to the police, I could see elements and things that he wanted me to do that I had refused—sexually.

It was almost like he was training her to take my place, but doing it right this time instead. (We'd been divorced for several years at that point.) Both kids were cooking and cleaning and painting and doing that kind of thing for him. This was just a part of it. With both kids, their relationship was getting very bad—with him, the father, not with each other. The only reason that my son wanted to go to visit his father was because his best friend lived a few blocks away, and he would go and would spend the whole weekend with his friend. He would treat my son very badly—angry, yelling at him; he ran away once.

Part of the way that I handled the relationship with my son was—"He's your father, he loves you; you and he have a life together that doesn't involve me." So I didn't ask any questions. If they came home and said, "Daddy took us to the zoo," I'd say, "Did you have fun? Did you have popcorn?" That kind of thing. He would always quiz them about my life. So I tried to short-circuit that by saying to them, if they started talking about Daddy's new girlfriend, "I don't want to hear about that stuff; it's none of my business." They'd come home and they'd complain, "Boy, mean Daddy, he did that." I don't want to hear that because that's Daddy. I don't want them going to him and saying, "Oh, that nasty mother—she made us eat dinner!" Who's the person you trust the most with your kids? The other parent!

He used to beat me, but he didn't beat my daughter. When we were divorced, his anger at them would get really strong, but he never beat them. Looking back on it, I don't think I would have handled it any differently. It was his problem. I think the reason that she hid it for so long was because he was telling her there would be trouble. I knew that something was wrong with her because that Fall, her relationship and mine was just incredibly bad. You would ask her to do something; she would say I'll do it; she wouldn't do it and I'd ask her to do it again, and finally I'd get angry. Simple things, like clean up your room, or simpler than that—take your socks from here to there—simple stuff. I'd get angry and I'd wind up screaming at her. She had a terrible time at school and her grades were just awful and she had an awful teacher—a very rigid, authoritarian teacher, which didn't help matters at all. And so she is still having difficulties in school. She tends to act out, particularly against men.

I've been reading about the mother-daughter relationships. She'll do the passive bit first, but then she'll act out against me. She has almost no friends. So, she hadn't really had a chance to develop a lot of friends. And then going to Daddy's every weekend to spend time with him, she didn't have the weekends for her friendships. She had one very, very, good girlfriend and they're still friends. She told her after. But she never told anyone at the time. She had a girlfriend in the city, who lived next door to her father who had as many troubles in her own way. She was a very, very, troubled little kid. They were fairly close and I don't know what kind of closeness it was. I think they just sort of clung to each other. But they didn't talk about what was going on. The other girl was a battered child. She would come to my husband's for protection. I have the feeling, because of something that was said, that he might have been beginning to encourage the two kids to do sexual play around him because one of his defenses was that my son was organizing these girls to prostitute for him. My son was thirteen at the time. That was just a statement in the defense. I don't know what was happening—it may not have been anything, except for some fantasies.

My son was never really involved, never really aware of it, until just a few days before they told me. She had some object that her father had given her to masturbate with and my son found this and said what's this for? My daughter doesn't lie—she's incapable of lying. She will hedge and evade and not say anything, but ask her point blank and she can't lie. So he knew that there was something wrong. He asked her and she started getting evasive. He got enough sense of what it was about that he really couldn't handle it. And he insisted, he forced her, to come to me.

We've talked about it a lot (mother and daughter), and yet there's a lot of information that just . . . I'm very uncomfortable with it and she knows this. And there are just things that I can't ask her.

My first response was to kill him.

This was lovely. It was three days before Christmas. My daughter and I had had a nasty fight—a verbal knock-down, drag-down fight. I knew something was wrong and I would say to her, "What is wrong? There's something wrong." As I said, she can't lie and she holds things inside of her. She just becomes the most obnoxious person in the world. You cannot stand to be around her. Her behavior; she's passive resistant to the point that if you want her to do something I think you could beat her to death and she'd just take it! My psychologist was saying, Jesus Christ, what is going on with this child? She and I didn't have enough of a trust relationship at that point for me to get through. Anyway, she and I just had this fight and my son was home during the fight, and he hauled her downstairs to me and said, "Mom, there's something you've got to know." This was on Monday or Tuesday. They had gone to their father's that weekend. Then she said, "I don't want my brother here. I'll tell you about it, but I don't want him here." Well, that was fine with him. And then she told me—I can't remember exactly what she said—that Daddy's been playing with me, that indication. I questioned her just enough to figure out that he had had intercourse with her. But I didn't get a lot of details from her. I just wanted enough to know what my next step was going to have to be.

I said to her, "As far as I'm concerned, you're never going to see him again." She was very relieved. My son, too. He didn't want to see him anyways, because their relationship was so bad. What they'd do—during a period of a few weeks— they'd come back from seeing him and say they'd never want to see him again. Then come Friday, he would come to pick them up and they would go. That afternoon when she told me, I was seeing someone for counseling; I needed to have some fairly objective person who knew me to ask, what's the next step? Well, she helped me to reduce my anger over the phone. She asked: "How are you doing? Are you ready to kill him?" I said, "Yes, that's my main emotion." So that helped to sort it out. I said to her: "I need somebody—a counselor in a clinic, who can deal with this." She decided she would do it, so she went the next night to see my daughter. They spent a lot of time together (she's a doctor) alone and just immediately had a good relationship.

The rule at the clinic was that the counselor stay with you during examination, but my daughter also wanted me there. So there was me and (M.) and a doctor who was a man. He was the most gentle—he was so good with her. He told me later that he had daughters of his own. This thing really hit everybody. He said to be sure that if I went to court that he would testify—not to worry about that—that his office was just five minutes away from the courtroom and all that it would take would be a phone call and he would be right there. Which surprised me because I was afraid a doctor would not want to testify. They tested her for pregnancy, for V.D.—I remembered she had had a period in the summer. So they tested her for everything.

These were the questions that came up. I said to my daughter, "What would happen if you'd gotten pregnant?" She said, "Well, Daddy said I could have an abortion." The doctor also tested for sperm, but of course there wasn't any, because it was the weekend. But just from the muscle structure, he was willing to testify that she had definitely been penetrated a number of times, apparently by an adult penis. I felt that was pretty strong. I called my lawyer. Somewhere along the line during this my first impulse was to not prosecute, not go through the criminal system because I still don't believe this is a crime. What I wanted to do was have the divorce decree modified so that he couldn't ever see the children. I feel it's a symbol of his emotional problem. I don't think he's helped at all by being treated as a criminal. I think I'd feel this way whether I'd been married to him or not. I just feel it's not a cruel kind of thing—I think it's an emotional sort of thing.

My lawyer informed me that on the books this is a crime. Knowledge of the crime is in itself a crime and we couldn't go to public court until we'd been through the criminal court. So, at that point I reported it to the police. I reported it myself; I didn't have my daughter with me. They told me to come back, with her, at a time when there would be a policewoman on duty and so forth. My treatment by the police was pretty sensitive. I was surprised. By this time it was Christmas Eve day so we couldn't come back till the day after Christmas because there would be no policewoman on duty and so forth. I'd also had my lawyer call my husband. I couldn't deal with that at all. My lawyer called my husband into his office and said, "We have reason to believe that you have committed a crime where your children are concerned and your children are not going to be visiting you for Christmas."

We went back the day after Christmas to see the policewoman and at that time I was a little bit hassled by a cop who said, "Why didn't you come sooner?" It had been about a week, with Christmas in between and all that. But I just kind of ignored him. That was the only insensitive thing that we ran into.

My daughter spent four hours with the policewoman. We dealt with it as something that had to be done—your father has done this—it's his responsibility—and we have to do what needs to be done to get him to take the responsibility for this. She was willing to go through each step of the way. The policewoman was fantastic—really sensitive, but really firm with my daughter. They threw me out of the room. She said she didn't want mother in the room to hear this. So I went out. Four hours of dragging every little detail out of her—just the policewoman and my daughter. She went to court with her—she was just incredible. And yet, I know that she was really firm with my daughter in terms of you've got to tell me. She asked questions and got all the details. I sat on a bench out in the other room. The cops in the other room were really nice to me. They gave me coffee; they gave me a newspaper; they said don't worry, we see these cases all the time.

After she wrote the statement, I had to sign it as the parent. So I had to read it. I'm glad I was out of the room and I kept hoping I wouldn't have to read it. Every little detail was in there. It was just terrible.

Then we had to come back a few days later because my daughter had to be examined by the police doctor. She turned out to be a woman and was very gentle. That was not a bad experience either, and her findings corroborated with the family-planning doctor. So we had two doctors, both of whom would testify in court. And while we were there, when we came back for the exam with the doctor, there was another family: a mother and two little girls. One of the girls was about my daughter's age. The policewoman said to my daughter, "You're obviously nervous . . . these girls are here for the same thing." Another separated or divorced parent.

Then I started the process of getting my daughter into counseling. That took a long time to find a counselor who was willing to work with her, who felt comfortable working with her. I didn't want someone who was going to try to get her to adjust to her role as a woman. I was looking and that took months. And then finding funding for it was hard because any of the agencies that were available I didn't really want to go to for a lot of reasons. The welfare department told me that they would fund counseling—no low-income requirement because this was a protective thing. Then when I finally found somebody they wouldn't pay for it because it was a social worker in private practice. But that took months. M. counseled with my daughter for a while just as sort-of a holding action—because at least they had a good relationship. M. said that she didn't feel qualified to deal with it, but at the same time, my daughter needed some type of a supportive relationship. She was really very good. She was with her from about January to June. Then M. terminated her, but she said she could come back. She said that at the end of those six months my daughter was just a normal, obnoxious thirteen-year-old.

A lot of the problems between my daughter and I were normal and would have been there anyhow. M. helped me to sort out what were my daughter's emotional problems and what were just developmental stages. I thought the social worker was the ideal person to be working with her, because she had a real understanding of family process, developmental, and yet she wasn't an old-line social worker. But, that was close to a year later before we finally found somebody.

My daughter was also tested by a psychologist who saw lot of depression, some not necessarily suicidal but . . . I also got her a CORE evaluation through 766 and she is still a 766 student. So, she's gotten some help from the school, because she was having some trouble—she's still having some trouble in her schoolwork. But that's improving. She has many more friends now. She probably will never be popular, but she has one or two really close friends. It's the first time ever her closest friends are not losers. She's fourteen now.

They had a warrant for his arrest—this was by now a Saturday (Christmas was on Thursday). By the way, his parents were coming on *that* Saturday to visit him and the kids for Christmas. I left it up to him to deal with why the kids weren't there. Luckily, they left before the police showed up to arrest him. The police came on Saturday night. He had a male friend visitng him who tried to stop the police from coming in. So he (the friend) was arrested for assault and battery on a police officer!

Three cops show up at the door with a warrant for your friend's arrest—what do you do? You say—there he is, officer, I'll see you later and you leave! But he tried to fight the cops off! So, I think because of this, because they made such a big deal out of this, the court reporter got hold of it. I since found out that the only information available to the court reporter from the police is name, address—that kind of stuff. Somebody talked to him. Even my husband, which really surprised me, or the police or somebody talked to him. He was a high school teacher; this is why a reporter picked up on it. And the reason the newspaper had a file on him was because he was assaulted by a student about a year before that and so his name was in the paper on that.

Three-column, two-line headline—"Ex-teacher on morals charge." He was an ex-teacher as soon as his school system found out about that. He was only substituting. He didn't have a regular job at that point. He was a permanent substitute. But the reporter called up the school personnel department, who said, "Well, he *was* working for us." Then they found out that he worked in another city as a regular teacher and they called the school system there. I don't think they were told about the assault. But, if he ever tried to get a new job—he can't use them as references because they both know. Then the article in the paper listed all the charges. One of them was incest with an eleven-year-old daughter. They charged him with . . . I said to the police, "What did you do? The shot-gun approach so that something will stick?"

It hit the newspapers. He was charged with sexual assault on a child under a certain age, lewd and lascivious conduct . . . There were five charges. One of them was the incest, which of course the whole world now knew. Well, I walked into work that morning and everybody came up to me looking as though somebody had died. They said, "We're so sorry." And I said, "What?" And they led me into the kitchen and there was the newspaper spread out on the table. People cared because they had known us previously. It was hard. On one level it was a help because we couldn't hide it and we couldn't act like we felt guilty about it.

My daughter had a little bit of trouble with the kids teasing her because the parents told their kids. Later, a representative from the Office for Children and I—they asked me if I would do this—went to the editor of the paper and discussed this with him: the effects that it had and how it wasn't protective of the child involved. We made some suggestions of how they could put the same article in and yet protect the child. He took it to a New England newspaper editors' conference and it is now policy throughout New England.

When he was finally convicted, the paper said he pleaded guilty to a half-dozen charges of sexual assault on *an* eleven-year-old child. He was arrested on Saturday night and they set $10,000.00 bail. His friend was released on a number of recognizances that night—the one that battered the police officer. He stayed until Monday, until he saw the judge, and then was released on several recognizances.

Then we had to go to District Court. That was just a few weeks. What the District Court does—the judge decides that there was evidence enough of a crime having been committed and he turns it over to Superior Court. So we had a hearing in District Court. It was a small courtroom. My daughter was there. They locked the courtroom so there were no spectators, but there were still about twenty-five people. The room was full of people—stenographers, etc. M. took a day off from work and went with us. The policewoman was there. My lawyer was there. My lawyer was one of the least supporting people and I really felt this with him. He really would have liked me to drop the charges and deal with it in some other way. And I refused. He was not comfortable. We're pretty good friends and we've dealt with this issue. But he was very uncomfortable. We tried to get his lawyers and him (my husband) to agree to the lawyer interviewing my daughter privately—without having to have her testify. The lawyer refused. Even my husband refused.

His story through the whole thing was that my daughter was lying, that I put her up to it because I wanted to ruin him. This is what he told his parents, his family, everybody. They crossed us off for a year and a half—they had nothing to do with us.

A short time later we appeared before the Grand Jury. That was horrible! Nobody prepared us for that. You go alone, into this room, without your lawyer, without nobody. My daughter went by herself, into this room. Twenty-two or -three jurors were there. They sit around the edges of this huge room. You stand up with a microphone in front of you. I'm not even sure who asked the questions. I had to testify, too. I'm comfortable in court. My lawyer says I've been in court more times than some attorneys he knows! I was intimidated by this scene—microphone stuck in your face, in this enormous room, the person who's asking the questions is *behind* you. So if you turn to look at him, you're turning away from the mike.

Then it was a year later before we were scheduled for court. And the night before, it was continued because his attorney (by this time he had changed attorneys) wanted a psychiatric exam of my daughter to find out—I guess the defense was going to be that she was crazy and fantasizing and all that stuff. I guess one of the things that kept coming up was: where did this child get this vocabulary? Well, she's my daughter and she has a tremendous vocabulary. Of all kinds of things. A lot of the words she used for a lot of things were very adult. Although, in the hearing she was unbelievable—you just knew that every word out of her mouth was the truth. In fact, the Assistant D.A. leaned over to me at one point and said, "You know, she's an absolutely devastating witness." Anyway, I had gotten called at work from the Assistant D.A., who was going to be prosecuting, that it might be continued and this was set for the next day. I finally had to leave work. I couldn't even work that day. And then I had to stay home the next day in case I got called. Meanwhile, a year later, my daughter had to memorize all of the details.

The policewoman sent me a copy of the statement. I called M. and told her I can't do this; there was no way that I could sit down with this child and go over this with her. So M. said do you want me to do it? M. went over the statement with her, item by item. By the time they got back I knew that we weren't going to go to court. That pissed me off. I spent most of that day trying to find a psychiatrist that we could get in quickly, hoping that maybe we could see someone right away and go ahead and have the trial anyway. It didn't work. We had to wait. And then I was really angry at the psychiatrist. He talked about it to me, and my daughter took an instant dislike to him. So when he was talking to me, in front of her, he said, "You know, she's such an awfully hostile child you have there." Well, she was hostile because she hated him. And he went on and on to me that for the good of this child you should drop the case.

Anything about the case—I was the one who found him; it wasn't the defense that found somebody. And he said that little girls at this age are very seductive to-wards their fathers. And I said, "Yeah, but most fathers don't do anything about it." So I was hostile towards him, too. When we were in the room I said to my daughter, "You know, we could drop this." She said, "No, we've come this far; we're going to finish it." She has always been really ambivalent towards him (her father). She loves him—hates him. But I was such a nut on taking responsibility that whenever I was ready to falter, she was ready to go on. So, that was December and we didn't hear a thing for months. And I kept after my lawyer and the only thing he could find out was that maybe they were going to continue it as long as he stayed out of trouble.

Finally, I got a call from the Assistant D.A. By this time my husband had a third lawyer who turned out to be this real hot lawyer.

My husband's father paid for this. Well, this lawyer apparently went over everything and recommended that he plead guilty. So, I got this call saying, "How would you feel about it? (They're beginning to do some plea bargaining.)" I said, "I want to protect my daughter. I would prefer not to go to court and go through a trial." I knew what a trial was going to be like. I knew that I would be on trial, my lifestyle. As much as the D.A. might try to protect her, they still would try to get things—and particularly through me. I would just see all kinds of questions. Did I have a man over and this type of thing. It would be totally irrelevant, but I knew they would drag this type of stuff in. I was really afraid—for my daughter, too. But I said I want my husband to take responsibility. If we can work it out without having to be in court, then fine.

So then I didn't hear anything for several weeks. Then a friend of mine saw something in the paper that said my husband pled guilty. So I called the D.A. on Monday and said, "What's the story?" He had tried to reach me to let me know. What had happened was they got it in originally, to the judge, to do some plea bargaining. My husband started waffling—he does this—he gets judges pissed off at him and he comes out in worse shape than he would have. So the D.A. said to the judge, this doesn't sound like a plea to me. The judge said—it doesn't to me, either. So they started talking about a state penitentiary. At that point his attorney asked for a recess and they went out, came back in and he pleaded guilty

to everything. He was sentenced to two years in the County House of Correction.
He'll be there to next June unless he gets some kind of (early) release. I seriously
doubt he's getting any help at all. I don't talk to his parents about it a lot—they
just can't. They resumed the relationship before he left, which I thought was interesting. They go visit him in jail and they see us, but they don't really talk about it
much. They don't know what kind of help he's getting, if any. I assume he's not
getting any help. We did go to probate court—it was November—eleven months
after we finally had a hearing date for that. They were building a new court structure and they lost our card—it was a big mess. A lot of people aren't aware that
even though one parent has custody of the children, the other parent is the legal
guardian. If the parent with custody dies, the children automatically go to the
other parent unless the court says remove that parent as guardian. You can't even
move out of state with your children without the court's permission. The first thing
I did was change my will. But he could have contested it in court. He probably
wouldn't have wanted it, but it was a contestable issue until we got it changed. The
way the divorce decree reads now is he still has no visitation privileges but he still
has the responsibility to support them financially. Not unless by some miracle he
discovers he is wrong and his behavior changes, but I can't see that ever.

She (my daughter) went through boy-crazy—well, she still is; she has a crush on
this one boy. Kids this age are really pretty sexually active. She came home from a
school activity recently and had apparently gone outside to the school parking lot
with a boy and they were petting. He was pushing her to have intercourse and she
absolutely refused. She had seen him at school a couple of times since then and he
won't speak to her. She saw him last night and I said, "Maybe he's embarrassed."
She's almost normal in that sense, but also she's really develped a good feeling of
herself as a person. And she can say no to the boys and not feel pressured. Everybody's attitude was, you're an eleven-year-old kid, you're not responsible for these
things. When she said to me, "He says that we will be in trouble if I tell anybody,"
I said, "No! *He* is in trouble, not you, *he!*"

She was seen last year at school by a social worker of 766 kids who is a male. He
said she kind of flirted with him. I told the man that I felt he could deal with her
very openly about that. Just tell her to cut it out. There was a man that I was involved with for a long time. Whenever he came to the house she would be absolutely obnoxious in various ways. Finally, I said to her, "You always act this way
whenever he is here. What the hell is going on?" And then she cut it out.

My ex-husband did not have good relations with either of his parents. His father
is very rigid, demanding and overbearing. His mother is helpless. They have the
most incredibly symbiotic kind of relationship with each other. If anything happened to him, she could not support herself. She has never done anything inde-
pendently. He has a sister a couple of years younger. By the way, she (the wife)
had a hysterectomy about thirteen years ago and she still hasn't recovered from it.
When she was in the hospital for the hysterectomy, her husband ran out of clean
socks, couldn't figure out how to run the washer and went out and bought new
ones.

I think his mother is an alcoholic. I think she's one of these quiet housewives who never has a drink before five o'clock, but she's got to have those two drinks. I don't know if she sneaks drinks during the day, but they have happy hour every day at five and she cannot survive without happy hour. The father's not an alcoholic. My husband tells stories of a period of several years where his father slept in a chair in the living room. He doesn't know what was going on. I know she was incredibly upset about our marriage. I was three years older than my husband. And we found out many years later that she was three years older than her husband. That was one of the things that she had fits about. The other thing—she found out that we had sex before we were married and she blew a fuse over that. We discovered after we were married several years, that she and her husband had only been married six months when my husband was born. It was a really strange relationship all around. We didn't get along at all. I don't particularly like them and my kids don't particularly like them, but they were the grandparents so we kind of go through the motions.

My mother and I have a really good adult relationship now. I wasn't a bad child, just totally insecure. I was an only child. But I have a really powerful mother who all those years played the game of the passive, quiet, good wife. Any time I fight with my father it was always because I did something wrong. We've finally worked a lot of these things out. My parents were really supportive through this whole thing. Before my Dad died he did say that he really admired me and my strength. They rarely will say good things about me—our relationship got pretty good. But it took his death to do it.

We dealt very openly with it. I said something to Mother on the phone about the situation with my daughter and I told her how I was talking with a friend about this. My mother said, "You really shouldn't talk to people about this." I said, "Mother, we have nothing to feel guilty about here. My daughter has nothing to feel guilty about. She did *nothing* wrong." And I wrote Mother a four-page letter shortly after it happened—just laying it on the line: what my feelings were on this and why I was handling it the way I did. After I wrote this to them, they called me and said, "You're right, we're sorry."

Appendix B

A MULTIPROBLEMED WOMAN*

Why don't I begin with how old I am. I think I'm forty-two because I'll be forty-three in October.

I was brought up in a wealthy suburban home. Both my parents were teachers. My parents were very strict disciplinarians. Their expectations of me were always more than I could meet. Nothing that I did academically was quite good enough. If I brought home a B, it should have been an A. If it was a C, forget it! That meant I couldn't listen to the radio or I couldn't do whatever—couldn't go outdoors and play. I didn't have very many friends when I was growing up. But I've had a couple of relationships that were very intimidating that I remember. My mother was one and another was a music teacher that I had probably from the time I was eight until maybe fourteen.

He was a very authoritarian reference who used to get very angry with me when I came in and what I played was not how he wanted me to play. He would write all over my music with his pencil. He would yell and scream and then leave the room and I'd sit there in the dark until he got through with his temper tantrum and would come back in. Sometimes my lessons would last ten or fifteen minutes. Then he would send me downstairs because I couldn't play the way he wanted me to—it was in a music studio. I was terrified of him, and it wasn't until I was thirteen or fourteen that I finally said to my parents "no more" ... I won't play the piano any more, and because this man thought I had a great deal of talent he was very upset that I wanted to leave but I think a lot of my love of music was destroyed by his kind of verbal assaults on me.

He'd take music and rip it up in shreds and then I'd have to go buy more, and my parents never thought anything of it. I'd come home with my music in pieces or written over in such a way that I couldn't read the notes any more but that was what I was supposed to practice. Out of my allowance I'd have to go buy more and they didn't see it as anything unusual. I'd have a lot of trouble with them just kind of accepting that behavior. I would tell them but they didn't listen.

I would be sick to my stomach before I'd go and see him every time—twenty-four hours before my music lesson I would not want to go. I'd start talking about it and it was like nobody heard me, and until I just said I wasn't going to go any more, and they could take me there and I was going to sit on the street corner, and I guess they believed me because they got me another music teacher, and as hard

* A verbatim interview.

as she tried, the love that I had, something happened to it and it was difficult for me to be spontaneous any more. Something had happened in my relationship with him that had kind of killed it. And so I tried more piano lessons with other teachers. All of them tried to make up for what he did, my first piano teacher, but it was sort of like something was missing.

And when I talk about my mother and her verbal abuse, it's hard for me now to focus on that very much because the last six months I had with her were good compared to all the rest of my life when I hated her. And I don't want to go back to that place of hating her, but I do remember her rampages. I remember her going through the house and seeing that this wasn't done or that wasn't done. I remember when I was a freshman at college and I received three obscene letters in my mailbox at college and I was very upset about it, and the person whom I was dating and who ended up being my husband saw the letters and felt I should take them to the FBI. I did. A couple of months later the FBI called me back into their office and had traced the letters. They were from my mother and they wanted to talk to her.

They (the letters) were very judgmental. They, I don't remember words except that there was a lot of obscenity in them. And they talked of how awful a person I was because I was going out with this man and there were allusions to my being a prostitute. But there must have been enough material, because whatever there was in the letters was sufficient for the FBI to investigate. I kind of blocked the letters out. This person would get to me somehow if I didn't stop what I was doing. And then when I was married and carrying my oldest son I got more of those kinds of letters—four- and five-page letters. I finally took them to the obstetrician. He was horrified and said I was going to lose the baby if this didn't stop. He called my mother and said that he had told me that any more letters I got from her were to be burned. And he was telling her to cut the crap.

He was my first doctor to intervene in my relationship with my mother. But it's like he and I never talked about these things. My mother wanted to hear what she wanted to hear and anything else she didn't hear. And so I sifted out a lot of what I shared with her. She decided where I was going to college. She decided where my sister was going to college. I didn't fight her—my sister did. My sister was a senior in high school and sent in her application to Russell Sage in September and when it got to be April, and everyone was hearing from their respective colleges, Maria heard nothing, and so she put a phone call through to Russell Sage and they never received her application. We found the application and the check my sister had written out in my mother's drawer. She had confiscated the mail and not sent it. I had a lot of trouble with my mother's anger towards my sister because my sister rebelled a lot more than I did, and so the two of them clashed a lot more. I had conformed until I left. The relationship was disruptive with my mother. I knew it was disruptive. I kept wanting it to be different, wanted her to meet my needs so I kept going back and looking for something else even though it was continually rejected.

The relationship with my husband, although I wasn't aware of it when it began, was not overly different from my relationship with my mother except that it contained physical abuse in addition to the emotional abuse. And it also contained sexual abuse, although I never saw it *then* as sexual abuse—I see it now. The physical abuse started when our marriage was probably two months along. I don't remember the incident except that he wanted something and I couldn't do it then and there, and I was hit with his hand. I couldn't believe it. I had not been hit in a long time and I tried to talk to him about it. He never apologized for any of the abuse in the thirteen-and-a-half years we were married, "I am sorry" was not part of his vocabulary.

The physical abuse probably accelerated, although I've blocked a lot out, to a place where when Sarah was two or three months old—that was the time I fought back. Sarah was my next to oldest. She was three months old and was on the bath mat. I was changing her, and he wanted a particular set of underwear washed and ironed right then and there. It wasn't that he didn't have any underwear, of course he did, but he wanted this particular set, this particular color. I said, "No, I'm changing the baby right now and I'm not going to do it." I was sent across the room. The baby fell on the floor. I went after him and I was knocked out. I came to. He was in the other room and the baby was still on the floor screaming.

He used karate or judo or something like that because I don't know what he did. I was no physical match for him. I had resisted and whatever I did was not effective enough. It was the first time I was aware that his physical strength was bigger than mine. He had hit me before. It's hard for me to remember the frequency of physical abuse. I know that I would follow the preventive, "What can I do not to have him hit me." If I had the house cleaned. If I had the kids in bed when he came home. If I kept the kids out of his way—on and on went the list of if I did this then I wouldn't get hit.

That I know stopped, some of it, except that the verbal abuse would be a result. I didn't have to do anything. I sometimes believed that there wasn't anything I did that deserved what was happening, but not very often. I remember like in the middle of the winter at three or four in the morning his wanting me to go out and get him some juice, pushing me out of the door with no coat on. It was like 20 degrees outside. There were no stores open—there weren't any 7 Eleven's then. Nothing was open at night—at least that I knew about, and I had to go to friends of ours and wake them up and ask if they had any juice. This was how frightened I was, and I remember that as a clear incident where I felt really trapped. My kids were in the house and he was in the house and he locked the door and said he would not let me back in until I had that juice. That is kind of an example of the emotional abuse—that he would tell me how stupid I was, that I was a lousy mother, that he could take the kids away from me if I ever left him and prove that I was an unfit mother, and I heard it often enough so that I believed it.

He would twist my arm. He never did anything that would show. He would punch me. He would pull my hair. He would pinch—but my mother had done that. My mother—oh, yes—as a kid. We would be somewhere and I wasn't smiling enough or I was fidgeting or something and she would pinch me. That was something my husband did, also.

I was very frightened. I don't think I did anything. Oh, yes. I went and washed his pants and ironed them dry. I don't remember telling very many people about it. I went to the minister of the Methodist church we attended and talked to him about it. And he said something like, "My dear, we all at times have to suffer. It sounds like your life has more suffering than a lot of us but that's the cross you must bear." And when I told him about what was happening in my relationship with him sexually, his answer was, "Well this is how you take care of it. You lessen the abuse if you make him feel like a man so you make lots of noises and sounds of pleasure when you're having intercourse." I said, fine, that's how you handle it. It didn't make any difference.

I didn't know very much about sex at all. I didn't even know how babies were created until I was sixteen. My uncle had sort of played with me since I was about nine. He would take me off somewhere and pretend to be on this spiritual level of discussion, and he would tell me that he wanted to just hold me and touch me and because he was my uncle this was how relationships were. And it didn't feel right. I had no sense of where this fit in relationships but something about it just didn't seem right.

I was nine. I was at camp with my parents. I was sick in bed. He had come up to see us. He came in the bedroom and said something about what a young lady I was getting to be and ran his hands up and down inside my blouse. When in my teens, I attempted to tell my parents that I didn't feel like his behavior was right. They didn't believe me because he was a Baptist minister and people just don't do things like that. So it was all my imagination.

I know that I had a lot of difficulty with men in my teens as far as what was real and what wasn't. And I think it started with my trying to say what was real and people not believing me. I know that I had an incident when I was fifteen, sixteen—somewhere in there—where I made up this scene about this delivery man again at this camp where my parents were and said he had tried to molest me in the refrigerator. Well, he hadn't done anything to me. It ended up involving the camp director and my parents. I stuck to my story. The man was fired from his job. Well, that was the only situation that anyone believed me and something was done, but it was never real.

My uncle was the only male who ever kissed me on the mouth. I have never had that experience with any kind of relative that I remember. Yes, always when my parents were not around. I remember his coming to my house when my oldest was little—three years old. He came when my husband wasn't there. He cornered me and was breathing heavy—and of course I had been married at that point so I had a little bit of knowledge about what was happening, and it was, "Oh, my God—this man is going to rape me. I've got to get myself out of here." I was terrified. It was the first time that I knew that all the fears I had as a teenager were real—that this man had been after me. But it was sort of like, since I didn't have anybody to validate it for me and say, "Yes, you're right," I had to test it out again when I was twenty-nine and I was up in Maine. He took me to his church and then blatantly said, "Why don't you take your clothes off. Let's make love on the bench." And it was like that was reality, and I ran out of the building and knew that I wasn't crazy—that the stuff that had been happening to me was real.

I became very rigid and very stiff, which is exactly what happened in my relationship with my husband. Initially, the first couple of months, our sexual relationship was good, I think. At least I found pleasure in it—that I know, but I was pregnant immediately, and the bigger I got, the more he wanted intercourse, and even when the doctor said I wasn't to have any more, that didn't make any difference. And I had a lot of difficulty believing he was that insensitive. Even after I had the baby and I was to wait six weeks. I wasn't out of the hospital more than twenty-four hours and he forced me to have sex with him. And that went on periodically. I would go in to have surgery and come out and he would want sex. Probably within the first year, whatever pleasure I had experienced sexually changed.

I think as far as sexual arousal was concerned, I became very passive—but not totally and completely desensitized until the last six months of my marriage in which I had experiences where I felt like I was being raped. My husband would take my clothes off and then stand there and look at me and say, "Do you know the sight of you disgusts me," and then proceed to have intercourse. That kind of experience was totally humiliating, and probably the first time I realized the extent of the damage was my first sexual experience maybe three years after my marriage and I realized I was totally numb. If a man was to touch my breasts, there was no sense of feeling. I didn't even know someone was touching me. Parts of me had gone completely dead. There was no sensation at all. And that never came until about three years ago—the sensational feeling.

When I think in terms of my knowledge now of what he could have done—No! He asked to have anal intercourse. I said, "No." He accepted that. He asked me to suck his penis. I did it once and refused to do it again. He was willing to accept some limits from me and was perfectly content with the traditional role of intercourse—as long as I let him do it whenever he wanted, that was fine. How often? Once or twice a week throughout the marriage—sometimes more often depending on him and whether he was working or not.

Somewhere in all this I have to say there is something about my father and sexual abuse that I have not been able to put together. There are some feelings about his behavior in my early teens that made me feel like whatever he wanted to do was not right. There is a difference again between reality and fantasy, and I'm not sure where that line crosses except that I was afraid of him like I was afraid of my uncle. Whether I did a transference job, I don't know except they were both in the same category even though I can't recall any specific instances. I find it very interesting that my sister is frigid at this point, too, which says to me something of our relationships with our parents that we had in common. She was too young—had a lot more healthy relationships with men than I did. I can't account for the way she is today.

Every time I saw my uncle he wanted to take me off somewhere, and my parents thought it was marvelous because they felt guilty about themselves and Christian education, and he supposedly was taking care of that. And they just—until I was in my late twenties and described the incident in the church—then they believed me. When I described the incident in my house they started to believe, well, maybe there was something there. I told them, and it was interesting because after I told my parents about the last incident in the church they started putting things together. "Oh, that's why the girls who came from the university never stayed very long." They didn't even finish a semester and one would disappear, and they could never figure it out. Now, my aunt was dead and she didn't catch a lot of things that happened between people. So, whether or not she knew or how long it had been going on none of us know. Except I know what was part of it. They and their children are missionaries—one is off in China, the other is in Spain. They left home fairly young. Women or men? One of each—and I don't have any sense of what his relationship with them was like. I only know what it was like with me, but it was not like that with my sister because I talked to her about it.

Something happened with my father. I know there was something that happened in a car. I can't say what it was now. Whether it was a feeling of not trusting him at that point. The car had an unusual smell that I couldn't associate with anything else. He seemed extremely tense and I was very frightened. I know my father was sexually frustrated. My mother had a lot to say about men and what they were good for. Something about marriage and sexuality—a fix it book. And her attitude toward men and sex was very clear. Men only wanted one thing from you and that was a lot. That gave me a sense of what she felt like in their relationship sexually and how she must have reacted, and I don't know what he did about it.

I remember coming into the bedroom once. I must have been more than eight. The room was dark and he was on top of her, and I didn't know what that meant. I remember I was very upset by the incident—that something was happening that didn't feel right. My whole exposure to sexual relationships was not a very pleasant exposure. I was told by a couple of farm girls who showed me how cows did it and that it was what people did. And I couldn't believe it. I immediately thought of my minister and said, "Oh, my God, he does something like this." It was a very degrading, debasing kind of action.

I was sixteen then. I thought babies came from kissing. I couldn't understand why I wasn't pregnant because my uncle had kissed me lots of times and I was afraid of that on a very regular basis, until the young lady clarified for me, the kissing on the lips was what he would do when he would meet me. I think basically I just froze and I let him do whatever it was he wanted but he didn't get any response from me. I guess I thought if I made myself stiff enough, then whatever was happening wouldn't make any difference anyway. So, I was sort of like blocking it when it happened. We were alone a lot—out in the woods, in his church, in his office, in the car—places he could get me out away from where everyone was. And we'd be gone for a couple of hours—I don't remember. The only penis I ever saw was my father's—he wouldn't wear a pajama bottom. He just wore a pajama top. He would run around and hold on to himself while he hit us. Well, I was obviously big enough to know that when he came into the room and again I was older than eight when he was still doing that. I knew he was trying to hide something but I wasn't sure what it was. He was trying to hide it—it was usually at night and we were in bed acting up.

So, probably the first picture I saw of one was when I came to college and had biology. I had been dating at that point and we had done some heavy petting but it had never gone far enough to expose genitals.

With my husband, we probably had intercourse within the first week we met each other. I had been doing a lot of dating on campus. One in particular I was madly in love with from October of my freshman year to January, and he would go to this man on campus I was seeing for therapy and say, "She is too much for me. I can't handle what she wants." Well, I didn't know what I wanted, but he seemed to have a clear idea what it was I wanted. I wanted to get away. I wanted to leave what was going on at home and I didn't much care what was happening in classes because my brain pooped out. I don't know how many classes I flunked my first term, but it was one—maybe two, which were the first F's I ever had. But I was not attending classes—I was out having a good time.

I think he (the therapist) told him to leave me alone—I had enough problems without his making more—because our relationship stopped, and I was very angry and very upset. But then I met my husband and he was two years out of the service and very anxious to find somebody and establish security and all the rest that he thought he was going to find. We ran away to get married the first time within two months of the time period we had met and the second time two months after that. The second time we succeeded—the first time we did not.

My mother found out where I was and called me up and told me that my father had a heart attack and was dying and that I needed to come home. I did. My father was fine. That was a story she made up. I was in New York. She had called my husband's mother and they had tracked me down. The second time we went nobody knew where we were. My mother located me that time, too. I wasn't the only one to hear the phone ring at two o'clock in the morning. I knew it was her, and it was, but nobody answered the phone. And the next day we were married and then it was too late and I was fine because I didn't want her to get me. I was eighteen and I had enough.

Periodically through my marriage I did go back home. I went home when the gas was turned off and I had a three-month-old baby and it was winter. My husband wasn't working and I was. So, my parents took us in until we got the gas turned back on. They took me in again when I had major surgery and had three kids. The doctor put some pressure on them because at that point I was jaundiced and the doctor told them I might not live through surgery. My parents were not being very helpful—they were just angry. So he called. I had $500 that was mine. We each had $500—my sister and I. They had given her hers to buy a car. I wanted mine to use toward surgery and they wouldn't give me the money. I guess the doctor told them like it was, because I got the money, and they said I could come there after surgery and stay for a while.

I don't know what I would have done if I didn't have any drugs around then unless it was to take aspirin. I can't even remember if suicide was part of [the reason for] therapy when I came on campus. I don't think I really associated the attempt with suicide that was in my head until I was at my parents' house after the marriage. It's not clear whether I was suicidal in my marriage. I probably was. I had access to drugs. My husband had me drugged periodically throughout the last couple of years of our marriage. He was into pharmaceutical therapy, and he discovered the way to keep me quiet was to put me on some kind of barbiturate that I didn't even know was a barbiturate then. It made me very dopey, very lethargic. My memory went in and out. And when I was eight months pregnant he pushed me down the stairs. That was one of the last incidents of physical violence that I remember. I was at the bottom of the stairs. I was hysterical. He called my gynecologist and told him I had fallen down a few stairs. There weren't a few—more like fifteen or sixteen stairs. The gynecologist put me on liquid phenobarbitol. Here I am eight months pregnant and this guy puts me on liquid phenobarbitol along with whatever else my husband was doing. No wonder my daughter had seizures when she was a baby. I never correlated the two.

. . . Like it was all my fault that I became pregnant. Contraceptives didn't work. I used a diaphragm. The pill that you're not supposed to get pregnant on—well, I did. You're not supposed to get pregnant when you're nursing. Well, I did. I used the diaphragm on a regular basis with jelly. The doctor just said I was very fertile. I was like a cow. I was built to have lots of babies, and I could have as many as I wanted.

I didn't like myself much as a mother because I didn't have all those nice, motherly feelings about having babies. I tried to get rid of all of them except one—I didn't succeed.

Took lots of laxatives, jumped off of high places . . . I didn't want to be a mother. Now I didn't think that was a bad thing . . .

My husband repeatedly spoke scripture at me about what a wife's responsibility was. She was supposed to do things—she was supposed to be submissive, and he would quote Paul, verse after verse after verse. I didn't feel like I had very much to fight with.

On campus he was student representative of whatever Christian organization they had.

I looked up to him and felt that here was somebody that had arrived sort of safe. I don't recall any clergy person I went to—and I went to more than one—being supportive of my feelings about not continuing the marriage, of not wanting the abuse to continue. I got no support at all from any clergyman—I think I saw three. We went to marriage counseling.

He distorted everything. Even if the marriage counselor said something, he would take it home and it would come out different. It was amazing how he could do it.

I think I shared some of it [with my parents] and my mother's response was that it's your bed. You made it. *You* lay in it. You wanted this bad enough so it's your problem. She didn't want me to get married in the first place and since I chose to do this, then I had to suffer.

My parents weren't particularly upset about any of this. I came to them when I was pregnant with Anne [third child]. I asked them if I could come home.

I had talked to my father-in-law. I had talked to all the relatives, and everybody was very supportive of my getting out of the marriage. My father-in-law would bring me and all my stuff home. My mother said no. And it wasn't as if my parents didn't have the room. They had a four-bedroom house. My sister was gone. There was nobody else in there but the two of them. And it took their coming out to New York State and finding me in this zombie-like state where I didn't get dressed. I didn't pull the shades up. I just wandered around in a daze, and they came out and found me like that.

Then my mother said, "Do you want to come home?" I wanted to get out of the marriage. I couldn't stand what was happening to the kids. Yes, he beat them. My oldest one was a baby. He didn't want his son to cry so he would put his hand over his mouth. My son would continue to cry but you couldn't hear him any more. He didn't care where he did it. We were in my parents' house and my son would start to cry and he'd do the same thing. People were horrified when they saw him do that. My son was going to conform, and if I attempted to interfere I got hit and so did my son. And by the time my son was four I couldn't handle him. I went to a Child and Family Services and said, "I have this four-year-old and I don't know what I can do with him." Told them a little bit about the marriage—what was going on. They got him into nursery school and attempted to add some support to me and the relationship, and attempted to get my son out of the house away from his father. That was a place I found support but the minute my husband discovered an agency was involved, he decided to go back to New York state and his home town, and we couldn't stay here any longer.

My oldest son was periodically hit in the area of his head and ears and his face. When I started having him tested around nine or ten, I felt like his apparent brain damage did not start from birth or any defects before but from his father's blows. That was very hard for me to accept—that as a mother I allowed these things to go on. The one final blow was that my kids were hungry and there was no food. My kids were cold and there was no heat.

He was very angry when my son was two-and-a-half and I got a teaching job. That was a big threat to him, and I taught for nearly three years, and even though that made *me* feel better, it was one of the worst times in our marriage because I was beaten even more then. His behavior then was horrendous and the thing I talked about—his shutting me out of the house happened then while I was teaching.

He probably had anywhere from twenty-five to fifty jobs during our marriage. Out of the last five years he worked one year. The rest of the time he didn't work. He had all these pipe dreams about what he was going to do. He was going to Alaska and homestead, and if I was a good enough wife, then I would see that this was what I was supposed to do with him. But here we are in western New York, he has a hunting license, and all kinds of animals, and we have no dinner and he won't go out and catch anything and we're supposed to go to Alaska and homestead. But he didn't push it because we didn't have the money to go anyway. When he got rich, then we'd go. As I say over and over again when I talk, I wish I could have left because I had enough of his abuse, but it wasn't that—because my kids were abused and they were being physically deprived of the basic necessities. That was the bottom line. I could not tolerate my kids being hungry, even though I didn't want to be a mother. I would have done anything to get them out. And there were times when I've been very protective of them, especially in their relationship with their father when I felt he was angry. I would get them out of the way so that his anger wouldn't be released. I would attempt to be a middle person. My third child got abuse, but she was a girl so she got less.

At fourteen my son (oldest one) was violent. I had bought my own home then and we were in the kitchen and I wanted him to go to school. He said no, he wasn't going to school and I said, yes, he was. He came after me and I knew he was going to hit me and I couldn't believe it. Here was my own son I was afraid of. And I went and locked the door, called the family doctor and arranged an appointment with him. Within a week or so my son was committed. His anger at that point was completely uncontrollable. He lashed out at his younger brother so that they could hardly stay in the same house together. He tormented his sisters unmercifully. But his attack on me was more than I was going to stand for. He was into drugs somewhat then, but I didn't know to what extent.

He never came back to live with me after that. He did come home on visits. He went to detention homes for stealing a car. He left school at ninth grade, but Roy couldn't read beyond second. grade so school was a waste of time. He didn't understand what was going on so he left. He went to one group home but didn't stay there long. It was like there was no place for him. At one point the hospital wanted to send him home and I refused and called the director of the hospital and said that if he came home and became violent, I would kill him, and it was just that simple.

My older son looked more like my father. My younger son looks like my husband—almost the spitting image of his father. But he was a very different youngster. He kept stuff in. My older boy let everything out. He was very angry from the time he was little and it all came out at me. I don't know how many times he ran away from home when he was nine, ten, or eleven. He'd go to my mother's house. My mother took him for a while. He was good with her. He listened to her—that was the only person he would listen to.

He married another person from the mental hospital he was in. He was nineteen. The marriage lasted maybe about a month. He abused her physically. She ended up back in the hospital and they're divorced now. He talks now about it with a great deal of sadness that his anger got that much out of control—that he would hurt anyone, because he was aware that he did. They did not have any kids because I made a very big fuss . . . that these things could go on from generation to generation. It was like, "Oh, my God, there will be a third generation. I won't have it." So I contacted his therapist and he arranged a meeting and talked about children and what was the likelihood if they were to have kids. . . .

My oldest daughter had had an abortion that was encouraged by me. She was seventeen. She physically abuses her dog, and I am very glad she doesn't have a kid because I know very well that kid would be physically abused just like that dog. The only time she takes the dog to the vet is when the dog's half dead. I'm saying, "Oh, my God, if she had kids she'd be doing the same thing." Now, I didn't know this. My younger daughter told me. My younger two and their relationships to people are very different from the older two. There is no sense of anger out of control. There isn't that much difference in ages, and yet the older two had a lot more contact with their father than the younger two. I protected the younger two. I hid them away, sort of. The oldest one I did—not the next because she was . . . sick most of the time—and not my younger son because he was very passive. I'm not so sure he (oldest son) got as much physical punishment from me. He always seemed to try my patience to get to me somehow, when I would lose control. And I remember once when he was about five and I got angry and I picked up something and was going to heave it at him. I looked down and saw that I had this enormous glass ash tray in my hand. I couldn't throw it. I realized then how much anger I had for this child . . . I attempted to work on my relationship with him, but it didn't do a whole lot of good. I did the best I knew how.

When I was in the eighth grade, I went to the minister of our church because I knew I was having problems with my parents and I didn't know how to talk about it, but I was in trouble and I knew it. And his response was quoting the scriptures—honor your mother and father like you're supposed to do—you'll outgrow it. Just a general kind of pacification, and so it was another four or five years after that before I attempted to see anybody else. But there was a lot of underlying anger that I was feeling against myself.

Seems like I was suicidal during that time period but I can't remember. I was unhappy until I lost that thirty pounds that summer I was seventeen. But I began that kind of dual personality stuff at that time where I lost thirty pounds. I went back to school, I smiled and was pleasant to everybody and all of a sudden being in a high school class of twenty-four, from not having any friends at all, being a social outcast through seventeen years, I worked for the yearbook, had the lead in the class play, *Boyfriend*. I mean, something happened that year that was completely inconsistent with anything I had done before then.

Spending a lot of time alone and feeling awful about myself, I lived with those feelings a heck of a lot. I can't recall anything consistent, anything concrete. I think in terms of my manipulation with pills after I left my husband.

I know that when I had surgery I didn't want to live. I didn't do anything helpful . . . but of course my husband didn't help either.

I had gall bladder surgery. The stones had moved out from the gall bladder and were in ducts and apparently they had begun to disintegrate the gall bladder itself. Jaundice had set in. I had a temperature of 104 when they took me in on an emergency basis. The doctor said he didn't think I was going to pull through because I didn't want to. I didn't want to live—that was very clear. I don't recall any clear attempts at suicide—just feelings that I didn't want to live—over and over again. Towards the end of my marriage I remember one very cold night. Climbing out a window in bare feet, no coat on—I think I was in a nightgown. There was a lot of snow and I went up into the woods, and I was going to stay there and die. Now, there may have been [other] attempts like that. That isn't the same as taking pills, but the intent is still the same. I didn't want to live, and I was actively doing something about that. All I managed to do was get a nasty case of bronchitis. I went back. I mean, I had read stories about what happened to people. They went to sleep and that was the end. It didn't happen that way—I got cold so I came back. I know I've done other things like that. . . .

I associated the pill stuff because that's what I did constantly on a long-term basis—very regularly. That started when I was living with my parents. I had been there a year and a half, maybe. I was in therapy and I started taking massive doses of aspirin—thirty or forty of them at a time. It was something—I didn't develop a physical something or other because I did this for three or four months. I was very suicidal during that time period and did not want it to stop . . .

I went to see a therapist when I lived alone. The therapist had become sort of like a father to me and he took care of me, gave me lots of attention. He had me come to his house—came into my house—starting buying me presents. One day in his office he kissed me and it was not a fatherly kiss. This was during a weight-loss reduction time period, and he was supposed to give me rewards for losing weight. And he promised me that he would take me to bed with him as soon as I got down to one hundred twenty-nine pounds.

I wasn't really sure that was what I wanted but I had very mixed feelings about my relationship with him. He knew that, and the last six months of therapy with him were very conflicting . . . because I wanted the relationship with him at any cost. I would have been his mistress. I would have been his cleaning lady—anything he wanted. He was very domineering, very demanding—his word was everything and I knew anything he asked of me I couldn't refuse.

He came to the house one Sunday and was sitting on my couch, and he put his arm around me and he asked if I would do anything he asked of me. I said, "Well, probably." And then sometime later on in the conversation, he asked me for the first time in those two-and-one-half years, was there anything in my husband's and my relationship—sexual relationship that I couldn't do. I said yes, recalling an incident where my husband asked me to suck his penis, which was very disgusting to me.

I was afraid of what he had on his mind that I had no control over and no power to do anything about. His assistant was a very close friend of mine. I called her up that night and told her the essence of what had happened in our conversation. She said, "But you do have control. You can say no." I knew I couldn't. I felt really hooked in this relationship, and felt that whatever he told me to do I would do because I had to. I felt really relaxed in the two-and-one-half years we had worked together.

So, sure enough three or four days later, I guess—I had called him for something. I was upset. He had told me to call him at any time. He said that it sounded like my problem was that I was sexually frustrated. I didn't know what that meant because I really hadn't thought of that sort of thing.

I basically believe I don't have high sex urges. He told me to see him, and we would work on the problem. I did, and I think he had his recording machine on at that point. He not only was a photographer, but he was playing around with electronics. He had lots of machines around with lights and things that I didn't understand, but there was one machine that had a red light on so I knew something was on that had not been on when I'd been there before. I did what he said I was supposed to do, and whatever I was supposed to feel and wasn't. I said I didn't want to do it any more. We came into a living room and he sat down in his chair and told me to come over and sit on his lap. I did, and he pulled out his penis. That's interesting because I don't know what I did then. The only thing I can remember right now is that I cried.

He patted me and told me to go home and I would feel better and to calm down. I went to his assistant's house—oh, I wasn't supposed to tell anybody what happened. I went to his assistant's house, which was only three houses away and I told her what happened. While I was there the phone rang. It had been ten minutes—he was on the phone . . . I had done what I wasn't supposed to do—I was not supposed to tell anybody, and therefore he was referring me to someone else. I couldn't believe it had happened. I couldn't believe he was sending me away. It didn't make any sense to me.

My behavior in the next few years was horrible. I went to bars on a very regular basis—picked up men I didn't know—went to bed with them—persisted in one blow job after another. I would tell the men that I was frigid and they were going to cure my frigidity. Then they would go through their routine—whatever routine—and then I'd laugh. Then I'd go home and and take a bunch of pills.

This went on for I don't know how long. Periodically, it went on for five to six years. I don't remember the length of time it took. It was a long time, though, on a very regular basis.

In therapy recently, the abuse I had received in my marriage and the abuse I had earned from my mother—I see them all as part of a pattern where I would become involved with someone who had a strong personality, whom I would care about and allow them to become strong and more dominant; then they would become abusive, and I would become helpless and passive and fearful and consequently did not move in any direction at all.

That pattern has stopped. The suicide attempts have stopped. The drug overdosing has stopped. And I never thought any of that would.

The other therapist felt very guilty that she had taken me to him in the first place. She had difficulty in believing that I would let myself do this, so I think she had problems with her husband, too.

Her husband had been taking care of my finances for me, and when she was away out in New York there were some bills that needed paying, so I called him up and said that I wanted to come over and pay some bills because I had gotten a check in.

He said, "Well, I'm here alone," and I said, "So, what else is new?" Somehow or other I never saw him as a man, and he said that I wouldn't want to let them know I'm horny. Talk about being naive. I didn't even know what the word meant. I had never heard it before. I couldn't associate it with anything I knew. I didn't look it up in the dictionary. I should have. So I went over there, and we did the bills and I got ready to go home. He put his arms around me and said, "Let's go downstairs," and I said, "What are you talking about?" He said, "We can go downstairs and sleep together." I said, "Oh, my God, here's another one."

I was very suicidal at the time. I think my therapist said I provoked it (abuse). I think he said by being helpless I was going to drag men into this kind of behavior. That's a bunch of hogwash—but, anyway, I think that's what he said.

The second therapist told me she loved me. I was in a little bit of trouble then with my relationships—personal relationships. I had two men who were chasing after me, both of them married. Both of the relationships were sick. I couldn't seem to get rid of them, so I figured, what the hell, I'll try something different. How can I lose? But I did.

At first she accepted my manipulations. She went to live with me. We built a house together, and I lived with her for like three years—two-and-one-half—until I could no longer tolerate her alcoholism. Yes, I suppose she did abuse me but it was a much lower degree of abuse than I had seen before—emotional abuse—not physical. When somebody ignores you—says they're going to go and smash all the pictures in the house you just sent them—I don't know if that's abuse or not. I just wanted her to pay attention to me, but she was interested in her book and her bottle and I was ignored, and that isn't a direct attack. I don't remember her ever directly attacking me. She would just go away . . . so I would fix it that I got the attention I needed. My husband didn't drink. I never had anything to do with an alcoholic before until I was with this woman. This is the first time I had gone into alcoholism and felt what it was like to live with one, and I know I would never do it again. I broke up with this woman because I didn't like what was happening to me. Not only was I drug dependent and I already knew about that—that was bad enough. But I was also becoming an alcoholic and I mixed them frequently. Heavy depressants, barbiturates, tranquilizers, and mixing with alcohol whenever I felt like it. Took overdoses of all sorts of drugs—took massive overdoses. I had large quantities of them.

If I felt like I wasn't getting enough attention, feeling rejected, then I would take a bunch of pills and go to sleep. I continued that with the alcohol added to it until my relationship with her ended.

I knew I was destroying myself in the process of living with her, even though I cared about her. I think I cared about myself a little bit at that point, and decided I didn't want to stay there any more. And that was very different for me to make that move rather than wait until I lost everything. It seems that I was learning. And that felt good—that I could make that decision and know that it didn't mean the end of the world.

I don't know much about my oldest's (daughter's) relationship except that it was with an older man. She was about sixteen when it started. It was only last year that I heard it was hooked up with sexual abuse—that he would beat her before they had intercourse. I didn't know that—I just knew that he beat her, and that made me very, very mad. She lived with him periodically for a couple of years. She has severed the relationship now. I don't know if it's permanent.

I had difficulties with my youngest one, but she has been very headstrong and very independent.

My daughter was fourteen. She was a very happy-go-lucky, trusting individual. She had no reason not to be. She's been brought up in a fairly sheltered environment with lots of love, lots of attention—a beautiful young lady. She did very dangerous things like accepting rides from people, even though I told her not to. She was raped twice within a six-month period. The first time she blocked it out, the second time made the first time real. During this time period she ran away from home a few times, and I didn't know what was going on. Tried Family Service—I called in Juvenile Court because I wanted her to have a structure to work within. I called in the Rape Crisis Center, so she was exposed to a lot of different options. What were the circumstances of the rape? She was hitchhiking and picked up—early afternoon as she left school. On her way home he took her to the drive-in before the drive-in was open—maybe winter and he raped her there. That was the first time.

The second time was an old boyfriend whom she hadn't seen in like a year, and she was again hitchhiking. She kept saying in the six months following that she couldn't believe people were like this—that they would really hurt people.

She has a very philosophical way to life. She was very warm and loving and giving and the idea that people were hurting other individuals she had a hard time in grasping.

She was naive. I didn't help her in any of that. I wanted to protect her from the world—she was my baby, and she was not going to see any of the bad stuff. And so, by the time I started saying, "You shouldn't do this—this will happen," she didn't believe me.

I felt that something was happening. Then, she called me and told me what had happened after the second rape. We went to the police. That was when I called the Rape Crisis Center. We had a rough few months. She was very angry with me. She blamed me for everything. She said that it was because I was a lesbian that she couldn't have healthy relationships. I knew that none of this was true—that she was just angry and hurt, but I was the one who was attacked.

Then she came to the house and took a lot of my stuff. She was living with her older brother. Then I found out that her older brother, within the last year, had sexually molested her periodically from the time she was little on up. I was not aware of it. Not actual penetration—oral. I was very upset with it. I knew my older son had problems but I didn't know they went that far, and she was living with him during the time period when all this was happening. She lived with him for three months—not very long—and she was out on the street for a while. Then she went to live with her other sister. She's been there for about a year now. She'd come home and then leave again. She was just a very upset young lady, and I didn't know how I could help her. So eventually I got her into an adolescent psychiatric clinic. She was there for three months. We had family therapy.

I thought that this doctor was very liberal but he wasn't. One of his questions to me when Anne and I were in therapy with him was, "Because you've had experience making love to other women, does this mean you want to make love to your daughter, too?" I couldn't believe it—I mean, here was another one. One track mind.

When I lived with the therapist, the children thought I was happier than I had been in any of my relationships with men—so that was okay. They were upset by her drinking, but they liked her and were close to her.

My second lesbian relationship—when they saw me? It was like they called her their second mother. They were close to her and very accepting. My oldest daughter has had trouble with that. She's talked about it, thinking maybe the same thing will happen to her. And we talked about it. She has some real mixed feelings about herself, her relationships and her sexuality. So I can understand how she's the most threatened by it. But I felt she could talk about it, and that we could talk about it and try to deal with it constructively.

My kids have been very supportive of me in my lesbian relationships. I think their main concern is that I'm a happy human being, and they've seen that and that's all that matters, and they say that over and over again and defend my relationships to their friends. And their friends accept my relationships without any difficulty.

They're moving along in the right direction. I feel better about them now than I did five years ago. Our relationships have changed. They've grown in a good way. I don't think I was as terrible a mother as I thought.

I think when I see abused women today and they're able to get out of the marriage early and the kids are relatively unaffected—I envy them. They're seeing a lot more clearly than I did. But abuse was not reason enough for me to leave.

It was made very clear to me why I deserved it. I mean I obviously must have because I got it in various forms over and over again. So it was like I didn't have any messages of consistent caring except in certain therapeutic relationships.

I am very much concerned that I cannot be in any kind of relationship where there is some kind of power struggle. But the minute I feel this might be happening, I jump right in and say—hey, none of this—you're making me feel like a child. That I can say that means I'm feeling stronger. And it feels good that I can settle in and say I don't want any of that because I couldn't for a long time.

I don't think it was because we have been close as sisters, but there has been such a sense of competition that was set up right from the time I was younger. My sister always did things better than I did. She learned things easier. She got straight As without working hard. She excelled in sports—I did not. Even though she and my mother related like two bulls in a pen, I could see she was much healthier than I and there was always a need for me to achieve to meet whatever standards she set. She was the one to set the standards. That I could get a diploma and have it magna cum laude and hers was only cum laude was marvelous. I was one up. There is still that sense of competition that goes way back. Even though I'm aware of it and can talk about it, it's real hard for me to change that pattern. And it interfered with our ability to share and be honest with one another.

I don't want to know and I'm not sure she would tell me because she doesn't even want to admit that there's a drinking problem. I've had to press to get her to talk about that, but any further and she'd just shut off, but I try to let her know I'm willing to talk about it if she wants to. I start with the alcoholism and leave plenty of open doors for her. She doesn't open any of them—I have to egg her on, and even then she's reluctant to talk about it. That would make her a failure, and failure was not something my parents accepted in any way. You have to succeed. You have to excel, and both of us have that in us. Having to meet their expectations, but competing against each other, makes it real hard now to undo this.

I think some people ask why women stay in an abusive relationship. A sense of repeated fear, the sense of being helpless, the lack of self-image does not perpetuate mobilization, so that you can move in any direction, if you feel paralyzed. That fear paralyzes you, that not having a very big sense of self paralyzes you, and your ability to free yourself becomes more entangled the longer the relationship goes on.

I'm lucky that the kids were hungry when I got out of there. Otherwise, I'd still be there. I saw no way of getting out. I felt completely trapped. And when no one will listen to you, when you feel like this horrendous secret you're not sure whom you can trust with—if there was anybody who would listen and try to work with you and come out on the other side. When divorce, for me, was a big stigma; in that day and age you divorced and got a lot of other labels attached to you. When statistics say if you're a divorced mother bringing up kids alone, the possibility of your kids being drug addicts and all the rest of that—they had lots of percentages. I just didn't want to be another percentage. It was very hard for me coming from where I did economically, and that hurt more than the emotional and physical abuse because I was already used to that. I had it before in varying degrees.

INDEX

Abortion, xii, 257
  deaths due to, 259
  and medicaid, 258
  violence in abortion clinics, 259
  as a woman's right, 256
Abrahamsen (1960), 146–147
Abramowitz (1976), 211
Abuse syndrome, 177–178
Abused women. *See* Incest; Rape; Wife
  battering
Adams et al. (1973), 296
Adams and Neel (1967), 113
Adams and Ware (1979) xix, xx
Adenocarcinoma of the vagina. *See*
  Cancer
Adler (1975), 150
Adolescents. *See* Teenagers
Adrenogenital Syndrome (AGS), 34–35
Advertising
  and drug prescriptions, 282
  violence in, xiv
Aeschylus, 11
Affirmative action, x
Against Our Will, 75
Aging process
  and Aphrodite complex, 17
  and beauty, 332
  and hormone therapy, 16
  and plastic surgery, 329–330
Agoraphobia, 197–199
Aggression
  and adrenogenital syndrome, 34–35
  angry, 23, 24
  in animals, 30, 33–34
  definition of, 21, 22–24
  and encephalitis, 33
  genetically determined, 3, 30–31
  and hormones, 3, 33–34, 36–39
  and hostility, 22, 25
  instrumental, 23
  and intent, 22, 23
  as learned behavior, 30, 39
  in males vs. females, 3, 4, 33–34
  and parental reinforcement, 4, 39–40
  and premenstrual syndrome, 37–39
  and rabies, 33
  and rapists, 93
  role of brain in, 30–31, 32

  sex and, 40
  and societal values, 23
  theories of, 24–42
  therapy for, 31
  and violence, 24
  and watching violence, 40–41
Aggression instinct. *See* Instinct theory of
  aggression
AGS. *See* Adrenogenital Syndrome
Albrecht (1973), 267, 272
Alcoholics Anonymous, 267
Alcoholism
  and bar prostitutes, 60
  definitions of, 265–266
  determining factors, 267–268
  and drugs, 283, 287, 288–289
  as coping mechanism, 265, 271
  and homicide, 152
  and incest, 125
  as learned behavior, 271, 273, 275
  and marriage, 269–271
  and mental illness, 274
  reasons for, 268–269, 271–274
  and self-destruction, 265
  societal values of, 278–279
  statistics of, 266–267
  and suicide, 300
  and violence, 32
  and wife battering, 176
Alexander and Selesnick (1966), 192, 193,
  194
"Alleged Psychogenic Disorders in
  Women," 209
Allison v. U.S., 83–85
Altruistic suicide, 291
Always Ask a Man, 310
Amazons, 2
American Cancer Institute, 251, 252
American Civil Liberties Union, 163
American College of Surgeons, 253
American Criminal Law Review, 49
American Humane Society, 111
American Journal of Public Health, 258
American Medical Association, ix, 253,
  266, 281, 326
American Psychiatric Journal, The, 213
American Psychological Association, 212,
  213